GEORGIAN COLLEGE LIBRARY

$ 88.29
GEOB-BK

MW01518321

IBM DB2 9.7 Advanced Application Developer Cookbook

Over 70 practical recipes for advanced application
development techniques with DB2

Sanjay Kumar

Mohankumar Saraswatipura

Library Commons
Georgian College
One Georgian Drive
Barrie, ON
L4M 3X9

[PACKT] enterprise
PUBLISHING
professional expertise distilled

BIRMINGHAM - MUMBAI

IBM DB2 9.7 Advanced Application Developer Cookbook

Copyright © 2012 Packt Publishing

All rights reserved. No part of this book may be reproduced, stored in a retrieval system, or transmitted in any form or by any means, without the prior written permission of the publisher, except in the case of brief quotations embedded in critical articles or reviews.

Every effort has been made in the preparation of this book to ensure the accuracy of the information presented. However, the information contained in this book is sold without warranty, either express or implied. Neither the authors, nor Packt Publishing, and its dealers and distributors will be held liable for any damages caused or alleged to be caused directly or indirectly by this book.

Packt Publishing has endeavored to provide trademark information about all of the companies and products mentioned in this book by the appropriate use of capitals. However, Packt Publishing cannot guarantee the accuracy of this information.

First published: March 2012

Production Reference: 1050312

Published by Packt Publishing Ltd.
Livery Place
35 Livery Street
Birmingham B3 2PB, UK.

ISBN 978-1-84968-396-8

www.packtpub.com

Cover Image by Artie Ng (artherng@yahoo.com.au)

Credits

Authors

Sanjay Kumar

Mohankumar Saraswatipura

Reviewers

Nadir Doctor

Saurabh Jain

Eldho Mathew

Acquisition Editor

Rukhsana Khambatta

Lead Technical Editor

Dayan Hyames

Technical Editors

Manasi Poonthottam

Lubna Shaikh

Mohammed Sahil

Copy Editors

Leonard D'silva

Neha Shetty

Aaron Rosario

Project Coordinator

Michelle Quadros

Proofreader

Sandra Hopper

Indexer

Monica Ajmera

Graphics

Valentina D'souza

Manu Joseph

Production Coordinator

Alwin Roy

Cover Work

Alwin Roy

About the Authors

Sanjay Kumar has been working as a database developer and architect for seven years. He has a lot of expertise in data modeling and performance tuning for business intelligence systems. He is an IBM certified advanced database administrator, application developer, and solution developer. He also has a 'PUBLISH' rated disclosure on data compression, and is an active member of the DB2 community.

He started his career with IBM India Software Labs as part of the DB2 development team. After working with IBM for five years, he moved to work for an investment bank as a data architect.

First of all, I would like to thank my lovely wife for supporting me throughout several months; without your support, I wouldn't have been able to accomplish this.

I would also like to thank the Packt Publishing staff for their help and support in getting this book published. I am especially grateful to Rukhsana who helped me understand the structure of cookbooks and professional writing. I would also like to thank Zainab, Dayan, and Michelle for keeping track of the schedule and reviews. Special thanks to Lubna and Manasi for making my book look professional.

I would also like to thank the technical reviewers, Saurabh Jain and Eldho Mathew for providing excellent suggestions. Last, but not least, I would like to thank Packt Publishing for getting my first book published. It was a pleasure working with Packt Publishing.

Mohankumar Saraswatipura started his career in DB2 8.1. He has worked as a database application developer and a performance consultant in High Performance On Demand Solutions (HiPODS) for IBM Software Labs, India. He is currently working as a Lead DB2 database administrator, helping application developers on Balanced Warehouse D5100, Siebel 8, and SAP ECC implementations. He is experienced in DB2 application performance tuning and database design. He is an IBM certified application developer, InfoSphere solution designer, XML solution developer, and Advanced DB2 database administrator.

He is an active member of IDUG India and an IBM Information Champion. Mohan completed his Master's of Technology in computer science in 2004, and Executive MBA from IIMC in 2007.

Mohan has also worked on the following articles:

- *DB2 performance tuning using the DB2 Configuration Advisor*, which was published in *IBM's developerWorks*. You can find this article at: `http://www-128.ibm.com/developerworks/db2/library/techarticle/dm-0605shastry/`

- *How to go hand-in-hand with DB2 and Informix*, which was published in *IBM's developerWorks*. You can find this article at: `http://www-128.ibm.com/developerworks/db2/library/techarticle/dm-0701shastry/index.html`

- *What's new in IDS 11*, which was published in *IBM's developerWorks*. You can find this article at: `http://www.ibm.com/developerworks/data/library/techarticle/dm-0705saraswatipura/`

- *Understanding the advantages of DB2 9 autonomic computing features*, which was published in *IBM's developerWorks*. You can find this article at: `http://www.ibm.com/developerworks/db2/library/techarticle/dm-0709saraswatipura/`

- *Effectively use DB2 data movement utilities in a data warehouse environment*, which was published in *IBM's developerWorks*. You can find this article at: `http://www.ibm.com/developerworks/data/library/techarticle/dm-1111movementdatawarehouse/index.html`

I work for an incredible organization, with brilliant people, where I've had opportunities to learn and grow. Thanks to Nelson Coish, and the higher management for helping me all the way. Thanks also to my wife, Dr. Nirmala Kammar, for being so kind when things were needed. Thanks, of course, to all at Packt Publishing group, especially Rukhsana, Zainab, Dayan, Michelle, Lubna, and Manasi. It was a great experience working with you all.

About the Reviewers

Saurabh Jain is part of the IBM tech sales team, covering the DM portfolio from IBM with a significant focus on DB2. Earlier, he was a part of the DB2 engineering lab, where he worked on the DB2 product. He is a DBA and field expert, having a significant amount of practical knowledge about DB2. He has done extensive work on database architecture, design, and development, with an emphasis on implementation best practices and evangelizing the product. He has co-authored some DB2 best practices documents published in IBM's developerWorks, and also has a couple of patents.

Eldho Mathew is a DB2 LUW, Linux, and AIX certified administrator, with eight years of proven expertise in various aspects of building, administering, and supporting highly complex 24x7 operational and warehouse database servers. He has handled highly complex and critical systems for many top branded customers in the UK.

www.PacktPub.com

Support files, eBooks, discount offers and more

You might want to visit www.PacktPub.com for support files and downloads related to your book.

Did you know that Packt offers eBook versions of every book published, with PDF and ePub files available? You can upgrade to the eBook version at www.PacktPub.com and as a print book customer, you are entitled to a discount on the eBook copy. Get in touch with us at service@packtpub.com for more details.

At www.PacktPub.com, you can also read a collection of free technical articles, sign up for a range of free newsletters and receive exclusive discounts and offers on Packt books and eBooks.

http://PacktLib.PacktPub.com

Do you need instant solutions to your IT questions? PacktLib is Packt's online digital book library. Here, you can access, read and search across Packt's entire library of books.

Why Subscribe?

- ▸ Fully searchable across every book published by Packt
- ▸ Copy and paste, print and bookmark content
- ▸ On demand and accessible via web browser

Free Access for Packt account holders

If you have an account with Packt at www.PacktPub.com, you can use this to access PacktLib today and view nine entirely free books. Simply use your login credentials for immediate access.

Instant Updates on New Packt Books

Get notified! Find out when new books are published by following @PacktEnterprise on Twitter, or the *Packt Enterprise* Facebook page.

Table of Contents

Preface

Welcome to the DB2 9.7 Advanced Application Developer Cookbook. DB2 9.7 is a truly incredible database product from IBM, which offers an excellent mix of application performance, reliability, and ease of development enablement.

In this cookbook, you can find both: hands-on and real world practical application development examples, as well as key references that provide a context for what you are learning.

As a reader, you will find several examples on new features in DB2 9.7 edition, including the following:

- A quick summary on new application development enhancements
- A step-by-step approach to port an Oracle 11g database to DB2 9.7
- Very generic application development techniques
- More detail on application designs
- A complete discussion on advanced OLAP functions
- Systematic approach in building stored procedures, functions, triggers,and modules
- Helping application developers to monitor the database performance and tuning for the better

What this book covers

Chapter 1, Application Development Enhancements in DB2 9.7, introduces the application development enhancements in DB2 9.7, which help most of the developer community to use the existing DB2 features, instead of building the application logic.

Chapter 2, DB2 Application Techniques, introduces all the basic techniques and aspects of application development that are very generic, and can be used with any programming language.

Chapter 3, General Application Design, introduces some advanced techniques that can be used to design efficient applications, including security aspects in a three-tier architecture, various methods of data encryption, extending the data type support, and so on.

Chapter 4, Procedures, Functions, Triggers, and Modules, introduces the different types of functional database objects that can be used to encapsulate business logic at the database server, including stored procedures, user defined functions, triggers, and modules.

Chapter 5, Designing Java Applications, introduces Java as a programming language, focusing on advanced topics, such as different ways of connecting to data sources, designing enhanced security in Java applications, handling XML data, and so on.

Chapter 6, DB2 9.7 Application Enablement, provides DB2 9.7 application enablement recipes, along with step-by-step instructions to port Oracle 11g database objects to DB2 9.7 using the IBM DataMovementTool (DMT). It also illustrates, with examples, how to use new functionalities, such as ROWNUM, DUAL, CUR_COMMIT isolation level, and ANONYMOUSPL/SQL blocks.

Chapter 7, Advanced DB2 Application Features and Practices, introduces some advanced DB2 features that are useful for analysing and troubleshooting application performance. This chapter also discusses some OLAP functions, which are very powerful for computing complex use cases in a very simple manner.

Chapter 8, Preparing and Monitoring Database Applications, discusses various tips and techniques that can be used to prepare an application environment. This chapter also focuses on the latest monitoring techniques introduced in DB2 9.7.

Chapter 9, Advanced Performance Tuning Tips, focuses on various tips and techniques that can be used to enhance application performance. It also discusses some best practices that should be followed while writing SQL statements for better performance.

What you need for this book

Ensure that the system meets the necessary operating system, memory, and disk requirements for a DB2 9.7 installation. The most recent requirements for DB2 9.7 data server installations are available on the Web at http://publib.boulder.ibm.com/ infocenter/db2luw/v9r7/topic/com.ibm.db2.luw.qb.server.doc/doc/ r0025127.html.

Along with DB2 9.7 code base, ensure that the system also meets the requirements for the IBM Data Movement Tool installation. The most recent update is available at: http://www. ibm.com/services/forms/preLogin.do?lang=en_US&source=idmt.

Who this book is for

If you are an IBM DB2 application developer who would like to exploit the advanced features provided by DB2 to design and implement high quality applications, then this book is for you.

This book assumes you have a basic understanding of DB2 application development.

Conventions

In this book, you will find a number of styles of text that distinguish between different kinds of information. Here are some examples of these styles, and an explanation of their meaning.

Code words in text are shown as follows: "We can include other contexts through the use of the include directive."

A block of code is set as follows:

```
<?xml version="1.0" encoding="UTF-8"?>
<OPTPROFILE VERSION="9.1.0.0">
<!-- Global optimization guidelines section. -->
<OPTGUIDELINES>............</OPTGUIDELINES>

<!-- Statement profile section. -->
<STMTPROFILE ID="Guidelines for Q1">
<STMTKEY SCHEMA="TEST">
<![CDATA[SQL Query]]>
</STMTKEY>
<OPTGUIDELINES>...........</OPTGUIDELINES>
</STMTPROFILE>
</OPTPROFILE>
```

When we wish to draw your attention to a particular part of a code block, the relevant lines or items are set in bold:

```
<OPTGUIDELINES>
<MQTENFORCE>
<NAME='MQT1'/>
<TYPE='REPLICATED'/>
</MQTENFORCE>
<OPTGUIDELINES>
```

Any command-line input or output is written as follows:

```
CREATE TABLE REPLACE1 (c1 INT, c2 INT)

CREATE TABLE REPLACE2 (c1 INT, c2 INT)

CREATE VIEW v1 AS SELECT * FROM REPLACE1

CREATE VIEW v2 as SELECT * FROM v1

CREATE FUNCTION fun1()
LANGUAGE SQL
RETURNS INT
RETURN SELECT c1 FROM v2

CREATE OR REPLACE VIEW v1 AS SELECT * FROM REPLACE2
```

New terms and important words are shown in bold. Words that you see on the screen, in menus or dialog boxes for example, appear in the text like this: "In the previous section, we can observe following information for **Operator#2**:".

Warnings or important notes appear in a box like this.

Tips and tricks appear like this.

Reader feedback

Feedback from our readers is always welcome. Let us know what you think about this book— what you liked or may have disliked. Reader feedback is important for us to develop titles that you really get the most out of.

To send us general feedback, simply send an e-mail to feedback@packtpub.com, and mention the book title via the subject of your message.

If there is a book that you need and would like to see us publish, please send us a note in the **SUGGEST A TITLE** form on www.packtpub.com or e-mail suggest@packtpub.com.

If there is a topic that you have expertise in and you are interested in either writing or contributing to a book, see our author guide on www.packtpub.com/authors.

Customer support

Now that you are the proud owner of a Packt book, we have a number of things to help you to get the most from your purchase.

Downloading the example code

You can download the example code files for all Packt books you have purchased from your account at `http://www.PacktPub.com`. If you purchased this book elsewhere, you can visit `http://www.PacktPub.com/support` and register to have the files e-mailed directly to you.

Errata

Although we have taken every care to ensure the accuracy of our content, mistakes do happen. If you find a mistake in one of our books—maybe a mistake in the text or the code—we would be grateful if you would report this to us. By doing so, you can save other readers from frustration and help us improve subsequent versions of this book. If you find any errata, please report them by visiting `http://www.packtpub.com/support`, selecting your book, clicking on the **erratasubmissionform** link, and entering the details of your errata. Once your errata are verified, your submission will be accepted and the errata will be uploaded on our website, or added to any list of existing errata, under the Errata section of that title. Any existing errata can be viewed by selecting your title from `http://www.packtpub.com/support`.

Piracy

Piracy of copyright material on the Internet is an ongoing problem across all media. At Packt, we take the protection of our copyright and licenses very seriously. If you come across any illegal copies of our works, in any form, on the Internet, please provide us with the location address or website name immediately so that we can pursue a remedy.

Please contact us at `copyright@packtpub.com` with a link to the suspected pirated material.

We appreciate your help in protecting our authors, and our ability to bring you valuable content.

Questions

You can contact us at `questions@packtpub.com` if you are having a problem with any aspect of the book, and we will do our best to address it.

1
Application Development Enhancements in DB2 9.7

In this chapter, we will focus on the following recipes related to application development enhancements in DB2 9.7 that help the application developer community to use DB2 features, instead of application logic:

- ▶ Changing column names online using the ALTER TABLE operation
- ▶ Using the CREATE OR REPLACE clause while creating objects
- ▶ Using the ALTER TABLE operation in a single transaction
- ▶ Using the CREATE WITH ERROR support
- ▶ Using the soft invalidation and automatic revalidation support
- ▶ Using the ALTER COLUMN SET DATA TYPE extended support
- ▶ Using the new TRUNCATE statement
- ▶ Using the AUTONOMOUS transactions
- ▶ Using implicit casting during application enablement
- ▶ Using the DEFAULT values and NAMED arguments in procedures

Introduction

DB2 9.7 provides many enhanced application features that make an application developer's life easier. In this chapter, we will focus on most of the new application features and their usage along with examples. This helps developers to understand the new features with respect to improving the application portability. The chapter is divided into various recipes and each recipe is followed by an example that helps in understanding the concept better.

Changing column names online using the ALTER TABLE operation

To rename a column in earlier versions of DB2, we used to recreate the table with a new column name and then insert the data from the earlier table on to a newly created table. The catch here is that while renaming the table, the source table should not have any references such as views, indexes, MQTs, functions, triggers, and constraints. This makes an application developer depend on a database administrator while changing the database object, based on the business requirement. In DB2 9.7, renaming a column is made extremely easy with just a single command inside the application code.

Getting ready

You need to have the ALTER privilege on the table that needs to be altered.

How to do it...

You can rename an existing column in the table to a new name without losing the data, privileges, and LBAC policies.

The DB2 command syntax to rename the column is as follows:

```
ALTER TABLE <SCHEMAS>.<TABLENAME> RENAME COLUMN <COLUMN> TO <NEW COLUMN >
```

For example:

```
ALTER TABLE DBUSER.DEPARTMENT RENAME COLUMN LOC TO LOCATION
```

After renaming the column, the application can start accessing the table without a table REORG requirement.

```
C:\>db2 "DESCRIBE TABLE DBUSER.DEPARTMENT"

                             Data type                   Column
Column name                  schema    Data type name    Length     Scale Nulls
---------------------------- --------- ----------------- ---------- ----- ------
DEPTNO                       SYSIBM    CHARACTER                  3     0 No
DEPTNAME                     SYSIBM    VARCHAR                   36     0 No
MGRNO                        SYSIBM    CHARACTER                  6     0 Yes
ADMRDEPT                     SYSIBM    CHARACTER                  3     0 No
LOC                          SYSIBM    CHARACTER                 16     0 Yes

  5 record(s) selected.

C:\>db2 "ALTER TABLE DBUSER.DEPARTMENT RENAME COLUMN LOC TO LOCATION"
DB20000I  The SQL command completed successfully.

C:\>db2 "DESCRIBE TABLE DBUSER.DEPARTMENT"

                             Data type                   Column
Column name                  schema    Data type name    Length     Scale Nulls
---------------------------- --------- ----------------- ---------- ----- ------
DEPTNO                       SYSIBM    CHARACTER                  3     0 No
DEPTNAME                     SYSIBM    VARCHAR                   36     0 No
MGRNO                        SYSIBM    CHARACTER                  6     0 Yes
ADMRDEPT                     SYSIBM    CHARACTER                  3     0 No
LOCATION                     SYSIBM    CHARACTER                 16     0 Yes

  5 record(s) selected.
```

How it works...

When an ALTER TABLE RENAME COLUMN command runs on the system, DB2 will rename the column in the table and invalidate the dependent objects (if any) such as views, functions, procedures, materialized query tables (MQT), and so on. Invalidated objects would get validated when the dependent objects are being accessed within the application or outside the application by a user. This automatic revalidation of invalid database objects depends on the value of the database configuration parameter, auto_reval.

See also

Refer to the *Using the CREATE WITH ERROR support* recipe for more details on automatic revalidation of invalid database objects, discussed in this chapter.

Using the CREATE OR REPLACE clause while creating objects

In DB2 9.7, we can create new database objects, such as aliases, procedures, functions, sequences, triggers, views, nicknames, and variables, with a CREATE OR REPLACE clause. These clauses would replace an object if it's already present; otherwise, they create a new object.

The privileges are preserved while replacing an object. In the case of modules, all of the objects within the module are dropped and the replaced version contains no objects.

The main benefit of using this feature is that DB2 doesn't have to wait for a lock on the database object being replaced. Without this feature, we cannot drop an object that is being used. Now DB2 is very intelligent and capable of making a judgment and recreating the object, even if it's been locked.

Getting ready

For the existing database objects, we need the CONTROL privilege, as the objects will be dropped and recreated.

How to do it...

When we use CREATE OR REPLACE, it replaces the earlier object, if it already exists; otherwise, it creates the object. This feature helps application developers not to worry about existing objects, but the production support team should be very cautious while using this.

1. The following set of SQL statements demonstrates the usage of the CREATE OR REPLACE statement.

```
CREATE TABLE REPLACE1 (c1 INT, c2 INT)

CREATE TABLE REPLACE2 (c1 INT, c2 INT)

CREATE VIEW v1 AS SELECT * FROM REPLACE1

CREATE VIEW v2 as SELECT * FROM v1

CREATE FUNCTION fun1()

LANGUAGE SQL

RETURNS INT

RETURN SELECT c1 FROM v2

CREATE OR REPLACE VIEW v1 AS SELECT * FROM REPLACE2
```

Downloading the example code

You can download the example code fles for all Packt books you have purchased from your account at http://www.PacktPub.com. If you purchased this book elsewhere, you can visit http://www.PacktPub.com/support and register to have the fles e-mailed directly to you.

2. As we replaced the VIEW v1 with a different base table, VIEW v2 and the function fun1 would get invalidated. The following screenshot shows the sample output for the preceding statements:

```
C:\>db2 "CREATE TABLE REPLACE1 (c1 INT, c2 INT)"
DB20000I  The SQL command completed successfully.

C:\>db2 "CREATE TABLE REPLACE2 (c1 INT, c2 INT)"
DB20000I  The SQL command completed successfully.

C:\>db2 "CREATE VIEW v1 AS SELECT * FROM REPLACE1"
DB20000I  The SQL command completed successfully.

C:\>db2 "CREATE VIEW v2 as SELECT * FROM v1"
DB20000I  The SQL command completed successfully.

C:\>db2 CREATE FUNCTION fun1() \
db2 (cont.) => LANGUAGE SQL \
db2 (cont.) => RETURNS INT \
db2 (cont.) => RETURN SELECT c1 FROM v2
DB20000I  The SQL command completed successfully.

C:\>db2 "SELECT SUBSTR(VIEWNAME, 1,20) VIEW, VALID FROM SYSCAT.VIEWS WHERE VIEWNAME='V2'"

VIEW                 VALID
-------------------- -----
V2                   Y

  1 record(s) selected.

C:\>db2 "CREATE OR REPLACE VIEW v1 AS SELECT * FROM REPLACE2"
DB20000I  The SQL command completed successfully.

C:\>db2 "SELECT SUBSTR(VIEWNAME, 1,20) VIEW, VALID FROM SYSCAT.VIEWS WHERE VIEWNAME='V2'"

VIEW                 VALID
-------------------- -----
V2                   N

  1 record(s) selected.
```

How it works...

The CREATE OR REPLACE command will create the object specified, if it doesn't exist, or drop and recreate the object, if it's already present. During this process of recreation, it invalidates any dependent objects. Based on the AUTO_REVAL parameter settings, DB2 will automatically revalidate the dependent objects after recreating the objects with the new definition.

```
C:\>db2 "SELECT * FROM v2"

C1          C2
----------- -----------

  0 record(s) selected.

C:\>db2 "SELECT SUBSTR(VIEWNAME, 1,20) VIEW, VALID FROM SYSCAT.VIEWS WHERE VIEWNAME='V2'"

VIEW                 VALID
-------------------- -----
V2                   Y

  1 record(s) selected.
```

Using the ALTER TABLE operation in a single transaction

When we perform the ALTER TABLE operations, such as dropping a column, in earlier versions of DB2, modifying the data types would force the database administrator to perform REORG on the table before any application would work on the table. Now in DB2 9.7, one can perform an unlimited number of table alterations within a single unit of work. This will allow a data modeler to manage the alteration of the column easily.

Getting ready

By default, autocommit is ON in DB2. That means each SQL statement we execute is a unit of work or a transaction. There are many ways to execute the unit of work; the simplest one is to turn off autocommit, or use db2 + c at the beginning, or use atomic procedures.

The different options available for the DB2 command can be listed using the following command:

```
C:\>db2 "? options"
db2 [option ...] [db2-command | sql-statement |
    [? [phrase | message | sqlstate | class-code]]]
option: -a, -c, -d, -e{c|s}, -finfile, -i, -lhistfile, -m, -n, -o,
        -p, -q, -rreport, -s, -t, -td;, -v, -w, -x, -zoutputfile.
```

Option	Description	Default Setting
-a	Display SQLCA	OFF
-c	Auto-commit	ON

How to do it...

In this section, we'll see how multiple ALTER TABLE operations are allowed in three different units of work. This can be implemented in any language, but the user must have privileges to alter a table.

For demonstration purposes, we have created the EMPLOYEEE table, which is a replica of EMPLOYEE of the sample database without the dependent objects. If there are dependent objects, we may have to drop them and perform the ALTER TABLE statement.

1. Set autocommit to ON: This is the default behavior for the DB2 prompt, but it can be explicitly specified as follows:

   ```
   C:\>db2 +c
   ```

2. Alter a table: Since autocommit is set to ON, it means that every statement executed is a transaction in itself. We will alter the same table in different transactions.

```
ALTER TABLE EMPLOYEEE DROP COLUMN SALARY

ALTER TABLE EMPLOYEEE ALTER COLUMN EDLEVEL DROP NOT NULL

ALTER TABLE EMPLOYEEE DROP COLUMN SEX
```

3. Reorganize the table: Since we have dropped some columns from the table, the table goes into the REORG PENDING state. To bring the table out of the REORG PENDING state, we can use the REORG command as follows:

```
REORG TABLE EMPLOYEEE
```

The following screenshot shows the sample output for the preceding statements:

```
C:\>db2 "ALTER TABLE EMPLOYEEE DROP COLUMN SALARY"
DB20000I  The SQL command completed successfully.

C:\>db2 "ALTER TABLE EMPLOYEEE ALTER COLUMN EDLEVEL DROP NOT NULL"
DB20000I  The SQL command completed successfully.

C:\>db2 "ALTER TABLE EMPLOYEEE DROP COLUMN SEX"
DB20000I  The SQL command completed successfully.

C:\>db2 "INSERT INTO EMPLOYEEE (EMPNO, FIRSTNME, LASTNAME) VALUES (1200,'ROGER','WILLIAM')"
DB21034E  The command was processed as an SQL statement because it was not a
valid Command Line Processor command.  During SQL processing it returned:
SQL0668N  Operation not allowed for reason code "7" on table
"MOHAN.EMPLOYEEE".  SQLSTATE=57016

C:\>db2 "REORG TABLE EMPLOYEEE"
DB20000I  The REORG command completed successfully.

C:\>db2 "INSERT INTO EMPLOYEEE (EMPNO, FIRSTNME, LASTNAME) VALUES (1200,'ROGER','WILLIAM')"
DB20000I  The SQL command completed successfully.
```

How it works...

When a table is altered with operations, such as dropping a column, altering a column data type, or altering the nullability feature of a column, the table may be placed in a REORG PENDING state. While the table is in the REORG state, no queries can be run until the table is brought online from the REORG PENDING state by executing the REORG command. Starting with DB2 9.7, one can perform an unlimited number of ALTER TABLE statements in a single transaction with a maximum of three transactions in a row before the need for table reorganization. This reduces the maintenance window requirement, in the case of a huge data warehouse environment.

Using the CREATE WITH ERROR support

The `AUTO_REVAL` database configuration parameter controls the revalidation and invalidation semantics in DB2 9.7. This configuration parameter can be altered online without taking the instance or the database down. By default, this is set to `DEFERRED` and can take any of the following values:

- `IMMEDIATE`
- `DISABLED`
- `DEFERRED`
- `DEFERRED_FORCE`

Now that we know all of the `REVALIDATION` options available in DB2 9.7, let's understand more about the `CREATE WITH ERROR` support. Certain database objects can now be created, even if the reference object does not exist. For example, one can create a view on a table which never existed. This eventually errors out during the compilation of the database object body, but still creates the object in the database keeping the object as `INVAILD` until we get the base reference object.

How to do it...

First, we will look at the ways in which we can change the `AUTO_REVAL` configuration parameter.

```
UPDATE DB CFG FOR <DBNAME> USING AUTO_REVAL [IMMEDIATE|DISABLED|DEFERRED|
DEFERRED_FORCE]
```

`CREATE WITH ERROR` is supported only when we set `AUTO_REVAL` to `DEFERRED_FORCE` and the `INVALID` objects can be viewed from the `SYSCAT.INVALIDOBJECTS` system catalog table.

1. Update the database configuration parameter `AUTO_REVAL` to `DEFERRED_FORCE`.

   ```
   UPDATE DB CFG FOR SAMPLE USING AUTO_REVAL DEFERRED_FORCE
   ```

2. Try to create a view `v_FMSALE`, referring to the `FMSALE` base table. Since we do not have the base table currently present in the database, DB2 9.7 still creates the view, marking it as invalid until we create the base reference object. This wasn't possible in the earlier versions of DB2.

   ```
   CREATE VIEW c_FMSALE AS SELECT * FROM FMSALE
   ```

3. How do you verify if the object is invalid? The following SQL query on the system catalog table, `SYSCAT.INVALIDOBJECTS`, shows why the database object is in an invalid state:

   ```
   SELECT OBJECTNAME, SQLCODE, SQLSTATE FROM SYSCAT.INVALIDOBJECTS
   ```

4. Once you create the base reference object and access the invalid object, DB2 revalidates and marks it as valid.

5. The following screenshot illustrates the sample output for the preceding statements:

```
C:\>db2 "UPDATE DB CFG USING AUTO_REVAL DEFERRED_FORCE"
DB20000I  The UPDATE DATABASE CONFIGURATION command completed successfully.

C:\>db2 "CREATE VIEW v_FMSALE AS SELECT * FROM FMSALE "
SQL20480W  The newly defined object "MOHAN.V_FMSALE" is marked as invalid
because it references an object "MOHAN.FMSALE" which is not defined or is
invalid, or the definer does not have privilege to access it.  SQLSTATE=0168Y

C:\>db2 "SELECT SUBSTR(OBJECTNAME,1,10) OBJECTNAME, SQLCODE, SQLSTATE FROM SYSCAT.INVALIDOBJECTS WHERE SQLSTATE=42704"

OBJECTNAME SQLCODE     SQLSTATE
---------- ----------- --------
V_FMSALE          -204 42704

  1 record(s) selected.

C:\>db2 "CREATE TABLE FMSALE (PRODUCT VARCHAR(10), SKUID INT, REVENUE INT, REGION VARCHAR(10))"
DB20000I  The SQL command completed successfully.

C:\>db2 "SELECT SUBSTR(OBJECTNAME,1,10) OBJECTNAME, SQLCODE, SQLSTATE FROM SYSCAT.INVALIDOBJECTS WHERE SQLSTATE=42704"

OBJECTNAME SQLCODE     SQLSTATE
---------- ----------- --------
V_FMSALE          -204 42704

  1 record(s) selected.

C:\>db2 "SELECT * FROM v_FMSALE"

PRODUCT    SKUID       REVENUE     REGION
---------- ----------- ----------- ----------

  0 record(s) selected.

C:\>db2 "SELECT SUBSTR(OBJECTNAME,1,10) OBJECTNAME, SQLCODE, SQLSTATE FROM SYSCAT.INVALIDOBJECTS WHERE SQLSTATE=42704"

OBJECTNAME SQLCODE     SQLSTATE
---------- ----------- --------

  0 record(s) selected.
```

How it works...

When we create an object without a base reference object, DB2 still creates the object with a name resolution error such as the table does not exist (SQLCODE: SQL0204N SQLSTATE: 42704).

1. DB2 creates an object even if the reference column does not exist with the error codes (SQLCODE: SQL0206N SQLSTATE: 42703).

2. If the referenced function is not present, we get SQLCODE: SQL0440N SQLSTATE: 42884.

3. When AUTO_REVAL is set to IMMEDIATE, all of the dependent objects will be revalidated as soon as they get invalidated. This is applicable to ALTER TABLE, ALTER COLUMN, and OR REPLACES SQL statements.

4. When AUTO_REVAL is set to DEFERRED, all of the dependent objects will be revalidated only after they are accessed the very next time; until then, they are seen as INVALID objects in the database.

5. When AUTO_REVAL is set to DEFERRED_FORCE, it is the same as DEFERRED plus the CREATE WITH ERORR feature is enabled.

There's more...

Let's have a quick look at the difference between AUTO_REVAL settings and behavior.

Case 1: AUTO_REVAL=DEFERRED

1.   When the table T1, on which the view V1 depends, is dropped, the drop would be successful, but V1 would be marked as invalid.

2.   After creating T1, V1 would still be marked as invalid until explicitly used.

Case 2: AUTO_REVAL=DEFERRED_FORCE

1.   One can create an object without having the base reference object present in the database; this only happens when we set AUTO_REVAL to DEFERRED_FORCE.

2.   Object revalidation happens when an object is being accessed.

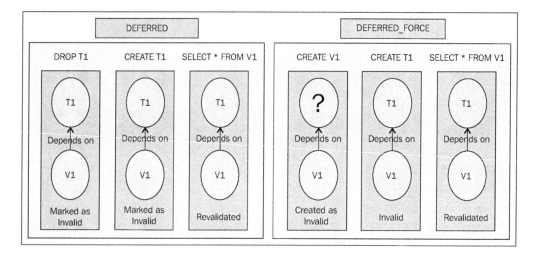

Using the soft invalidation and automatic revalidation support

In the earlier versions of DB2, whenever an object was altered or dropped, an exclusive lock was applied to ensure that no user accessed the object. This locking resulted in lock-waits or the rolling back of the transaction because of the deadlocks.

Getting ready

We need the SYSADM authority to modify the values for DB2 registry variables.

How to do it...

To enable or disable soft invalidation at the instance level, use the DB2 registry variable, `DB2_DDL_SOFT_INVAL`.

- To enable soft invalidation at the instance level, set the value of the `DB2_DDL_SOFT_INVAL` registry variable to `ON`.

```
db2set DB2_DDL_SOFT_INVAL=ON
db2stop
db2start
```

- To disable soft invalidation at the instance level, set the value of the `DB2_DDL_SOFT_INVAL` registry variable to `OFF`.

```
db2set DB2_DDL_SOFT_INVAL=OFF
db2stop
db2start
```

How it works...

In DB2 9.7, we have the soft invalidation feature to avoid these lock-waits or deadlocks. Upon activating soft invalidation using the registry variable `DB2_DDL_SOFT_INVAL=ON` in any transaction, the DDL operations, such as `DROP TABLE`, `ALTER TABLE`, and `DETACH` partitions on database objects will not be stuck because of a lock-wait (`SQL0911N Reason Code 68`) or a deadlock (`SQL0911N Reason Code 2`) while the modifying objects are being accessed by other transactions. This is because the current transaction will continue to access the original object definition while the new transaction will make use of the changed object definition of `ALTER`, `DROP`, or `DETACH` if the object being accessed is altered. During the `DROP` statement, the current transaction would still see the object until the completion of the execution of the transaction and all new transactions would fail to find the dropped object. This way, DB2 9.7 improves the application concurrency for DDL statements.

The following is the list of DDL statements for which soft invalidation is supported in DB2 9.7:

- CREATE OR REPLACE ALIAS
- CREATE OR REPLACE FUNCTION
- CREATE OR REPLACE TRIGGER
- CREATE OR REPLACE VIEW
- DROP ALIAS
- DROP FUNCTION
- DROP TRIGGER
- DROP VIEW

There's more...

As discussed in the earlier recipe, DB2 9.7 supports automatic object revalidation, based on the database configuration parameter's AUTO_REVAL setting.

Normally, the object would get revalidated whenever the application or the user accesses the invalid object, if AUTO_REVAL is set to DEFERRED. If we set AUTO_REVAL to IMMEDIATE, the objects get revalidated immediately after they become invalid.

Using the ALTER COLUMN SET DATA TYPE extended support

ALTER COLUMN SET DATA TYPE was present in the earlier versions of DB2 as well, supporting SMALLINT to INTEGER, INTEGER to BIG, REAL to DOUBLE, and BLOB(n) to BLOB(n+m) conversions; data types could not be cast to smaller data types. In DB2 9.7, the ALTER TABLE statement is extended to support all compatible types, from casting to small data types.

In some cases, data may be truncated upon altering the column data type such as DECIMAL to INTEGER. To avoid the data loss issues, DB2 9.7 scans the column data before the change and writes the error messages, such as overflow errors and truncation errors, into the notification log.

The column data type is set to a new data type only if there is no error reported during the column data scan phase.

Getting ready

To perform the ALTER COLUMN SET DATA TYPE action, the user needs to have one of the following authorizations on the object:

- ▸ ALTER privilege
- ▸ CONTROL privilege
- ▸ ALTERIN privilege on the schema
- ▸ DBADM authority

How to do it...

We can do it using ALTER COLUMN SET DATA TYPE as follows:

```
ALTER TABLE SALES ALTER COLUMN SALES SET DATA TYPE SMALLINT
ALTER TABLE EMPLOYEE ALTER COLUMN COMM SET DATA TYPE INTEGER
```

The preceding SQL statements try to change the data type from one to another.

```
C:\>db2 "DESCRIBE TABLE SALES"

                          Data type              Column
Column name               schema   Data type name Length   Scale Nulls
-----------------------   -------- -------------- -------   ----- -----
SALES_DATE                SYSIBM   DATE               4       0 Yes
SALES_PERSON              SYSIBM   VARCHAR           15       0 Yes
REGION                    SYSIBM   VARCHAR           15       0 Yes
SALES                     SYSIBM   INTEGER            4       0 Yes

  4 record(s) selected.

C:\>db2 "ALTER TABLE SALES ALTER COLUMN SALES SET DATA TYPE SMALLINT"
DB20000I  The SQL command completed successfully.

C:\>db2 "ALTER TABLE EMPLOYEE ALTER COLUMN COMM SET DATA TYPE INTEGER"
DB21034E  The command was processed as an SQL statement because it was not a
valid Command Line Processor command.  During SQL processing it returned:
SQL0270N  Function not supported (Reason code = "21").   SQLSTATE=42997
```

The reason for the failure in the case of second ALTER COLUMN statement is because an MQT "ADEFUSR" is referring to the base table EMPLOYEE.

```
db2 "? SQL0270N"

        21
```

A column cannot be dropped or have its length, data type, security, or nullability altered on a table that is a base table for a materialized query table.

We can change the COLUMN type in the base table as follows:

```
CREATE TABLE BTABLE (C1 INT, C2 INT);
CREATE VIEW v1 AS SELECT C1, C2 FROM BTABLE;
CREATE VIEW v2 AS SELECT C1, C2 FROM V1;
ALTER TABLE BTABLE ALTER COLUMN C1 SET DATA TYPE SMALLINT;
REORG TABLE BTABLE;
SELECT SUBSTR(OBJECTNAME,1,20) NAME, SQLCODE, SQLSTATE, \
OBJECTTYPE FROM SYSCAT.INVALIDOBJECTS WHERE OBJECTNAME IN ('V1','V2')
SELECT * FROM v2;
```

How it works...

The ALTER COLUMN SET DATA TYPE statement downcasts the data type INT to SMALLINT, which invalidates the views V1 and V2. Since we have AUTO_REVAL set to DEFERRED, the dependent objects become invalid until used.

```
C:\>db2 -tvf altertable.db2
CREATE TABLE BTABLE (C1 INT, C2 INT)
DB20000I  The SQL command completed successfully.

CREATE VIEW v1 AS SELECT C1, C2 FROM BTABLE
DB20000I  The SQL command completed successfully.

CREATE VIEW v2 AS SELECT C1, C2 FROM V1
DB20000I  The SQL command completed successfully.

ALTER TABLE BTABLE ALTER COLUMN C1 SET DATA TYPE SMALLINT
DB20000I  The SQL command completed successfully.


C:\>db2 "REORG TABLE BTABLE"
DB20000I  The REORG command completed successfully.

C:\>db2 "INSERT INTO BTABLE VALUES (1,2),(3,4),(5,6),(7,8)"
DB20000I  The SQL command completed successfully.
C:\>db2 SELECT SUBSTR(OBJECTNAME,1,20) NAME, SQLCODE, SQLSTATE, \
db2 (cont.) => OBJECTTYPE FROM SYSCAT.INVALIDOBJECTS WHERE OBJECTNAME IN ('v1','v2')

NAME                 SQLCODE     SQLSTATE OBJECTTYPE
-------------------- ----------- -------- ----------
V2                         - -            V
V1                         - -            V

  2 record(s) selected.
```

As soon as we access the dependent objects after altering the column data type, objects become valid and you won't see them in the SYSCAT.INVALIDOBJECTS system catalog table.

```
C:\>db2 "SELECT * FROM v1"

C1      C2
------- -----------
      1           2
      3           4
      5           6
      7           8

  4 record(s) selected.

C:\>db2 "SELECT * FROM v2"

C1      C2
------- -----------
      1           2
      3           4
      5           6
      7           8

  4 record(s) selected.

C:\>db2 SELECT SUBSTR(OBJECTNAME,1,20) NAME, SQLCODE, SQLSTATE, \
db2 (cont.) => OBJECTTYPE FROM SYSCAT.INVALIDOBJECTS WHERE OBJECTNAME IN ('v1','v2')

NAME                 SQLCODE     SQLSTATE OBJECTTYPE
-------------------- ----------- -------- ----------

  0 record(s) selected.
```

There's more...

- Casting of VARCHAR, VARGRAHIC, BLOB, CLOB, and DBCLOB data types to types smaller than the current one will not scan the table for a compatibility check, as this casting is not supported by DB2 9.7

- In the case of range partitioning tables, the string data type cannot be altered if it's a part of the range partitioning key

- The identity column cannot be altered in DB2 9.7

- In the case of the database partitioning feature, if the altering column is a part of the distribution key, then the new data type must meet the following listed conditions:

    - Same data type as the current one

    - Same column length

    - FOR BIT DATA cannot be modified in the case of CHAR and VARCHAR

Using the new TRUNCATE statement

In the earlier version of DB2, in order to empty the tables, we used the DELETE statement. The DELETE statement logs everything, so it's not efficient when we are dealing with a large volume of data. An alternate solution is to load the table using a null file and replacing the table data with it. In DB2 9.7, the TRUNCATE command is introduced, which deletes the data from a table quickly and does not log the activity, resulting in very good performance.

Getting ready

We need one of the following privileges to execute the TRUNCATE command:

- DELETE privilege

- CONTROL privilege

- DATAACCESS authority

How to do it...

TRUNCATE is just a simple command that can also be embedded in any host language.

- Truncating a table with DROP STORAGE: The TRUNCATE command deletes all the rows from a table. We have the option to retain or drop the space allocated for the table. The default is to drop the storage.

```
TRUNCATE TABLE <SCHEMA>.<TABLE> DROP STORAGE IMMEDIATE
TRUNCATE TABLE EMPLOYEEE DROP STORAGE IMMEDIATE
```

> ▸ Truncating a table with `REUSE STORAGE`: We can use the `REUSE STORAGE` clause in the `TRUNCATE` command, if we do not want to drop the storage. In this case, the space remains allocated to the table and can be used for the new data.

```
TRUNCATE TABLE <SCHEMA>.<TABLE> REUSE STORAGE IMMEDIATE

TRUNCATE TABLE EMPLOYEEE REUSE STORAGE IMMEDIATE
```

The following screenshot illustrates the sample output for the `TRUNCATE` command:

```
C:\>db2 -x "SELECT COUNT(*) FROM EMPLOYEEE"
      220160

C:\>db2 "TRUNCATE TABLE EMPLOYEEE DROP STORAGE IMMEDIATE"
DB20000I  The SQL command completed successfully.

C:\>db2 -x "SELECT COUNT(*) FROM EMPLOYEEE"
      0
```

How it works...

The `TRUNCATE` statement cannot be rolled back, as with the `DELETE` statement. This is very useful if you have tons of records to be deleted, saving archive log space and time.

The sample table used in this recipe had 0.2 million rows. `TRUNCATE` deleted all rows in a second, where the same set of records `DELETE` would take 10 seconds or more on an average-performing system, and sometimes we may hit the condition when the transaction log is full and may need to change the `LOGSECOND/LOGFILSZ` parameter.

```
DELETE FROM EMPLOYEEE
```

```
C:\>db2 "DELETE FROM EMPLOYEEE"
DB21034E  The command was processed as an SQL statement because it was not a
valid Command Line Processor command.  During SQL processing it returned:
SQL0964C  The transaction log for the database is full.  SQLSTATE=57011
```

One can use `TRUNCATE` on a table, which is present on the current server. The `TRUNCATE` statement cannot be used against the following database objects:

- ▸ Cataloged table
- ▸ Nickname
- ▸ View
- ▸ Sub table
- ▸ Staging table
- ▸ System MQT
- ▸ Range Clustered table

If the table that we are truncating is a root table in the hierarchy, then all tables in the hierarchy are truncated.

The DROP STORAGE or REUSE STORAGE clause specifies whether to drop or reuse the existing allocated storage space for the table.

The IMMEDIATE clause is mandatory, where it specifies if the TRUNCATE operation is processed immediately and cannot be undone. Always and always, the TRUNCATE statement should be the first statement in the transaction. If we have many statements inside the transaction, other operations can be undone, except the TRUNCATE operation.

IGNORE DELETE TRIGGERS or RESTRICT WHEN DELETE TRIGGERS specifies if any delete triggers, which are defined on the table, would not be activated by the TRUNCATE operation and is the default behavior. Otherwise, an error is returned in the case of RESTRICT WHEN DELETE TRIGGER.

There's more...

There are different ways to delete the data without logging the activity in the transaction logs other than TRUNCATE. They are explained as follows:

- Disable logging for a table: ACTIVATE NOT LOGGED INITIALLY is an attribute of the table for a unit-of-work operation. During this, any changes made to the table by INSERT, UPDATE, DELETE, CREATE INDEX, DROP INDEX, and ALTER TABLE are not logged.

  Now let's see how we can delete the table data without logging:

  db2 +c "ALTER TABLE EMPLOYEEE ACTIVATE NOT LOGGED INITIALLY"

  db2 "DELETE FROM EMPLOYEEE"

  db2 "COMMIT"

```
C:\>db2 +c "ALTER TABLE EMPLOYEEE ACTIVATE NOT LOGGED INITIALLY"
DB20000I  The SQL command completed successfully.

C:\>db2 "DELETE FROM EMPLOYEEE"
DB20000I  The SQL command completed successfully.

C:\>db2 "COMMIT"
DB20000I  The SQL command completed successfully.

C:\>db2 -x "SELECT COUNT(*) FROM EMPLOYEEE"
         0
```

- Using LOAD with REPLACE: Another method is to use the LOAD command to delete the data where 1.del is an empty file.

  db2 "LOAD FROM 1.del OF DEL REPLACE INTO EMPLOYEEE"

> ▶ Replace the data with an empty table: Yet another method is to use NOT LOGGED INITIALLY WITH EMPTY TABLE.
>
> ```
> db2 +c "ALTER TABLE EMPLOYEEE ACTIVATE NOT LOGGED INITIALLY WITH
> EMPTY TABLE"
> db2 "COMMIT"
> ```

```
C:\>db2 -x "SELECT COUNT(*) FROM EMPLOYEEE"
    176128

C:\>db2 +c "ALTER TABLE EMPLOYEEE ACTIVATE NOT LOGGED INITIALLY WITH EMPTY TABLE
DB20000I  The SQL command completed successfully.

C:\>db2 COMMIT
DB20000I  The SQL command completed successfully.

C:\>db2 -x "SELECT COUNT(*) FROM EMPLOYEEE"
    0
```

Now that we know we have many ways to delete data, we should be using the right method in the right situation. For example, when one uses the ACTIVATE NOT LOGGED INITIALLY option and the unit of work fails, the table has to be rebuilt and the data is lost. In any DB2 High Availability and Disaster Recovery (HADR) setup, be very sure that only tables (the data of which can be easily reproducible) can be marked as NOT LOGGED INITIALLY if required, else we may end up losing the data upon a DR switch. Also, be very cautious while working in a huge data warehouse environment in LOAD with the REPLACE clause. When the data is distributed across multiple partitions, one can expect the APPLHEAPSZ error and the table may go inaccessible. There is also the issue of running out of the utility's heap space UTIL_HEAP_SZ, if you have many data range partitions.

Using AUTONOMOUS transactions

DB2 9.7 provides ways to execute and commit a block of SQL statements independent of the outcome of invoking a transaction. For example, if transaction A invokes transaction B, which is AUTONOMOUS in nature, transaction B commits its work even if transaction A fails.

This feature enables application portability from any RDBMS that supports AUTONOMOUS transactions to DB2 9.7.

How to do it...

Let's understand the concept and the usage part of the AUTONOMOUS transaction with an example.

In an organization, the HR director wants to make sure all the salary updates are captured for audit purposes. To fulfill this request, the application developer provides an AUTONOMOUS-based code to capture the salary updates and the HR director who performs the change.

The salary, which is greater than 400,000 should only be updated by the HR director after the executive committee's approval is received, but the attempt should be captured in case anyone other than the director tries to update it.

To implement an autonomous transaction, use the AUTONOMOUS keyword while creating the procedure. The AUTONOMOUS procedure runs in its own session independent of the calling procedure. A successful AUTONOMOUS procedure commits implicitly at the end of the execution and an unsuccessful one will roll back the changes.

1. Create two new tables to capture the update activity on an employee's salary. The table eLogData is to log the autonomous transaction activity and the table eNoLog is to log the non-autonomous transaction activity. This is explained in the following code:

```
CREATE TABLE eLogData
   (LOGINID VARCHAR(10),
    EMPCODE VARCHAR(6),
    QUERYTIME TIMESTAMP,
    OLDSALARY DECIMAL(9,2),
    NEWSALARY DECIMAL(9,2))@


CREATE TABLE eNoLog
   (LOGINID VARCHAR(10),
    EMPCODE VARCHAR(6),
    QUERYTIME TIMESTAMP,
    OLDSALARY DECIMAL(9,2),
    NEWSALARY DECIMAL(9,2))@
```

2. Create an AUTONOMOUS transaction procedure, logData, and a non-autonomous transaction procedure, noLog, as follows:

```
CREATE OR REPLACE PROCEDURE
logData (IN hrLogin varchar(10),
    IN empNo VARCHAR(6),
    IN queryTime TIMESTAMP,
    IN oldSalary DECIMAL(9,2),
    IN newSalary DECIMAL(9,2))
LANGUAGE SQL
AUTONOMOUS
BEGIN
INSERT INTO eLogData VALUES
```

```
        (HRLOGIN,
         EMPNO,
         QUERYTIME,
         OLDSALARY,
         NEWSALARY);
    END@


    CREATE OR REPLACE PROCEDURE
    noLog (IN hrLogin varchar(10),
        IN empNo VARCHAR(6),
        IN queryTime TIMESTAMP,
        IN oldSalary DECIMAL(9,2),
        IN newSalary DECIMAL(9,2))
    LANGUAGE SQL
    BEGIN
    INSERT INTO eNoLog VALUES
        (HRLOGIN,
         EMPNO,
         QUERYTIME,
         OLDSALARY,
         NEWSALARY);
    END@
```

3. Create a procedure to update the salary, and if the salary is more than 400,000, the update would roll back, as this needs an approval from the executive committee.

```
    CREATE OR REPLACE PROCEDURE
    UpdateSalary (IN empCode VARCHAR(6),
            IN newSalary DECIMAL (9,2))
    LANGUAGE SQL
    BEGIN
    DECLARE oldSalary DECIMAL(9,2);
    DECLARE eSal DECIMAL(9,2);
    DECLARE QueryTime TIMESTAMP;
    SET QueryTime= CURRENT TIMESTAMP;
    SELECT salary INTO eSal FROM EMPLOYEE WHERE empNo=empCode;
    SET oldSalary=eSal;
```

```
CALL logData ('Tim Wilc', empCode, QueryTime, oldSalary, newSalary
);

CALL noLog ('Tim Wilc', empCode, QueryTime, oldSalary, newSalary
);

UPDATE EMPLOYEE SET SALARY=newSalary WHERE EMPNO=empcode;

IF newSalary > 400000 THEN

ROLLBACK;

ELSE

COMMIT;

END IF;

END@
```

The sample output of the preceding example looks similar to the following screenshot:

```
C:\>db2 -td@ -f Autonomus.db2
DB20000I  The SQL command completed successfully.

DB20000I  The SQL command completed successfully.

DB20000I  The SQL command completed successfully.

DB20000I  The SQL command completed successfully.

DB20000I  The SQL command completed successfully.


C:\>db2 "CALL UpdateSalary ('000010',280000.00)"

  Return Status = 0

C:\>db2 "CALL UpdateSalary ('000010',480000.00)"

  Return Status = 0

C:\>db2 "SELECT * FROM eLogData"

LOGINID     EMPCODE QUERYTIME                      OLDSALARY    NEWSALARY
----------  ------- -------------------------- ----------- -----------
Tim Wilc    000010  2011-05-21-22.07.37.805000    220000.00    280000.00
Tim Wilc    000010  2011-05-21-22.07.46.164000    280000.00    480000.00

  2 record(s) selected.

C:\>db2 "SELECT * FROM eNoLog"

LOGINID     EMPCODE QUERYTIME                      OLDSALARY    NEWSALARY
----------  ------- -------------------------- ----------- -----------
Tim Wilc    000010  2011-05-21-22.07.37.805000    220000.00    280000.00

  1 record(s) selected.
```

How it works...

This sample demonstrates how an AUTONOMOUS transaction differs from the standard stored procedure transaction. When Tim Wilc updates the salary of CHRISTINE to 280000 in the employee table of the sample database, both the procedures caught the change. However, while updating the salary of CHRISTINE to 480000, this activity is only caught in the AUTONOMOUS transaction, as it executes the procedure, independent of the invoking procedure.

Using implicit casting during application enablement

Typecasting is very common in application development. It means changing the data type from one to another. This is required in assignment operations and comparisons.

The necessity of type casting lies in the database or programming language. In this section, we will only focus on databases. Prior to DB2 9.7, databases supported strong typing for comparisons and assignments. For example, you could assign only an integer value to an integer data type. It didn't allow you to assign any other numeric data type to an integer variable without casting it to the integer explicitly. This restriction is known as **strong typing**.

Starting from DB2 9.7, it indirectly supports weak typing (from a user's point-of-view) but internally it casts the value to the required data type implicitly. This is commonly known as **implicit casting**. Implicit casting is the automatic conversion of one data type into another. During any comparison operation or assignment operation, if DB2 encounters different data types, then it uses implicit casting to do the required conversion. Implicit casting is based on a predefined set of conversion rules.

Getting ready...

In this section, we will see a few examples where we can exploit implicit casting between different data types. However, the support of implicit casting is not limited to the following scenarios. All of the following examples use the SAMPLE database.

How to do it...

We have many types of casting available in DB2, including casting numeric to string, string to numeric, and casting in the BETWEEN predicate and arithmetic operations. We will discuss each one of them in detail with an example.

> ▸ **Casting numeric to string data types**: The EMPNO column in the EMPLOYEE table is of CHAR (6) data type. You can either pass the parameter as a string or as a numeric value and DB2 takes care of implicitly casting it.

```
SELECT EMPNO, FIRSTNME, LASTNAME FROM EMPLOYEE WHERE EMPNO = '000250';
SELECT EMPNO, FIRSTNME, LASTNAME FROM EMPLOYEE WHERE EMPNO = 000250;
```

```
C:\>db2 "SELECT EMPNO, FIRSTNME, LASTNAME FROM EMPLOYEE WHERE EMPNO = '000250'"

EMPNO  FIRSTNME      LASTNAME
------ ------------- ----------------
000250 DANIEL        SMITH

  1 record(s) selected.

C:\>db2 "SELECT EMPNO, FIRSTNME, LASTNAME FROM EMPLOYEE WHERE EMPNO = 000250"

EMPNO  FIRSTNME      LASTNAME
------ ------------- ----------------
000250 DANIEL        SMITH

  1 record(s) selected.
```

▶ **Casting string to numeric data types**: The DEPTNUMB column in the ORG table is of the SMALLINT data type. Let's see how DB2 converts a string value to an integer value:

```
SELECT * FROM ORG WHERE DEPTNUMB=10;
SELECT * FROM ORG WHERE DEPTNUMB='10';
```

```
C:\>db2 "SELECT * FROM ORG WHERE DEPTNUMB=10"

DEPTNUMB DEPTNAME        MANAGER DIVISION    LOCATION
-------- --------------- ------- ----------- --------------
      10 Head Office         160 Corporate   New York

  1 record(s) selected.

C:\>db2 "SELECT * FROM ORG WHERE DEPTNUMB='10'"

DEPTNUMB DEPTNAME        MANAGER DIVISION    LOCATION
-------- --------------- ------- ----------- --------------
      10 Head Office         160 Corporate   New York

  1 record(s) selected.
```

▶ **Implicit casting in the BETWEEN predicate**: The DEPTNUMB column in the ORG table is of the SMALLINT data type. Let's see how we can exploit implicit casting in the BETWEEN predicate of a SELECT query:

```
SELECT * FROM ORG where DEPTNUMB BETWEEN 10 AND 50;
```

```
SELECT * FROM ORG where DEPTNUMB BETWEEN '10' AND '50';
```

```
C:\>db2 "SELECT * FROM ORG where DEPTNUMB BETWEEN 10 AND 50"

DEPTNUMB DEPTNAME        MANAGER DIVISION  LOCATION
-------- --------------- ------- --------- -----------
      10 Head Office         160 Corporate New York
      15 New England          50 Eastern   Boston
      20 Mid Atlantic         10 Eastern   Washington
      38 South Atlantic       30 Eastern   Atlanta
      42 Great Lakes         100 Midwest   Chicago

  5 record(s) selected.

C:\>db2 "SELECT * FROM ORG where DEPTNUMB BETWEEN '10' AND '50'"

DEPTNUMB DEPTNAME        MANAGER DIVISION  LOCATION
-------- --------------- ------- --------- -----------
      10 Head Office         160 Corporate New York
      15 New England          50 Eastern   Boston
      20 Mid Atlantic         10 Eastern   Washington
      38 South Atlantic       30 Eastern   Atlanta
      42 Great Lakes         100 Midwest   Chicago

  5 record(s) selected.
```

▶ **Using implicit casting in arithmetic operations**: Implicit casting is also supported in arithmetic operations. The SALARY column in the EMPLOYEE table is DECIMAL(9,2). Let's apply some calculations on SALARY using different data types:

```
SELECT EMPNO, SALARY FROM EMPLOYEE WHERE EMPNO = '000200';
```

```
UPDATE EMPLOYEE SET SALARY = SALARY + '1000' + 1500 + BIGINT(2000)
WHERE EMPNO = 000200;
```

```
SELECT EMPNO, SALARY FROM EMPLOYEE WHERE EMPNO = '000200';
```

```
C:\>db2 -x "SELECT EMPNO, SALARY FROM EMPLOYEE WHERE EMPNO = '000200'"
000200    57740.00

C:\>db2 -x "UPDATE EMPLOYEE SET SALARY = SALARY + '1000' + 1500 + BIGINT(2000) WHERE EMPNO = 000200"
DB20000I  The SQL command completed successfully.

C:\>db2 -x "SELECT EMPNO, SALARY FROM EMPLOYEE WHERE EMPNO = '000200'"
000200    62240.00
```

How it works...

In DB2 9.7, application development is made a lot easier with the help of implicit casting. It allows data types to be compared, even if the data types are of a different kind. Prior to DB2 9.7, DB2 would normally raise an error stating data type mismatch. In the current version, DB2 will automatically convert the data types to a common, more appropriate format.

There's more...

- Implicit casting is also used during function resolution. For instance, if the data types of function parameters do not match with the data types of arguments supplied during the function call, then the data types of arguments are implicitly cast to the data types of the parameters.

- Implicit casting becomes very handy during application migration. If you have an application that runs on any other database other than DB2, then the effort required to modify such applications to run on DB2 reduces significantly.

- Implicit casting is also supported in federation.

Using the DEFAULT values and NAMED arguments in procedures

When we define a stored procedure, it also has IN and OUT parameters associated with it. The stored procedures can be invoked from any host language or by command line. To call a stored procedure, we need to provide the procedure name and parameters. Since we need to process the IN and OUT parameter values, we will have to use host language variables. To make this happen, we can use parameter markers.

A **parameter marker** acts as a place holder in an SQL statement. Normally, parameter markers are identified by question marks (?). DB2 9.7 also provides support for named parameter markers. It means that we can assign names to the parameter markers and refer to them by using these names. We can also assign DEFAULT values for these parameter markers while creating the procedure.

Getting ready

In this section, we will see a few examples where we can use named and default parameters in the SQL stored procedure. We need the following privileges or authorities to create a stored procedure:

- CREATIN or IMPLICIT schema privilege, whichever is applicable
- Privileges needed to execute all the SQL statements used in the procedure

How to do it...

In this example, we will create a procedure with named/default parameters and will see how we can use named parameters while invoking the procedure.

> ▶ **Creating a stored procedure with named parameters**: We will create a stored procedure with two input parameters, both defined with DEFAULT values. The first input parameter accepts a DATE value and another parameter accepts an offset value. The procedure calculates the month by adding up the date and offset. As we are aware, in DB2 9.7, when defining the stored procedure, the application developer can provide default values so that if there is no input from the user while invoking the procedure, it uses the default set values.

```
CREATE PROCEDURE namedParmDefault (    OUT out_month SMALLINT,
                                    IN in_date DATE DEFAULT '1900-
01-01',
                IN in_offset INT DEFAULT 0)
LANGUAGE SQL
BEGIN
   SELECT MONTH(in_date + in_offset DAYS)
     INTO out_month
     FROM SYSIBM.SYSDUMMY1;
END @
```

```
C:\>db2 -td@ -f NamedParamDefault.db2
DB20000I  The SQL command completed successfully.

C:\>db2 "CALL NamedParmDefault(?, CURRENT DATE, 50)"

  Value of output parameters
  --------------------------
  Parameter Name  : OUT_MONTH
  Parameter Value : 7

  Return Status = 0

C:\>db2 "VALUES (CURRENT DATE)"

1
----------
05/23/2011

  1 record(s) selected.
```

- ▸ **Calling the procedure with named parameters**: In the preceding example, we illustrated how to call a normal procedure in any DB2 version. With the default and named parameters, we need not provide all input values in the procedure call statement. We also don't have to use the same order of values as the parameters are defined in the procedure. Consider the following examples where both these cases are illustrated:

```
CALL NamedParmDefault(?)@

CALL NamedParmDefault(?, in_offset=>100, in_date=>CURRENT DATE)@
```

```
C:\>db2 "CALL NamedParmDefault(?)"

Value of output parameters
--------------------------
Parameter Name  : OUT_MONTH
Parameter Value : 1

Return Status = 0
C:\>db2 "CALL NamedParmDefault(?, in_offset=>100, in_date=>CURRENT DATE)"

Value of output parameters
--------------------------
Parameter Name  : OUT_MONTH
Parameter Value : 8

Return Status = 0
```

How it works...

In the earlier examples, we had learnt that in addition to providing the default values, DB2 9.7 also provides the flexibility for a developer to change the parameter order in which the procedure can be invoked. With this new capability of DB2 9.7, the application developer can code less error-prone SQL procedures.

- ▸ We don't need to specify the parameters in the order of procedure definition.
- ▸ We can also define the DEFAULT values for parameters.
- ▸ We don't need to specify all parameters in the procedure call statement. In such cases, the default values will be used.
- ▸ Applications become easier to read and understand.

2

DB2 Application Techniques

In this chapter, we will focus on the following recipes describing the common DB2 techniques for application development:

- ▶ Granting and revoking instance-level authorities
- ▶ Granting and revoking database-level authorities
- ▶ Granting and revoking object privileges
- ▶ Implementing static SQL in DB2
- ▶ Implementing dynamic SQL in DB2
- ▶ Creating Declared Global Temporary Tables (DGTTs)
- ▶ Using XML in a declared temporary table
- ▶ Improving performance by creating indexes on a DGTT
- ▶ Creating Created Global Temporary Tables (CGTT)
- ▶ Using generated columns in tables
- ▶ Creating a savepoint
- ▶ Using savepoints in JDBC
- ▶ Using savepoints in SQLJ
- ▶ Creating a sequence object
- ▶ Modifying a sequence object
- ▶ Referencing a sequence object

Introduction

DB2 provides many features that an application developer can use. In this chapter, we will focus on all the basic techniques and aspects of application development that are very generic and can be used with any programming language. It will also help developers to design their applications in an efficient manner and to use the database features efficiently. The chapter is divided into various recipes and each recipe includes appropriate examples that help to understand the concept better.

Granting and revoking instance-level authorities

Authorization is a security mechanism by which DB2 determines whether a user is allowed to perform a certain action or not. DB2 provides various authorities for the administration of databases and their environment. We can grant these authorities to different users to perform a certain set of operations. These operations could be installation, migration, backups, maintenance activities, data loads, so on and so forth. The authorities comprise certain privileges that are necessary to perform a certain task. DB2 provides two levels of authorities:

- ▸ Instance-level authorities
- ▸ Database-level authorities

Instance-level authorities allow the user to perform the instance-level activities, such as upgrading databases, instance performance monitoring, managing disk space, and so on. This level of authorization doesn't provide access to data in the database.

DB2 provides four types of instance-level authorities:

- ▸ SYSADM: This is the highest level of administrative authority in DB2. It is assigned to the group specified by the sysadm_group database manager configuration parameter.
- ▸ SYSCTRL: This is the highest level of system control authority. It is assigned to the group specified by the sysctrl_group database manager configuration parameter.
- ▸ SYSMAINT: This is the second level of system control authority. It is assigned to the group specified by the sysmaint_group database manager configuration parameter.
- ▸ SYSMON: This authority provides only the ability to perform monitoring activities for the instance or its databases. It is assigned to the group specified by the sysmon_group database manager configuration parameter.

Getting ready

We need SYSADM authority to update the database manager configuration parameters, which in turn, are required to grant instance-level authorities.

How to do it...

Let's see how we can grant and revoke instance-level authority. The process is the same for all instance-level authorities.

Granting instance-level authorities

All instance-level authorities can only be granted to groups and not individual users. For each of the four authorities, there is a corresponding database manager configuration parameter. To grant the required authority to any group, this database manager configuration parameter is updated with the group name.

1. Create a group (or choose an existing group) that you would like to grant an authority to.

   ❏ For Windows (Server Edition): Use the following steps to create a group on Windows:

      i. Right-click on **My Computer** and click on **Manage**

      ii. Under **System Tools**, expand **Local Users and Groups**

      iii. Right-click on **Groups** and select **New group**

      iv. Fill the details and click **Create**

   ❏ For UNIX: Use the groupadd command to create a group on the UNIX operating systems. For example:

      ```
      groupadd devgrp
      ```

2. Update the corresponding database manager configuration parameter value as:

   ```
   UPDATE DBM CFG USING <DBM CFG parameter> <group_name>
   ```

3. For example, to grant SYSADM authority to the db2grp1 group, use the following command:

   ```
   UPDATE DBM CFG USING SYSADM_GROUP db2grp1
   ```

4. Add all users to whom you would like to grant the authority to this group. One user could be a part of multiple groups and hence a user can have multiple authorities. The membership in this group is controlled outside DB2 through the security facility provided by the operating system.

5. You can add users to the group as follows:

   ❑ For Windows: Use the following steps to add a user to a group on Windows:

      i. Right-click on **My Computer** and click on **Manage**

      ii. Under **System Tools**, expand **Local Users and Groups**

      iii. Double-click on the group name to which users are to be added

      iv. Click on **Add** and enter usernames

6. Click on **Ok**

   ❑ For UNIX: Use the `usermod` command to add a user to a group. The following command adds the `joe` user to the `devgrp` group:

```
usermod -G devgrp joe
```

   Alternatively, we can also add a user to a group manually in the `/etc/groups` file against the desired group. This file can be edited in any text editor such as the "vi" editor.

Revoking authorities

To revoke any instance-level authority from a user, change its group membership. This can be done by using the security facility of the operating system.

Use the following steps to remove a user from a group:

▸ For Windows: Use the following steps to remove a user from a group on Windows: ·

   ❑ Right-click on **My Computer** and click on **Manage**

   ❑ Under **System Tools**, expand **Local Users and groups**

   ❑ Double-click on the user from the **Users** list

   ❑ Go to the **Member of** tab

   ❑ Select the group name that needs to be removed for this user

   ❑ Click on the **Remove** button

   ❑ Click **Ok.**

▸ For UNIX: Use the `usermod` command to change the group membership of a user. We need to pass all the group names that the user should be part of. Any group which is not in the list, will be removed from that group. For example:

```
usermod -G devgrp, dbctrl, dbmon joe
```

How it works....

DB2 does not maintain any user itself. It uses the operating system users and groups. To grant or revoke any authority to or from any user, we need to use operating system security facility to create new users, or modify group membership of any user. Once the users and groups have been configured in an operating system, they can be used in DB2.

The users and groups created at the operating system needs to follow certain naming conventions; otherwise, they can't be used in DB2. These are:

- Length of group names should be within the SQL limit of 128 characters
- Usernames on UNIX systems can have up to 8 characters
- Usernames on Windows systems can have up to 30 characters
- Usernames and group names cannot begin with IBM, SQL, or SYS
- Usernames and group names cannot be USERS, ADMINS, GUESTS, PUBLIC, LOCAL or any reserved SQL word

There's more...

When a user with SYSADM authority creates a database, that user is automatically granted ACCESSCTRL, DATAACCESS, DBADM, and SECADM authority on the database. If we want to prevent that user from accessing the database as a database administrator or a security administrator, then we must explicitly revoke these database authorities from the user.

 On Windows systems, when the sysadm_group database manager configuration parameter is not specified, the Local System account is considered a system administrator (holding SYSADM authority).

What changed in DB2 9.7

In DB2 9.7, the authorization model has been changed to separate the duties of the system administrator, database administrator, and security administrator. As part of this change, the SYSADM authority no longer has implicit DBADM authority as opposed to earlier versions of DB2. If the SYSADM authority needs similar permissions to those in earlier versions of DB2, then SECADM must explicitly grant him DATAACCESS and ACCESSCTRL authorities.

We can use the SYSPROC.AUTH_LIST_AUTHORITIES_FOR_AUTHID table function to retrieve the authorities for any user. This function accepts the authorization and the authorization ID type.

For example, to view the authorizations for the ADMINISTRATOR user, we can use following query:

```
SELECT CHAR(AUTHORITY, 30), D_USER, D_GROUP, D_PUBLIC,
       ROLE_USER, ROLE_GROUP, ROLE_PUBLIC, D_ROLE
  FROM TABLE (SYSPROC.AUTH_LIST_ AUTHORITIES_FOR_AUTHID ('ADMINISTRATOR',
'U') ) AS T;
```

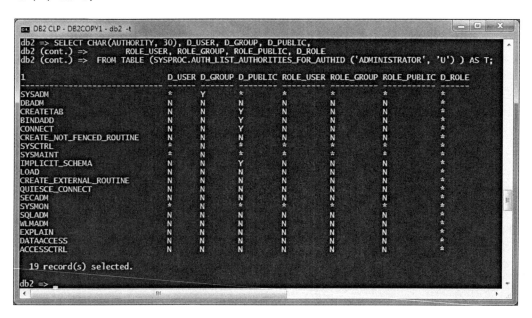

The following table summarizes all activities that can be performed by each authority:

Authority	Activities that can be performed
SYSMON	▸ Using GET DATABASE MANAGER MONITOR SWITCHES
	▸ Using GET MONITOR SWITCHES
	▸ Using GET SNAPSHOT
	▸ Using LIST commands
	▸ Using RESET MONITOR
	▸ Using UPDATE MONITOR SWITCHES
	▸ APIs that can be used: db2GetSnapshot and db2GetSnapshotSize, db2MonitorSwitches, db2mtrk, and db2ResetMonitor
	▸ All snapshot table functions
	▸ Connect to the database

Authority	Activities that can be performed
SYSMAINT	▸ Includes all activities that SYSMON can perform
	▸ Backing up a database or table space
	▸ Restoring to an existing database
	▸ Rolling to a forward recovery
	▸ Starting or stopping an instance
	▸ Restoring or quiescing a table space, and querying its state
	▸ Running tracing
	▸ Database system monitor snapshots
	▸ Reorganizing tables
	▸ Using RUNSTATS and updating the log history files
SYSCTRL	▸ Includes all activities that SYSMAINT can perform
	▸ Updating a database, node, or distributed connection services (DCS) directory
	▸ Restoring to a new or existing database
	▸ Forcing the users off the system
	▸ Creating or dropping a database
	▸ Creating, dropping, or altering a table space
	▸ Restoring to a new or existing database
	▸ Using any table space
SYSADM	▸ Includes all activities that SYSCTRL can perform
	▸ Updating and restoring database manager configuration parameters
	▸ Granting and revoking table space privileges
	▸ Upgrading and restoring a database

Granting and revoking database-level authorities

This category of authorities allows a user to perform activities specific to a database. These activities are viewing/modifying data in the database, granting and revoking privileges to users, performing data load operations, running maintenance activities like collecting statistics, backups and restores, and so on.

Getting ready

▸ We need SYSADM authority to grant DBADM or SECADM authority

▸ We need SYSADM or DBADM authority to grant other database authorities

How to do it...

Let's see how we can grant and revoke database-level authorities. The process is the same for every type of database-level authority.

Granting database-level authorities

▸ All database-level authorities can be granted to groups and roles as well as to individual users except SECADM, which can only be granted to a user.

Use the following command to grant any authority to user/role/group:

```
GRANT <authority_name> ON DATABASE <db_name> to USER/ROLE/GROUP
<name>
```

For example, to grant DBADM authority to a user user_dba on SAMPLE database, use the following command:

```
GRANT DBADM ON DATABASE SAMPLE TO USER USER_DBA
```

▸ We can also grant multiple authorities simultaneously in a single SQL command. For example, to grant DBADM, ACCESSCTRL, and DATAACCESS authorities to user user_dba on SAMPLE database, use the following command:

```
GRANT DBADM, ACCESSCTRL, DATAACCESS ON DATABASE SAMPLE TO USER
USER_DBA
```

Revoking authorities

▸ Use the following command to revoke the database-level authority from a user or group or role:

```
REVOKE <authority_name> ON DATABASE <database_name> FROM <user/
group/role name>
```

For example, to revoke DBADM authority on SAMPLE database from user user_dba, use the following command:

```
REVOKE DBADM ON DATABASE SAMPLE FROM USER USER_DBA
```

▶ Similar to GRANT, REVOKE can also include multiple authorities at a time. For example, to revoke DBADM, DATAACCESS and ACCESSCTRL authorities from user user_dba, use the following command:

```
REVOKE DBADM, ACCESSCTRL, DATAACCESS ON DATABASE SAMPLE FROM USER
USER_DBA
```

How it works...

1. DB2 does not maintain any user itself. It uses the operating system users and groups. To grant or revoke any authority to or from any user, we need to use the operating system security facility to create new users, or modify group membership of any user. Once the users and groups have been configured in the operating system, they can be used in DB2.

   The users and groups created by the operating system need to follow certain naming conventions; otherwise, they can't be used in DB2. These are:

   ❑ Length of group names should be within the SQL limit of 128 characters

   ❑ Usernames on UNIX systems can have up to 8 characters

   ❑ Usernames on Windows systems can have up to 30 characters

   ❑ Usernames and group names cannot begin with IBM, SQL, or SYS

   ❑ Usernames and group names cannot be USERS, ADMINS, GUESTS, PUBLIC, LOCAL, or any reserved SQL word

2. Database-level authorities can also be granted to roles along with groups and users. Only a system administrator can modify users and groups within an operating system. This adds a dependency on database administrators and security administrators of DB2 database to rely on the system administrator. To overcome this dependency, DB2 provides DATABASE ROLES. These are very similar to groups in the operating system except that they exist at database level. We can assign a database role to any set of users and grant authorities or privileges to the role. Now, the system administrator only needs to create new users at an operating system level and the rest can be taken care of by the database administrators or security administrators.

There's more...

The DB2 authorization model has been updated to separate the duties of system administrators, database administrators, and security administrators. The DBADM authority no longer has the ability to access data (DATAACCESS), to grant/revoke privileges, authorize (ACCESSCTRL), or define security policies (SECADM). If the DBADM authority needs these authorities, then the SECADM will have to explicitly grant these authorities to DBADM.

Only authorization IDs with the SECADM authority can grant the ACCESSCTRL, DATAACCESS, DBADM, and SECADM authorities. All other authorities can be granted by authorization IDs that hold ACCESSCTRL or SECADM authorities.

We can use the SYSPROC.AUTH_LIST_ROLES_FOR_AUTHID table function to retrieve the authorities for any user. This function accepts the authorization and authorization ID type. For example, to view the roles for the ADMINISTRATOR user, we can use following query:

```
SELECT CHAR(GRANTOR, 30) GRANTOR, GRANTORTYPE, CHAR(GRANTEE, 30)
       GRANTEE, GRANTEETYPE, CHAR(ROLENAME, 30) ROLENAME,
       CREATE_TIME, ADMIN
FROM TABLE(SYSPROC.AUTH_LIST_ROLES_FOR_AUTHID('ADMINISTRATOR','U')) AS T;
```

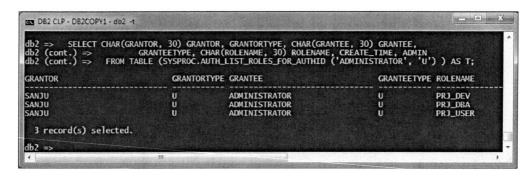

The following table summarizes the activities performed by each database authority:

Authority	Activities that can be performed
ACCESSCTRL	▶ Using SELECT on system catalog tables and views ▶ Granting and revoking SQLADM, WLMADM, EXPLAIN, BINDADD, CONNECT, CREATETAB, CREATE_EXTERNAL_ROUTINE, CREATE_NOT_FENCED_ROUTINE, IMPLICIT_SCHEMA, LOAD, QUIESCE_CONNECT ▶ Granting and revoking all privileges on global variables, indexes, nicknames, packages, routines (except system-defined audit routines), schemas, sequences, servers, tables, table spaces, views, and XSR objects

Authority	Activities that can be performed
SECADM	▸ All activities that ACCESSCTRL can perform
	▸ Creating, altering, dropping, and commenting on security objects
	▸ Granting and revoking all privileges and authorities
	▸ Using TRANSFER OWNERSHIP
	▸ Using EXECUTE on audit system-defined routines
	▸ Granting the EXECUTE privilege on audit system-defined routines
	▸ Using the AUDIT statement
	▸ Using the CONNECT authority
DATAACCESS	▸ Using the LOAD authority
	▸ Using SELECT, INSERT, UPDATE, and DELETE privileges on all tables, views, MQTs, and nicknames
	▸ Using SELECT on system catalog tables and views
	▸ Using EXECUTE on all routines (except system-defined audit routines)
	▸ Using EXECUTE on all packages
EXPLAIN	▸ Using the EXPLAIN statement
	▸ Using the PREPARE statement
	▸ Using EXECUTE system-defined explain routines
SQLADM	▸ Includes all activities that EXPLAIN can perform
	▸ Using CREATE EVENT MONITOR
	▸ Using DROP EVENT MONITOR
	▸ Using FLUSH EVENT MONITOR
	▸ Using SET EVENT MONITOR STATE
	▸ Using FLUSH OPT. PROFILE CACHE
	▸ Using FLUSH PACKAGE CACHE
	▸ Using PREPARE
	▸ Using REORG INDEXES/TABLES
	▸ Using RUNSTATS
	▸ Using EXECUTE on all system-defined routines (except audit routines)
	▸ Using SELECT on system catalog tables and views
	▸ Using EXPLAIN
	▸ Certain clauses of ALTER SERVICE CLASS, ALTER THRESHOLD, ALTER WORK ACTION SET, ALTER WORKLOAD

Authority	Activities that can be performed
WLMADM	► Creating, altering, and commenting on, and dropping workload manager objects
	► Granting and revoking workload privileges
	► Using EXECUTE system-defined workload management routines
	► Granting USAGE privilege on workloads
DBADM	► Includes all the activities that WLMADM, SQLADM, and EXPLAIN can perform, except granting USAGE privilege on workloads
	► Creating, altering, and dropping non-security-related objects
	► Reading log files
	► Creating, activating, and dropping event monitors
	► Querying the state of a table space
	► Updating log history files
	► Quiescing a table space
	► Reorganizing indexes/tables
	► Using RUNSTATS
	► Using the BINDADD authority
	► Using the CONNECT authority
	► Using the CREATETAB authority
	► Using the CREATE_EXTERNAL_ROUTINE authority
	► Using the CREATE_NOT_FENCED_ROUTINE authority
	► Using the IMPLICIT_SCHEMA authority
	► Using the LOAD authority
	► Using the QUIESCE_CONNECT authority
BINDADD	► Creating new packages in the database
CONNECT	► Connecting to the database
CREATETAB	► Creating tables in the database
CREATE_EXTERNAL_ROUTINE	► Creating procedures
CREATE_NOT_FENCED_ROUTINE	► Creating "not fenced" UDFs or procedures
IMPLICIT_SCHEMA	► Creating the schema implicitly (schema will be created automatically if it doesn't exist)
LOAD	► Loading data in the table
QUIESCE_CONNECT	► Accessing the database while it is quiesced

Granting and revoking object privileges

Privileges are the next level of security mechanism that can be implemented at database object level. A privilege determines the permission of performing a task on an object. A user who creates an object in the database implicitly acquires all the privileges associated with that object. Privileges can be divided into three categories:

1. **Individual object privileges**: Such privileges allow a user to perform different actions on the object. These privileges don't allow a user to grant or revoke similar privileges to or from other users. Example of such privileges can be: SELECT, EXECUTE, UPDATE, and so on. Only a user with CONTROL, ACCESSCTRL, or SECADM can grant these privileges to another user.

2. **CONTROL privilege**: This privilege allows users to grant and revoke privileges to or from other users. The CONTROL privilege is implicitly granted to the creator on the newly-created tables, indexes, and packages. It is implicitly granted on newly-created views if the object owner has the CONTROL privilege on all the tables, views, and nicknames referenced by the view definition. A user with CONTROL privilege can extend the ability to grant and revoke privileges to and from other users by using WITH GRANT OPTION in the GRANT command.

3. **Privileges for objects inside a package or routine**: Once a package is created, only the EXECUTE privilege on that package is needed for a user to execute this package. Users need not have any other privilege on objects referenced in the package or routine. If the package or routine contains static SQL, then the privileges of the package or routine owner are considered at the time of execution. If it contains dynamic SQL, then it depends on the DYNAMMICRULES BIND option of the package.

WITH GRANT OPTION does not allow the person granting the privilege to revoke the privilege, once granted. We must have the SECADM authority, the ACCESSCTRL authority, or the CONTROL privilege to revoke the privilege.

Getting ready

To grant privileges on any object, we need to have SYSADM, DBADM, or CONTROL privilege on that object, or the user must hold that privilege with WITH GRANT OPTION.

Also, to grant CONTROL privilege, we need to have the SYSADM or DBADM privilege.

How to do it...

Let's see how to grant and revoke object privileges to and from users, roles, or groups.

Granting privileges

- ▸ Any object privilege can be granted to groups and roles as well as to individual users.

- ▸ Use the following command to grant any privilege to a user/role/group:

```
GRANT <privilege> ON <object_type> <object_name> to USER/ROLE/
GROUP <name>
```

For example, to grant the SELECT privilege to a user user_dev on the TEST. EMPLOYEE table, use the following command:

```
GRANT SELECT ON TABLE TEST.EMPLOYEE SAMPLE TO USER USER_DEV
```

- ▸ We can also grant multiple privileges simultaneously in a single SQL command. For example, to grant SELECT, INSERT, DELETE, and UPDATE privileges to user user_dev on TEST.EMPLOYEE table, use the following command:

```
GRANT SELECT, INSERT, UPDATE, DELETE ON TABLE TEST.EMPLOYEE TO
USER USER_DEV
```

Revoking privileges

- ▸ Use the following command to revoke privileges on an object from a user/group/role:

```
REVOKE the <privilege> ON <object_type> <object_name> FROM <user/
group/role name>
```

For example, to revoke SELECT privilege on the TEST.EMPLOYEE table from user user_dev, use the following command:

```
REVOKE SELECT ON TABLE TEST.EMPLOYEE SAMPLE FROM USER USER_DEV
```

- ▸ Similar to GRANT, REVOKE can also include multiple privileges at a time. For example, to revoke SELECT, INSERT, UPDATE, and DELETE privileges on the TEST.EMPLOYEE table from the user 'user_dev', use the following command:

```
REVOKE SELECT, INSERT, UPDATE, DELETE FROM USER USER_DEV
```

There's more...

We can use the SYSIBMADM.PRIVILEGES administrative view to retrieve the privileges on any database object. For example, to view the privileges on the EMPLOYEE table, we can use the following query:

```
SELECT CHAR(AUTHID, 10) AUTHID, AUTHIDTYPE, CHAR(PRIVILEGE, 10)
PRIVILEGE,
       CHAR(OBJECTNAME, 10) OBJECTNAME,
       CHAR(OBJECTSCHEMA, 10) OBJECTSCHEMA,
      CHAR(OBJECTTYPE, 10) OBJECTTYPE
  FROM SYSIBMADM.PRIVILEGES
  WHERE OBJECTNAME='EMPLOYEE';
```

The following table summarizes all privileges available for different types of database objects:

Object type	Privilege	Additional information
Authorization ID	SETSESSIONUSER	Allows the holder to switch identities to any of the authorization IDs on which the privilege was granted.
Schema	CREATEIN	Allows the user to create objects within the schema.
	ALTERIN	Allows the user to alter objects within the schema.
	DROPIN	Allows the user to drop objects from within the schema.
Table space	USE	Allows the user to create tables in a table space.
Table and View	CONTROL	Provides the user with all the privileges for a table or view, including the ability to drop it, and to grant and revoke individual table privileges.
	ALTER	Allows the user to modify a table. A user with an ALTER privilege can also COMMENT on a table, or on columns of the table.
	DELETE	Allows the user to delete rows from a table or view.
	INDEX	Allows the user to create an index on a table.
	INSERT	Allows the user to insert a row into a table or view and run the IMPORT utility.
	REFERENCES	Allows the user to create and drop a foreign key, and specify the table as the parent in a relationship. The user might have this privilege only on specific columns.
	SELECT	Allows the user to retrieve rows from a table or view, to create a view on a table, and to run the EXPORT utility.
	UPDATE	Allows the user to change an entry in a table, a view, or one or more specific columns in a table or view. The user may have this privilege only on specific columns.
Package	CONTROL	Provides the user with the ability to rebind, drop, or execute a package, as well as the ability to extend those privileges to others
	BIND	Allows the user to rebind or bind that package and to add new package versions of the same package name and creator
	EXECUTE	Allows the user to execute or run a package.
Index	CONTROL	Allows the user to drop the index.

Object type	Privilege	Additional information
Sequence	USAGE	Allows the user to use NEXT VALUE and PREVIOUS VALUE expressions for the sequence.
	ALTER	Allows the user to perform tasks, such as restarting the sequence or changing the increment for future sequence values.
Routine	EXECUTE	Allows the user to invoke that routine.
Workload	USAGE	Allows the user to use a workload.

Implementing static SQL in DB2

When the complete SQL statement is known at pre-compile time, it is known as static SQL. All aspects of the SQL statement, such as the table name, column names, filter criteria, and so on must be specified at pre-compile time. The only thing that can be passed at the time of execution are host variables. Even if we have host variables, the complete information such as data type, length, and so on, must be available at the pre-compile time. Static SQL statements can be embedded in all languages except interpreted languages. At the time of pre-compilation, the language pre-processor converts the static SQL code into database manager run-time service API calls which the compiler can understand. In the case of interpreted languages, there is no concept of pre-processing, so everything becomes dynamic SQL there. In this section, we will see how to implement static SQL.

The advantages of static SQL are:

- Relatively simpler programming effort
- End user doesn't need a direct privilege to execute SQL statements because DB2 uses the authorization ID of the person binding the application.
- Static SQL statements are persistent, which means that the statements last for as long as the package exists.
- Static SQL statements are precompiled and are ready for execution. This provides performance benefits as it saves SQL compilation time.

Getting ready

You can only implement static SQL if you know the complete SQL statement at pre-compile time.

We'll also need a host language which can be precompiled. We will use SQLJ for this recipe.

How to do it...

Let's see how static SQL can be implemented in SQLJ. The following example assumes that we have a database named SAMPLE. We will use the below query in our example:

```
SELECT EMPNO, FIRSTNME, LASTNAME, SALARY
    INTO :empNo:firstName:lastName:salary
    FROM EMPLOYEE
    WHERE EMPNO = '200340'
```

Implementing static SQL mainly involves the following steps:

1. **Connecting to the database**: Before we can execute any SQL against the database, we need to establish a connection. In SQLJ, we first need to load the database driver, and then create a connection object and a connection context object:

   ```
   Use Class.forName() method to load the database driver.
   Class.forName ("COM.ibm.db2.jdbc.app.DB2Driver").newInstance();

   Use getConnection() method to get the connection.
   String url = "jdbc:db2:sample";
   Connection con = DriverManager.getConnection(url);

   Use setDefaultContext() method to set the default context
   DefaultContext ctx = new DefaultContext(con);
   DefaultContext.setDefaultContext(ctx);
   ```

2. **Declaring the host variables**: In this section, we will declare all the host variables that we need. Because we want to fetch the employee name, first name, last name, and salary from the EMPLOYEE table, we need four host variables:

   ```
   String empNo, firstName, lastName;
   Float salary;
   ```

3. **Executing the SQL statements**: This is the most crucial section. In this section, we will execute SQL statements statically. To do that, we need an SQL statement, which is complete in nature. All the statements that are enclosed in #sql {} are preprocessed by the pre-compiler and are replaced with the corresponding language API calls that the compiler can understand.

   ```
   #sql { SELECT EMPNO, FIRSTNME, LASTNAME, SALARY
               INTO :empNo, :firstName, :lastName, :salary
               FROM SANJU.EMPLOYEE
               WHERE EMPNO = '200340'};
   ```

4. **Processing the results if needed**: Once we have the results from the SQL statement, we can process them as needed:

```
System.out.println ("\nEmployee Num: " + empNo +
                    "\nFirst Name: " + firstName +
                    "\nLast Name: " + lastName +
                    "\nSalary: " + salary);
```

5. **Disconnecting from the database**: Once we are done with the application, we need to disconnect the database connection. Use the `close()` method to disconnect from the database:

```
con.close();
```

Sample output for the previous example is shown next:

```
c:\Users\Sanju\Desktop\Programming\sqlj>java staticSql
THIS EXAMPLE SHOWS HOW TO USE STATIC SQL

Employee Num: 200340
First Name: ROY
Last Name: ALONZO
Salary: 31840.0

c:\Users\Sanju\Desktop\Programming\sqlj>
```

How it works...

When a static SQL statement is prepared, an executable form of the statement is created and stored in the database package. The package contains access plans selected by the DB2 optimizer for the static SQL statements in our application. The access plan contains the information required by the database manager to issue the static SQL statements in the most efficient manner as determined by the optimizer. The executable form can be constructed either at the pre-compile time, or at a later bind time. In either case, the preparation occurs before runtime. Because the access plan is created at pre-compile time, the DB2 optimizer uses the statistics available at that time.

There's more...

Starting with DB2 9.7, the access plan for static SQL can be reused. DB2 provides the mechanism to lock down the access plans for static SQL. Once an access plan is locked down, the DB2 optimizer attempts to reuse the same access plan across binds or rebinds, resulting in a predictable performance. The users can also ensure very similar performance across the fix pack upgrades and statistics updates. They can also expect some configuration-parameter changes as well. The locked access plan might not be the best access plan (maybe after statistics are updated), but still, it will ensure the same performance as earlier. The following is applicable for an access plan reuse:

▶ To enable access plan reuse, use the ALTER PACKAGE command or use the APREUSE option for BIND, REBIND, and PRCOMPILE commands.

▶ If significant changes are made to the schema or the environment, then it might not be possible to reuse the same access plan. Such changes could be dropping of an index, recompiling the statement at a different optimization level, and so on.

▶ The statement-level optimization guideline takes precedence over access plan reuse.

▶ A statement profile with empty guideline can be used to disable access plan reuse for a particular statement, keeping it still available for other statements.

▶ If the access plan cannot be reused, a warning is raised (SQL20516W).

The isolation level for static SQL statements is specified as an attribute of a package and applies to the application processes that use that package. It can be specified by using the ISOLATION option in BIND or PRECOMPILE commands. The isolation clause in a select statement overrides all other isolation levels.

Over a period of time, static SQL packages become inefficient due to old statistics. In such cases, we can REBIND the package after updating the statistics. REBIND will create a fresh access plan based on the latest statistics.

If the static SQL statements has host variables or global variables, we can defer the compilation of these statements till EXECUTE or OPEN. We can use the REOPT bind option to specify when to compile such statements. The advantage of this approach is that the statements will be compiled with real values of the variables, which mean the access plan chosen would be better. We can choose between REOPT ONCE and REOPT ALWAYS. With REOPT ONCE, the access plan is cached after the first OPEN or EXECUTE request and will be available for the subsequent execution of this statement. With REOPT ALWAYS, the access plan is generated for every OPEN or EXECUTE statement using the latest value for the variables, resulting in even better access plans but at the cost of the recompilation time.

We can use the DEGREE option of BIND and PREP commands to control the degree of intra-partition parallelism for static SQL.

Implementing dynamic SQL in DB2

When an SQL statement or some part of it is not known until the execution time, then these statements are executed dynamically. In the case of dynamic SQL, the statement is compiled at runtime. It also means that the access plan is created at runtime, which can benefit from the latest statistics. When the database manager runs a dynamic SQL or XQuery statement, it creates an access plan based on the current system statistics and current configuration parameters. This access plan might change from one execution of the statements, application program to the other.

Dynamic SQL can be used when:

▶ A complete SQL statement or some part of it is not known at compile time

▶ Objects referenced in the SQL statement are not available at compile time

▶ We want to use the latest statistics available to optimize the access plan

▶ We might change the environment such as the changing database or database manager configuration parameters, special registers, and so on, which might improve the performance

How to do it...

To implement dynamic SQL, an SQL statement is first prepared and then executed. This preparation and execution happens at runtime. It is also possible to prepare a statement once and execute it multiple times.

Every language provides the means to prepare and execute SQL statements. In this recipe, we will see how to implement dynamic SQL in Java. We will also see how to use parameter markers.

1. **Creating a database connection**: Before we can execute any SQL statement against the database, we need to create a connection object. For that, we need to load the database driver first, and then create a connection object:

    ```
    Use Class.forName() method to load the database driver.
    Class.forName("COM.ibm.db2.jdbc.app.DB2Driver").newInstance();

    Use getConnection() method to get the connection.
    String url = "jdbc:db2:sample";
    Connection con = DriverManager.getConnection(url);
    ```

2. **Declaring a variable**: Because we are trying to get results from a query, we need variables to store the results. Let's declare a few variables that we might need:

    ```
    String empNo, firstName, lastName;
     Float salary;
    ```

3. **Preparing a statement**: To run an SQL statement dynamically, we first need to prepare it. Once a statement is prepared, we can run it multiple times. The SQL statement to be used for preparing the statement need not be available at compile time. We can use the `PreparedStatement` class to store a prepared statement. We can either use a string or a variable to pass the SQL query to the `prepareStatement()` method:

```
PreparedStatement pstmt1 = con.prepareStatement("select
empno, firstname, lastname, salary from employee where empno =
'200310'");
```

4. **Executing a statement**: Now, we have a prepared statement. We can execute it as many times as we want. We can use the `executeQuery()` method to execute a prepared statement and process the results as desired:

```
ResultSet rs1 = pstmt1.executeQuery();

while (rs1.next())
{
  empNo = rs1.getString(1);
  firstName = rs1.getString(2);
  lastName = rs1.getString(3);
  salary = rs1.getFloat(4);
  System.out.println("EmpNo: " + empNo +
                     "; First Name: " + firstName +
                     "; Last Name: " + lastName +
                     "; Salary: " + salary);
}
```

5. If we have an SQL statement that has to be executed multiple times with different values of variables, then we can use parameter markers. The parameters are identified by a question mark (?) in the SQL statement. Once an SQL statement with parameter markers is prepared, it can be executed against different values for a parameter marker without having to prepare it again:

```
PreparedStatement pstmt2 = con.prepareStatement("select empno,
firstname, lastname, salary from employee where empno = ?");
pstmt2.setString(1, "200310");
ResultSet rs2 = pstmt2.executeQuery();
pstmt2.setString(1, "200330");
ResultSet rs3 = pstmt2.executeQuery();
pstmt2.setString(1, "200340");

ResultSet rs4 = pstmt2.executeQuery();
```

6. The sample output for our example looks as follows:

```
C:\Program Files (x86)\IBM\SQLLIB\samples\java\jdbc>java DynamicSql
THIS EXAMPLE SHOWS HOW TO USE DYNAMIC SQL.
EmpNo: 200310; First Name: MICHELLE; Last Name: SPRINGER; Salary: 35900.0
EmpNo: 200330; First Name: HELENA; Last Name: WONG; Salary: 35370.0
EmpNo: 200340; First Name: ROY; Last Name: ALONZO; Salary: 31840.0

C:\Program Files (x86)\IBM\SQLLIB\samples\java\jdbc>_
```

How it works...

DB2 provides Dynamic SQL support statements, which are required to transform the host variable containing SQL text into an executable form. These statements can be directly embedded into any host language. These support statements are:

*   EXECUTE IMMEDIATE: Prepares and executes a statement that does not use any host variables. This can also be used as an alternative to PREPARE and EXECUTE statements.

*   PREPARE: Turns the character string form of the SQL statement into an executable form of the statement. It assigns a statement name, and optionally places information about the statement in an SQLDA structure.

*   EXECUTE: Executes a previously prepared SQL statement. The statement can be executed repeatedly within a connection.

*   DESCRIBE: Places information about a prepared statement into an SQLDA.

Dynamic SQL statements are prepared from an SQL statement and a statement name. We can also have an SQL statement in a variable. The SQL statements are not processed when the application is pre-compiled. This also means that the SQL statement need not even exist at pre-compile time. Because the host variable information, such as the data type, length, and so on, is not available during the pre-compilation time, and we cannot use host variables in dynamic SQL, we can use parameter markers instead of host variables. A parameter marker is indicated by a question mark (?) or a colon followed by a name (:name). This indicates where to substitute a variable inside the SQL statement. We can have more than one parameter marker in an SQL statement. In such cases, the values of the variables will be substituted in the order of parameter markers.

There's more...

Similar to Static SQL, we can use the REOPT option in BIND or PREPARE to control the access plan generation of dynamic SQL statements. If the SQL statements have parameter markers or global variables, we can postpone the compilation of these statements until OPEN or EXECUTE statements are encountered. The benefit of using the REOPT option is that the statements will be compiled with the real values of the variables, which means the access plan chosen would be better. We can choose between REOPT ONCE and REOPT ALWAYS. With REOPT ONCE, the access plan is cached after the first OPEN or EXECUTE request and will be available for subsequent execution of this statement. With REOPT ALWAYS, the access plan is generated for every OPEN or EXECUTE statement using the latest value for the variables, resulting in even better access plans but at the cost of recompilation time. With REOPT ALWAYS, the statement concentrator is disabled.

DB2 can avoid recompiling a dynamic SQL statement that has been run previously by caching the access section and statement text in the dynamic statement cache. A subsequent PREPARE request for this statement will attempt to find the access section in the dynamic statement cache, avoiding compilation. However, statements that differ in literals used in predicates will not match.

> If the FLUSH PACKAGE CACHE statement is issued, then all the cached dynamic SQL statements are removed. When these statements are invoked again, they are recompiled implicitly.

Statement concentrator for dynamic SQL

The dynamic SQL statements are compiled at the execution time. In an OLTP environment, we have a large number of similar SQL statements executed dynamically. They only differ in the literal values. DB2 9.7 introduced a statement concentrator for dynamic SQL statements, which can share the access plan for such statements. This saves a lot of compilation time. This behavior can be enabled by setting the value for the stmt_conc database configuration parameter as follows:

```
UPDATE DB CFG FOR SAMPLE USING STMT_CONC LITERALS
```

This is disabled or set to OFF by default.

When enabled, the following SQL statements will share the same access plan:

```
SELECT DEPTNAME, MGRNO FROM DEPT WHERE DEPTNO='A00';

SELECT DEPTNAME, MGRNO FROM DEPT WHERE DEPTNO='B01';
```

Choosing between static and dynamic SQL

Static SQL statements are precompiled while dynamic SQL statements are compiled at runtime which is an overhead. It's a tradeoff between a better access plan and the compilation time. If our SQL query is pretty complex and its execution time is much greater than compilation time, then we might want to use dynamic SQL, as it will add compilation time as an overhead; but in return, it will result in a better access plan and hence lesser execution time, resulting in a better overall response time. In general, if the expected runtime is less than 2 seconds, static SQL can be used, and if it is higher than 10 seconds, then dynamic SQL would be a better choice. For intermediate ones, we can choose either.

Static SQL works better when underlying data distribution is uniform.

If the query has many range predicates, then dynamic SQL would perform better.

If the SQL statement is likely to run multiple times (like more than 10), then dynamic SQL can be preferred, as the compilation time becomes less as compared to multiple execution times.

If the query is very random in nature, then dynamic SQL will be better.

Creating Declared Global Temporary Tables (DGTTs)

Declared Global Temporary Tables (also known as DGTTs) are used to store temporary results within an application. Because these tables are only used for temporary storage, they do not persist. They do not appear in the system catalog either. And because they don't persist, they can't be shared with other applications. When the application using this table terminates, any data in the table is deleted and the table is dropped.

Another key difference between DGTTs and regular tables is that the rows in a DGTT cannot be locked, as the temporary tables can't be shared among different applications. In this recipe, we will create a declared global temporary table.

Getting ready

- To create a declared global temporary table, we need a user temporary table space.
- To create a declared global temporary table, we need at least one of the following authorities/privileges:
    - USE privilege on USER TEMPORARY TABLE SPACE
    - DBADM authority
    - SYSADM authority
    - SYSCTRL authority

How to do it...

In this section, we will see how to create the declared global temporary tables:

1. Before we can create any temporary table, we need a user temporary table space. It's always recommended to create temporary table spaces as `MANAGED BY SYSTEM`. If this clause is specified, then the table space is controlled by the operating system. Use the `CREATE TABLESPACE` command to create a temporary tablespace:

   ```
   CREATE USER TEMPORARY TABLESPACE user_temp_tbsp
     MANAGED BY SYSTEM
     USING ('c:\user_tbsp')
   ```

2. Use the following command to create a DGTT. This statement defines a temporary table called `sal_rise_temp`:

   ```
   DECLARE GLOBAL TEMPORARY TABLE sal_rise_temp
     (empno INT,
      sal_rise_date DATE,
      updated_sal BIGINT,
      manager_empno INTEGER)
     ON COMMIT DELETE ROWS
     NOT LOGGED
     IN user_temp_tbsp
   ```

3. We can also use the `LIKE` clause to create a temporary table similar to the existing regular table:

   ```
   DECLARE GLOBAL TEMPORARY TABLE emp_temp LIKE EMPLOYEE
     ON COMMIT DELETE ROWS
     NOT LOGGED
     IN user_temp_tbsp
   ```

How it works...

► `ON COMMIT DELETE ROWS`: If this option is specified, then the rows in the temporary table are deleted on every `COMMIT`.

► `NOT LOGGED`: If this option is specified, the insert, update, and delete operations are not logged. Only creation and dropping are logged. If this option is specified, then DB2 uses an internal `TRUNCATE` to delete the rows in the table. If any cursor with the `WITH HOLD` clause is open, then DB2 will delete one row at a time. The default is `LOGGED`, which logs everything.

If the temporary table is defined without specifying any table space name, then DB2 looks for the existing user's temporary table space that has the smallest sufficient page size over which the user has USE privilege. If table spaces with these criteria are present more than once, then DB2 decides which to choose.

There's more...

We can create more than one temporary table with the same name in different applications unlike regular tables. This becomes very advantageous in designing applications for concurrent users.

The temporary tables can also get benefits from row compression. The compression is enabled for a declared temporary table. If DB2 thinks it can benefit from the compression of a temporary table, then the data will be compressed. This is completely transparent to the user and nothing's especially needed to enable the compression for temporary tables. The indexes on the temporary tables are also eligible for compression.

The errors in operation during a unit of work using a declared temporary table do not cause the unit of work to be completely rolled back. However, an error in operation in a statement changing the contents of a declared temporary table will delete all the rows in that table.

Referencing a declared global temporary table

The schema for declared global temporary table is always SESSION. We always need to qualify a temporary table with this schema or else DB2 will look for a table in the current schema.

To select the data from a temporary table temp_tbl, we can use following command:

```
SELECT * FROM SESSION.temp_tbl
```

The preceding statement selects all records from the temp_tbl temporary table.

For all declared global temporary tables, the schema name is always SESSION. We can also create a regular table with the schema name as SESSION. In such cases, if we have a regular table (as in SESSION schema) and a temporary table with the same name, then DB2 will resolve the reference to the temporary table rather than the regular table. Hence, it is never recommended to create regular tables in the SESSION schema to avoid confusion.

Dropping a declared temporary table

The declared temporary tables are dropped when the application terminates the database connection. We can also drop them explicitly, by using the DROP command. For example:

```
DROP TABLE SESSION.temp_tbl
```

To drop a temporary table, we must specify SESSION as a schema name. Once the temporary table is dropped, it can no longer be referenced even if the transaction is not committed.

Using declared temporary tables across transactions

If a temporary table is defined within a transaction, then with the ROLLBACK command, the temporary table is also dropped. Otherwise, it is available until the application disconnects from the database. If we want to use a temporary table and its data across the transactions, then there is only one thing to think about, which is whether or not we want to preserve the data in the temporary table once it exits a transaction. This behavior can be specified by using the ON COMMIT clause:

```
DECLARE GLOBAL TEMPORARY TABLE sal_rise_temp

    (empno INT,

     sal_rise_date DATE,

     updated_sal BIGINT,

     manager_empno INTEGER)

  ON COMMIT DELETE ROWS

  NOT LOGGED

 IN user_temp_tbsp
```

If the ON COMMIT DELETE ROWS clause is specified, then the rows will be deleted on COMMIT. This is the default. If the ON COMMIT PRESERVE ROWS clause is specified, then the rows will not be deleted on COMMIT.

Using Admin views to view temporary tables information

We can use the SYSIBMADM.ADMINTEMPTABLES administrative view and the SYSPROC. ADMIN_GET_TEMP_TABLES table function to get information about the temporary table present in the database. The results can be filtered by specifying conditions, such as TEMPTABTYPE='D' or TEMPTABTYPE= 'C'. We can also filter the results through the application handle or application name:

```
SELECT TABSCHEMA, TABNAME, ONCOMMIT, ONROLLBACK,

    INSTANTIATION_TIME

  FROM SYSIBMADM.ADMINTEMPTABLES
```

```
    WHERE TEMPTABTYPE = 'D' AND INSTANTIATOR = SYSTEM_USER
SELECT TABSCHEMA, TABNAME, ONCOMMIT, ONROLLBACK, INSTANTIATION_TIME
    FROM TABLE (SYSPROC.ADMIN_GET_TEMP_TABLES(APPLCATION_HANDLE,
TABSCHEMA, TABNAME))
AS T
```

The sample output is as follows:

Using XML in a declared temporary table

Starting from DB2 9.7, we can create declared temporary tables with XML columns in them. DGTTs can contain XML data and they can be used just like regular tables.

How to do it...

Let's see how we can create a declared temporary table with an XML columns:

1. Create a declared temporary table with XML column in it:

    ```
    DECLARE GLOBAL TEMPORARY TABLE sample_xml (empno INT,
                                        sal_rise_date DATE,
                                        sal_dtls XML)

        ON COMMIT DELETE ROWS
        NOT LOGGED
        IN user_temp_tbsp;
    ```

2. Insert an XML document in the temporary table. To do that, use the XMLPARSE function. This function converts a serialized string value to an XML document. In case of any errors in the XML document, an error is returned:

    ```
    INSERT INTO SESSION.sample_xml
        VALUES(1007,
    ```

```
                CURRENT DATE,
                XMLPARSE(document'<salary_revision sal_dtl_key = "5099">
                        <old_salary>
                          <monthly_salary>30000</monthly_salary>
                          <effective_date>24-11-2010</effective_date>
                        </old_salary>
                          <new_salary>
                           <monthly_salary>40000</monthly_salary>
                            <effective_date>24-11-2011</effective_date>
                          </new_salary>
                        </salary_revision>'));
```

3. Let's see the data in the table:

```
SELECT * FROM SESSION.sample_xml;
```

How it works...

Prior to DB2 9.7, since XML was not supported in the temporary tables, the user had to use regular tables as a workaround. Now, we can use the XML data in temporary columns just like any other relational column. The XML data uses its own storage, which is different from the relational data. If the `INLINE` length is specified, then the XML is stored in the base table as long as its length is smaller than the inline length. This works very well if the XML documents are small in size as in-lining gives performance benefits.

There's more...

Starting from DB2 9.7, we can also create declared temporary tables with LOB columns. In such cases, the LOB data is also stored in the same table space as the temporary table:

1. The following example creates a declared global temporary table with LOB columns:

```
DECLARE GLOBAL TEMPORARY TABLE sample_lob
        (empno INT,
         resume_posting_dt DATE,
         resume CLOB(6000))
        ON COMMIT DELETE ROWS
        NOT LOGGED
        IN user_temp_tbsp;
```

2. Once we have created a declared temporary table with LOB columns, the rest is very similar to regular tables. We can process LOB columns just like any other column. Let's insert some LOB data in our temporary table. In this example, we will insert the resumes from the EMP_RESUME table in our temporary table:

```
INSERT INTO SESSION.sample_lob (empno, resume_posting_dt, resume)
    SELECT EMPNO, CURRENT DATE, RESUME FROM EMP_RESUME;
```

Improving performance by creating indexes on a DGTT

If we are processing a large amount of data from a temporary table, then we can use indexes to get performance benefits. We can create indexes on regular columns as well as on XML columns. The indexes will also be stored in the same table space in which the temporary table is defined.

How to do it...

Index creation on a DGTT is very similar to regular tables. Let's see how to do that:

1. Create a declared global temporary table:

```
DECLARE GLOBAL TEMPORARY TABLE sample_xml (empno INT,
                                           sal_rise_date DATE,
                                           sal_dtls XML)

ON COMMIT DELETE ROWS

NOT LOGGED

IN user_temp_tbsp;
```

2. Create an index on a relational column: Just like a regular table, use the CREATE INDEX statement to create an index on a temporary table. The following command creates an index on a relational column of a temporary table:

```
CREATE INDEX SESSION.TEMP_REL_IDX ON SESSION.SAMPLE_XML (EMPNO);
```

3. Create an index on an XML column: We can also create indexes on XML columns. To create an index on an XML column, we need to provide the XML pattern expression on which we want to create the index. In this example, we will create an index on sal_dtl_key:

```
CREATE UNIQUE INDEX SESSION.TEMP_TEMP_XML_IDX ON SESSION.SAMPLE_
XML (sal_dtls)

GENERATE KEY USING XMLPATTERN '/salary_revision/sal_dtl_key'

AS SQL DOUBLE
```

How it works...

Once we have created indexes on temporary tables, they are available to the optimizer. The DB2 optimizer uses cost-based optimization techniques to find the best access plan. If the optimizer thinks using indexes will improve performance, then it will use it. As a best practice, we should create indexes on only those columns that appear in the WHERE clause of the query.

There's more...

In a partitioned environment, we can define our temporary table to take advantage of database partitioning. We can also create a temporary table with XML data in a partitioned environment.

We can use the DISTRIBUTE BY HASH clause to define a partitioning key for a temporary table:

```
DECLARE GLOBAL TEMPORARY TABLE temp_partitioned (ID INT, DOC XML)
    ON COMMIT DELETE ROWS
    IN user_temp_tbsp
    DISTRIBUTE BY HASH (ID)
```

The column specified in the DISTRIBUTE BY HASH clause is the partitioning key. The temporary tables also use the same algorithm of data partitioning as a regular table. A hash function that determines the partition in which a particular record will go is applied on the partitioning key. If the table is defined in a table space which spans across multiple partitions and no partitioning key is defined, then DB2 chooses the first column that is a valid partitioning key. If we plan to join a temporary table with a regular partitioned table, then we should always prefer the same partitioning key as the other table. This will ensure collocated joins, which are better in terms of performance.

Creating Created Global Temporary Tables (CGTT)

DB2 9.7 introduced a new type of temporary table: **Created Global Temporary Table**, also known as CGTT. The purpose of using a created global temporary table is the same as a declared global temporary table, which is to store the intermediate results within an application. There are some key differences between the two. The biggest difference between a CGTT and a DGTT is the existence in system catalogs. The definition of the created global temporary tables are stored in system catalogs, while it's not done for a DGTT. The content of a CGTT is still private to a session. Because the definitions of a CGTT is present in system catalogs, it persists. The advantage of its persistence is that it is usable in functions, procedures, and so on. Also, we don't need to declare the table every time in our application before using it. In this recipe, we will see how to create a created global temporary table (CGTT).

Getting ready

▸ To create a declared global temporary table, we need a user temporary table space.

▸ To create a declared global temporary table, we need at least one of the following authorities/privileges:

  ❑ USE privilege on USER TEMPORARY TABLE SPACE

  ❑ DBADM authority

  ❑ SYSADM authority

  ❑ SYSCTRL authority

How to do it...

1. Use the CREATE GLOBAL TEMPORARY TABLE command to create a CGTT. The following example creates a temporary table called sal_rise_temp:

```
CREATE GLOBAL TEMPORARY TABLE user1.sal_rise_temp
    (empno INT,
     sal_rise_date DATE,
     updated_sal BIGINT,
     manager_empno INTEGER)
    ON COMMIT DELETE ROWS
    NOT LOGGED
    IN user_temp_tbsp
```

2. We can also use the LIKE clause to create a temporary table similar to an existing regular table:

```
CREATE GLOBAL TEMPORARY TABLE user1.emp_temp LIKE EMPLOYEE
    ON COMMIT DELETE ROWS
        NOT LOGGED
        IN user_temp_tbsp
```

How it works...

▸ Unlike DGTT, we can create a CGTT in the user schema as well.

▸ ON COMMIT DELETE ROWS: If this option is specified, then the rows in the temporary table are deleted on every COMMIT.

▸ NOT LOGGED: If this option is specified, the insert, update, and delete operations are not logged. Only creation and dropping are logged. If this option is specified, then DB2 uses an internal TRUNCATE to delete the rows in the table. If any cursor with the WITH HOLD clause is open, then DB2 will delete one row at a time. The default is LOGGED, which logs everything.

There's more...

Created temporary tables do appear in system catalogs just like a regular table. They have TYPE as G in SYSCAT.TABLES catalog view. Since a CGTT is persisted in system catalogs, it can only be created on primary server in HADR (high availability and disaster recovery) setup. Once created, its definition is replicated to the standby server. However, we cannot access it directly on standby server. Attempts to reference a CGTT on standby server will receive an error SQL1773N.

Referencing a CGTT

We can reference a CGTT just like a regular table. We can qualify the table name with its schema. For example, if we want to select the data from a temporary table, we can use the following command:

```
SELECT * FROM user1.emp_temp;
```

The first implicit or explicit reference of a created temporary table by an application creates an empty instance of that temporary table. Once this instance is created, subsequent operations on the temporary table are executed against this instance, which is completely isolated from other applications. This instance of the temporary table persists only till the connection is live.

Dropping a CGTT

When an application using a created temporary table disconnects from the database, the instance of the temporary table which was created for this application sure. The temporary table definition still exists in the system catalogs and it can be instantiated again by any application. It needs to be dropped explicitly. Once a created temporary table is dropped explicitly, then its definition is also deleted from the catalogs and it cannot be referenced anymore.

To drop a created temporary table, we need the CONTROL privilege on it. We can use the DROP TABLE command to drop a created global temporary table:

```
DROP TABLE user_name.temp_tbl
```

Using generated columns in tables

Generated columns are special types of columns in a table whose values are generated by an expression. In this recipe, we will talk about how to create tables with generated columns and will see the use cases for it. In this recipe, we will create a table with a generated column.

Getting ready

We need the privileges to create a table.

How to do it...

1. Use the GENERATED clause in CREATE TABLE to create the generated columns:

    ```
    CREATE TABLE tab1 (c1 INT,
                       c2 INT,
                       max_col GENERATED ALWAYS AS
                           (CASE WHEN c1 > c2 THEN c1 ELSE c2 END));
    ```

2. Let's see how DB2 populates the values for generated columns automatically:

    ```
    INSERT INTO tab1(c1, c2) VALUES(5, 10);
    INSERT INTO tab1(c1, c2) VALUES(30, 20);
    SELECT * FROM tab1;
    ```

    ```
    Results:
    C1          C2          MAX_COL
    ------      -------     --------
             5          10          10
            30          20          30
    ```

How it works...

- GENERATED ALWAYS: If this clause is specified, then the column value is always generated automatically.

- GENERATED BY DEFAULT: If this option is specified and if the column value is not supplied in the INSERT statement, then a value is generated automatically.

- All the columns referenced in the generated column must appear BEFORE the generated column in the CREATE TABLE statement.

There's more...

DB2 automatically computes values for generated columns; hence these columns are not specified in the INSERT statements while inserting rows in table. Apart from the value generation, these columns are very similar to regular table columns.

LOAD and IMPORT considerations for generated columns

When loading or importing data in a table having generated columns, we need to consider how we want to load the generated column values. The data file may or may not have the values for the generated columns. We can either accept the values from the data file or we can let the LOAD or IMPORT utility generate the values for the generated columns automatically. DB2 provides three options to handle this:

▶ GENERATEDIGNORE: If the values for the generated columns are present in the data file, they are ignored and LOAD/IMPORT utility generates the values automatically.

▶ GENERATEDMISSING: If this clause is specified, then the LOAD/IMPORT utility assumes that there is no data for the generated columns in the data file and the utility generates the values for them.

▶ GENERATEDOVERRIDE: If this clause is specified, then the LOAD/IMPORT utility accepts the values available in the data file. The table is placed in SET INTEGRITY PENDING state after the LOAD operation. We need to run the SET INTEGRITY command once the load completes. However, if the generated column is part of partitioning key, dimension, or distribution key, then this option is ignored and the load utility generates these values similar to the GENERATEDIGNORE option.

These options can be specified in the MODIFIED BY clause of the LOAD or the IMPORT utility. For example:

```
LOAD FROM datafile.dat OF DEL MODIFIED BY GENERATEDOVERRIDE INSERT
INTO tab1;
```

Using a generated column as range partitioning key

We can also use GENERATED columns to control the granularity for table partitions. We can define a GENERATED COLUMN with an expression on another column resulting in coarsification of the new column, which could be a better partitioning key:

```
CREATE TABLE sales_part(business_date DATE,
                        sales_amount DECIMAL(27,2),
                        sales_month SMALLINT GENERATED ALWAYS AS
                                     (MONTH(business_date)))
PARTITION BY RANGE (sales_month)  STARTING FROM 1 ENDING AT 12 EVERY 1);
```

Because we have specified GENERATED ALWAYS, we don't need to worry about the column data population, as this will be taken care of by DB2 automatically.

Using generated columns as MDC dimensions

Just like range partitions, we can also use GENERATED columns as dimensions for an MDC. For an MDC, the dimension should neither have very high cardinality, nor too small cardinality. In such cases, we can use GENERATED columns to coarsify columns resulting in better candidates for dimension:

```
CREATE TABLE T1 (col1 INT,
                 col2 INT,
                 col3 DATE,
                 col_dim_month INT GENERATED ALWAYS AS (MONTH(col3)),
                 col_dim_year INT GENERATED ALWAYS AS (YEAR(col3)))
  ORGANIZE BY DIMENSIONS (col_dim_year, col_dim_month);
```

With the previous table definition, the clustering will be based on YEAR and MONTH. The DB2 optimizer has the capability to recognize the generated columns used as dimensions, so we will also get the performance benefit.

Using generated columns for performance

Generated columns can be used for performance improvements as well. If we have any derivation logic in SQL, and if any part of the derivation can be stored as a GENERATED column, then the optimizer can benefit from it. If we have an expression that we include in queries very often, then we can eliminate the overhead of expression calculation by adding an extra column in the table, so that we will have the expression value pre-computed.

For example, if we compare two columns of a table very often in queries, then we can create a generated column as shown:

```
CREATE TABLE tab1 (col1 INT,
                   col2 INT,
                   col_max INT GENERATED ALWAYS AS
                   (CASE WHEN col1 > col2 THEN 1 ELSE NULL END));
CREATE INDEX idx1 ON tab1(col_max);
```

In this example, the following query will perform better because of the generated column and the index on it:

```
SELECT COUNT(*) FROM tab1 WHERE col1 > col2;
```

The DB2 optimizer has the capability to observe the generated columns and exploit them for better performance if they can. In the previous example, query rewrite will rewrite the query similar to:

```
SELECT COUNT(*) FROM tab1 WHERE col_max IS NOT NUNLL;
```

Similarly, if we have a column of string type in a table and we expect values to be in a mixed case, it becomes tricky when we want to compare the same string with a different casing. Typically, we would use the UCASE or LCASE function and do the comparison. With this approach, the index will not be used, as DB2 wouldn't support creating indexes on the column expression. As an alternative, we can add a GENERATED column that stores a UCASE (or LCASE) equivalent and creates an index on it. Now, DB2 should be able to use this index even if we don't reference the generated column explicitly.

Creating a savepoint

The savepoints are used to divide a big transaction into smaller sub-transactions. It gives the developer the ability to do partial rollbacks, saving re-execution time. Multiple savepoints can be created in a transaction and we can roll back to any savepoint without affecting the processing done before the savepoint. In this recipe, we will see how to create a savepoint.

How to do it...

We can use a SAVEPOINT statement to create a savepoint. This statement can be embedded in any host language within a transaction:

```
SAVEPOINT svpnt_temp
  UNIQUE
  ON ROLLBACK RETAIN CURSORS
  ON ROLLBACK RETAIN LOCKS
```

How it works...

- ▶ UNIQUE: If this clause is specified, then we cannot create another savepoint with the same name until the savepoint is still active. We can always create more than one savepoint in multiple transactions. The savepoint level is started when the transaction starts, and finishes when the transaction completes.

- ▶ ON ROLLBACK RETAIN CURSORS: The cursors are unaffected if a rollback to a savepoint is performed. Cursors are open and positioned to the record where they were.

- ▶ ON ROLLBACK RETAIN LOCKS: The locks are not released even if the application performs a rollback to a savepoint. Locks are not released until the transaction is committed or rolled back completely.

There's more...

If we no longer wish to use any savepoint, we can release it explicitly. Once a savepoint is released, it can't be referenced anymore but it can be created and used again regardless of whether the UNIQUE keyword was specified on the earlier SAVEPOINT statement.

We can use the RELEASE SAVEPOINT statement to release a savepoint:

```
RELEASE SAVEPOINT savepoint_name;
```

Rolling back to a savepoint

As we discussed in the previous recipe, the motivation behind creating savepoints is to divide a transaction into sub-tasks. It allows us to partially roll back a transaction, saving total execution time. Once a transaction is rolled back to a savepoint, the savepoint still exists but all nested savepoints no longer exist. In this recipe, we will see how to use savepoints in a ROLLBACK statement.

How to do it...

Use the ROLLBACK TO SAVEPOINT statement to roll back to a savepoint. To understand better, we will create a test table and use multiple savepoints in a single transaction, and observe the effect of rolling back to different savepoints.

In this example, we will create a table and insert a few records in the table. Then we will see how savepoints work:

1. Create a test table:

```
CREATE TABLE TEST_SVPT (
    EMPNO    INTEGER,
    EMPNAME VARCHAR(20),
    MGRNO    INTEGER);
```

2. By default, the DB2 prompt is enabled for auto commit. For savepoints, we need to maintain an open transaction, so let's disable the auto commit. We can do it by updating the command options, as follows:

```
UPDATE COMMAND OPTIONS USING c OFF;
```

3. Insert a record in the table and create a savepoint:

```
INSERT INTO TEST_SVPT VALUES (1, 'Bob', 101);
SAVEPOINT SAVEPOINT1 ON ROLLBACK RETAIN CURSORS;
```

4. Insert another record in the table and create one more savepoint:

```
INSERT INTO TEST_SVPT VALUES (2, 'Mat', 102);
SAVEPOINT SAVEPOINT2 ON ROLLBACK RETAIN CURSORS;
```

5. To understand better, let's create another savepoint:

```
INSERT INTO TEST_SVPT VALUES (3, 'Joe', 103);
SAVEPOINT SAVEPOINT3 ON ROLLBACK RETAIN CURSORS;

INSERT INTO TEST_SVPT VALUES (4, 'Pat', 104);
```

6. By now, we have inserted four rows on the table and we have three savepoints. Let's see the impact of rolling back to a savepoint. Before we proceed, let's view the table contents at this point:

```
SELECT * FROM TEST_SVPT;
```

EMPNO	EMPNAME	MGRNO
1	Bob	101
2	Mat	102
3	Joe	103
4	Pat	104

```
  4 record(s) selected.
```

7. Roll back to a savepoint and view the results:

```
ROLLBACK TO SAVEPOINT SAVEPOINT3;
SELECT * FROM TEST_SVPT;
```

EMPNO	EMPNAME	MGRNO
1	Bob	101
2	Mat	102
3	Joe	103

```
  3 record(s) selected.
```

8. Roll back to another savepoint and view the results:

```
ROLLBACK TO SAVEPOINT SAVEPOINT1;
SELECT * FROM TEST_SVPT;
```

EMPNO	EMPNAME	MGRNO
1	Bob	101

```
  1 record(s) selected.
```

9. Complete the transaction by either committing or rolling it back:

```
COMMIT;
```

Using savepoints in JDBC

JDBC drivers available in DB2 provide the `setSavepoint()` method to create a savepoint. In this recipe, we will use savepoints in a JDBC application.

Getting ready...

▶ We will use the same table `TEST_SVPT` created in the previous example. The following command can be used to create it:

```
CREATE TABLE TEST_SVPT (
    EMPNO    INTEGER,
    EMPNAME  VARCHAR(20),
    MGRNO    INTEGER);
```

▶ The methods used will be:

- ❑ `Connection.setSavepoint(String name)`
- ❑ `Connection.rollback(Savepoint savepointName)`
- ❑ `Connection.releaseSavepoint(Savepoint savepointName)`

How to do it...

In this example, we will create a transaction having multiple savepoints and we will see how to use them.

1. Creating a connection object: A database connection is required before we execute any SQL statement against the database. To create a connection object, we first need to load the database driver and then create a connection object.

   Use the `Class.forName()` method to load the database driver:

   ```
   Class.forName("COM.ibm.db2.jdbc.app.DB2Driver").newInstance();
   ```

   Use the getConnection() method to get the connection:

   ```
   String url = "jdbc:db2:sample";
   Connection con = DriverManager.getConnection(url);
   ```

2. Autocommit: To keep the transaction open, we need to set the auto commit option to false. Use the `setAutoCommit()` method to disable the auto commit option:

   ```
   con.setAutoCommit(false);
   ```

3. Create a statement object, which we will use to execute the INSERT queries:

```
Statement stmt = con.createStatement();
```

4. Let's INSERT a row in the table:

```
stmt.executeUpdate("INSERT INTO TEST_SVPT VALUES (1, 'Bob',
101)");
```

5. Create a savepoint: To create a savepoint in the transaction, use the Savepoint class:

```
Savepoint savept1 = con.setSavepoint();
```

6. Let's insert a few more rows and create a couple of more savepoints:

```
stmt.executeUpdate("INSERT INTO TEST_SVPT VALUES (2, 'Mat',
102)");

Savepoint savept2 = con.setSavepoint();


stmt.executeUpdate("INSERT INTO TEST_SVPT VALUES (3, 'Joe',
103)");

Savepoint savept3 = con.setSavepoint();

stmt.executeUpdate("INSERT INTO TEST_SVPT VALUES (4, 'Pat',
104)");
```

7. By now, we have three savepoints. We can use the rollback() method to roll back to any savepoint:

```
con.rollback(savept3);

con.rollback(savept2);

con.rollback(savept1);
```

8. The sample output for our example, is as shown:

```
C:\Program Files (x86)\IBM\SQLLIB\samples\java\jdbc>java Savepoints
THIS EXAMPLE SHOWS HOW TO USE SAVEPOINTS.
EMPNO     EMPNAME      MGRNO
-----     --------     -------
    1        Bob         101
    2        Mat         102
    3        Joe         103
    4        Pat         104


EMPNO     EMPNAME      MGRNO
-----     --------     -------
    1        Bob         101
    2        Mat         102
    3        Joe         103


EMPNO     EMPNAME      MGRNO
-----     --------     -------
    1        Bob         101
```

Using savepoints in SQLJ

We can directly embed `SQL SAVEPOINT` commands to implement savepoints in SQLJ. Let's see how to do it.

Getting ready...

- We will implement savepoints in SQLJ using the same example as before.
- We will use the same table `TEST_SVPT` created in the previous example. We can use the following command to create it:

```
CREATE TABLE TEST_SVPT (
    EMPNO    INTEGER,
    EMPNAME VARCHAR(20),
    MGRNO    INTEGER);
```

How to do it...

In this example, we will create a transaction having multiple savepoints and we will see how to use them:

1. Creating a connection object and a connection context: Before we can execute any SQL statement against the database, we first need to set up the database connection. To do that, we need to load the database driver and then create a connection object:

   Use the `Class.forName()` method to load the database driver:

   ```
   Class.forName("com.ibm.db2.jcc.DB2Driver ").newInstance();
   ```

   Use the `getConnection()` method to get the connection:

   ```
   String url = "jdbc:db2:sample";
   Connection con = DriverManager.getConnection(url);


   Use setDefaultContext() method to set the default context
   DefaultContext ctx = new DefaultContext(con);
   DefaultContext.setDefaultContext(ctx);
   ```

2. AutoCommit: Disable the AutoCommit option by using the `setAutoCommit()` method:

   ```
   con.setAutoCommit(false);
   ```

3. In SQLJ, we can directly embed the SQL statements. Let's insert a few records in a test table and create a few savepoints:

```
#sql {INSERT INTO TEST_SVPT VALUES (1, 'Bob', 101)};

#sql {SAVEPOINT SAVEPOINT1 ON ROLLBACK RETAIN CURSORS};

#sql {INSERT INTO TEST_SVPT VALUES (2, 'Mat', 102)};

#sql {SAVEPOINT SAVEPOINT2 ON ROLLBACK RETAIN CURSORS};

#sql {INSERT INTO TEST_SVPT VALUES (3, 'Joe', 103)};

#sql {SAVEPOINT SAVEPOINT3 ON ROLLBACK RETAIN CURSORS};

#sql {INSERT INTO TEST_SVPT VALUES (4, 'Pat', 104)};
```

4. By now, we have inserted four records in the table and we have three savepoints. We can use a ROLLBACK TO command to roll back to any savepoint:

```
#sql {ROLLBACK TO SAVEPOINT SAVEPOINT3};
#sql {ROLLBACK TO SAVEPOINT SAVEPOINT1};
```

5. The sample output for our example is as shown:

```
C:\Users\Sanju\Desktop\Programming\sqlj>java Savepoints sanju sanju
THIS SAMPLE SHOWS HOW TO USE SAVEPOINTS
EMPNO      EMPNAME        MGRNO
-----   ----------   --------
    3           Joe        103
    4           Pat        104
    1           Bob        101
    2           Mat        102

EMPNO      EMPNAME        MGRNO
-----   ----------   --------
    3           Joe        103
    1           Bob        101
    2           Mat        102

EMPNO      EMPNAME        MGRNO
-----   ----------   --------
    1           Bob        101
```

Creating a sequence object

Many applications require sequential numbers to be generated for key values such as the item number, invoices, and so on. Sequences offer a very good solution to such applications. Sequences are database objects that allow a user to generate key values automatically. Because these values are generated within the database, there is no chance of the duplicate values being present. DB2 keeps track of the values being generated and knows the next values, so even in the case of a crash or a failure, the new values are correct. It also gives better performance as compared to other approaches of generating the values manually. In this recipe, we will see how sequences can be created and used, and we will also see how it is different from an identity column. In this recipe, we will see how to create sequence objects.

Getting ready

The key aspect to consider before creating a sequence is the sequence behavior. DB2 automatically increments the sequence value based on the criteria on which it was created. As a user, we can control the behavior of the sequence.

How to do it...

Use the following command to create a sequence object that starts at 1 and is incremented by 1:

```
CREATE SEQUENCE item_num
    AS INTEGER
    START WITH 1
    INCREMENT BY 1
    MINVALUE 1
    MAXVALUE 2000
    NO CYCLE
    CACHE 20
    ORDER
```

How it works...

▸ By default, a sequence starts at 1 and is incremented by 1.

▸ We can create a sequence with numeric data types (SMALLINT, INTEGER, BIGINT, DECIMAL, and NUMERIC).

- ▶ START WITH: This clause specifies the first value of the sequence. The default is MINVALUE for the ascending sequences and MAXVALUE for descending sequences.

- ▶ INCREMENT BY: Allows us to specify the interval between two consecutive values generated.

- ▶ MINVALUE: Allows us to specify the minimum value a sequence can generate.

- ▶ MAXVALUE: Allows us to specify the maximum value a sequence can generate.

- ▶ CYCLE or NO CYCLE: Allows us to specify the behavior once MINVALUE or MAXVALUE are reached. If CYCLE is specified, then the new values will be generated in cyclic order, and it generates duplicate values.

- ▶ CACHE: This option is used for performance reasons. It allows us to specify the number of values to be pre-generated and kept in memory for faster access. Pre-allocation and storing values in cache reduces synchronous IO. By implementing a cache, DB2 does not have to go to the system catalogs to get the next value again and again, hence resulting in better performance. The default CACHE is 20. Only when all the values in the cache are used will DB2 create the next set of cache.

- ▶ ORDER: Allows us to specify whether the values need to be generated in order. The default is NO ORDER.

There's more...

We can use sequence objects to store the constant values as well. In that case, INCREMENT BY should be zero.

If we are using sequence values outside the database, we should not recover the database to a prior point in time, as it might give duplicate values.

The sequence counter value is recoverable, as it can be reconstructed from database logs in case of recovery.

If cache is enabled for a sequence, then there is a possibility of gaps in the generated values in the case of a database crash. Once the sequence cache is built, system catalogs will have the information to generate the next value for the sequence. In the case of a crash, DB2 will start with the information available in the catalogs to generate the next value and hence there could be gap in the values.

We can query the SYSCAT.SEQUENCES system catalog table to see the available sequences in the database. The information available in this system table includes all sequence attributes:

```
SELECT SEQSCHEMA, SEQNAME, INCREMENT, START, CACHE,
NEXTCACHEFIRSTVALUE FROM SYSCAT.SEQUENCES WHERE OWNERTYPE='U';
```

The sample output is as shown:

```
DB2 CLP - DB2COPY1 - db2 -t                                        _ □ X

db2 => SELECT CHAR(SEQSCHEMA, 10), CHAR(SEQNAME, 20), INT(INCREMENT),
db2 (cont.) =>          INT(START), INT(CACHE), INT(NEXTCACHEFIRSTVALUE)
db2 (cont.) =>     FROM SYSCAT.SEQUENCES WHERE OWNERTYPE='U';

1            2                    3            4            CACHE          6
------------ -------------------- ------------ ------------ ------------ ------------
SANJU        SAMPSEQUENCE                    1            1           20            1
SANJU        ITEM_NUM                        1            1           20            1
SANJU        ITEM_SEQ                        5         1000           20         1000

   3 record(s) selected.

db2 =>
```

We can use the DROP command to drop a user-defined sequence object. The system-generated sequence object for identity columns cannot be dropped. For example:

```
DROP SEQUENCE item_num;
```

Modifying a sequence object

We can alter a sequence object to perform tasks, such as restarting the sequence, changing the sequence behavior like increment interval and other attributes. We cannot change the sequence data type once it is created. In such cases, we need to drop the sequence and recreate with the new definition. If a sequence is altered, then all the values present in cache are also lost.

Getting ready

We need the ALTER privilege on the sequence object to alter a sequence. The creator of the sequence automatically gets USAGE and ALTER privileges on the sequence. The ALTER statement can be embedded in an application program or can be issued as simple SQL.

How to do it...

We can use the ALTER SEQUENCE command to modify a sequence object. Let's see a few examples of sequence modification:

  ▶ In the following example, ALTER is a sequence with a new MINVALUE:

      ```
      ALTER SEQUENCE item_num MINVALUE 1000;
      ```

  ▶ In the following example, RESTART is a sequence with a numeric value:

      ```
      ALTER SEQUENCE item_num RESTART WITH 1001;
      ```

How it works...

▸ The ALTER SEQUENCE command can be embedded in any host language and can be prepared dynamically. We cannot alter a sequence generated by the system for an identity column.

▸ Only future values are affected by the ALTER SEQUENCE command.

▸ After restarting a sequence object, it is possible to get duplicate values of the ones previously generated.

Referencing a sequence object

The sequence objects create values that get incremented under the application control. We can use NEXT VALUE and PREVIOUS VALUE commands to use sequence values. Alternatively, we can also use NEXTVAL and CURRVAL instead of NEXT VALUE and PREVIOUS VALUE respectively. These alternatives are only for compatibility with the previous versions of DB2 and are not recommended to be used.

Getting ready

We need the USAGE privilege on a sequence object to use the sequence. The creator of the sequence object automatically gets USAGE and ALTER privileges.

How to do it...

▸ We can use the NEXT VALUE command to get the next value generated by the sequence object:

```
VALUES NEXT VALUE FOR item_num;

VALUES item_num NEXTVAL;
```

▸ We can also use sequence values in SQL statements like INSERT, UPDATE, and so on:

```
INSERT INTO item_tbl(ITEM_NUM) VALUES (NEXT VALUE FOR item_num);

INSERT INTO item_tbl(ITEM_NUM) VALUES (item_num NEXTVAL);
```

▸ We can use the PREVIOUS VALUE command to get the previous value of the sequence:

```
VALUES PREVIOUS VALUE FOR item_num;

VALUES item_num CURRVAL;
```

How it works...

- The NEXT VALUE generates and returns the next value for the sequence referenced.

- The PREVIOUS VALUE returns the most-recently generated value for the sequence referenced.

- The PREVIOUS VALUE can only be used if the NEXT VALUE expression for that sequence has already been referenced in the current application, whether in the current transaction or the previous transaction.

There's more...

- The PREVIOUS VALUE function can be used multiple times in an application and will always return the last value generated by the sequence in that application. Even if the sequence value is already incremented by some other application, the PREVIOUS VALUE will still be the same. This becomes very handy if we need to use the same generated value at multiple places. The value of the PREVIOUS VALUE persists until the next value is not generated in the current session.

- In a partitioned environment, PREVIOUS VALUE may not return the most-recently generated value.

- If there are multiple NEXT VALUE functions in a single query, then the value of a sequence is incremented only once throughout the query and all instances of NEXT VALUE will return the same value.

- When a value of a sequence is generated against the NEXT VALUE function, it is consumed and a new value will be generated. Even if the transaction is rolled back, the sequence will generate the next value on subsequent NEXT VALUE function calls.

- If the NEXT VALUE function is used in a SELECT statement of a cursor, then a new value will be generated for each row in the result set.

- If the PREVIOUS VALUE function is used in the SELECT statement of a cursor, then it refers to the recent value that was generated prior to the opening of the cursor.

3
General Application Design

In this chapter, we will focus on the following recipes related to advanced application development:

- ▶ Improving concurrency by using a connection concentrator
- ▶ Using trusted contexts for improved security
- ▶ Using trusted connections in JDBC
- ▶ Using trusted connections in PHP
- ▶ Securing data using DB2 encryption
- ▶ Improving concurrency by using enhanced optimistic locking
- ▶ Working with user-defined types (UDT)
- ▶ Working with structured types

Introduction

In this chapter, we will look at some advanced techniques that can be used to design efficient applications. We will see how we can improve security in 3-tier architecture applications. We will also look at the various methods of data encryption provided by DB2. Thereafter, we will see how we can extend the data type support provided by DB2 and apply them in our application design.

Improving concurrency by using a connection concentrator

The first step in any database application is establishing a connection to the database. When an application attempts to connect to a database, DB2 allocates an agent to service the request. This agent services all requests coming from this application. Once the application disconnects from the database, this agent is released. Allocating agents for every connection request may cause a bottleneck when the number of incoming connections increases. This overhead becomes more significant if the application executes small transactions. In such cases, the time required to get a connection is much higher than executing the entire transaction. To overcome this overhead, DB2 provides connection pooling.

Connection pooling is a technique which provides ready-to-use connections available for applications. DB2 provides techniques to preserve a connection after an application disconnects from the database. Once an application disconnects from the database, DB2 keeps the agents in the agent pool instead of terminating them. These agents are now free for the next incoming application. If the connection pool is exhausted, a new connection is created. Connection pooling saves the overhead of closing connections and creating new connections. This process is completely transparent to the applications. Many application servers, such as the WebSphere, also provide a connection pooling infrastructure. Connection pooling is enabled by default in DB2.

However, connection pooling doesn't help much when the number of connection requests is very high. We come across many situations where we anticipate a very high number of incoming connections that have very short transactions. An example of such a scenario could be any OLTP system. In such cases, if we increase the connection pool size, then it would simply consume a lot of resources. To overcome such situations, DB2 provides the connection concentrator.

The connection concentrator allows us to accommodate more connections than the number of agents available. This way, DB2 can service more connections with lesser resources. The connection concentrator follows multiplexing architecture where it manages more application connections with less database agents. When the connection concentrator is enabled, DB2 makes use of the idle agents as well. This means, if an application connection is idle, DB2 attempts to use the assigned agents to service other requests. Hence the system resources are used to their full potential and nothing is idle. Just like connection pooling, the connection concentrator is also transparent to the application and the application doesn't even know if its agents are serving other applications.

Getting ready

Before we enable the connection concentrator, we need to know what the following database manager configuration parameters means:

- `NUM_POOLAGENTS`: Maximum number of idle agents in the agent pool
- `NUM_INITAGENTS`: Number of idle agents created in the agent pool when an instance is started
- `MAX_CONNECTIONS`: Maximum number of client connections allowed, per database partition
- `MAX_COORDAGENTS`: Maximum number of coordinating agents

How to do it

In this recipe, we will see how to find the appropriate values for these parameters and how to set them.

1. **Enabling connection pooling**: Before we enable the connection concentrator, we first need to enable connection pooling. DB2 enables connection pooling by default. Even if it's not enabled, we can do it by setting the `NUM_POOLAGENTS` database manager configuration parameter.

2. Use the following command to see the current value of the `NUM_POOLAGENTS` configuration parameter:

   ```
   SELECT NAME, VALUE FROM SYSIBMADM.DBMCFG WHERE NAME = 'num_
   poolagents'
   ```

3. Use the following command to set the value for the `NUM_POOLAGENTS` configuration parameter:

   ```
   UPDATE DBM CFG USING NUM_POOLAGENTS 200 AUTOMATIC
   ```

   When set to `AUTOMATIC`, the database manager automatically manages the number of agents in the agent pool.

4. **Enabling connection concentrator**: To enable the connection concentrator, set the value of the `MAX_CONNECTIONS` database manager configuration parameter to be greater than the `MAX_COORDAGENTS` configuration parameter.

5. Use the following command to see the current values of the `MAX_COORDAGENTS` and `MAX_CONNECTIONS` configuration parameters:

   ```
   SELECT * FROM SYSIBMADM.DBMCFG WHERE NAME IN ('max_coordagents',
   'max_connections');
   ```

6. Use the following command to set the value of the MAX_CONNECTIONS configuration parameter:

   ```
   UPDATE DBM CFG USING MAX_CONNECTIONS 1000 AUTOMATIC
   ```

7. **Tuning the values**: Now, we have a connection concentrator enabled, but we don't have optimized values. For better optimization, we need to know the maximum number of agents we need. We are basically looking for the maximum number of agents we need simultaneously during our peak time. We have already enabled the connection concentrator with the current system settings. Now, when the connection concentrator is enabled, a smaller number of database agents will be spawned for application requests. So, by looking at the database snapshot, we should be able to find out the maximum number of coordinating agents, which will, in turn, tell us the highest number of agents needed to fulfill all application requests.

8. Use the following command to take the database manager snapshot:

   ```
   db2 => GET SNAPSHOT FOR DATABASE MANAGER;


                   Database Manager Snapshot


   Node name                               =
   Node type                               = Enterprise Server
   Editionwith local and
   remote clients
   Instance name                           = DB2
   .

   .

   .

   Agents assigned from pool               = 4
   Agents created from empty pool          = 14
   Agents stolen from another application  = 0
   High water mark for coordinating agents = 11
   Hash joins after heap threshold exceeded = 0
   OLAP functions after heap threshold exceeded = 0
   ```

9. See the value of **High water mark for coordinating agents**. This shows the maximum number of agents required at peak time. We can set the MAX_COORDAGENTS to be a little higher than this value. Once we have an optimum value of MAX_COORDAGENTS, we can increase the MAX_CONNECTIONS value to accommodate more client connections.

How it works...

When the connection concentrator is enabled, db2agents are freed when transaction boundaries are reached (**COMMIT** or **ROLLBACK**). Once the agent is freed, it can be used by any other request. If there are no more incoming service requests, then the dispatcher process determines whether this agent can be terminated or not. If connection pooling is enabled, this agent goes into the connection pool; otherwise, it gets terminated. However, the maximum number of agents is governed by the NUM_POOLAGENTS configuration parameter setting. If this value is reached, the extra agents are terminated.

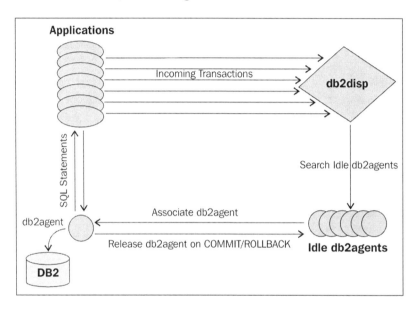

The connection concentrator revolves around the dispatcher process (**db2disp**). This process controls the assignment of **DB2** agents to the incoming service requests. It keeps track of all idle agents. If it doesn't find any agent in the agent pool, it spawns a new one for the incoming request. The maximum number of agents is governed by the MAXAGENTS configuration parameter.

Multithreaded architecture was introduced in DB2 9.5 on all platforms, where all database-manager-engine-component processes are now executed as threads in the main process.

There's more...

If the dispatcher process **(db2disp)** does not find any agent available for a new incoming request, then this incoming transaction appears to be in the *hang* state. This is because the dispatcher process is waiting for an agent. This also means that all agents are busy serving other transactions. In such situations, the database manager configuration parameters might not be appropriate for such a workload. We might need to increase MAX_COORDAGENTS or lower the MAX_CONNECTIONS parameter value. It is also a best practice to commit or roll back transactions as soon as possible. This is because unless a transaction is completed, the associated agents are not set free, which in turn can result in agent contention.

Differences between connection pooling and the connection concentrator

Connection pooling and the connection concentrator work hand-in-hand, but are very different in terms of their behavior. The following points highlight the main differences between these two:

► Connection pooling reduces the overhead of creating and terminating database agents against the application connection/disconnection requests, whereas the connection concentrator helps in utilizing idle database agents.

► Connection pooling is associated with the creation and termination of the database agents for database connections, whereas a connection concentrator is associated with context switching of agents when a transaction is committed or rolled back.

► Connection pooling acts upon connection and disconnection, whereas the connection concentrator acts upon transaction commit or rollback.

Using trusted contexts for improved security

DB2 provides various levels of security like authorization, authentication, privileges, roles, and so on. We can limit user access by setting the proper restrictions at any level. We can only apply these restrictions to a user, a role, or a group. It also means that if we use generic authorization IDs, then we cannot provide granular security. This is the exact problem we face in 3-tier architecture. In this architecture, we have the application server between the database and the application. The application server runs all the queries against the database on behalf of the application and this is done by the authorization ID, available at the application server. Because we also want this authorization ID to be able to perform all the tasks, we end up giving most of the privileges to this generic authorization ID and hence we are exposed to a security compromise.

To overcome this situation, DB2 provides a new functionality, known as trusted connections. Trusted connections provide us with means to retain the authorization ID indirectly that initiated the request up to the database. Once we have the authorization ID available at the database, we can control access in a desired manner.

A trusted context is a database object that defines a trust relationship between the middleware and the database. This relation is based on the following attributes:

- **Authorization ID**: The user ID that establishes the connection to the database (mostly the authorization ID at the application server)

- **IP Address**: The network address of the client from which the connection is established

- **Encryption**: Whether or not the communication between the database and the client is encrypted

Once a trusted context is created, it can be used by applications. In this recipe, we will focus on how to create a trusted context, and in the next recipe, we will see how we can use this trusted context in applications.

Getting ready

We need the SECADM authority to create a trusted context.

How to do it

1. We can use the following command to create a trusted context:

   ```
   CREATE TRUSTED CONTEXT <trusted_context name>
   BASED UPON CONNECTION USING SYSTEM AUTHID <System authorization ID>
   ATTRIBUTES (ADDRESS '<IP Address>',
              ENCRYPTION '<encryption parameter>')
   DEFAULT ROLE <role_name>
   ENABLE
   WITH USE FOR <user authorization ID>
   ```

2. If we want to create a connection context where the system authorization ID is `appservuser` and we want this context to be available for PUBLIC usage, then we can use the following command:

   ```
   CREATE TRUSTED CONTEXT ctx_common
   BASED UPON CONNECTION USING SYSTEM AUTHID appservuser
   ATTRIBUTES (ADDRESS '192.168.0.1',
              ENCRYPTION 'LOW')
   ENABLE
   WITH USE FOR PUBLIC WITHOUT AUTHENTICATION
   ```

3. We can also define our trusted context in such a manner that it requires authentication for one set of users and not for the other set of users.

```
CREATE TRUSTED CONTEXT ctx_common

BASED UPON CONNECTION USING SYSTEM AUTHID appservuser

ATTRIBUTES (ADDRESS '192.168.0.1',

            ENCRYPTION 'LOW')

ENABLE

WITH USE FOR BOB WITH AUTHENTICATION,

            TINA WITHOUT AUTHENTICATION
```

4. We can also define database roles for trusted contexts, so that any user connected by using this trusted context will automatically acquire this database role.

```
CREATE TRUSTED CONTEXT ctx_common

BASED UPON CONNECTION USING SYSTEM AUTHID appservuser

ATTRIBUTES (ADDRESS '192.168.0.1',

            ENCRYPTION 'LOW')

DEFAULT ROLE DEV_ROLE

ENABLE

WITH USE FOR PUBLIC WITHOUT AUTHENTICATION
```

How it works...

By creating trusted contexts, we establish a trust relationship between the application server and the client application. Now, the application server has the ability to switch user ID on connecting to a different user ID with or without authentication, depending on the trusted context definition. The security administrator can assign the required privileges to a database role and define a trusted context with this role. Now, only the trusted connections can make use of these privileges, which, in turn, means we can control when the privileges would be available to the user, resulting in better system security.

Once a trusted context is created, it can be used by the client applications. If the application connection request matches the trusted context attributes, the connection is said to be trusted. Once a trusted connection is established, the application can switch the connection to users allowed by the trusted context and then run SQL queries on behalf of this user. A trusted context can also be defined on a database role instead of a user ID.

When any database request is issued, the privileges and authorities held by the context-assigned role or authorization ID are considered in addition to the other privileges held directly by the authorization ID of the statement. However, the privileges held by the context authorization ID are not considered when issuing any DDL statement. For example, the user can create an object in the database only if they have direct privileges to create database objects.

Only one uncommitted SQL statement can be executed at a time across all database partitions in a trusted context. If there are multiple SQL statements, then the subsequent statements will wait until the current statement is committed or rolled back.

Acquiring role membership through a trusted context

When a user establishes a trusted connection with the database by using a defined trusted context, they automatically acquire the role on which the trusted context was defined. This happens for all trusted context users, by default. The security administrator can also use a trusted context to specify a role for a specific user.

Consider the following trusted context definition:

```
CREATE TRUSTED CONTEXT ctx_common
BASED UPON CONNECTION USING SYSTEM AUTHID appservuser
ATTRIBUTES (ADDRESS '192.168.0.1',
           ENCRYPTION 'LOW')
DEFAULT ROLE DEV_ROLE
ENABLE
WITH USE FOR PUBLIC WITHOUT AUTHENTICATION
```

In this example, any user connected by this trusted connection will inherit the DEV_ROLE role, by default. This is true even if the user ID is switched to any other user ID.

Now consider the following trusted context definition:

```
CREATE TRUSTED CONTEXT ctx_common
BASED UPON CONNECTION USING SYSTEM AUTHID appservuser
ATTRIBUTES (ADDRESS '192.168.0.1',
           ENCRYPTION 'LOW')
DEFAULT ROLE DEV_ROLE
ENABLE
WITH USE FOR BOB WITH AUTHENTICATION,
             TINA ROLE ADMIN_ROLE WITHOUT AUTHENTICATION
```

With this trusted context, if TINA is connected to the database, then she will inherit the ADMIN_ROLE role instead of the default role, DEV_ROLE.

Enhancing performance

The trusted connections also have some performance benefits:

- Because trusted connections provide us with the ability to switch user IDs without creating a new connection, they save the overhead associated with creating and dropping database connections, resulting in improved performance.

- We can also define a trusted context to switch user IDs without the need for authentication, which again saves the overhead of authentication.

Altering a trusted context

We can also change the attributes of a trusted context by using the ALTER TRUSTED CONTEXT command. We may choose to disable the trusted context, or change its usage or any attribute:

```
ALTER TRUSTED CONTEXT ctx_common
  ALTER DISABLE;


ALTER TRUSTED CONTEXT ctx_common
  ADD USE FOR JOE WITH AUTHENTICATION;


ALTER TRUSTED CONTEXT ctx_common
  ALTER ATTRIBUTES (ADDRESS '192.168.0.4');
```

If a trusted context is changed and there are some connections using this trusted context, then these connections remain trusted until the connection terminates or the user ID is switched. This holds even if a trusted context is disabled.

Using trusted connections in JDBC

In the previous recipe, we saw why trusted contexts are needed and we also saw how to create a trusted context. Once a trusted context is created, it can be used in various languages to create trusted connections. The infrastructure to create trusted connections is provided by the database drivers for that language. DB2 provides the following drivers that support trusted connections (as of DB2 9.7 GA):

- IBM DB2 Driver for JDBC and SQLJ (Type-4 and Type-2 connectivity)
- IBM_DB Driver for Ruby
- IBM Data Server Provider for .NET
- ibm_db2 Driver for PHP
- CLI/ODBC

In this recipe, we will see how we can establish trusted connections in Java and switch user IDs within a connection. In this recipe, we will use the IBM DB2 driver for JDBC and SQLJ to connect to the database.

Getting ready

The following are the prerequisites for this recipe:

1. Java should be set up and the IBM DB2 driver for JDBC and SQLJ should be available (this driver is shipped with DB2, by default).

2. Create a trusted context in the database. We will use the trusted context created in the previous section. We can use the following command to create the trusted context for our recipe:

   ```
   CREATE TRUSTED CONTEXT ctx_common
   BASED UPON CONNECTION USING SYSTEM AUTHID db2admin
   ATTRIBUTES (ADDRESS '192.168.0.1',
              ENCRYPTION 'LOW')
   ENABLE
   WITH USE FOR PUBLIC WITHOUT AUTHENTICATION
   ```

How to do it

In this recipe, we will use a trusted context to establish a trusted connection with the database and we will see how we can switch to different user IDs using the same connection:

1. **Importing the required classes**: We need the following classes for trusted connections:

   ```
   import java.net.InetAddress;
   import com.ibm.db2.jcc.*;
   import com.ibm.db2.jcc.DB2Connection;
   import com.ibm.db2.jcc.DB2ConnectionPoolDataSource;
   ```

2. **Establishing a connection to the database**: To establish a connection to the database, we need a data source. To define a data source, we need a hostname (or its IP address) of the database server, database port number, and the database name. We will use type-4 connectivity. We can create a data source as follows:

   ```
   com.ibm.db2.jcc.DB2ConnectionPoolDataSource ds1 = new com.ibm.db2.jcc.DB2ConnectionPoolDataSource();
   ds1.setServerName('localhost');
   ds1.setPortNumber(Integer.valueOf(50000).intValue());
   ds1.setDatabaseName('sample');
   ds1.setDriverType (4);
   ```

3. **Establishing an explicit trusted connection**: We can use the
`getDB2TrustedPooledConnection()` method to establish a trusted connection.
This method returns an `Object` array with the connection instance as the first
element and a unique cookie for the connection instance as the second element.

```
System.out.println("Create a trusted connection...");
Object[] objects = new Object[6];
byte[] cookie = new byte[1];
java.util.Properties properties = new java.util.Properties();
com.ibm.db2.jcc.DB2PooledConnection pooledCon =
(com.ibm.db2.jcc.DB2PooledConnection)objects[0];
objects = ds1.getDB2TrustedPooledConnection(authid, authid_pwd,
properties);
pooledCon = (com.ibm.db2.jcc.DB2PooledConnection)objects[0];
cookie = (byte[])objects[1];
```

4. **Verifying the trusted connection**: By now, we have established a trusted connection
with the application server authorization ID. We can see the current authorization ID
by executing following query:

```
Connection con = null;
con = pooledCon.getDB2Connection(cookie, newUser, newPassword,
null, null, null, properties);
Statement stmt = con.createStatement();
Resultset rs = stmt.executeQuery("values SYSTEM_USER");
rs.next();
sqlid = rs.getString(1);
System.out.println("\tCurrent user connected to database = " +
sqlid);
```

5. **Switching to a different user ID using the same trusted connection**: We can use
the `getDB2Connection()` or `reuseDB2Connection()` method to switch to a
different user.

```
System.out.println("Switch to '" + tcUser + "' userID");
con = pooledCon.getDB2Connection(cookie, newUser, newPassword,
null, null, null, properties);
stmt = con.createStatement();
System.out.println("\tCheck who is currently connected to
database...");rs = stmt.executeQuery("values SYSTEM_USER");
rs.next();
sqlid = rs.getString(1);
System.out.println("\tCurrent user connected to database = " +
sqlid);
```

6. **Setting up additional privileges to the roles for trusted connections**: As we discussed in the previous section, using trusted connections can also provide additional privileges to the user. To see it in action, let's create a test table and grant `SELECT` privileges to the role `DEV_ROLE`. We will then define the trusted context to use this role, once a trusted connection is established.

Create a test table as follows:

```
CREATE TABLE TC.TEST_TC_TABLE (a INT, b INT);
```

Insert some data in this table as follows:

```
INSERT INTO TC.TEST_TC_TABLE VALUES (1,1), (2,2), (3,3);
```

Grant the `SELECT` privilege on this table to the role `DEV_ROLE`:

```
GRANT SELECT ON TC.TEST_TC_TABLE TO ROLE DEV_ROLE;
```

Update the trusted context to add this role:

```
ALTER TRUSTED CONTEXT ctx_common
  ALTER DEFAULT ROLE DEV_ROLE;
```

7. **Using trusted connections to inherit additional privileges**: With the set up in the previous step, the user `tempuser` should not have the `SELECT` privilege on `TC.TEST_TC_TABLE` when accessed directly, but should have the `SELECT` privilege when using a trusted connection. We will first connect to the database without a trusted connection, and then we will establish a trusted connection and see the difference in privileges:

An example of a non-trusted connection is as follows:

```
Connection con1 = DriverManager.getConnection("jdbc:db2:sample",
tempUser, tempUserpasswd );
int cnt = 0;

stmt = con1.createStatement();
try
{
rs = stmt.executeQuery("SELECT COUNT(*) as COUNT FROM TC.TEST_TC_
TABLE");
while (rs.next())
{
  cnt = rs.getInt(1);
}
} catch (SQLException sqle)
{
```

```
System.out.println("\tSelect without using trusted connection
fails as expected: \n" + "----------------------------------------
-------------------\n" + sqle + "\n----------------------------
----------------------------");
}
```

The previous code throws an exception as the user doesn't have the required privilege. Now, let's use a trusted connection and run the same query again:

```
Connection con2 = pooledCon.getDB2Connection(cookie, tempUser,
null, null, null, null, properties);
stmt = con2.createStatement();
rs = stmt.executeQuery("SELECT COUNT(*) as COUNT FROM TC.TEST_TC_
TABLE");
while (rs.next())
{
  cnt = rs.getInt(1);
  System.out.println("\tSelect using trusted connection is
successful");
}
```

8. The sample output for the previous example is as shown in the following screenshot:

How it works...

The trust relationship between the application server and the database is established when the first connection is created. This relationship lasts till the connection is terminated. Once this trust relationship is made, then the application server can use the database connection under different user IDs with or without the need for authentication at the database server.

The infrastructure required to establish and switch users over a trusted connection is provided by the underlying database driver.

- `DB2ConnectionPoolDataSource`: This class provides the `getDB2TrustedPooledConnection` method to create a trusted connection.

- `DB2XADataSource`: This class provides `getDB2TrustedXAConnectionMethod` to create a trusted connection.

When the application server calls any of these methods, it receives an `Object` array with two elements:

- A connection instance.

- A unique cookie for this connection instance. This cookie is used by the JDBC driver for authentication during a subsequent connection reuse.

The connection reuse facility is also provided by the database driver:

- `DB2PooledConnection`: This class provides the `getDB2Connection()` method to reuse a trusted connection.

- `DB2Connection`: This class provides the `reuseDB2Connection()` method to reuse a trusted connection.

These methods use the cookie and the new connection properties to reuse the connection or to switch to a different user ID on the same connection. The database drive checks the supplied cookie and ensures that it matches the cookie of an underlying trusted connection and only then allows the switch.

Using trusted connections in PHP

In the previous recipe, we saw how we can use trusted connections in Java. In this recipe, we will use trusted connections in PHP. Starting from DB2 9.5 FP3, the `ibm_db2` extension for PHP supports trusted connections. We will use this extension to see how we can create trusted connections and how we can switch user IDs on an established trusted connection.

Getting ready

1. To establish trusted connections, we need the `IBM_DB2` extension configured in PHP.

2. We need a trusted context to be created at the database. We can use the following command to create the trusted context:

```
CREATE TRUSTED CONTEXT ctx_common
BASED UPON CONNECTION USING SYSTEM AUTHID db2admin
ATTRIBUTES (ADDRESS 'localhost',
```

```
                    ENCRYPTION 'NONE')
ENABLE

WITH USE FOR tcuserwoa WITHOUT AUTHENTICATION,

                    tcusera WITH AUTHENTICATION;
```

This trusted context will allow tcuserwoa to use a trusted context without authentication and tcuserwa to use a trusted context with authentication.

How to do it...

By now, we have a trusted context created in the database. As explained in the previous sections, if the connection request matches the trusted context attributes, then a trusted connection will be created.

1. **Creating a trusted connection**: We can use the db2_connect() method to establish a trusted connection. To use this method, we need to create a connection string that has all the needed attributes defined for a trusted connection.

2. **Creating a connection string**: We need to use the same authorization ID for which the trusted context was defined, which is db2admin, in our case:

    ```
    $conString = "DATABASE=$database;HOSTNAME=localhost;PORT=50000;PRO
    TOCOL=TCPIP;UID=db2admin;PWD=db2admin;";
    ```

    To enable trusted connections, we need to pass the DB2_TRUSTED_CONTEXT_ ENABLE connection option. This option cannot be set by using the db2_set_ option() method.

    ```
    $options = array ("trustedcontext" => DB2_TRUSTED_CONTEXT_ENABLE);
    ```

3. Establish a trusted connection by calling the db2_connect() method.

    ```
    echo "\n_____ \n";
    echo "\n--- Creating a Trusted Connection --- \n";

    $tc_conn = db2_connect($conString, "", "", $options);
    if($tc_conn) {
      echo "Explicit Trusted Connection succeeded.\n";
    }
    else {
      echo "Explicit Trusted Connection failed.\n";
    }
    ```

4. **Verifying the current user ID against which the trusted connection is established**: In our case, we should get `db2admin` as the current user.

```
$trusted_user = db2_get_option($tc_conn, "trusted_user");
echo "\tCurrent user: " . $trusted_user . "\n";
```

5. **Switching to a different user ID with authentication**: To switch the user ID with authentication, we need to set the connection options with the new user credentials. In our case, we will switch to `tcuser`. As per the trusted context definition, this user is only allowed to use this trusted context with authentication.

```
echo "\n_____ \n";
echo "\n--- Switching user ID on a trusted connection with
authentication --- \n";
$userBefore = db2_get_option($tc_conn, "trusted_user");
$parameters = array("trusted_user" => $tcuser,
                    "trusted_password" => $tcuser_pass);
$res = db2_set_option ($tc_conn, $parameters, 1);

$userAfter = db2_get_option($tc_conn, "trusted_user");
echo "\tBefore user: " . $userBefore . "\n";
echo "\tAfter user: " . $userAfter . "\n";

if($userBefore != $userAfter) {
   echo "User has been switched." . "\n";
}
else {
   echo "User is not switched" . "\n";
   echo db2_conn_errormsg() . "\n";
   }
```

6. **Switching to a different user ID without authentication**: To switch the user ID without authentication, we only need to set the user ID in the connection options. In this example, we will switch the user to `tcuserwoa`, which is allowed to use this trusted context without authentication, as per the trusted context definition.

```
echo "\n_____ \n";
echo "\n--- Switching userID without authentication --- \n";

$userBefore = db2_get_option($tc_conn, "trusted_user");

$res = db2_set_option ($tc_conn, array("trusted_user" =>
$tcuserwoa), 1);

$userAfter = db2_get_option($tc_conn, "trusted_user");
echo "\tBefore user: " . $userBefore . "\n";
echo "\tAfter user: " . $userAfter . "\n";
```

```
          if($userBefore != $userAfter) {
            echo "User has been switched." . "\n";
          }
          else {
            echo "User is not switched" . "\n";
            echo db2_conn_errormsg() . "\n";
          }
```

7. **Closing the trusted connection**: A trusted connection can be closed just like any other connection:

    ```
    db2_close($tc_conn);
    ```

8. The sample output for our example is as shown in the following image:

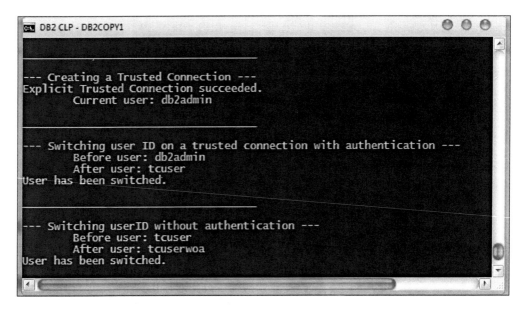

Securing data by using DB2 encryption

Data encryption becomes very crucial in handling confidential data. Data can be encrypted during transit and at storage level. In this recipe, we will focus on encrypting the stored data. DB2 provides various functions that can be used to encrypt and decrypt the data. These functions can be embedded in any host language, just like a regular function or statement. Data is encrypted into BIT DATA, so before we can use encryption, we should have the target table designed to support the encrypted data.

Getting ready

We will use DB2 encryption functions to encrypt and decrypt the data in a test table. The following statement creates a test table that we will use in our recipe:

```
CREATE TABLE TEST_ENCRYPTION
  (ID INTEGER,
   NAME VARCHAR(30),
   CONFIDENTIAL_INFO VARCHAR(100) FOR BIT DATA);
```

Because the encrypted data is BIT DATA, we need to define our target column as FOR BIT DATA.

How to do it...

In this recipe, we will see how we can use encryption functions provided by DB2 to encrypt the data:

1. **Setting the encryption password**: The data encryption provided by DB2 encryption functions is password-based, which means we need a password to encrypt and decrypt the data. We can use the SET ENCRYPTION PASSWORD statement to set the password:

```
SET ENCRYPTION PASSWORD 'myPassword';
```

2. This statement sets the encryption password in a special register known to encryption and decryption functions. This statement is not under transaction control and is not tied to DB2 authentication.

3. **Encrypting the data**: We can encrypt the data by using the ENCRYPT function. This function uses a password-based encryption. It accepts three arguments: data string expression, password string expression, and a password-hint string expression. We can pass the encryption password as a parameter to this function or else it will take the password from a special register whose value can be set by the SET ENCRYPTION PASSWORD command.

4. The following statement uses an encryption password from the special register, which in our case should be mypassword.

```
INSERT INTO TEST_ENCRYPTION VALUES (101, 'Daniel K',
ENCRYPT('ACSX1001'));
```

We can also supply the password explicitly as:

```
INSERT INTO TEST_ENCRYPTION VALUES (102, 'Daniel K',
ENCRYPT('ACSX1001', 'Daniel K'));
```

The ENCRYPT function also provides means to supply password hints, which can be useful if the owner forgets the password.

```
INSERT INTO TEST_ENCRYPTION VALUES (103, 'Daniel K',
ENCRYPT('ACSX1001', 'Daniel K', 'Name'));
```

5. The result of the ENCRYPT function is VARCHAR FOR BIT DATA. We can only encrypt CHAR, VARCHAR, and FOR BIT DATA.

6. **Verifying the encryption**: Once the data is encrypted, it can only be used after decryption. Let's see the data looks like in the table without decryption:

```
SELECT * FROM TEST_ENCRYPTION;
```

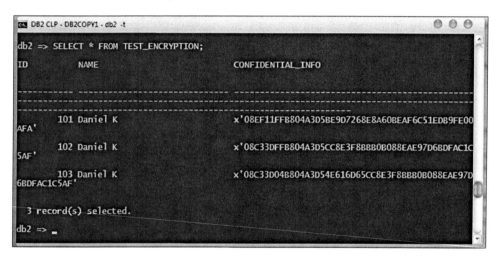

7. **Decrypting the data**: We can use the DECRYPT_BIN and DECRYPT_CHAR functions to decrypt the encrypted data. The data can only be decrypted by using the same password that was used at the time of encryption. The DECRYPT_BIN function returns VARCHAR FOR BIT DATA and the DECRYPT_CHAR function returns VARCHAR.

```
SELECT ID, NAME, DECRYPT_CHAR(CONFIDENTIAL_INFO) FROM TEST_
ENCRYPTION WHERE ID = 101;
```

```
SELECT ID, NAME, DECRYPT_CHAR(CONFIDENTIAL_INFO, 'Daniel K') FROM
TEST_ENCRYPTION WHERE ID IN (102, 103);
```

```
DB2 CLP - DB2COPY1 - db2 -t                                    ● ● ●
db2 => SELECT ID, NAME, DECRYPT_CHAR(CONFIDENTIAL_INFO) FROM TEST_ENCRYPTION WHERE ID = 10
1;
ID          NAME                       3
----------- -------------------------- ------------------------------------------------
--------------------
        101 Daniel K                   ACSX1001

  1 record(s) selected.
db2 => SELECT ID, NAME, DECRYPT_CHAR(CONFIDENTIAL_INFO, 'Daniel K') FROM TEST_ENCRYPTION W
HERE ID IN (102, 103);
ID          NAME                       3
----------- -------------------------- -------------------------
--------------------------------
        102 Daniel K                   ACSX1001
        103 Daniel K                   ACSX1001

  2 record(s) selected.
```

8. **Getting the password hint**: In case we forget the password, we can see the password hint (only if provided at the time of encryption) by using the GETHINT function. It will return NULL if the hint wasn't provided during the encryption. The hint is embedded in the encrypted data.

```
SELECT GETHINT(CONFIDENTIAL_INFO) FROM TEST_ENCRYPTION;
```

```
DB2 CLP - DB2COPY1 - db2 -t                                    ● ● ●
db2 => SELECT ID, GETHINT(CONFIDENTIAL_INFO) FROM TEST_ENCRYPTION;

ID          2
----------- -------------------------------------------
        101 -
        102 -
        103 Name

  3 record(s) selected.

db2 =>
```

How it works...

The ENCRYPT function uses an RC2 block cipher with padding. The 128-bit secret key is derived from the password using an MD5 message checksum. The encrypted data is longer than the original string value, so we need to ensure that the target is big enough to accommodate encrypted data.

Length of encrypted data with the password hint = Length of unencrypted data + 8 bytes + 32 bytes + bytes until the next 8-byte boundary

Length of encrypted data without the password hint = Length of unencrypted data + 8 bytes + bytes until the next 8-byte boundary

There's more...

Once the data is encrypted, it can only be decrypted by using the same password, so we should plan how to manage forgotten passwords. As a best practice, the password should not be provided explicitly in the ENCRYPT function and the SET ENCRYPTION PASSWORD statement should be used. Also, we should use a host variable while setting the encryption password, instead of using a literal string in applications.

Improving concurrency by using enhanced optimistic locking

When a record is selected for updating a table, a lock is acquired. This lock will be released only when the transaction ends. When this lock is acquired by a transaction, no other transaction can update or delete this record. In other words, the second transaction assumes that the first transaction may update the record and hence it waits until the lock is released. This is also known as pessimistic locking. The biggest downside of this type of locking is reduced concurrency.

To overcome such situations, optimistic locking has been introduced. Optimistic locking provides techniques that do not require locks to be held between selecting and updating/ deleting the records. When optimistic locking is used, the application releases the lock immediately after the read operation. If optimistic locking is implemented, then the application assumes that this row will not be updated/deleted by other transactions and releases the lock. Before committing the update or delete operation, it checks whether this row was updated by any other application or not. If not, then the transaction completes successfully; otherwise, it retries the same transaction. The advantage of this approach is that because the resources are locked for a shorter time, concurrency improves.

The application has to ensure that the rows are not updated by some other transaction; it should have a proper retry logic designed. In this recipe, we will see how we can implement optimistic locking in database applications.

How to do it...

Optimistic locking is based on finding out whether a row has been changed from the last fetch or not. This can be achieved by using ROW CHANGE TOKEN and ROW CHANGE TIMESTAMP. Optimistic locking can be implemented in any host language. In this recipe, we will focus on implementing the concept in CLP:

1. **Schema changes**: To implement optimistic locking, we need to make some changes to the table to support optimistic locking. We need a column generated as ROW CHANGE TIMESTAMP in the table:

```
CREATE TABLE TEST_OL
    (ID INT,
     NAME VARCHAR(100),
     SALARY DECIMAL(6,2),
     RCT_COL TIMESTAMP NOT NULL
            GENERATED ALWAYS FOR EACH ROW ON UPDATE AS ROW CHANGE
TIMESTAMP
    );
```

For existing tables, we can also ALTER the table and add this extra column. For example:

```
ALTER TABLE TEST_OL
   ADD COLUMN RCT_COL TIMESTAMP NOT NULL
            GENERATED ALWAYS FOR EACH ROW ON UPDATE AS ROW CHANGE
TIMESTAMP;
```

2. **Selecting the data for UPDATE or DELETE**: The test table we created has a generated column as ROW CHANGE TIMESTAMP. The reason we added this column was to check if the row has changed between SELECT and UPDATE/DELETE. This check will be based on the ROW CHANGE TOKEN value. We will compare the ROW CHANGE TOKEN values between SELECT and UPDATE/DELETE. This means we will again have to locate that row. To make this search more efficient, we can use a row identifier (RID_BIT). To do so, we first need to read the ROW_BIT and ROW CHANGE TOKEN in a host variable. We can use following query to do so:

```
SELECT ID, NAME, SALARY,
       RID_BIT(t1),
       ROW CHANGE TOKEN FOR t1
   FROM TEST_OL t1;
```

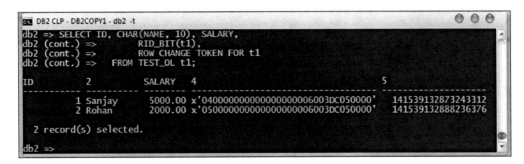

We can keep these values in the host variables to use them in later steps.

3. **Releasing the locks**: The whole idea behind optimistic locking is to provide ways to keep the resources free for other applications. When we are in a transaction, the locks are not released until the transaction is committed or rolled back. We can safely release the locks on selected rows because we have a way to check whether the row is changed or not. The locks can be released by disconnecting from the database or by committing/rolling back the transaction. In our example, we will commit the transaction.

   ```
   COMMIT;
   ```

4. **Searched UPDATE**: Now we have already released the locks and this row is available to other transactions. Now we want to update this row. To do that, we can use searched UPDATE by using RID_BIT, which we captured in a previous step, and we will use ROW CHANGE TOKEN to identify whether the row was changed or not.

   ```
   UPDATE TEST_OL t1
   SET SALARY = SALARY + 100
   WHERE RID_BIT(t1) = x'04000000000000000006003DC050000' AND
           ROW CHANGE TOKEN FOR t1 = 141539132873243312
   ```

5. We are using the row identifier for a search, which will make the search very fast as the row ID has the physical address of the row. It has the page number and the row offset within that page, so the search becomes very fast. We are comparing the ROW CHANGE TOKEN value with the value that we read before. If the row wasn't changed between SELECT and UPDATE, the ROW CHANGE TOKEN will remain the same; otherwise it will change. We can capture the return code to see whether UPDATE succeeded or failed.

6. **Retry logic**: If the previous step failed, then we need to handle the retry logic. We again have to select the row and use the same logic again to do the UPDATE/DELETE.

How it works

DB2 provides new SQL functions to support optimistic locking. Optimistic locking implementation can be divided into two areas:

1. **Searched Update**: Since the locks are released between SELECT and UPDATE/DELETE, we need to locate the row again while updating. This means additional traversal of the table or index. To ease this process, DB2 provides a technique to locate the row by its physical address, which is the most efficient way of doing it. DB2 provides the RID() and RID_BIT() functions to get the physical address of a row. These functions can be used in the SELECT list or as predicates.

2. **Time-based UDPATE detection**: Since optimistic locking releases the locks between `SELECT` and `UPDATE/DELETE`, we need some way to figure out whether the row was changed after the `SELECT`.

   ❑ The first thing DB2 provides to achieve this is the `ROW CHANGE TOKEN` expression. This token represents a relative point in the modification sequence of a row or page. If any row changes in a page, this token value also changes. We can compare this new token value with the one at the time of using `SELECT` and we can find whether any row changed on this page. Since there can be multiple rows on a page, this token value will change with every update on any row in that page. This behavior causes false negatives. **False negative** is a scenario where by looking at a `ROW CHANGE TOKEN` value, we conclude that a row has changed even though it hasn't.

   ❑ To overcome this, we can use `ROW CHANGE TIMESTAMP`. If we have a column which is generated as `ROW CHANGE TIMESTAMP`, `ROW CHANGE TOKEN` will be based on this timestamp. Since the timestamp for all the rows in a page will be different, the `ROW CHANGE TOKEN` will also be different, and hence there will not be any false negatives.

There's more...

There are some key points to consider before implementing optimistic locking in applications:

▸ If the table does not have a generated column as `ROW CHANGE TIMESTAMP`, then the application can get many false negatives. If the number of false negatives is higher, then the application might not perform well because of too many retries.

▸ If `REORG` is performed between `SELECT` and `UPDATE`, then the update will fail because of a false negative. This should be handled in the application retry logic.

▸ For compatibility reasons, we can also have the generated column as an implicitly hidden column. If a column is defined as implicitly hidden, then these columns are not externalized, unless referenced explicitly. For example, such columns will not appear in `SELECT *` against the table. This is also true while inserting rows in a table.

Working with user-defined types (UDT)

In any business, there are many entities or objects. There is no default way to represent a business object in a database. For example, currency is a business entity and there is such a thing in the database that can represent currency directly. To support such requirements, DB2 provides user-defined types (also known as UDTs). A **user-defined type** is a data type which is derived from the existing data types and is treated as a separated data type.

As a user, we can define our own data types based on in-built data types provided by DB2. A simple example would be, we can define USD as DECIMAL (10, 2) and use this across our application or schema. Similarly, we can define a type as CLOB (32K) and resume, and so on. Even if we define multiple user-defined types based on the same underlying DB2 data type, they are still treated as separate data types. The key advantage of such a design is consistency. Because we can define our own data type for a business object, this ensures that every instantiation of this business object will have similar attributes. This also reduces human errors. We can also define functions and operators on distinct data types and hence we can control the way they operate, resulting in consistent behavior.

How to do it...

In this recipe, we will focus on how to create and manipulate distinct data types and how to use them in tables and applications:

1. **Defining a distinct type**: We can use the CREATE DISTINCT TYPE command to create a user-defined type. For example, if we want to create a user-defined type for USD, we can define a distinct type as:

   ```
   CREATE DISTINCT TYPE USD AS DECIMAL(10, 2) WITH COMPARISONS;
   ```

2. Let's create another distinct type that we will use in our recipe:

   ```
   CREATE DISTINCT TYPE EURO AS DECIMAL(10, 2) WITH COMPARISONS;
   ```

3. When we create a distinct type, DB2 generates some cast functions automatically to support casting of a base type to a user-defined type and vice versa. These functions can be used for manipulation of data between these two types. When the WITH COMPARISONS clause is added to the statement, it means that two instances of this user-defined type can be compared with each other. If this clause is specified, then DB2 also generates comparison operators for this type. This option cannot be specified if the base data type is BLOB, CLOB, or DBCLOB.

4. **Creating tables with distinct types**: Once we have created a user-defined type, we can use it just like any other data type. For example, we can create a table with the aforementioned created user type as:

   ```
   CREATE TABLE US_Sales
     (SALES_DT DATE,
     DIVISION VARCHAR(30),
     SALE_VALUE USD);


   CREATE TABLE EU_Sales
     (SALES_DT DATE,
     DIVISION VARCHAR(30),
     SALE_VALUE EURO);
   ```

5. **Comparing distinct types and constants**: Just like any other data type, we may also need to compare the user-defined types with constants in our applications. All user-defined types are strongly typed. This means that they can only be compared with the same data type. So, if we want to compare a user-defined type with a constant, then we need to cast any one of them to change it to the same type as the other. We can either use the `CAST` function or we can use DB2-generated casting functions. For example:

```
SELECT SALES_DT, DIVISION
   FROM    US_Sales
   WHERE   SALE_VALUE > USD(10000);
```

6. **Casting between distinct types**: As mentioned in the previous step, all user-defined types are strongly typed, which means even if we want to compare two different user-defined types, we need to use proper casting. To do that, we need to define some casting functions, which will allow us to cast one user-defined type to another.

7. In our example, if we want to compare the sales between the US and the EU, then we need to use casting functions. During this casting, we need to take care of currency exchange rates. For simplicity, we will assume the following exchange rate:

   1 EURO = 1.45 USD;

   We can define the casting function as:

```
CREATE FUNCTION USD(val EURO)
   RETURNS USD
   RETURN USD(DECIMAL(val) * 1.45);
```

   Similarly, we can define one casting function for USD to EURO also:

```
CREATE FUNCTION EURO(val USD)
   RETURNS EURO
   RETURN EURO(DECIMAL(val) / 1.45);
```

Once we have defined the casting functions, we can use them in comparisons and assignment operations.

```
DB2 CLP - DB2COPY1 - db2 -t

db2 => SELECT US.SALES_DT, US.DIVISION, US.SALE_VALUE - EU.SALE_VALUE
db2 (cont.) =>    FROM US_Sales US, EU_Sales EU
db2 (cont.) =>    WHERE US.SALE_VALUE > EU.SALE_VALUE;
SQL0401N  The data types of the operands for the operation ">" are not
compatible or comparable.  SQLSTATE=42818
db2 =>
db2 =>
db2 => SELECT US.SALES_DT, US.DIVISION, DECIMAL(US.SALE_VALUE) - DECIMAL(USD(EU.SALE_VALUE
))
db2 (cont.) =>    FROM US_Sales US, EU_Sales EU
db2 (cont.) =>    WHERE US.SALE_VALUE > USD(EU.SALE_VALUE);

SALES_DT    DIVISION                              3
---------- ----------------------------- --------------
02/03/2011 Home & Decor                       2000.00

  1 record(s) selected.

db2 =>
```

8. **Creating UDFs involving distinct types**: To extend the functionality of any user-defined type, we can also define functions on them. These functions are also known as sourced UDFs. SUM is a very common operation that we do on many data types. We can create a similar SUM function for our user-defined type.

9. In our example, we can define a SUM function that calculates the SUM for USD values and returns the value in USD.

    ```
    CREATE FUNCTION SUM (USD)

    RETURNS USD

    SOURCE SYSIBM.SUM (DECIMAL());
    ```

    We can directly use this function like a built-in SUM function:

    ```
    SELECT SALES_DT, DIVISION, SUM(SALE_VALUE)

      FROM US_Sales;
    ```

10. **Using distinct types in UNION**: The user-defined types are union-compatible only for the same distinct type. So, if we want to use UNION on different distinct types, we need to use proper casting. For example:

    If we want to do a union on both tables, then we need to use casting functions to cast one of them.

    ```
    SELECT SALES_DT, DIVISION, SALE_VALUE FROM US_Sales

    UNION

    SELECT SALES_DT, DIVISION, USD(SALE_VALUE) FROM EU_Sales;
    ```

11. **Dropping distinct types**: If we no longer need a user-defined type, we can drop it by using the DROP command.

```
DROP DISTINCT TYPE USD
```

A user-defined type cannot be dropped if it has any dependency. For example, if a user-defined type is being used in a table or typed view or another structured type, then we cannot drop it.

There's more...

As mentioned earlier, all user-defined types are strongly typed. This means that we can only compare two objects of the same distinct type. Strong typing guarantees that only functions and operators defined explicitly on the distinct type can be applied to its instances.

Consider a case where we define two user-defined types with the same base data type. For example, US Dollar and Canadian Dollar. Now, because these two currencies have different exchange rates, we do not want any operation that compares these two as that would be wrong. If we want this comparison, then we need to define functions that can cast one distinct type to another and then they can be compared. This restriction is also there for assignment operations for the same reasons.

Working with structured types

In an object-oriented design, we have business objects as entities and each entity has a set of attributes. A structured type is a user-defined special data type, consisting of one or more data types. To represent an entity in DB2, we can use structured types.

A **structured type** is a user-defined data type consisting of one or more data types defined as its attributes. For example, in a school, a room can be one entity and its attributes can be length, width, and height. In this example, we can create a structured type as room and define its attributes as width, height, and length. Once we have created a structured type, we can use it as a regular built-in data type. DB2 also provides ways to define its behavior. In this recipe, we will see how to create structured types and use them in our applications.

Getting ready

In this recipe, we will take a scenario of a high school where we have faculty members and students.

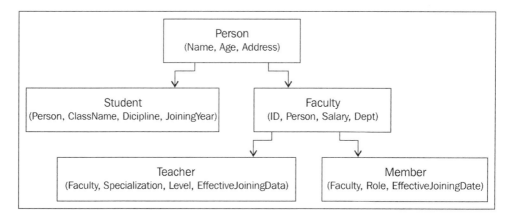

How it works...

1. **Creating a structured type**: Before we proceed with the implementation, we need to have the logical model ready. We will follow the relationship hierarchy as shown in the previous diagram. In our scenario, we have Person as an entity. Let's create a structured type for Person. We can use the CREATE TYPE statement to create a structured type:

```
CREATE TYPE Person_t AS
      (Name VARCHAR(20),
       Age INT,
       Address VARCHAR(200))
       MODE DB2SQL;
```

Just like distinct types, DB2 automatically creates casting functions for structured types that can cast values between the structured type and its representation type and vice versa. In addition to these casting functions, DB2 also creates functions that let us compare structured types by using comparison operators like =, <, >, <>, so on. In our example, DB2 creates the following casting functions by default:

```
CREATE FUNCTION VARCHAR(REF(Person_t))
    RETURNS VARCHAR;


CREATE FUNCTION Person_t(VARCHAR(20))
    RETURNS REF(Person_t);
```

Along with the casting functions and operator functions, DB2 also creates a constructor function for a structured type and mutator and observer methods for its attributes, which are as follows:

- **Constructor function**: This is used to create an instance of the structure type. The constructor function for our example (`Person_t`) looks as follows:

```
CREATE FUNCTION Person_t ( ) RETURNS Person_t
```

- **Mutator method**: This exists for each attribute of the structure type. This method can be used to set the values of attributes in a structured type. When we invoke a mutator method on an instance of the structured type and specify a new value for its associated attribute, then this method returns a new instance with the updated attribute value. For example:

```
ALTER TYPE Person_t
       ADD METHOD AGE(INT)
       RETURNS Person_t;
```

- **Observer method**: This method also exists for each attribute. On invocation, this method returns the value of an attribute. For example:

```
ALTER TYPE Person_t
       ADD METHOD AGE()
       RETURNS INTEGER;
```

2. **Creating a structured type hierarchy**: Using the same method, we can implement the complete object hierarchy in the database. While defining the hierarchy object, we specify the parent object and some additional attributes. When we define an object based on some other object, then it automatically inherits all the properties of its parent objects. Let's create all the objects in our hierarchy.

```
CREATE TYPE Person_t AS
        (Name VARCHAR(20),
        Age INT,
        Address VARCHAR(200))
        INSTANTIABLE
        REF USING INT
        MODE DB2SQL;


   CREATE TYPE Student_t UNDER Person_t AS
  (ClassName VARCHAR(30),
  Descipline VARCHAR(30),
   JoiningDate DATE)
  MODE DB2SQL;
```

```
CREATE TYPE Faculty_t UNDER Person_t AS

    (ID INT, Dept VARCHAR(30), BaseSalary DECIMAL(9,2), Allowances
DECIMAL(9,2))

    MODE DB2SQL;


CREATE TYPE Teacher_t UNDER Faculty_t AS

    (Specialization VARCHAR(50), Level INT, EffectiveJoiningDate
DATE)

    MODE DB2SQL;


CREATE TYPE Member_t UNDER Faculty_t AS

    (Role VARCHAR(20), EffectiveJoiningDate DATE)

    MODE DB2SQL;
```

3. **Defining behavior for structured types:** We can create user-defined methods to extend the functionality and usability of the structured types. These methods are tightly integrated with the structured type. Defining a user-defined method involves two steps. We first need to associate a method specification with the structured type and then define the method.

   The following statement adds the method specification for a method called TOTAL_INCOME to the Faculty_t type:

```
ALTER TYPE Faculty_t

    ADD METHOD TOTAL_INCOME ()

    RETURNS INT;
```

   Once a method is associated with the type, it can then be defined as any SQL or external method.

   For example, the following statement registers an SQL method called TOTAL_INCOME, which returns the total income of the type Faculty_t:

```
CREATE METHOD TOTAL_INCOME ()

    RETURNS INT

    FOR Faculty_t

    RETURN (SELF..BaseSalary + SELF..Allowances);
```

   We can create many methods with the same name for different objects, but they should have different signatures.

4. **Overriding methods from the parent type**: The child object inherits the methods of the parent type and these methods can be used against both types. If we do not want a method defined for a parent type to be used for its child type, then we can override the parent method. This is done by re-implementing the same method but for the given child type. This facilitates polymorphism, where only the specific method is invoked, depending upon the type of object. To define an overriding method, use the OVERRIDING clause in the CREATE TYPE statement.

For example, if we have defined a method as Test_Override_Function for the Faculty_t type, then this can be invoked against the Teacher_t and Member_t types as well. If we want to override this method for the Teacher_t type, then we can define it as follows:

```
ALTER TYPE Faculty_t
    ADD METHOD Test_Override_Function ()
    RETURNS VARCHAR(100);


ALTER TYPE Teacher_t
    ADD OVERRIDING METHOD Test_Override_Function ()
    RETURNS VARCHAR(100);


CREATE METHOD Test_Override_Function ()
    RETURNS VARCHAR(100)
    FOR Faculty_t
    RETURN 'This is Faculty';


CREATE METHOD Test_Override_Function ()
    RETURNS VARCHAR(100)
    FOR Teacher_t
    RETURN 'This is Teacher';
```

5. **Creating tables with structured types**: A structured type is a database representation of a business object. A structured object can be stored either as a row in a table or as a column in a table. If it is stored as a row in a table, then each of its attributes becomes the columns of that table. We can use the following statement to create a table with a structured type:

```
CREATE TABLE Person OF Person_t
    (REF IS Oid USER GENERATED);
```

Each column in this table derives its name and data types based on the structured type. Such tables are also known as typed tables.

We can also store a structured type, stored as a table column. In this case, we will define the column as a structured type instead of a regular DB2 data type.

```
CREATE TABLE Test_student
    (RollNum INT,
     Class VARCHAR(20),
     details Person_t);
```

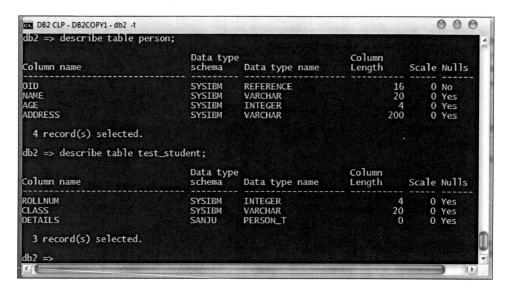

6. **Creating a table hierarchy**: With typed tables, we can also create a table hierarchy, similar to the structured type hierarchy. In every hierarchy, we have a root, tables, and sub tables.

   To create a child table, we need to mention its immediate parent:

   ```
   CREATE TABLE Person OF Person_t
       (REF IS Oid USER GENERATED);


   CREATE TABLE Student OF Student_t UNDER Person
       INHERIT SELECT PRIVILEGES;


   CREATE TABLE Faculty OF Faculty_t UNDER Person
       INHERIT SELECT PRIVILEGES;


   CREATE TABLE Teacher OF Teacher_t UNDER Faculty
       INHERIT SELECT PRIVILEGES;
   ```

```
CREATE TABLE Member OF Member_t UNDER Faculty
    INHERIT SELECT PRIVILEGES;
```

7. **Inserting data in typed tables**: When a structured type is stored as a row in a table, then each attribute of this structured type is a column in that table. Now this table can be used just like a regular table. For example, we have created the table `Person` from the type `Person_t`. Now this table will have all the attributes of the `Person_t` type.

The first column in this table is the OID column. This column is a reference column, which takes an object of the same type. To insert a row in this table, we can use the following query:

```
INSERT INTO Person (Oid, Name, Age, Address) VALUES(Person_t(1),
'John', 31, '23/7, Markham, Ontario(Canada)');
```

Let's insert a few more rows in our tables:

```
INSERT INTO Person (Oid, Name, Age, Address) VALUES (Person_t(2),
'Daniel', 29, '2 NY Plaza');
```

```
INSERT INTO Student (Oid, Name, Age, Address, ClassName,
Descipline, JoiningDate) VALUES (Student_t(3), 'Dan', 54,
'Andheri, Mumbai, India',  '3rd Year', 'Information Technology',
'2011-06-01');
```

```
INSERT INTO Teacher (OID, Name, Age, Address, ID,
Dept, BaseSalary, Allowances, Specialization, level,
EffectiveJoiningDate) VALUES (Teacher_t(4), 'Shyam', 34, 'Banjara
Hils, Hyderabad', 101, 'IT', 20000.00, 15000.00, 'Databases', 2,
'2005-01-15');
```

On the other hand, if a structured type is stored as a column in a table, then we need to use the mutator and observer methods to insert/select records. For example, let's say our table is something like:

```
CREATE TABLE Test_student
    (RollNum INT,
    Class VARCHAR(20),
    details Person_t);
```

In this case, we need to cast the input parameter values to a `Person_t` type before inserting.

```
INSERT INTO Test_student (RollNum, Class, details)
    VALUES(23, '3rd Grade', Person_t..Name('Sanjay')..Age(23)..
Address('Wadala, Mumbai, 400032'));
```

If we want to update this record, then we can use its mutator function:

```
UPDATE Test_Student
   SET details..Age = 25
   WHERE RollNum = 23;
```

8. **Selecting data from typed tables**: When a SELECT, INSERT, or UPDATE is applied on a typed table, the operation is also applied on all its sub tables as well. For example, if we run a SELECT query against our main table Person, then the results will also contain results from its sub tables, which include the Student, Faculty, and Assistant tables.

```
db2 -t

db2 => SELECT OID, NAME, AGE, SUBSTR(ADDRESS, 1, 30) FROM Person;

OID          NAME                    AGE          4
------------ ----------------------- ------------ ------------------------------
          1 John                      31 23/7, Markham, Ontario(Canada)
          2 Daniel                    29 2 NY Plaza
          3 Dan                       54 Andheri, Mumbai, India
          4 Shyam                     34 Banjara Hils, Hyderabad

  4 record(s) selected.

db2 =>
```

We can restrict the results to only the main table by using the ONLY keyword.

```
SELECT * FROM ONLY(Person);
```

```
DB2 CLP - DB2COPY1 - db2 -t

db2 => SELECT OID, NAME, AGE, SUBSTR(ADDRESS, 1, 30) FROM ONLY(person);

OID          NAME                    AGE          4
------------ ----------------------- ------------ ------------------------------
          1 John                      31 23/7, Markham, Ontario(Canada)
          2 Daniel                    29 2 NY Plaza

  2 record(s) selected.

db2 =>
```

If a structured type is defined as a column in a table, then we need some transformation to display or select the value. For example, consider the following example where we have `Address` as a structured type. In such a case, we might want to concatenate all fields and generate a string result for display.

```
CREATE TYPE Address_t AS
   (town VARCHAR(20),
    city VARCHAR(50),
    state VARCHAR(30),
    country VARCHAR(30))
MODE DB2SQL;
```

```
CREATE TABLE test_transform (id INT, name VARCHAR(20), add
Address_t);
INSERT INTO test_transform VALUES (1, 'Bob', Address_t..
town('Andheri')..city('Mumbai')..state('MH')..country('India'));

INSERT INTO test_transform VALUES (2, 'Pat', Address_t..
town('Downtown')..city('Toronto')..state('ON')..
country('Canada'));

INSERT INTO test_transform VALUES (3, 'Joe', Address_t..
town('Indra Nagar')..city('Bangalore')..state('KA')..
country('India'));
```

Now if we run the `SELECT *` query, we will get the following error because we haven't defined the way it should be displayed.

```
SELECT * FROM test_transform;
```

```
SQL20066N  The "FROM SQL" transform function is not defined in the
transform
group "DB2_PROGRAM" for data type "SANJU.ADDRESS_T".
SQLSTATE=42744
```

One way of selecting is to use the observer methods for individual attributes. The other method to display the entire structure is by defining a transform function. Using a transform function, we can format the layout for display.

```
CREATE FUNCTION transform_address (add Address_t) RETURNS
VARCHAR(150) LANGUAGE SQL
  RETURN add..town || ', ' || add..city || ', ' || add..state || ',
' || add..country;


CREATE TRANSFORM FOR Address_t DB2_PROGRAM (FROM SQL WITH FUNCTION
transform_address);
```

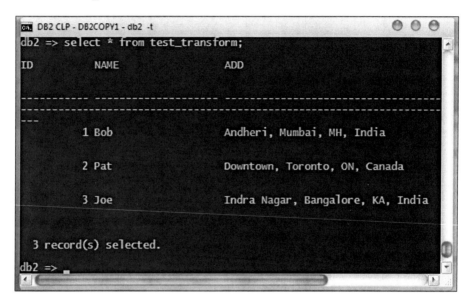

Dropping typed tables

A typed table can only be dropped if it doesn't have any sub table associated. It can be dropped just like a regular table by using the DROP command.

```
DROP TABLE Test_Student;
```

We can also drop the complete hierarchy of tables in a single statement by adding the HIERARCHY keyword in the DROP command and providing the name of the root table.

```
DROP TABLE HIERARCHY Person;
```

Defining constraints on object identifier columns

We can also create referential constraints in typed tables, just like we do for regular tables. We can use the `OID` column as a key column of the parent table in a referential constraint. To do that, we first need to define the OID column in the parent table as the primary key or unique key. Consider the following tables:

1. Create a structured type `Dept` as follows:

   ```
   CREATE TYPE Dept_t AS
   (DeptName VARCHAR(30))
   MODE DB2SQL;


   CREATE TYPE Employee_t AS
   (Name VARCHAR(30), DeptID REF(Dept_t))
   MODE DB2SQL;
   ```

2. Create typed tables for the `Dept_t` and `Employee_t` types:

   ```
   CREATE TABLE Dept OF Dept_t (REF IS OID USER GENERATED);
   CREATE TABLE Employee OF Employee_t(REF IS OID USER GENERATED);
   ```

3. Add the `UNIQUE` constraint to the `OID` of the parent table:

   ```
   ALTER TABLE Dept ADD CONSTRAINT uk1 UNIQUE(OID);
   ```

4. Add a referential constraint by using the OID:

   ```
   ALTER TABLE Employee ADD CONSTRAINT fk1 FOREIGN KEY(DeptID)
   REFERENCES Dept (OID);
   ```

4
Procedures, Functions, Triggers, and Modules

In this chapter, we will focus on the following recipes related to DB2 routines, triggers, and modules:

- ▶ Creating a simple stored procedure
- ▶ Using dynamic SQL in stored procedures
- ▶ Working with result sets in stored procedures
- ▶ Using ARRAY objects in stored procedures
- ▶ Handling errors in stored procedures
- ▶ Designing external stored procedures
- ▶ Using PL/SQL exception handling in a procedure
- ▶ Working with the message buffer in stored procedures
- ▶ Planning and designing triggers
- ▶ Using scalar user-defined functions
- ▶ Writing external user-defined functions
- ▶ Designing external table functions
- ▶ Working with modules in DB2

Introduction

In this chapter, we will look at the different types of functional database objects that can be used to encapsulate business logic at the database server. We will discuss stored procedures and user-defined functions that can be used for better application management and for secure and robust application design. We will also discuss how we can use triggers to enforce business policies seamlessly. This chapter will also include the concept of modules, which was introduced in DB2 9.7.

Creating a simple stored procedure

Stored procedures are database objects that allow us to encapsulate a set of SQL statements and execute them directly on a server. A stored procedure resides in a database server, so when we execute it, it is executed locally. We can implement any business logic or application logic inside a stored procedure and keep it in the database. It can be invoked from any client application. Stored procedures can accept input parameters and return output parameters or result sets or both. In this recipe, we will see how to create a simple stored procedure.

We can define a stored procedure in the following three ways:

- External procedures: The procedure body is written in a high-level programming language for external procedures
- Sourced procedures: They are also known as **federated procedures**, where the definition of a procedure is based on another procedure that resides on a different server, accessible via federation
- SQL: The procedure body is written in SQL

Getting ready

We need the following privileges to create a stored procedure:

- `CREATIN` or `IMPLICIT` schema privilege, whichever is applicable
- Privileges needed to execute all SQL statements used in the procedure

How to do it...

1. Define the input and output parameters as follows:

```
CREATE PROCEDURE SP_Update_Salary
    (IN percentage DECIMAL(5,2), OUT extraCost DECIMAL(11,2))
```

2. Add any optional clauses as appropriate. In this example, we intend to modify the data, so we should specify MODIFIES SQL DATA:

```
MODIFIES SQL DATA
LANGUAGE SQL
```

3. **Compound statement**: This is the actual functionality of the procedure.

```
BEGIN
```

❑ Declare the variables as follows:

```
DECLARE v_sumOldSalaries DECIMAL(11,2) DEFAULT 0;
DECLARE v_sumNewSalaries DECIMAL(11,2) DEFAULT 0;
DECLARE stmt VARCHAR(1000);
```

❑ Processing is carried out as follows:

```
-- Select the total value of current salaries
SELECT SUM(salary) INTO v_sumOldSalaries FROM EMPLOYEE;

-- Update the salary with given input parameter
SET stmt = 'UPDATE EMPLOYEE SET SALARY = SALARY * (100 + ?)/100';
PREPARE s1 FROM stmt;
EXECUTE s1 USING percentage;

-- Select the total value of new salaries
SELECT SUM(salary) INTO v_sumNewSalaries FROM EMPLOYEE;
```

❑ Return the results as follows:

```
-- Set the OUT parameter as the difference of two salaries.
SET extraCost = v_sumNewSalaries - v_sumOldSalaries;
END @
```

How it works...

We can create a procedure either in SQL or in any external host language, such as C, C++, Java, and so on. In this recipe, we will focus on SQL stored procedures.

The `CREATE PROCEDURE` statement can be used to create a stored procedure. The basic structure of this statement is as follows:

```
CREATE PROCEDURE <proc_name> (parameters)
  OPTIONAL CLAUSES
 PROCEDURE BODY
```

Parameters: Stored procedures can have the following three types of parameters:

▸ `IN`: This is the input parameter, which can be supplied at the time of calling the procedure by the client.

▸ `OUT`: This is the output parameter, which is returned to the client or caller.

▸ `INOUT`: This parameter can serve the purpose of both `IN` and `OUT` parameters. This parameter can be used to pass in the input values to the procedure as well as to get the output from the procedure.

Optional clauses: We can use any combination of the following options in the `CREATE PROCEDURE` statement:

▸ `SPECIFIC NAME`: This is a unique name for the stored procedure, which can be used to alter or drop a procedure. We can create multiple stored procedures with the same procedure name, but with different signatures. In such cases, we need to provide a different `SPECIFIC` name. DB2 generates a name of its own, if this is not specified explicitly. However, we cannot use this name to invoke a procedure.

▸ `DYNAMIC RESULTSETS`: This indicates the upper bound of result sets returned by the procedure.

▸ `CONTAINS SQL`, `READS SQL DATA`, and `MODIFIES SQL DATA`: These can be specified to specify the behavior of the procedure.

▸ `DETERMINISTIC` or `NON DETERMINISTIC`: Indicates whether the procedure produces the same results for given input values every time.

▸ `COMMIT ON RETURN`: This option indicates whether a commit should be issued when the procedure returns. The default is `NO`.

▸ `AUTONOMOUS`: Indicates whether the procedure should execute in its own transaction scope.

▸ `INHERIT SPECIAL REGISTERS`: If this clause is specified, then the procedure inherits the updatable special registers from the client environment from where the procedure is invoked.

▸ `LANGUAGE SQL`: This option indicates that this procedure is defined in SQL.

▸ `EXTERNAL ACTION` or `NO EXTERNAL ACTION`: Indicates whether the procedure changes anything that is not managed by DB2.

▸ `PARAMETER CCSID`: Indicates the encoding of string data passed in and out of the procedure.

Procedure body: We can use compound statements to define the stored procedure functionality. A compound statement has the following logical sections:

- ▸ Variable declaration section
- ▸ Condition declaration section
- ▸ Cursor declaration section
- ▸ Condition handler section
- ▸ SQL statements

Once a stored procedure is created, it gets registered on the database server. Now any client application can invoke this procedure by a `CALL` statement and the procedure gets executed on the server. The following diagram compares using stored procedures and not using stored procedures. If a procedure is not used, then every SQL statement needs to be passed over the network to DB2 and the results need to be retrieved. Passing the data over the network creates congestion and it is very expensive in terms of performance. Instead, if we use stored procedures, then the client can use the `CALL` statement to invoke the procedure. The procedure gets executed locally on the server and we only get the actual results and no intermediate results.

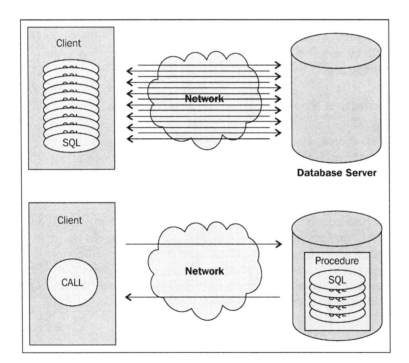

There's more

Since the procedures reside on the server, we have some key benefits to using stored procedures:

- Network traffic: All SQL statements are already present in the stored procedure definition, so the client application only has to send a command to invoke the procedure and get the results. There is no intermediate data transmission over the network, hence reducing the network traffic, which in turn gives better performance.

- Reusability: Once a procedure is created and registered on the server, it can be used in any application in any host language. This becomes very handy when different applications need to perform similar tasks. This approach also simplifies maintenance.

- Business logic encapsulation: We can embed our business logic within the stored procedure and use it in different applications just by invoking this procedure. It allows us to maintain business logic at one place instead of maintaining it in multiple applications and reusing the same business logic in all applications.

- Better performance: Stored procedures are precompiled and are ready for execution. Hence it saves compilation time, resulting in better performance.

- Access control: A user invoking a stored procedure only needs the EXECUTE privilege on the procedure and no other privilege on objects referenced by the procedure. This way, we can control the access to database objects.

Stored procedure execution

When a stored procedure is created, DB2 separates the SQL queries and the procedural logic. All SQL queries are compiled and access plans are generated for them. A package is created for this procedure and it has access plans for each SQL query. Within the package, these access plans are divided into sections. The procedural logic is compiled into a dynamic linkage library. During the execution of a procedure, whenever DB2 has to jump between SQL query and procedural logic, it has to make a context switch. If the procedure is running in *unfenced* mode, then it uses the same address space as DB2, so the context switch is between different parts of the memory and not on completely separate address space. We should always try to minimize the number of context switches. If there are too many context switches, performance will be affected. For example, if we have a stored procedure that processes too many records and does some kind of data manipulation or cleansing on them, then there will be many context switches between SQL and procedural logic causing slower performance.

> *When a stored procedure is defined to run in unfenced mode, then it uses the same memory space as that of the DB2 engine. It can result in problems like database crashes, memory faults, and the like in the database manager if there is any bug in the procedure. Hence it should be used with much caution and testing.*

Calling a stored procedure

Stored procedures can only be invoked by a CALL statement. We can embed a CALL statement in any host language or call it from a procedure, UDF, compound statement or trigger, or from CLP.

```
CALL SP_Update_Salary(20.00, ?) @
```

```
CALL SP_Update_Salary(20.00, ?)

  Value of output parameters
  --------------------------
  Parameter Name  : EXTRACOST
  Parameter Value : 488505.00

  Return Status = 0
```

Using named parameters

We can also use names and default values for parameters in stored procedures. If we use named parameters, then we don't need to specify the parameters in the order of the procedure definition. We also don't need to specify all the parameters in the CALL statement. In this case, the default values will be used for unspecified parameters.

In the preceding example, if we want to add a default value to any input parameter, it can be done as follows:

```
CREATE PROCEDURE SP_Update_Salary
  (OUT extraCost DECIMAL(11,2), IN percentage DECIMAL(5,2) DEFAULT 10.00 )
LANGUAGE SQL
```

The actual definition remains the same.

```
BEGIN
  -- Declare variables
  DECLARE v_sumOldSalaries DECIMAL(11,2) DEFAULT 0;
  DECLARE v_sumNewSalaries DECIMAL(11,2) DEFAULT 0;
  DECLARE stmt VARCHAR(1000);

  -- Select the total value of current salaries
  SELECT SUM(salary) INTO v_sumOldSalaries FROM EMPLOYEE;

  -- Update the salary with given input parameter
  SET stmt = 'UPDATE EMPLOYEE SET SALARY = SALARY * (100 + ?)/100';
  PREPARE s1 FROM stmt;
```

```
    EXECUTE s1 USING percentage;


    -- Select the total value of new salaries
    SELECT SUM(salary) INTO v_sumNewSalaries FROM EMPLOYEE;


    -- Set the OUT parameter as the difference of two salaries.
    SET extraCost = v_sumNewSalaries - v_sumOldSalaries;


END @
```

While calling the stored procedure, we can use parameter names instead of just values. This becomes very handy because we don't need to worry about parameter orders.

```
CALL SP_Update_Salary(?, percentage=> 20.00)@
CALL SP_Update_Salary(?)@
```

```
CALL SP_Update_Salary(?, percentage=> 20.00)

  Value of output parameters
  --------------------------
  Parameter Name  : EXTRACOST
  Parameter Value : 488505.00

  Return Status = 0
CALL SP_Update_Salary(?)

  Value of output parameters
  --------------------------
  Parameter Name  : EXTRACOST
  Parameter Value : 244252.50

  Return Status = 0
```

Using dynamic SQL in stored procedures

Dynamic SQL is used when the SQL statement is not known at compile time. In such cases, we use PREPARE and EXECUTE statements to execute a dynamic SQL, where we get the complete SQL statement at runtime. The prepared statement is based on either a host variable or a string expression. At runtime, we make this value available for DB2 to process it. We can implement dynamic SQL in stored procedures in the same manner as in other applications. In this recipe, we will focus on using dynamic SQL in stored procedures.

How to do it...

Executing an SQL statement dynamically: To execute an SQL statement dynamically, we need to first prepare it and then execute it. The statement can be prepared from a declared variable or directly from an SQL statement.

The following example prepares and executes an UPDATE statement on the EMPLOYEE table, based on input parameter value:

1. Define the input and output parameters of the procedure along with any optional clauses as appropriate:

```
CREATE PROCEDURE raise_salary(IN EMPNO CHAR(6), IN pct
DECIMAL(4,2))
LANGUAGE SQL
  BEGIN
   DECLARE stmt VARCHAR(1000);
   DECLARE temp DECIMAL(9,2) DEFAULT 0;
```

2. Create the SQL statement to be prepared as a string. We can use parameter markers as a placeholder for values:

```
    SET stmt = 'UPDATE EMPLOYEE SET SALARY = SALARY * (1 + ? /
100) WHERE EMPNO = ?';
```

3. Prepare the preceding SQL statement:

```
    PREPARE s1 FROM stmt;
```

4. Execute the statement using values for parameter markers:

```
    EXECUTE s1 USING pct, empno;
   ROLLBACK;
END @
```

Once a statement is prepared, we can execute it against the different values of parameter markers.

Executing an SQL statement using dynamic cursors: Just like a dynamic SQL statement, we can also define dynamic cursors. To do that, we declare the cursors on statement name and not on the SELECT query. This becomes very useful when we don't have the complete SQL statement ready at the time of cursor declaration. Since we cannot have any procedural logic before the cursor declaration section, we can use dynamic statements to define the cursors.

1. Consider the following example where the result set we are interested in is based on the `DEPT` values, which are passed in as the input parameter:

```
CREATE PROCEDURE SP_DynamicCursors(IN empno CHAR(6), OUT details
VARCHAR(1000))
    LANGUAGE SQL
BEGIN
    DECLARE v_sql varchar(200);
    DECLARE at_end INT DEFAULT 0;
    DECLARE v_firstName VARCHAR(20);
    DECLARE v_lastName VARCHAR(20);
    DECLARE v_sal DECIMAL(9,2);
    DECLARE not_found CONDITION FOR SQLSTATE '02000';
```

2. Declare the cursor against a statement name instead of the `SELECT` query:

```
    DECLARE c1 CURSOR FOR v_stmt;
    DECLARE CONTINUE HANDLER FOR not_found SET at_end = 1;
```

3. Create the `SELECT` query against which we want the cursor to be opened:

```
    SET v_sql ='SELECT FIRSTNME, LASTNAME, SALARY, WORKDEPT FROM
EMPLOYEE WHERE EMPNO = ''' || empno || '''';
```

4. Prepare the preceding SQL statement as follows:

```
    PREPARE v_stmt FROM v_sql;
```

5. Open the cursor. The cursor will point to the result set of the preceding prepared SQL statement.

```
OPEN c1;
```

6. Process the cursor as desired.

```
    ins_loop:
    LOOP
        FETCH c1 INTO v_firstName, v_lastName, v_sal;
        IF at_end = 1 THEN
            LEAVE ins_loop;
        END IF;
    END LOOP;
    SET details = 'Employee Num: ' || empno || ' ; First Name: ' ||
v_firstName || ' ; Last Name : ' || v_lastName || ' ; Salary: ' ||
CAST(v_sal AS VARCHAR(20));
END@
```

How it works...

When a stored procedure is registered in a database, it is compiled and a package is created. This package contains access plans for all static SQL statements contained in the procedure definition. Packages contain section entries for each SQL statement. This section entry has details of the respective SQL statement and its context. However, dynamic SQL statements are compiled at execution time. Section entries for dynamic SQL statements are present in the package but they are empty, as the SQL statements and their contexts are not available until execution time.

Working with result sets in stored procedures

We can get the results from a stored procedure either in the form of the OUT or INOUT parameters or as result sets. In this recipe, we will discuss returning result sets in stored procedures. A stored procedure can be invoked either from a client application or from another stored procedure. If we return a result set from a procedure, we need to decide where to return it. We can return the result set to its caller or to the client. If it's returned to CALLER, then the result sets are not available at the end client. In this recipe, we will discuss how we can return result sets from a stored procedure.

How to do it...

Returning a result set: To return a result set from a procedure, we need to declare a cursor with the required definition and leave the cursor OPEN. The cursor should be defined as WITH RETURN; otherwise, the result set will not be returned.

For example, if we want to return all the employees with a salary greater than 10,000, then we can use the following stored procedure:

```
CREATE PROCEDURE SP_Resultset()
RESULT SETS 1
LANGUAGE SQL
BEGIN
-- Declare the cursor as "WITH RETURN"
    DECLARE c1 CURSOR WITH RETURN FOR SELECT EMPNO, FIRSTNME, LASTNAME,
SALARY
                                FROM EMPLOYEE WHERE WORKDEPT =
'D11';
```

```
-- Leave the cursor opened.
    OPEN c1;
END@
```

```
CALL SP_Resultset()

Result set 1
-------------

EMPNO    FIRSTNME    LASTNAME         SALARY
------   ----------  -------------    ----------
000060   IRVING      STERN            72250.00
000150   BRUCE       ADAMSON          55280.00
000160   ELIZABETH   PIANKA           62250.00
000170   MASATOSHI   YOSHIMURA        44680.00
000180   MARILYN     SCOUTTEN         51340.00
000190   JAMES       WALKER           50450.00
000200   DAVID       BROWN            57740.00
000210   WILLIAM     JONES            68270.00
000220   JENNIFER    LUTZ             49840.00
200170   KIYOSHI     YAMAMOTO         64680.00
200220   REBA        JOHN             69840.00

11 record(s) selected.

Return Status = 0
```

Returning a result set to caller: A **caller** is the application or any entity that invokes a stored procedure. It may not be the end-client application. For example, if we have an application that calls a stored procedure, then this application is the client as well as the caller. However, if this application calls a procedure, which in turn calls another stored procedure, then this application is the client and the procedure is the caller. Depending on the requirements, we might want to return the result set to the client or to the caller. Return to caller is the default behavior.

If we take the preceding example, we will only get the result set at the caller side and not at the client side. To see this, let's create a nested stored procedure, which calls the previously-created procedure:

```
CREATE PROCEDURE SP_Resultset_Outer()
RESULT SETS 1
LANGUAGE SQL
BEGIN
    CALL SP_Resultset();
END@
```

Now if we call this procedure, then we will not have the result set from the OUT_MEDIAN procedure.

```
CREATE PROCEDURE SP_Resultset_Outer()
RESULT SETS 1
LANGUAGE SQL
BEGIN
    CALL SP_Resultset();
END
DB20000I  The SQL command completed successfully.

CALL SP_Resultset_Outer()

  Return Status = 0
```

Returning a result set to the client: If we want to return the result set to the client, then we need to declare the cursor as WITH RETURN TO CLIENT. Let's create a procedure that has a cursor defined as RETURN TO CLIENT:

```
CREATE PROCEDURE SP_Resultset_ToClient()

RESULT SETS 1

LANGUAGE SQL

BEGIN

    DECLARE c1 CURSOR

        WITH RETURN TO CLIENT

        FOR SELECT EMPNO, FIRSTNME, LASTNAME, SALARY

            FROM EMPLOYEE WHERE WORKDEPT = 'D11';

    OPEN c1;

END@
```

With the preceding definition, the result set will be returned to the client and not to the caller. To see it in action, let's create another procedure, which in turn calls this procedure.

```
CREATE PROCEDURE SP_Resultset_OuterClient()

RESULT SETS 1

LANGUAGE SQL

BEGIN

    CALL SP_Resultset_ToClient();

END@
```

Now if we call `return_to_client_sp`, which in turn is calling the `OUT_MEDIAN` procedure, the result set will be available to the client. In our case, we should see the result set on CLP, which is our client in this example:

```
CALL SP_Resultset_OuterClient()


Result set 1
---------------

EMPNO  FIRSTNME      LASTNAME          SALARY
------ ------------- ----------------- -----------
000060 IRVING        STERN             72250.00
000150 BRUCE         ADAMSON           55280.00
000160 ELIZABETH     PIANKA            62250.00
000170 MASATOSHI     YOSHIMURA         44680.00
000180 MARILYN       SCOUTTEN          51340.00
000190 JAMES         WALKER            50450.00
000200 DAVID         BROWN             57740.00
000210 WILLIAM       JONES             68270.00
000220 JENNIFER      LUTZ              49840.00
200170 KIYOSHI       YAMAMOTO          64680.00
200220 REBA          JOHN              69840.00

11 record(s) selected.

Return Status = 0
```

Using result sets from a nested stored procedure: In the previous steps, we saw how to return the result sets from a procedure to the caller and clients. In this step, we will see how to process the result set that is returned from another procedure. One way to share data between two procedures can be by storing the result set in a temporary table and using it in another procedure. Another approach could be to directly process the result set. To do that, we first need to declare a result set locator.

In this example, we will process the result set returned from the preceding sample procedure, `SP_Resultset`. We can use the following statement to declare a result set locator:

```
DECLARE rs_locator RESULT_SET_LOCATOR VARYING;
```

1. Now we can invoke the procedure by using the `CALL` statement:

   ```
   CALL SP_Resultset();
   ```

2. The next step is to associate this result set locator with the called procedure (whose result set is to be processed). We can use the following statement to make this association:

```
ASSOCIATE RESULT SET LOCATOR(rs_locator) WITH PROCEDURE SP_
Resultset;
```

3. Then we need to allocate the cursor that points to the result set returned. This can be done as follows:

```
ALLOCATE c1 CURSOR FOR RESULT SET rs_locator;
```

4. Now we can use this cursor to process the result set in the desired manner:

```
OPEN c1;
  sel_loop:
  LOOP
    FETCH c1 INTO v_empNo, v_firstName, v_lastName, v_salary;
    IF at_end = 1 THEN
      LEAVE sel_loop;
    END IF;


  END LOOP;
  CLOSE c1;
```

Returning multiple result sets: We can also return multiple result sets from a stored procedure. We just have to open multiple cursors and keep them open:

```
DECLARE c1 CURSOR
    WITH RETURN
    FOR SELECT EMPNO, FIRSTNME, LASTNAME, SALARY
        FROM EMPLOYEE WHERE WORKDEPT = 'D11';


DECLARE c2 CURSOR
    WITH RETURN
    FOR SELECT EMPNO, FIRSTNME, LASTNAME, SALARY
        FROM EMPLOYEE WHERE WORKDEPT = 'D21';
OPEN c1;
OPEN c2;
```

```
CALL SP_MultiResultset()

Result set 1
--------------

EMPNO  FIRSTNME     LASTNAME          SALARY
------ ------------ ----------------- -----------
000060 IRVING       STERN             72250.00
000150 BRUCE        ADAMSON           55280.00
000160 ELIZABETH    PIANKA            62250.00
000170 MASATOSHI    YOSHIMURA         44680.00
000180 MARILYN      SCOUTTEN          51340.00
000190 JAMES        WALKER            50450.00
000200 DAVID        BROWN             57740.00
000210 WILLIAM      JONES             68270.00
000220 JENNIFER     LUTZ              49840.00
200170 KIYOSHI      YAMAMOTO          64680.00
200220 REBA         JOHN              69840.00

11 record(s) selected.


Result set 2
--------------

EMPNO  FIRSTNME     LASTNAME          SALARY
------ ------------ ----------------- -----------
000070 EVA          PULASKI           96170.00
000230 JAMES        JEFFERSON         42180.00
000240 SALVATORE    MARINO            48760.00
000250 DANIEL       SMITH             49180.00
000260 SYBIL        JOHNSON           47250.00
000270 MARIA        PEREZ             37380.00
200240 ROBERT       MONTEVERDE        37760.00

7 record(s) selected.

Return Status = 0
```

How it works...

The only way to return result sets from a stored procedure is by using cursors. When a cursor is defined with a `WITH RETURN` clause and is left open the in the procedure definition, it can be retrieved at the client side or caller side, depending on the cursor definition. Separate cursors must be defined for every result set we need to return. Once a cursor is opened, it allows us to retrieve rows from it. If some rows are fetched from a cursor and the same cursor is used to return the result set, then only the unfetched rows will be returned to the client or the caller application. If we have multiple cursors open for multiple result sets, then the result sets will be returned in the order of opening the cursors.

There's more...

If we want to process the result sets outside the transactions, then we need to declare the cursors with the `WITH HOLD` option. If this option is not specified, then the cursor will be automatically closed when the transaction completes. This also means that if we have a stored procedure, which is defined as `AUTONOMOUS`, then we need to make sure that all the cursors which will be returned are declared as `WITH HOLD`. All cursors defined without hold are closed on `COMMIT` and all cursors (with or without hold) are closed on `ROLLBACK`. After a `COMMIT` or a `ROLLBACK` is made in a procedure, we can still open a cursor and return it as a result set to the caller.

When we declare a cursor for return, we can also fetch the data from this cursor. If we do that, then only the unfetched data is returned to the client or caller.

Using ARRAY objects in stored procedures

`ARRAY` as a data type was introduced in DB2 9.5. An **array** is a set of identical data elements. These base elements are based on inbuilt data types. Any element in an array can be identified by its index position. Arrays are very useful when we need to store a set of values. This becomes very useful when we need to pass a set of values to a procedure. Instead of passing many parameters simultaneously, we can pass one array to the procedure. For example, if we want to pass in a list of employee numbers as input to a procedure, then we can keep them in an array and pass this array as an input parameter. The same concept applies when getting the results from a procedure. In this recipe, we will see how we can create and use arrays in stored procedures.

How to do it...

1. Create a variable of the type ARRAY: The main use of the ARRAY type in a procedure is as an input or output parameter. Before we can define any procedure with ARRAY type parameters, we need to define an object of ARRAY type. We can use the CREATE ARRAY statement to create an array object:

    ```
    CREATE TYPE int_array AS INTEGER ARRAY[50]@
    ```

2. Create a procedure that accepts and returns an array: Once we have the array object defined, it can be used like a regular inbuilt data type:

    ```
    CREATE PROCEDURE SUM(IN numList INT_ARRAY, OUT total INTEGER)
    BEGIN
      DECLARE cnt INTEGER DEFAULT 1;
      SET total = 0;


    -- An array element can be referenced by using index values.
      WHILE (cnt <= CARDINALITY(numList)) DO
        SET total = total + numList[cnt];
        SET cnt = cnt + 1;
      END WHILE;
    END @
    ```

3. Since the input parameter of this procedure is of ARRAY type, we need to create an array before we can pass the values:

    ```
    CALL SUM(ARRAY[1,2,3,4,5,6,7,8,9], ?)@
    ```

There's more...

DB2 provides many helping scalar functions to use ARRAY type objects:

-   ARRAY_NEXT: To get the next value of an array relative to a given index
-   ARRAY_PRIOR: To get the previous value of an array relative to a given index
-   ARRAY_DELETE: To delete an element of an array
-   ARRAY_FIRST: To get the first element of an array
-   ARRAY_LAST: To get the last element of an array

Using procedures with ARRAY parameters in Java

If we have ARRAY type procedure parameters, then they need to be handled in the client application accordingly. Every language provides semantics to manipulate array objects. Using ARRAY type in any language involves declaring the variables in the host language and binding them as parameters to a procedure. As an example, let's see how we can handle them in Java:

- IN/INOUT parameters: The ARRAY type parameters IN, OUT, and INOUT can be represented as java.sql.Array objects. For IN and INOUT parameters, we can use the DB2Connection.createArrayOf method to create an ARRAY object. To assign values to the java.sql.Array objects, we can use the CallableStatement.setArray method.

- OUT parameter: For OUT parameters also, we need to define an ARRAY type host variable. We can use the CallableStatement.registerOutParameter method to register a host variable as an OUT parameter to a stored procedure.

Let's take the following stored procedure as an example that we will use in our Java example:

```
CREATE PROCEDURE SUM(IN numList INT_ARRAY, OUT total INTEGER)
BEGIN
  DECLARE cnt INTEGER DEFAULT 1;
  SET total = 0;

  WHILE (cnt <= CARDINALITY(numList)) DO
    SET total = total + numList[cnt];
    SET cnt = cnt + 1;
  END WHILE;
END @
```

The following is the sample Java code:

```
    // Prepare the call statement:
        String sql = "CALL SUM(?, ?)";
        CallableStatement callStmt = con.prepareCall(sql);

    // Create an array of values that should be passed as input parameter
    to the procedure.
    numList[0]=new Integer(1);
    numList[1]=new Integer(2);
    numList[2]=new Integer(3);
    numList[3]=new Integer(4);
    numList[4]=new Integer(5);

    // Create an array type using the above values.
```

```
        java.sql.Array numListArray = con.createArrayOf("INTEGER",
numList);

    // Set IN parameters
        callStmt.setArray(1,numListArray );

    // Register OUT parameter
        callStmt.registerOutParameter(2, java.sql.Types.INTEGER);

    // Call the procedure
        callStmt.execute();

    // Retrieve the OUT parameter
        val1 = callStmt.getInt(2);
```

Handling errors in stored procedures

Whenever any SQL statement is executed, it either succeeds or fails. As an application developer, we need to make sure that we handle all possible errors gracefully. To ease this task, DB2 provides various tools or methods that can be used for better error handling.

There are two types of errors. If an SQL statement literally fails, then that's an error. However, there could be cases where the SQL statement passes technically but the results are not proper from a business point of view. For example, if we are updating salaries of employees in the Employee table and if the new salary becomes negative somehow, then technically the update was successful, but we all know that negative salary is not valid. So we need to handle such error cases as well in our code.

In this recipe, we will focus on methods that can be used for error handling in stored procedures.

How to do it...

Error handling in stored procedures is very similar to what we do in programming languages. DB2 provides many tools or techniques to handle errors. We can control the application behavior based on these tools. At any point, we can check if the preceding statement failed or succeeded, and choose appropriate actions to handle the situation. In this recipe, we will look at all the options available to us that can help us identify the problems or errors.

1. Declare DB2 error code variables: Whenever DB2 executes an SQL statement, it returns an SQLCODE and SQLSTATE. Looking at these values, we can find whether the SQL statement succeeded, failed, or gave some warning. SQLCODE is the return code that indicates an error or warning or success status, along with a code that gives detailed information about the result. Every DBM has its own set of SQLCODES, so we cannot compare the SQLCODES from two different DBMSs. This becomes an issue when we have to migrate to another DBMS. To overcome this issue, we also have SQLSTATE variables, which are a standard code for an error. We can use SQLCODE or SQLSTATE or both in our application.

   SQLCODE: When SQLCODE is negative, it's an error. If it's positive, then it's a warning. If it is zero, then it represents a success status. To use them in stored procedures, we need to declare SQLCODE and SQLSTATE variables in the procedure body:

   ```
   DECLARE SQLCODE INTEGER DEFAULT 0;

   DECLARE SQLSTATE CHAR(5) DEFAULT '00000';
   ```

   DB2 automatically sets these values upon execution of SQL statements. When these values are accessed, they are reset back to default values, which are 0 and 00000.

2. Declare condition handlers: Once we have defined the preceding two variables, we can track the return codes. If we don't handle these errors (if any), then the procedure would fail. To handle these errors, we need to declare condition handlers. We can use condition handlers to control the behavior of the stored procedure. We can define these condition handlers on general conditions or on specific SQLSTATE values.

   If we have defined a condition handler for an SQL exception, and if that exception occurs, then DB2 passes the control to that condition handler. Once the control is with the condition handler, we can take appropriate action to address this exception.

   This is a two-step process. First we need to declare a condition and then we need to declare its handler.

   ```
   DECLARE <condition_name> CONDITION FOR SQLSTATE '<sqlstate>';

   DECLARE [CONTINUE/EXIT/UNDO] HANDLER FOR <condition_name>
   <action>;
   ```

- ❏ `CONTINUE`: After the handler, the control is passed back to the SQL statement next to the one that raised the exception

- ❏ `EXIT`: After the handler, the procedure ends

- ❏ `UNDO`: It rolls back all the changes made by the procedure (or compound statement)

We can define conditions based either on `SQLSTATE` or on generic conditions, such as `SQLEXCEPTION`, `SQLWARNING`, or `NOT FOUND`. For example:

```
DECLARE not_found CONDITION FOR SQLSTATE '02000';

DECLARE CONTINUE HANDLER FOR not_found SET at_end = 1;
```

With this example, if we are selecting rows from a cursor and if rows are not available, then this condition will arise and DB2 will pass the control to this condition handler. In this handler, we are setting a variable value to 1. We can use this variable value on our loop to fetch the rows and find out if there are no more rows. This way, we can handle all types of errors and warnings.

3. Raising user-defined exceptions: There could be situations where we need to define our own exceptions depending upon the business logic. For example, if we see any negative salary value, then that's an exception from a business point of view. To handle such cases, we need to check the exception use case and raise an exception. To raise exceptions, DB2 provides `SIGNAL` and `RESIGNAL` commands. We can use any valid `SQLSTATE` as an exception and we can also provide a custom error message.

   For example:

```
SIGNAL SQLSTATE '75002' SET MESSAGE_TEXT = 'Customer number is
not known';
```

A `RESIGNAL` statement is used within a condition handler to resignal an exception or maybe some other exception:

```
RESIGNAL SQLSTATE '22375';.
```

4. Get diagnostics: At any point, we can get the information about the last SQL statement executed. The following information can be retrieved by using the `GET DIAGNOSTICS` statement:

   - ❏ `DB2_RETURN_STATUS`: Returns the status of a procedure call

   - ❏ `DB2_NESTING_LEVEL`: Represents the level of nesting or recursion

   - ❏ `ROW_COUNT`: Number of rows associated with the previous SQL statement

   - ❏ `DB2_TOKEN_STRING`: Error or warning message token returned from the previous SQL statement

   - ❏ `MESSAGE_TEXT`: Error or warning message returned from the previous SQL statement

To get the diagnostic information, we can use the GET DIAGNOSTIC statement. For example:

```
GET DIAGNOSTICS row_count = ROW_COUNT;


GET DIAGNOSTICS EXCEPTION 1 msgtxt=MESSAGE_TEXT,
msgtxtlen=MESSAGE_LENGTH;
```

5. Return status: If any procedure doesn't succeed due to some exception, then we can return any custom integer as its return code. As a convention, we can use 0 if everything goes well and -1 f anything fails. If we return the proper return code, then this information can be used by the client to check whether the procedure succeeded or failed.

```
RETURN 0;
```

6. Putting it together: Consider the following example that puts everything together:

```
CREATE PROCEDURE SP_ERROR_HANDLING (IN empno VARCHAR(6), OUT
rowsUpdated INTEGER)
BEGIN
  DECLARE stmt VARCHAR(1000);


  -- Exit handler in case of no data found condition
  DECLARE EXIT HANDLER FOR NOT FOUND
    SIGNAL SQLSTATE '75000' SET MESSAGE_TEXT = 'Employee ID is not
known';


  SET rowsUpdated = 0;
  SET stmt = 'UPDATE EMPLOYEE SET SALARY = SALARY * 1.5 WHERE
EMPNO = ' || empno;
  PREPARE s1 FROM stmt;
  EXECUTE s1;
  GET DIAGNOSTICS rowsUpdated = ROW_COUNT;
END @


CALL SP_ERROR_HANDLING('000000', ?) @
```

```
db2 => CALL SP_ERROR_HANDLING('000000', ?) @
SQL0438N  Application raised error or warning with diagnostic text: "Employee
ID is not known".  SQLSTATE=75002
db2 =>
```

How it works...

When an SQL statement is executed, it can result either in success, failure, or success with a warning condition. This can be identified by examining the return code, which is also referred to as SQLCODE. If the SQLCODE is 0, that means the statement executed successfully. A negative value indicates failure and a positive value indicates success with warning. Apart from SQLCODE, DB2 also returns SQLSTATE, which is also an error code. SQLCODE is specific to a DB2 product, whereas SQLSTATE is common across the DB2 products family. We can use both SQLCODE and SQLSTATE values for identifying the errors. The entire exception handling process revolves around SQLCODE and SQLSTATE values. We can define exception handlers for known or expected errors identified by SQLSTATE values.

Designing external stored procedures

The stored procedures can be defined either in SQL or in a high-level programming language. If their definition is written in high-level language, then they are known as **external procedures**. Their definition is very similar to a normal program written in a language. There could be various reasons to prefer external procedures. For instance, if we want to perform actions external to the database, then external procedures can be very useful. It could be very useful in encapsulating complex business logic in an external procedure, where we can exploit all the features of a high-level programming language.

DB2 supports the following languages for external stored procedures:

* C/C++
* Java
* .NET common language runtime languages
* OLE
* Cobol

Getting ready

We need the following privileges to create a stored procedure:

* CREATIN or IMPLICIT schema privilege, whichever is applicable
* Individual privileges needed to execute all SQL statements used in the procedure

How to do it...

In this recipe, we will see how we can implement external stored procedures. As an example, we will create a stored procedure where its definitions will be written in Java. The procedure will accept an input parameter and return the count of employees and a result set with all employee details. The definition of the procedure will be a method in a class. While registering the procedure, we need to specify the class name and the method name.

1. Code the procedure definition: A method definition is just like a regular method in Java where we have a method defined in a class. We need to define one parameter for each `IN`, `OUT`, and `INOUT` parameter of the procedure. If we are returning a result set from the procedure, then we also need to define a parameter to the method as a result set object.

```
Import required packages
import java.sql.*;

Define the class as public
public class spdef
{

Define the method (or main function) as public.
  public static void SPExtern(String inDept, ResultSet[] outRes)
// CHAR(8)
  throws SQLException
  {
    try
    {

Get the caller's connection to the database.
Connection con = DriverManager.getConnection("jdbc:default:connect
ion");

Procedure functionality can be coded in this section. In our
example, we will prepare a statement and get the results from
database.
    // set the SQL statement that will return the desired result
set
    String sql = "SELECT EMPNO, FIRSTNME, LASTNAME, SALARY FROM
EMPLOYEE WHERE WORKDEPT = ?";

    // prepare the SQL statement
    PreparedStatement stmt = con.prepareStatement(sql);

    // set the value of the parameter marker (?)
    stmt.setString(1, inDept);
```

```
       // get the result set that will be returned to the client
       outRes[0] = stmt.executeQuery();
       stmt.close();
       con.close();
    }
    catch (SQLException sqle)
    {
       System.out.print(sqle.getErrorCode());
    }
  }

}
```

2. Compile the code: Once we have the procedure definition ready, we can compile it just like a regular Java class (or something similar, if any other language is chosen):

   ```
   javac spdef.java
   ```

3. Copy the object file: After compilation, we get the class file. This class should be copied to the `SQLLIB/FUNCTIONS` directory. This is the default location where DB2 expects the routine definition.

4. Register the procedure: Once we have the compiled code ready, we need to register the procedure. For an external procedure, certain clauses are mandatory. They are as follows:

   - `LANGUAGE` clause: Language in which the procedure is defined, such as Java, .NET, and so on.

   - `PARAMETER STYLE` clause: Parameter convention is followed in the procedure definition.

   - `EXTERNAL` clause: This indicates where the object file is located. We need to specify the class name and the method name that has the procedure definition.

   ```
   CREATE PROCEDURE SPExtern (IN inDept VARCHAR(20))
   DYNAMIC RESULT SETS 1
   DETERMINISTIC
   LANGUAGE JAVA
   PARAMETER STYLE JAVA
   NO DBINFO
   FENCED
   THREADSAFE
   READS SQL DATA
   PROGRAM TYPE SUB
   EXTERNAL NAME 'spdef.SPExtern'@
   ```

5. Call the procedure: We can invoke the external stored procedures as a regular procedure by using a CALL statement.

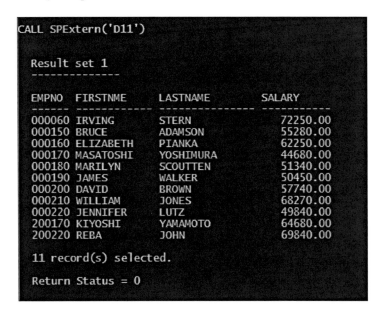

```
CALL SPExtern('D11')

Result set 1
--------------

EMPNO  FIRSTNME     LASTNAME          SALARY
------ ------------ ----------------- -----------
000060 IRVING       STERN             72250.00
000150 BRUCE        ADAMSON           55280.00
000160 ELIZABETH    PIANKA            62250.00
000170 MASATOSHI    YOSHIMURA         44680.00
000180 MARILYN      SCOUTTEN          51340.00
000190 JAMES        WALKER            50450.00
000200 DAVID        BROWN             57740.00
000210 WILLIAM      JONES             68270.00
000220 JENNIFER     LUTZ              49840.00
200170 KIYOSHI      YAMAMOTO          64680.00
200220 REBA         JOHN              69840.00

11 record(s) selected.

Return Status = 0
```

How it works...

When an external stored procedure is invoked, DB2 executes the compiled code as a procedure. While creating the procedure, we may have specified NO SQL, CONTAINS SQL or MODIFIES SQL. Since DB2 cannot know the procedure behavior while compiling the code, it does that while executing. If any violation is found, it gives an error (SQLCODE -579, SQLSTATE 38004). Parameters passed to an external procedure definition method cannot be used as host variables. If this is needed, then the method should declare its own variables and copy the parameter values to the host variables.

There's more...

A routine cannot establish any connection of its own; rather it uses the connection of the calling application. Also, we cannot terminate any connection in a procedure. The COMMIT and ROLLBACK statements can only be executed by procedures, which are defined with the MODIFIES SQL DATA clause.

Parameter styles in external stored procedures

An external procedure can be written in any programming language. While defining the procedure, we can choose between different ways to handle parameters. DB2 provides the following parameter styles:

- SQL: Apart from the procedure input and output parameters, the following parameters are also passed between DB2 and the external method:
    - Null indicator: This is used to indicate whether the input or output parameter is null.
    - An SQLSTATE which is returned to DB2: This can be used to raise an error with custom messages as well.
    - Qualified name of the procedure.
    - Specific name of the procedure.
    - SQL-diagnostic string which is returned to DB2.
    - DBINFO structure that contains database information.

    If this parameter style is used for external functions, then it can also include the following parameters in addition to the preceding ones:
    - Buffer for the scratchpad
    - Call type for the function

- DB2SQL: This is very similar to SQL style, but this can only be used for stored procedures.

- JAVA: This style uses the Java convention. All OUT and INOUT parameters are defined as single entry array variables. We also need to define the ResultSet objects, if we want to return any result set from the procedure (one for each result set).

- DB2GENERAL: This style accepts parameters, such as a JAVA parameter style. In addition, it has DBINFO as well.

- GENERAL: It receives parameters from the CALL statement. Depending on the DBINFO clause of the CREATE statement, it also passes DBINFO to the procedure.

- GENERAL WITH NULLS: This is similar to the GENERAL parameter style. In addition, it also includes a vector containing a null indicator for each parameter.

Using PL/SQL exception handling in a procedure

In object-oriented languages, we have the concept of exception blocks and catch blocks. The code in the exception block can raise an exception and the catch block handles this exception. We can implement a similar logic in DB2 by using exception blocks.

As part of PL/SQL support, DB2 9.7 extends the support for exception handling by providing the concept of exception blocks. We can define a set of possible exceptions and their respective handlers for a given set of SQL statements. In this recipe, we will discuss how we can design and implement exception handling by using PL/SQL exception blocks.

How to do it...

To implement PL/SQL exception handling, we need to declare all exceptions that we anticipate and want to handle. Then we need to provide the handlers for each type of exception. This complete task follows the following syntax:

```
DECLARE declarations
  BEGIN SQL statements
  EXCEPTION HANDLERS
  END
```

Let's discuss how to implement these sections:

- ► Declare exceptions: All exceptions that we want to handle are declared in this section. We can identify an exception in two ways: One by using system-defined exception names and the other by using specific error codes. DB2 provides some system-defined exception names, such as NO_DATA_FOUND, DUP_VAL_ON_INDEX, and so on that can be used directly to refer to a kind of exception.

  We don't need to declare any exception for system-defined exceptions. If we want to handle any other exception, then we must declare it. Once an exception is declared, it can be referred to by its name. We cannot handle any exception without an exception name. All exceptions are based on error codes. DB2's extended support for PL/SQL allows us to declare Oracle exceptions as well. If it's an Oracle error code, then we need to use the PRAGMA EXCEPTION_INIT() function. For DB2 error codes, we need to use the PRAGMA DB2_EXCEPTION_INIT() function.

```
DECLARE
    exception1 EXCEPTION;
    exception2 EXCEPTION;
    PRAGMA EXCEPTION_INIT(exception1,-942);
    PRAGMA DB2_EXCEPTION_INIT(exception2,'42884');
```

 DB2 only accepts a limited number of Oracle SQL code as arguments to the EXCEPTION_INIT() function.

▶ Statements section: This section has all the SQL statements that we want to execute.

```
BEGIN

  CALL SUM(ARRAY[1,2,3,4], ?);
```

▶ Exception handlers: In this section, we can provide handlers for all the exceptions declared along with some generic exceptions. For each exception, we can have corresponding handlers.

```
EXCEPTION

  WHEN exception1 THEN

      DBMS_OUTPUT.PUT_LINE('Exception 1 Error message');

  WHEN exception2 THEN

      DBMS_OUTPUT.PUT_LINE('Exception 2 Error message');
```

How it works...

If there is no error in SQL statements, then the control passes to the END after executing all SQL statements. If any error is encountered, then the control passes to the exception handler section. The WHEN clause in each handler is searched to find a match with the occurred error. If a match is found, then its corresponding handler statements are executed and then the control is passed to END. If a match is not found, then the procedure stops abruptly.

There's more...

Whenever any exception is caught, the value returned by SQLCODE is always a DB2 SQLCODE and not the Oracle SQLCODE, even if the exception is defined on Oracle SQLCODE. DB2 can only handle a set of Oracle SQLCODE and not all. If any exception is defined on Oracle code not supported by DB2, then the compilation fails.

Explicitly raising an exception

If DB2 encounters any error while executing any SQL statement, then it raises an exception which is then handled by our catch block. If we explicitly want to raise an exception, then we can use the RAISE statement or the RAISE_APPLICATION_ERROR procedure to raise an exception explicitly. With the RAISE statement, we can only raise a previously defined exception, while by using RAISE_APPLICATION_ERROR, we can raise an exception based on any user-provided error code and error message.

For example, if we want to raise an exception for the salary less than zero condition, we can use RAISE_APPLICATION_ERROR as follows:

```
IF v_sal < 0 THEN

    RAISE_APPLICATION_ERROR(-20140, 'Invalid Salary');

END IF;
```

The following table lists all system-defined exceptions available in DB2:

Exception	Description
CASE_NOT_FOUND	Nothing matched in the CASE statement
CURSOR_ALREADY_OPEN	Occurs when an opened cursor is attempted to open again
DUP_VAL_ON_INDEX	Duplicate values found for index
INVALID_CURSOR	Invalid use of cursor
INVALID_NUMBER	Invalid number
LOGIN_DENIED	Invalid username or password
NO_DATA_FOUND	No rows returned
NOT_LOGGED_ON	Data connection does not exist
OTHERS	This can be used to catch everything else which is not explicitly mentioned
SUBSCRIPT_BEYOND_COUNT	Array index out of range
SUBSCRIPT_OUTSIDE_LIMIT	Value cannot be assigned to an array because of data type limits
TOO_MANY_ROWS	More than one row returned when only one is expected
VALUE_ERROR	Invalid value
ZERO_DIVIDE	Division by zero was attempted

Working with the message buffer in stored procedures

DB2 9.7 introduced the module DBMS_OUTPUT, which provides a set of procedures that can be used to interact with the message buffer. There are many situations when we want to print something on screen from the procedure. This is very common when we are debugging a procedure. In this recipe, we will discuss different procedures available in the DBMS_OUTPUT module.

Getting ready

We need the EXECUTE privilege on the DBMS_OUTPUT module.

How to do it...

The `DBMS_OUTPUT` module provides a set of procedures that can be used as appropriate. All these procedures allow us to use the message buffer.

1. Before we can use any of the available procedures, we need to decide the way in which we want to handle the message buffer. The most common use would be to display the contents on the standard output. We can use the following commands to redirect the message buffer to the standard output:

   ```
   SET SERVEROUTPUT ON;
   SET SERVEROUTPUT OFF;
   ```

   When set to `ON`, the message buffer will be redirected to the standard output. Once done, all messages written to the message buffer will appear on screen. We can turn it off by using the `OFF` option. When set to `OFF`, the content of the buffer is erased and the buffer is released.

2. When the preceding command is run, it calls the `DBMS_OUTPUT.ENABLE` procedure, which created the message buffer with a default size of 20,000 bytes. If we want a bigger message buffer, we can explicitly call the `DBMS_OUT.ENABLE` procedure with the required buffer size.

   ```
   CALL DBMS_OUTPUT.ENABLE( 30000 );
   ```

   To disable the buffer, we can either use the `SET SERVEROUTPUT` command or we can call the `DBMS_OUTPUT.DISABLE` stored procedure.

3. The `PUT` procedure: This procedure adds a string to the message buffer.

   ```
   CALL DBMS_OUTPUT.PUT( 'HELLO' );
   CALL DBMS_OUTPUT.PUT( 'WORLD' );
   ```

   Now the message buffer should have `HELLOWORLD` in it. Note that this procedure does not add any new line character at the end.

4. The `PUT_LINE` procedure: This procedure adds a string to the message buffer followed by a new line character.

   ```
   CALL DBMS_OUTPUT.PUT_LINE( 'HELLO' );
   CALL DBMS_OUTPUT.PUT_LINE( 'WORLD' );
   ```

   Now the message buffer should have the following data:

   ```
   HELLO
   WORLD
   ```

5. The `NEW_LINE` procedure: This procedure adds a new line character at the end of character sequence in the message buffer.

```
CALL DBMS_OUTPUT.PUT( 'HELLO' );

CALL DBMS_OUTPUT.NEW_LINE;

CALL DBMS_OUTPUT.PUT( 'WORLD' );
```

With the preceding calls, the message buffer should look similar to the following:

```
HELLO
WORLD
```

6. The `GET_LINE` procedure: This procedure can be used to read a line from the message buffer. The line must have a new line character at the end.

```
CALL DBMS_OUTPUT.GET_LINE( v_text, v_status );
```

The line is stored in the `v_text` variable. The second parameter is the status parameter which is `0` if the line was returned and `1` when no line was returned. Once a line is retrieved from the message buffer, it is also removed from the buffer.

7. The `GET_LINES` procedure: This procedure can be used to get multiple lines from the message buffer. The number of lines to be retrieved is specified as a parameter to the procedure. The output lines can be retrieved in a collection object of type `DBMS_OUTPUT.CHARARR`. The `DBMS_OUTPUT.CHARARR` type is internally defined as `VARCHAR(32672)ARRAY[2147483647]`.

```
DECLARE v_line_array DBMS_OUTPUT.CHARARR;

CALL DBMS_OUTPUT.GET_LINES( v_line_array, num_lines );
```

How it works...

All procedures defined in `DBMS_OUTPUT` are intended to print useful text from within a procedure. These procedures interact with the message buffer. The `DBMS_OUTPUT` module provides routines to add text and retrieve text from the message buffer. When the output is redirected to the standard output device, we can see the text present in the message buffer. That makes this module very useful for debugging purpose and passing messages to the user. Consider the following example where it shows the sample output for the `DBMS_OUTPUT` module routines:

```
DROP PROCEDURE TEST()@

CREATE PROCEDURE TEST()

LANGUAGE SQL

BEGIN

  CALL DBMS_OUTPUT.ENABLE( 30000 );

  CALL DBMS_OUTPUT.PUT( '1. HELLO' );
```

```
    CALL DBMS_OUTPUT.PUT ( ' WORLD' );

    CALL DBMS_OUTPUT.NEW_LINE;

    CALL DBMS_OUTPUT.PUT_LINE ( '2. HELLO' );

    CALL DBMS_OUTPUT.PUT_LINE ( '3. WORLD' );

    CALL DBMS_OUTPUT.NEW_LINE;

END @

SET SERVEROUTPUT ON@

CALL TEST()@
```

```
db2 => SET SERVEROUTPUT ON@
DB20000I   The SET SERVEROUTPUT command completed successfully.
db2 => CALL TEST()@

  Return Status = 0

1. HELLO WORLD`
2. HELLO
3. WORLD

db2 =>
```

Planning and designing triggers

A trigger is a database object that can be used to perform some action in response to the INSERT, UPDATE, or DELETE operations. Triggers are very useful to enforce business rules. For example, if our business policy doesn't allow any employee's salary to be higher than his manager, then we can check the salaries before we actually make the change in the table and accept or reject the update. This also eases the application development, as we don't have to implement business policies in all applications and we can have them centralized in the database.

Multiple triggers can be specified for a combination of table, event (INSERT, UPDATE, or DELETE), or activation time (BEFORE, AFTER, or INSTEAD OF). When more than one trigger exists for a particular table, event, and activation time, the order in which the triggers are activated is the same as the order in which they were created. Thus, the most recently created trigger is the last trigger to be activated.

DB2 provides the following types of triggers:

- **BEFORE triggers**: These triggers run before the event (INSERT, UPDATE). We can check and modify the values before they are applied to the database. Data cleansing and transformation can be done before triggers.

- **BEFORE DELETE triggers**: These triggers run before the DELETE commands. This can be used to raise error conditions or alerts.

▶ **AFTER triggers**: These triggers run after the event (INSERT, UPDATE, or DELETE). This can be used to validate the data and raise alerts. The AFTER triggers can also be used to maintain audit data.

▶ **INSTEAD OF triggers**: These triggers are used to define how INSERT, UPDATE, and DELETE operations should be performed on a view. If we have a complex view and we want to use this view for INSERT, UPDATE, and DELETE operations, then we can define an INSTEAD OF trigger. The INSTEAD OF triggers usually have the inverse logic of a view definition. If the INSTEAD OF triggers are defined for a view, then modify operations on this view are replaced with the trigger definition. We can only have one INSTEAD OF trigger for one event.

Getting ready

We need one of the following privileges to create a trigger:

▶ The ALTER privilege on the base table

▶ The CONTROL privilege on view (for the INSTEAD OF trigger)

▶ The SYSADM or DBADM authority

▶ The CREATIN or IMPLICIT schema privilege

How to do it...

In this recipe, we will see how to design triggers and how to use different options to control their behavior.

The following is the syntax:

```
CREATE (OR REPLACE) TRIGGER <trigger name>
    <trigger event>
ON <table/view name>
    <optional clauses>
    <granularity>
    <action>
```

Basic trigger structure: The main attributes of a trigger are trigger name, triggering event, trigger action, and its granularity.

▶ Triggering event specifies when the trigger should be activated. It can either be INSERT, UPDATE, or DELETE

▶ Trigger granularity specifies whether the trigger will execute once per statement or once per row

▶ Trigger action specifies the action (trigger definition) that should be executed

The following trigger is an `INSERT` trigger that increments the total number of employees in the `HEADCOUNTS` table by one whenever a new employee is added to the `EMPLOYEE` table:

```
CREATE TRIGGER new_employee
  AFTER INSERT ON EMPLOYEE
  FOR EACH ROW
  UPDATE HEADCOUNTS SET NUMEMP = NUMEMP + 1
```

Conditional triggers: There could be cases when all the statements are not meaningful to a trigger. In such cases, we can use conditions in a trigger that can control the trigger execution. This condition is an optional clause in the trigger definition. If the condition is `true`, then the trigger executes; otherwise, it doesn't. If it's a statement trigger, then the condition is checked once, and if it's a row trigger, the condition is checked for each row. This becomes very useful when we want to enforce any data-dependent rule.

For example, the following trigger definition specifies that the trigger should only be activated for rows where the salary of the employee is higher than 1,000,000:

```
CREATE TRIGGER update_sal
  AFTER UPDATE OF salary ON EMPLOYEE
  REFERENCING NEW AS N_ROW
  FOR EACH ROW


  WHEN (N_ROW.salary > 1000000)
  BEGIN ATOMIC
      INSERT INTO SALARY_AUDIT (EMPNO, SALARY) VALUES (N_ROW.EMPNO, N_
ROW.SALARY);
  END
```

Referencing OLD and NEW values in a trigger: Consider an `UPDATE` trigger where we want to enforce a business rule and we want to do some checks before the change is actually made. In such cases, we can check the old and new values upfront. This option is applicable only for row triggers. We can use the `REFERENCING` clause in the trigger definition to refer to `OLD` and `NEW` rows.

Consider the following example:

```
CREATE TRIGGER update_salary
  AFTER UPDATE OF salary ON EMPLOYEE
  REFERENCING NEW AS N_ROW
  REFERENCING OLD as O_ROW
  FOR EACH ROW
  WHEN (N_ROW.SALARY > O_ROW.SALARY * 130)
```

```
    BEGIN ATOMIC

        INSERT INTO SALARY_AUDIT (EMPNO, OLD_SALARY, NEW_SALARY) VALUES
(N_ROW.EMPNO, O_ROW.SALARY, N_ROW.SALARY);

    END
```

Referencing OLD and NEW table result sets: If we want an original and modified result set in a trigger, we can use the REFERENCING clause to refer to them. These result sets can be referred to as OLD_TABLE and NEW_TABLE respectively. This is useful when we have to perform some result-set-level operations, such as doing some aggregation or getting MAX and MIN from it.

Consider the following example:

```
    CREATE TRIGGER update_inventory

        AFTER UPDATE OF quantity ON INVENTORY

        REFERENCING NEW_TABLE AS N_TABLE

        REFERENCING OLD_TABLE as O_TABLE

        FOR EACH ROW

        WHEN (SUM(NEW_TABLE.quantity) > SUM(OLD_TABLE.quantity) * 10)

        BEGIN ATOMIC

          INSERT INTO MSG_QUEUE (DATE, MESSAGE)

            VALUES (CURRENT DATE, 'Inventory limit exceeded');

        END
```

Note that NEW_TABLE always has the full set of updated rows, even on a FOR EACH ROW trigger. When a trigger acts on the table on which the trigger is defined, NEW_TABLE contains the changed rows from the statement that activated the trigger. However, NEW_TABLE does not contain the changed rows that were caused by statements within the trigger, as that would cause a separate activation of the trigger.

How it works...

We can create multiple triggers for a table for a given event. We can have a set of BEFORE and AFTER triggers for event on a table. In such cases, the BEFORE triggers are activated first, then the SQL (SQL that activated the trigger) is executed, then the constraints (if any) are checked, and finally, all the AFTER triggers are executed.

Apart from INSERT, UPDATE, and DELETE SQL statements, the MERGE statement can also activate a trigger. A MERGE statement eventually uses INSERT, UPDATE, and DELETE statements that cause triggers to activate. Triggers are not executed when the data is loaded by utilities such as LOAD.

There's more...

Triggers are very effective in enforcing business policies. Since the trigger is stored in the database, we don't need to code the business rules defined in the application. This gives another advantage of centralized business rules, where changing any policy at one place makes it effective for all applications. Triggers are automatically activated by DB2, which makes the maintenance simple.

Modifying and dropping triggers

A trigger definition cannot be modified. If we need to change the definition, then the only option is to drop and recreate it with a new definition. We can use the DROP statement to drop a trigger.

```
DROP TRIGGER update_inventory
```

A trigger can have dependency on many database objects. For example, if any table is referenced in a trigger, then this is a dependency. If any trigger dependency is dropped, the trigger becomes invalid. To revalidate the trigger, we must recreate it. With the DB2 9.7 autorevalidation feature, this is taken care of by DB2 automatically. DB2 uses the same definition stored in the system catalogs to recreate it at its first reference.

Similarly, when a trigger is dropped, it can cause its dependant packages to become invalid. Once a package is invalidated, it must be built again by binding the application or rebinding the package. A package can never reference a trigger, but in certain cases it can become invalid. They are explained as follows:

- If an UPDATE trigger that does not refer to any column explicitly is dropped, then the package that updates the target table is invalidated. If the trigger refers to any column explicitly and if the package also refers to the same column, then it will become invalid if the trigger is dropped.

- If an INSERT trigger is dropped, then the packages using INSERT on the target table become invalid.

- If a DELETE trigger is dropped, then the packages doing DELETE on the target table become invalid.

Using scalar user-defined functions

User-defined functions provide us with the ability to group a set of statements or instructions which can perform a task. A simple example would be a function that returns the sum of values. Functions can be designed to return a scalar value, a row, or a table. Similar to the stored procedures, user-defined functions can also be designed in SQL or any high-level programming language and they also accept input parameters and return the result. In this recipe, we will focus on the simplest form of functions, which is a scalar function. As the name suggests, a **scalar function** returns a scalar value. DB2 provides many scalar in-built functions like SUM(), AVG(), MAX(), MIN(), and so on. Scalar functions are commonly used for string manipulation, mathematical operations, and so on.

Getting ready

We need the following privileges to create a stored procedure:

▸ The CREATIN or IMPLICIT schema privilege, whichever is applicable

▸ The SELECT privileges on each table, view, or nickname referenced in the function

How to do it...

Let's write a simple function that accepts a date value and returns its integer form.

1. Define the function with a name and input parameters. In our example, we will accept a date as the input parameter.

   CREATE FUNCTION DATE_INT (inDate DATE)

2. Choose optional clauses: For a simple function, we must supply language at the minimum. In our example, since we will define the function in SQL, we can specify the LANGUAGE as SQL.

   LANGUAGE SQL

3. Return type: This is the type that we want to return from the function. In our example, this will be INTEGER.

   RETURN INTEGER

   ;

4. Definition: Now we have everything we need for a function, we need to provide its definition. The definition can be any SQL statement or a compound statement. The only additional attribute is the RETURN clause in the SQL statement. This clause is used to return values from the function. In our example, we will return the integer form of a given date. This can be defined as follows:

```
RETURN INT(inDate);
```

5. Since we are returning a scalar value, this function can only be used in the context of a scalar. For example:

```
SELECT CURRENT DATE, DATE_INT(CURRENT DATE) FROM SYSIBM.SYSDUMMY1;
```

How it works...

A user-defined function has the following components:

▸ Function name: This is the name of the function. Similar to stored procedures, we can create multiple functions with the same name, provided they have different signatures. In such cases, we can use SPECIFIC NAME to alter or drop the procedure.

▸ Input parameters: We can only have input parameters in user-defined functions. The results are received by the RETURN clause.

▸ Return type: This specifies the return options for the function. If it's a scalar function, then the corresponding data type and length needs to be mentioned against this clause. In the case of a table function, we need to provide the details of all the columns in the result set and their respective lengths.

▸ Optional clauses: Similar to stored procedures, we can have optional clauses for functions as well. They are as follows:

  ❑ SPECIFIC NAME: This is a unique name for the stored procedure which can be used to alter or drop a procedure. We can create multiple stored procedures with the same procedure name but with different signatures. In such cases, we need to provide a different SPECIFIC name. DB2 generates a name of its own, if this is not specified explicitly. However, we cannot use this name to invoke a procedure.

  ❑ CONTAINS SQL, READS SQL DATA, and MODIFIES SQL DATA: This can be used to specify the behavior of the procedure.

  ❑ DETERMINISTIC or NON DETERMINISTIC: This indicates whether the procedure produces same results for the given input values every time.

  ❑ INHERIT SPECIAL REGISTERS: If this clause is specified, then the procedure inherits the updatable special registers from the client environment from where the procedure is invoked.

  ❑ LANGUAGE SQL: This indicates that the procedure is defined in SQL.

❑ EXTERNAL ACTION or NO EXTERNAL ACTION: This indicates whether the procedure changes anything that is not managed by DB2.

❑ PARAMETER CCSID: This indicates the encoding of string data passed in and out of the procedure.

❑ CALLED ON NULL INPUT (or NULL CALL): This indicates whether the function can be called if any of the arguments is NULL.

▸ Function definition: A function definition can be a single statement or it could be a compound statement.

User-defined functions can be referenced in SQL statements. Their logic is executed on the server as part of the SQL statement. When functions are used in query predicates, it can filter the result set directly on the server, limiting the total number of rows, resulting in better performance. Scalar functions can return only a single value (which can't be a result set).

There's more...

Scalar functions can be applied anywhere in the SQL statement where a scalar value can be used. For example, we can use it while comparing some values:

```
SELECT * FROM EMPLOYEE WHERE EMPNO = MAX_EMPNO();
```

Using table functions: A **table function** can be referenced in the FROM clause, similar to a table.

```
SELECT * FROM TABLE(tableUDF('D11')) as T
```

Restrictions on user-defined functions

The following are the restrictions on user-defined functions:

▸ COMMIT and ROLLBACK statements cannot be included in UDFs

▸ In a DPF environment, UDFs cannot contain any SQL statements

▸ In a non-DPF environment, UDFs can contain SQL statements, but they cannot modify any tables in the database

Writing external user-defined functions

Just as with stored procedures, we can also define user-defined functions written in high-level programming languages. These are known as external UDFs. They can also be used in the same way as SQL functions. Complex business logic can be better implemented in high-level programming languages, hence giving better flexibility. By using external functions, we can maintain state between iterative invocations of the function. External functions can access external objects as well, such as a server filesystem, system calls, and so on. One limitation for external functions is that we cannot return result sets. In this recipe, we will see how we can design external user-defined functions.

External functions are supported in the following languages:

- C/C++
- Java
- OLE
- .NET common language runtime languages

How to do it...

Just like stored procedures, we need to define the function body in a programming language and register the function in DB2. We will use Java as an example in this recipe.

Define the function in the programming language:

1. Choose the parameter style: In the stored procedures section, we saw different parameter styles available in DB2. We can only choose any one of the following parameter styles for external functions:

   - SQL
   - JAVA
   - DB2GENERAL

   Based on these parameter styles, we need to define the arguments in the method definition.

2. Define the function: The function definition can be just like a regular Java method that accepts input parameters and returns the result. We cannot return the results directly. We need to define arguments for the method. The values can be returned by setting values for these arguments.

   Define the class and method as `public`. We need to specify one parameter for each input and return values. In our example, we will accept a parameter and return its square value. So we need to define two arguments in the method. To return any value, use the `set ()` method to set the values.

```
public class extfunc extends UDF
{
  public void sqval(int inval, int outval)
  throws Exception
  {
    // Use set() method to set the return values.
    set(2, inval * inval);
  }
}
```

3. Compile the code: Once we have the function definition ready, we can compile it, just like a regular Java class (or another similar language, if any other language is chosen).

    javac extfunc.java

4. Copy the object file: After compilation, we get the class file. This class should be copied to the SQLLIB/FUNCTIONS directory. This is the default location where DB2 expects the routine definition to be.

5. Register the function: Once we have the compiled code ready, we are ready to register the function.

    CREATE FUNCTION sqval(INTEGER)

    RETURNS INTEGER

    EXTERNAL NAME 'extfunc!sqval'

    DETERMINISTIC

    NO EXTERNAL ACTION

    FENCED

    NOT NULL CALL

    LANGUAGE JAVA

    PARAMETER STYLE DB2GENERAL

    NO SQL

    SCRATCHPAD 10

    FINAL CALL

    DISALLOW PARALLEL

    NO DBINFO@

6. Invoking the function: A function can be embedded in any SQL statement, as appropriate. Our example created a function that returns the square of input, so we can use it in the scalar context.

    VALUEs sqval(3);

How it works...

DB2 internally uses different call types to invoke an external function. For scalar functions, we can have the following call types:

 ▸ FIRST CALL: This is the first call which can be used to do initial processing. Arguments are accepted in this call and it can return as well.

 ▸ NORMAL CALL: This is where we can have our normal processing. This type of call is made for each invocation of the function until the last call is made. For example, if we have a scalar function that is applied to a column in a table, and if the result set is having 10 rows, then FIRST CALL will be made once and NORMAL CALL will be made nine times.

 ▸ FINAL CALL: This is the last call made after all the processing is done. We usually perform a resource clean up in this call type. Nothing is returned in this call.

We don't make any call explicitly; this is taken care of by DB2.

There's more...

Microsoft OLE DB is an OLE interface that provides uniform access to different data sources. DB2 allows us to create user-defined functions based on OLE data sources. OLE data sources are identified by an OLE DB provider connection string, which can be used in the EXTERNAL clause of the CREATE FUNCTION statement. Once a user-defined function is created on an OLE data source, it can then be used seamlessly with other data in DB2.

For example, if we want to create a user-defined function to get the data from the ref_data table from the Microsoft Access database, then we can define it as follows:

```
CREATE FUNCTION ref_geo_data ()
  RETURNS TABLE (geo_id INTEGER, geo_addr VARCHAR(100))
  LANGUAGE OLEDB
  EXTERNAL NAME '!orders!Provider=Microsoft.Jet.OLEDB.3.51;Data
Source=c:\testData.mdb';
  SELECT geo_id, geo_addr FROM TABLE(ref_geo_data()) AS t;
```

Now this function can be used as a regular table function in DB2.

Using scratchpad in external functions

An external function can use scratchpad to maintain the state between invocations.
Scratchpad is a memory area which is allocated for an external function. The scratchpad
applies only to the individual reference of the function. If there are multiple references of a
function in a statement, then each reference will have its own scratchpad area. We can use
this memory to store values that can be used between different invocations of the function.

The following is a simple Java function that gives a sequence number for every row fetched.
We will use the scratchpad area to preserve previous values for the next invocation.

1. Set up the scratchpad area:

   ```
   byte[] scratchpad = getScratchpad();
   ```

2. Set up the input stream to read data from the scratchpad:

   ```
   ByteArrayInputStream byteArrayIn = new ByteArrayInputStream(sc
   ratchpad);
   DataInputStream dataIn = new DataInputStream(byteArrayIn);
   ```

3. Set up the output stream to write in the scratchpad area:

   ```
   ByteArrayOutputStream byteArrayOut = new
   ByteArrayOutputStream(1000);
   DataOutputStream dataOut = new DataOutputStream(byteArrayOut);
   ```

4. Handle different `callTypes` in the `switch`/`case` statements:

   ```
   switch(getCallType())
   {
     case SQLUDF_FIRST_CALL:
     // initialize the result
   result = 1;

     // save data in back scratchpad area
       dataOut.writeInt(result);
       byteArrayCounter = byteArrayOut.toByteArray();
       for(i = 0; i < byteArrayCounter.length; i++)
       {
         scratchpad[i] = byteArrayCounter[i];
       }
       setScratchpad(scratchpad);
   break;

       case SQLUDF_NORMAL_CALL:
       // Read the last value from scratchpad and increment it by
         one to get the next value.
         result = dataIn.readInt();
   ```

```
        result = result + 1;
// save data back into scratchpad area
        dataOut.writeInt(result);
        byteArrayCounter = byteArrayOut.toByteArray();
        for(i = 0; i < byteArrayCounter.length; i++)
        {
           scratchpad[i] = byteArrayCounter[i];
        }
        setScratchpad(scratchpad);
    break;

    }
// Set the results
        set(1, result);
    }
```

Designing external table functions

Just like external scalar functions, we can also have external table functions. The external table functions return a table and can only be used in the FROM clause of a query. Even though it returns a result set, the association between DB2 and the function is at a row level. In other words, instead of returning all of the rows at a time, a function returns one row at a time. In this recipe, we will see how we can implement external table functions where they are defined in high-level languages.

How to do it...

When an external table function is invoked, it can internally make five types of calls to it. To define an external table function, we can get the entire result in the first call and return one row at each fetch call. Let's see how we can implement this.

As an example, we will create a table function that returns the names and salaries of employees filtered by their work department, which will be passed as an input to the function. We will define the example table function in Java for this recipe.

1. Define the structure of the returned table as arguments to the method. In our example, our table has two columns, namely, EmployeeName and Salary. We also have an input parameter, which is the work department for employees. We need to define all three parameters.

    ```
    public void tableUDF(String inDept,
                         String outempno,
                         double outNewSalary)
    ```

2. Create the scratchpad area, which we will use for maintaining the current row index.

```
byte[] scratchpad = getScratchpad();
```

3. Set up the input streams to read from the scratchpad area.

```
ByteArrayInputStream
byteArrayIn = new ByteArrayInputStream(scratchpad);
DataInputStream
dataIn = new DataInputStream(byteArrayIn);
```

4. Set up output streams to write into the scratchpad area.

```
ByteArrayOutputStream
byteArrayOut = new ByteArrayOutputStream(10);
DataOutputStream
dataOut = new DataOutputStream(byteArrayOut);
```

5. By now, we have done the ground work that we will use to build the table function. Now we need to handle different call types. We will use the `switch`/`case` statements to handle these calls. The call type can be identified by the `getCallType()` method, which is provided by the Java class, `COM.IBM.db2.app.UDF`.

```
switch (getCallType())
{
case SQLUDF_TF_FIRST:
  break;

case SQLUDF_TF_OPEN:
  break;

  case SQLUDF_TF_FETCH:
  break;

  case SQLUDF_TF_CLOSE:
  break;

  case SQLUDF_TF_FINAL:
  break;
}
```

`SQLUDF_TF_FIRST`: We can do any type of initialization in this call type.

`SQLUDF_TF_OPEN`: We will get the complete result set to be returned in this call type. Since we will return row by row on subsequent calls, we need a placeholder to store the results temporarily. We will use array objects to store these values. These array objects should be declared in the main class.

```
String[] empNameList;
double[] salList;
```

6. Before we can use these arrays, we need to instantiate them with the required size. To get the size required, we can get the number of rows to be returned. In our example, we are filtering the results based on the WORKDEPT value, passed in as input parameter to the function.

```
Connection con = DriverManager.getConnection("jdbc:default:connect
ion");
 String query = "SELECT count(*) FROM EMPLOYEE WHERE WORKDEPT =
?";
 PreparedStatement stmt = con.prepareStatement(query);
 stmt.setString(1, inDept);
 ResultSet rs = stmt.executeQuery();
 rs.next();
numRows = rs.getInt(1);
```

7. Now that we have the number of rows to be returned, we can initialize our array objects.

```
empNameList = new String[numRows];
salList = new double[numRows];
```

8. Now we can fetch the complete result set and store it in these array objects.

```
String query1 = "SELECT CONCAT(FIRSTNME, CONCAT(' ', LASTNAME)),
DOUBLE(SALARY) FROM EMPLOYEE WHERE WORKDEPT = ?";
PreparedStatement    stmt1 = con.prepareStatement(query1);
stmt1.setString(1, inDept);
rs = stmt1.executeQuery();
int counter = 0;
while(rs.next())
{
    empNameList[counter] = rs.getString(1);
    salList[counter] = rs.getDouble(2);
    counter ++;
 }
```

9. Now we have the complete result set in our temporary array objects. We can use them in subsequent calls. Before we can close this call type, we need to preserve the row number of the result set. This can be saved in the scratchpad area.

```
dataOut.writeInt(intRow);
byteArrayRow = byteArrayOut.toByteArray();
for(i = 0; i < byteArrayRow.length; i++)
{
   scratchpad[i] = byteArrayRow[i];
}
setScratchpad(scratchpad);
break;
```

SQLUDF_TF_FETCH: This call type is the actual fetch where we start sending the rows to the client. At every call, we will fetch the corresponding row from our array objects and send it to the client. To do that, we need to find the current row number.

```
intRow = dataIn.readInt();
if(intRow > numRows) {
   setSQLstate ("02000");
} else {
// Set the current output row and increment the row number
   set(2, empNameList[intRow - 1]);
   set(3, salList[intRow - 1]);
   intRow++;
 }
```

10. Now we can save the new row number in the scratchpad area for further use.

```
dataOut.writeInt(intRow);
byteArrayRow = byteArrayOut.toByteArray();
for(i = 0; i < byteArrayRow.length; i++) {
   scratchpad[i] = byteArrayRow[i];
}
setScratchpad(scratchpad);
```

SQLUDF_TF_CLOSE and SQLUDF_TF_FINAL: We can perform any kind of resource free up in these call types.

11. Register the function: Now we can compile the code and keep the class file in the SQLLIB/FUNCTION directory. We can use the following statements to register the function:

```
CREATE FUNCTION tab_func(VARCHAR(20))
  RETURNS TABLE ( EMPNAME VARCHAR(40), salary DOUBLE )
  EXTERNAL NAME 'udfsamp!tabFunc'
  LANGUAGE JAVA
  PARAMETER STYLE DB2GENERAL
  NOT DETERMINISTIC
  READS SQL DATA
  SCRATCHPAD 10
  FINAL CALL
  DISALLOW PARALLEL
  NO DBINFO@
```

Since this is a table function, we can use it in the FROM clause of the SELECT statement.

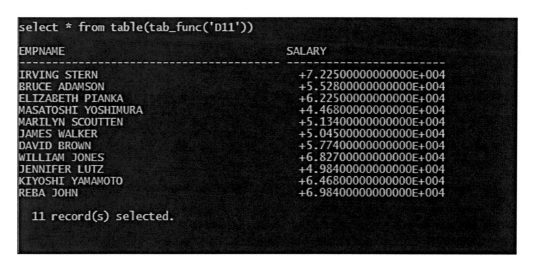

```
select * from table(tab_func('D11'))

EMPNAME                                      SALARY
-------------------------------------------  ------------------------
IRVING STERN                                 +7.22500000000000E+004
BRUCE ADAMSON                                +5.52800000000000E+004
ELIZABETH PIANKA                             +6.22500000000000E+004
MASATOSHI YOSHIMURA                          +4.46800000000000E+004
MARILYN SCOUTTEN                             +5.13400000000000E+004
JAMES WALKER                                 +5.04500000000000E+004
DAVID BROWN                                  +5.77400000000000E+004
WILLIAM JONES                                +6.82700000000000E+004
JENNIFER LUTZ                                +4.98400000000000E+004
KIYOSHI YAMAMOTO                             +6.46800000000000E+004
REBA JOHN                                    +6.98400000000000E+004

  11 record(s) selected.
```

How it works...

When an external table function is defined, it leverages the call type mechanism. It can have the following call types that control the behavior of the table function:

- FIRST CALL: This is the first call made. It accepts input parameters, but nothing is returned. All kinds of initialization can be done in this call. The scratchpad is cleared before this call, which can now be used until the final call. This call can only be made if the function was created with the FINAL CALL clause.

- OPEN CALL: This is when the cursor is opened. Nothing is returned in this call. The scratchpad is now available for use.

- FETCH CALL: This is when the function actually starts returning records. For each fetch call, one row is returned. We can use the scratchpad in any way we want. For example, if we want to keep track of the number of rows returned, we can use the scratchpad to track the counts.

- CLOSE CALL: This call is made when the scan is complete.

- FINAL CALL: This call is made at the end of the statement. We can clear up the resources in this call. This call can only be made if the function was created with the FINAL CALL clause.

Working with modules in DB2

Modules were introduced in DB2 9.7, which provide a way to group together related database objects in a separate box. We can create a collection of different database objects and wrap them in a module. A module itself is a database object that can have different database objects in it. Objects that can be encapsulated in a module can be functions, stored procedures, user-defined types, and variables. Modules are typically used to group together the objects that serve a similar business purpose. For example, we can group together a set of functions and procedures that are useful for sales. We can manage a module, just like any other database object, making management easy. Modules provide ways to add and remove database objects in them. They also allow us to publish only selective objects from the module to users. In this recipe, we will discuss how we can create modules and how we can use them.

Getting ready

To create a module, we need at least one of the following privileges:

▶ IMPLICIT_SCHEMA or CREATIN schema privilege, whichever is applicable
▶ DBADM authority

How to do it

We can consider a module as a wrapper around different database objects. Once the wrapper is defined, we can add and remove other database objects in it. Let's see how we can create and manage modules:

1. Create a module: The first step in this recipe is to create the module. This can be done by using the CREATE MODULE command.

   CREATE MODULE test_module@

   CREATE OR REPLACE MODULE test_module@

   If the OR REPLACE clause is specified, then the existing module (if any) will be dropped and a new module will be created. If we want to create the module in any specific schema, then we need to provide the fully qualified name for the module.

2. Add objects: Once a module is created, we can add any database object to it. To add a database object, we can use the ALTER MODULE statement. This statement allows us to add a database object as private or published. Only published objects can be referenced outside the module, whereas private objects can only be used within the module.

   ❑ Add a procedure with its definition.

   ALTER MODULE test_module

```
    PUBLISH PROCEDURE proc1()

    LANGUAGE SQL

BEGIN

    CALL DBMS_OUTPUT.PUT_LINE('******** Procedure 1
**********');

END@
```

❑ Add a user-defined type to the module.

```
ALTER MODULE test_module PUBLISH TYPE type_t

    AS ROW(ID INT, name VARCHAR(20))@
```

❑ Add a user-defined function to the module.

```
ALTER MODULE test_module PUBLISH FUNCTION square (val
INTEGER)

RETURNS INTEGER

BEGIN

    RETURN val * val;

END@
```

❑ Add another procedure to the module.

```
ALTER MODULE test_module

    PUBLISH PROCEDURE sum(IN val1 INT, IN val2 INT, OUT sum
INT)

    LANGUAGE SQL

BEGIN

    SET sum = val1 + val2;

END@
```

By now, we have the module created with four objects in it.

3. Prototypes new routines: We can add or define a function or procedure without its body. Such routines are also known as **prototypes**. We can add the routine body later. However, they cannot be invoked before their body is added. This can only be done for published routines.

```
ALTER MODULE test_module PUBLISH PROCEDURE proc2() LANGUAGE SQL@
```

Till now, we have only added a prototype of a procedure to the module. If we try to invoke it now without providing the definition, we will get the following error:

```
ALTER MODULE test_module PUBLISH PROCEDURE proc2() LANGUAGE SQL
DB20000I  The SQL command completed successfully.

CALL test_module.proc2()
SQL20496N  The routine "SANJU.TEST_MODULE.PROC2" cannot be invoked because it
is only a routine prototype.  SQLSTATE=55019
```

```
ALTER MODULE test_module ADD PROCEDURE proc2()
BEGIN
    CALL DBMS_OUTPUT.PUT_LINE('******** Procedure 2 **********');
END@
```

4. Referencing objects within a module: By now, we have created a module with some functions and procedures. They can be referenced or used within the module as well as outside, depending on whether they are made private or published. Private members can only be used within the module, whereas published objects can be used outside the routine as well. Within a module, we can use a one-part, two-part, or three-part naming convention to refer to any object in a module.

   ❑ Three-part naming convention: `<schema-name>.<module-name>.<object-name>`

   ❑ Two-part naming convention: `<module-name>.<object-name>`

   ❑ One-part naming convention: `<object-name>`

   In the preceding example, if we want to call the SUM procedure within the module, then this can be called in any of the following methods:

   ```
   CALL SANJU.TEST_MODULE.SUM(7, 9, ?);
   CALL TEST_MODULE.SUM(7, 9, ?);
   CALL SUM(7, 9, ?);
   ```

5. Referencing objects outside the module: Module objects can only be referenced outside the module by using a two-part or three-part naming convention.

   In the preceding example, if we want to call the SUM procedure outside the module, then this can be called in any of the following methods:

   ```
   CALL SANJU.TEST_MODULE.SUM(7, 9, ?);
   CALL TEST_MODULE.SUM(7, 9, ?);
   ```

6. Dropping a module object: We can use the ALTER MODULE statement to drop any object within it. If any object within a module is dropped, then its dependent objects are marked inoperative.

   For example, procedure sum can be dropped by executing the following statement:

   ```
   ALTER MODULE test_module DROP PROCEDURE sum @
   ```

We can also drop all private objects within a module by using the DROP BODY clause. It drops all private objects, bodies of published routines, private types, and global variables. The rest of the prototype remains along with the module itself.

```
ALTER MODULE test_module DROP BODY @
```

7. Dropping a module: A module, if no longer needed, can be dropped by using the DROP MODULE statement. If a module is dropped, then all objects within the module are also dropped.

How it works

Modules allow us to group logically related database objects together in a named set. It can group objects as stored procedures, user-defined functions, user-defined types, and global variables. Modules provide an abstraction layer where we can define private and public members. Private members are only accessible within the module, whereas public members are accessible outside the module as well. When any member is referenced within the module, we can use a two-part naming convention, whereas if any member is to be referenced outside the module, then we should use a three-part naming convention.

There's more...

A module can have a set of functions, procedures, global variables, and so on. Before we can use them, we might want to prepare our module or do some kind of preprocessing. For such situations, we can use a module initialization procedure. We can create a stored procedure with the name SYS_INIT (reserved name) and can have all setup instructions in this procedure. When any module object or any global variable is referenced outside a module for the first time, then DB2 implicitly looks for this procedure and executes it before anything else is done. This way, we can ensure that we have everything set up properly for the module to work. This procedure can also be invoked explicitly by using the CALL statement from within the module or outside the module. Some basic use cases for using the SYS_INIT procedure can be the initialization of global variables, creating temporary tables, opening cursors, and so on.

This procedure can be added to a module like a regular stored procedure by using the ALTER MODULE statement. This procedure can have SQL statements supported for compound statements. However, we cannot return result sets from the SYS_INIT procedure and it cannot have any parameters.

Module privileges

We can only grant the EXECUTE privilege on modules. It is not possible to grant privileges for individual objects within the module. We can use the GRANT statement to grant the privileges to a user, role, or a group.

```
GRANT EXECUTE ON MODULE test_module TO test_user@
```

Similarly, we can use the REVOKE statement to revoke privileges for a module.

```
REVOKE EXECUTE ON MODULE test_module FROM test_user@
```

Object name resolution

As mentioned earlier, an object within a module can be referenced by a two-part or one-part naming convention. If we are using the two-part naming convention, then there could be conflicts. For example, we can have another database object outside the module which has the same two-part name as the module object. In other words, `<module-name>.<object-name>` can be the same as `<schema-name>.<object-name>`. In such cases, DB2 uses the following rules to resolve the object name:

- If the object reference is within a module and if the first qualifier matches that module name, then this module is searched for a corresponding object (published or private). If a match is found, then this object is used.

- If the preceding search fails, then DB2 assumes that the first qualifier is a schema name and searches the schema with this name. If a schema is found, then the object is searched in this schema.

- If the schema is not found, or the object is not found in this schema, then DB2 looks for a module named as the first qualifier. If any such module is found, then it looks for published objects with the respective object name.

- If the name is still not resolved, then DB2 looks for a public synonym while considering the published module objects.

One-part naming conventions can only be used within a module. In the case of a one-part naming convention, the following rules are applied to resolve the object names:

- An object with a given name is searched for within the module

- If such an object is not found in the module, then the current schema (or the first schema in the SQL path) is searched with the given object name

- If the name is still not resolved, then the resolution fails

5
Designing Java Applications

In this chapter, we will focus on the following recipes related to development in Java:

- ▶ Creating connection objects in JDBC applications
- ▶ Creating connection objects in SQLJ applications
- ▶ Manipulating XML data in Java applications
- ▶ Batch processing in JDBC applications
- ▶ Batch processing in SQLJ applications
- ▶ Working with scrollable result sets
- ▶ Handling errors and warnings in JDBC applications
- ▶ Developing Java applications for high availability
- ▶ Using SSL in Java applications

Introduction

In this chapter, we will focus on Java as a programming language. Java is one of the most extensively-used programming languages, especially in database applications. This chapter focuses on some advanced topics, such as the different ways of connecting to data sources, designing enhanced security in Java applications, handling XML data, and so on.

Creating connection objects in JDBC applications

The first step in any database application is establishing a connection to the database. DB2 provides different methods to create a database connection. In general, we have two types of database connectivity:

- **Type-2 connectivity**: This type of connectivity needs a database client installed on the host machine. It can only connect to local databases. If we want to use this type of connectivity to connect to a database available over the network, then we need to catalog that database on the client application host and then use this type of connectivity. The only specification provided to establish a connection is that the database name should be available in a local database directory.

- **Type-4 connectivity**: This type of connectivity can be used to connect to any database over the network. It can also connect to a local database, but through its network address. The specification required to establish a connection includes a network address, a port number, and a database name.

Getting ready

DB2 supports the following database drivers for Java applications:

- **DB2 JDBC Type -2 driver**: This driver is deprecated and will not be supported in future versions. This driver is packaged as `db2java.zip`, available in the `SQLLIB/Java` directory. This driver uses the DB2 CLI interface to connect to the database server. Any application that uses this driver to connect to a database needs the DB2 client installed on the client's host machine and the target data base needs to be cataloged in the local directory.

- **IBM Data Server Driver for JDBC and SQLJ**: This driver is packaged as `db2jcc.jar` and `sqlj.zip` for JDBC 3.0 and as `db2jcc4.jar` and `sqlj4.zip` for JDBC 4.0. This driver allows us to use the type-2 and type-4 type connectivity.

These drivers are shipped with DB2.

How to do it...

Before we can execute any SQL statement, we need to establish a connection to the database. DB2 provides four ways to create a connection to the DB2 database:

Type-2 connectivity using DB2 JDBC Driver: This type of connectivity can be used when the database exists on the same host as the client application. This can also be used when DB2 connect is available at the client host. Connecting to DB2 using type-2 connectivity is done in two steps, and they are loading the database driver and creating a connection object.

1. **Loading the database driver**: Use the `Class.ForName()` method to load the driver.

```
try {
  Class.forName("COM.ibm.db2.jdbc.app.DB2Driver");
} catch (ClassNotFoundException e) {
  e.printStackTrace();
}
```

2. **Creating a connection object**: Once the database driver is loaded, we can use the `getConnection()` method of the `DriverManager` class to create a connection object. This method can be called in the following ways:

```
getConnection(String url);
getConnection(String url, user, password);
getConnection(String url, java.util.Properties prop);
```

The `url` identifies the data source.

URL for DB2 JDBC Type-2 driver: jdbc:db2:<database-name>

`prop` can be used to pass driver properties for the connection. Instead of passing the username and password directly to the `getConnection()` method, we can use properties to set them as connection attributes.

```
String url = "jdbc:db2:sample";
Properties prop = new Properties();
prop.put("user", "dbuser");
prop.put("password", "dbpassword");
```

We can use any of the following ways to create a connection object:

```
Connection con = DriverManager.getConnection(url);
Connection con = DriverManager.getConnection(url, "dbuser",
"dbpassword");
Connection con = DriverManager.getConnection(url, prop);
```

Type-2 connectivity using IBM DB2 Data Server for JDBC and SQLJ: This driver supports both type-2 and type-4 connectivity. Connecting to a database using this type of connectivity is also a two-step process that includes loading the database driver and creating a connection object:

1. **Loading the database driver**: Use the `Class.ForName()` method to load the driver.

```
try {
  Class.forName("com.ibm.db2.jcc.DB2Driver ");
} catch (ClassNotFoundException e) {
  e.printStackTrace();
}
```

2. **Creating a connection object**: Once the database driver is loaded, we can use the `getConnection()` method of the `DriverManager` class to create a connection object. This method can be called in the following ways:

```
getConnection(String url);
getConnection(String url, user, password);
getConnection(String url, java.util.Properties prop);
```

The URL for DB2 JDBC Type-2 driver is

```
jdbc:db2:<database-name>:[property=value]n
```

The connection attributes can also be specified by using properties within the connection URL.

```
String url = "jdbc:db2:sample:user=dbuser;password=dbpassword;";
Connection con = DriverManager.getConnection(url);
```

Other than this, we can explicitly pass the username and password directly to the `getConnection()` method.

```
String url = "jdbc:db2:sample";
String user = "dbuser";
String password = "dbpassword";
Connection con = DriverManager.getConnection(url, user, password);
```

The connection attributes can be passed as properties to the connection:

```
Properties properties = new Properties();
properties.put("user", "dbuser");
properties.put("password", "dbpassword");
String url = "jdbc:db2:sample";
Connection con = DriverManager.getConnection(url, properties);
```

Type-4 connectivity: This type of connectivity can be used when the target database is accessible over the network. Similar to type-2 connectivity, connecting to DB2 using type-4 connectivity also needs two steps that include loading the database driver and creating the connection object.

1. **Loading the database driver**: Type-4 connectivity is provided by the IBM Data Server Driver for JDBC and SQLJ.

```
try {
  Class.forName("com.ibm.db2.jcc.DB2Driver");
} catch (ClassNotFoundException e) {
  e.printStackTrace();
}
```

2. **Creating a connection object**: Once the database driver is loaded, we can use the `getConnection()` method of the `DriverManager` class to create a connection object.

The URL for the IBM Data Server Driver for JDBC and SQLJ Type-4 driver is `jdbc:db2//server:port/database:[property=value;]n`

The connection attributes can be specified by using properties within the connection URL:

```
String url = "jdbc:db2://localhost:50001/sample:user=dbuser;passwo
rd=dbpassword;";
Connection con = DriverManager.getConnection(url);
```

Other than this, we can explicitly pass the username and password directly to the `getConnection()` method.

```
String url = "jdbc:db2://localhost:50001/sample";
String user = "dbuser";
String password = "dbpassword";
Connection con = DriverManager.getConnection(url, user, password);
```

The connection attributes can also be passed in as properties to the connection.

```
Properties properties = new Properties();
properties.put("user", "dbuser");
properties.put("password", "dbpassword");
String url = "jdbc:db2://localhost:50001/sample";
Connection con = DriverManager.getConnection(url, properties);
```

Connecting using the DataSource interface: Connecting to a database using JDBC drivers reduces the application portability, as we need to use a specific driver class name and driver URL. If we plan to port this application to a new environment, then we should use the `DataSource` interface to connect to the database. We need a `DataSource` object created on the server. The applications can identity a `DataSource` object by its name. Using `DataSource` is a two-step process:

1. **Creating a DataSource object**: This can be done within the application or it can be created independently and deployed on the application server. This is a three-step process:

Create an instance of the appropriate `DataSource` implementation:

```
DB2SimpleDataSource dbDS= new com.ibm.db2.jcc.
DB2SimpleDataSource();
```

Set the properties of the `DataSource` object:

```
dbDS.setDatabaseName("sample");
 dbDS.setUser("dbuser");
dbDS.setPassword("dbpasswd");
```

Register the `DataSource` object with JNDI (Java Naming and Directory Interface)

```
Context ctx=new InitialContext();
Ctx.bind("jdbc/sampleDS",dbDS);
```

2. **Creating a connection object using the DataSource object**: Once the `DataSource` object is created and registered with JNDI, we can use this to create connection objects.

```
 Context ctx=new InitialContext();
DataSource ds=(DataSource)ctx.lookup("jdbc/sampleDS");
Connection con=ds.getConnection();
```

If the `DataSource` object is created within the application, then we don't need to register it at JDNI; it can be used directly to create connection objects:

```
Connection con=dbDS.getConnection();
```

> The DB2 JDBC driver for type-2 connectivity is deprecated and will not be supported in future versions of DB2.

How it works...

The IBM Data Server driver for JDBC and SQLJ provides the following interfaces for the `DataSource` implementation:

- ▶ `com.ibm.db2.jcc.DB2SimpleDataSource`: This interface can be used with type-2 and type-4 type connectivity. However, this does not support connection pooling.

- ▶ `com.ibm.db2.jcc.DB2ConnectionPoolDataSource`: This can be used with type-2 and type-4 type connectivity and it also supports connection pooling.

- ▶ `com.ibm.db2.jcc.DB2XADataSource`: This is only available with type-4 type connectivity. This is used in distributed applications. It supports connection pooling provided by the application server.

The DB2 JDBC type-2 driver provides the following interfaces for `DataSource` implementation:

- ▶ `COM.ibm.db2.jdbc.DB2DataSource`: This interface provides connection pooling that is transparent to the application.

- ▶ `COM.ibm.db2.jdbc.DB2XADataSource`: This is used in distributed applications and this does not provide any inbuilt support for connection pooling.

There's more...

Once we have created a connection object, we can set a number of connection properties that control the application behavior. Some of the commonly used connection attributes are:

1. **Auto commit mode**: This indicates whether all SQL statements executed under a given connection should be committed automatically. We can set it to `true` or `false` by using the `setAutoCommit()` method.

   ```
   con.setAutoCommit(false);
   ```

2. **Isolation levels**: This property sets the isolation level at which the statements would be executed on the database. This controls the locking behavior while selecting or processing the data. The isolation level can be changed any number of times in an application, if required.

   DB2 provides four isolation levels, as shown in the following table:

JDBC value	DB2 isolation level
TRANSACTION_SERIALIZABLE	Repeatable read
TRANSACTION_REPEATABLE_READ	Read stability
TRANSACTION_READ_COMMITTED	Cursor stability
TRANSACTION_READ_UNCOMMITTED	Uncommitted read

   We can use the `setTransactionIsolation()` method to set the isolation level for a connection.

   ```
   con.setTransactionIsolation(TRANSACTION_READ_COMMITTED);
   ```

3. Specifying the read only nature: If we do not intend to make any changes, then we can define the connection as read only. This helps in better optimization, resulting in better performance of read only queries. We can use the `setReadOnly()` method to set this property.

   ```
   con.setReadOnly(1);
   ```

Creating connection objects in SQLJ applications

To establish a connection to the database, we use connection contexts in the SQLJ application. A connection context specifies the database details, transaction behavior, and session to be used in the application. In this recipe, we will focus on the different ways of establishing database connections in SQLJ applications.

Getting ready

DB2 supports IBM Data Server Driver for JDBC and SQLJ for SQLJ applications. This driver is packaged as db2jcc.jar and sqlj.zip for JDBC 3.0 and as db2jcc4.jar and sqlj4.zip for JDBC 4.0. This driver allows us to use type-2 and type-4 type connectivity.

This driver is shipped with DB2.

How to do it...

The basic idea with all these techniques is to create a connection context based on an interface that can identify the database. The database can be represented by a DataSource interface or a DriverManager interface. We use these interfaces as arguments for the context class constructor method.

1. **Technique 1** : This technique uses the JDBC DriverManager interface to create a connection context for SQLJ applications. This can be done as follows:

    i. Declare a connection context :

    ```
    #sql context Ctx;
    ```

    ii. Load the database driver.

    ```
    Class.forName("com.ibm.db2.jcc.DB2Driver");
    ```
    Or
    ```
    Class.forName("COM.ibm.db2.jdbc.app.DB2Driver");
    ```

    iii. Create a connection context object: The constructor method of the context class can be invoked in any of the following ways:

    ```
    Ctx myctx=  new Ctx(String url, boolean autocommit);
    Ctx myctx=  new Ctx(String url, String user, String
        password, boolean autocommit);
    Ctx myctx=  new Ctx(String url, Properties info, boolean
        autocommit);
    ```

Now this connection context (`myct`) can be used to execute any SQL statement in the SQLJ application.

2. **Technique 2** : This technique uses the `DriverManager` interface for creating the connection. In this technique, the connection context is created by using a JDBC connection object.

    i.   Declare a connection context.

```
#sql context Ctx;
```

    ii.   Load the database driver, as shown:

```
Class.forName("com.ibm.db2.jcc.DB2Driver");
```

     Or:

```
Class.forName("COM.ibm.db2.jdbc.app.DB2Driver");
```

    iii.   Create a JDBC connection object by using the `DriverManager` interface.

```
Connection con = DriverManager.getConnection(url);
```

     We can use any form of the `getConnection()` method that can accept user credentials and properties information.

    iv.   Create a connection context object by using the previously-created connection object.

```
Ctx myctx=  new Ctx(con);
```

     Now this connection context (`myct`) can be used to execute any SQL statement in the SQLJ application.

3. **Technique 3** : This technique uses the `DataSource` interface to create a connection context. We use the `DataSource` interface to look up the data source from JNDI.

    i.   Declare a connection context.

```
#sql context Ctx;
```

    ii.   Get the logical name of the data source to which the connection is needed.

```
import javax.naming.*;
Context ctx=new InitialContext();
DataSource ds=(DataSource)ctx.lookup("jdbc/sampleDS");
Connection con=ds.getConnection();
```

    iii.   Create a connection context object by using the connection object we just created.

```
Ctx myctx=  new Ctx(con);
```

Now this connection context (`myct`) can be used to execute any SQL statements in the SQLJ application.

4. **Technique 4** : This technique is very similar to the preceding one, but instead of creating a connection object on the `DataSource` interface, we can use it directly to create the connection context object.

    i.   Declare a connection context: The connection context must be declared as public and static.

```
#sql public static context Ctx with (dataSource="jdbc/
    sampleDS");
```

    ii.   Create a connection context object: We can use the connection object we just created to create a connection context object.

```
Ctx myConnCtx=new Ctx(userid, password);
```

Now this connection context (`myct`) can be used to execute any SQL statement in the SQLJ application.

5. **Technique 5** : This technique uses a previously-created connection context. If we have created a connection context in a Java application, then we can use it in other applications as well. This context, in such cases, is passed as an argument to other programs.

    i.   Create a connection context in a separate program:

```
#sql context Ctx;
String userid="dbadm";
String password="dbadm";
String empname;
try {
   Class.forName("com.ibm.db2.jcc.DB2Driver");
}
catch (ClassNotFoundExcepti3.on e) {
   e.printStackTrace();
}
Ctx myConnCtx= new Ctx("jdbc:db2://localhost:50001/sample",
    userid,password,false);
```

    ii.   Use the connection context created in the previous program in our application (`useConCtx.sqlj`). This program should accept a connection context as a parameter.

```
void useContext(sqlj.runtime.ConnectionContext myConnCtx)
{
   Ctx myConnCtx = new Ctx(myConnCtx);

}
```

6. **Technique 6** : This technique uses the default context. This is useful only if the database threads are controlled by some resource manager that takes care of establishing a connection with the target database. In such cases, we don't specify any connection context while executing the SQL statements. If there is no context specified, then DB2 uses the default connection context, if available. For example, we can execute SQL statements as follows:

```
#sql {SELECT EMPNO INTO :empno FROM EMPLOYEE WHERE
EMPNO='000380'};
```

How it works...

SQLJ applications need a connection context to interact with databases. If a default context is not set explicitly, then SQLJ runtime does a JNDI lookup for `jdbc/defaultDataSource`. A context defines particulars of the connection for an SQL statement to be executed. It allows us to have multiple contexts within an application. If we have multiple contexts defined, then each context acts as a separate connection where changes made by one context are not visible to another, until committed. As a best practice, we should always define a default context.

Java packages for SQLJ applications

DB2 provides the following packages as part of the IBM Data Server driver for JDBC and SQLJ that can be used in SQLJ applications:

- `javax.sql`: This package provides APIs for server-side data source access
- `javax.naming`: This package provides classes and interfaces for JNDI (Java naming and directory interface) lookups
- `com.ibm.db2.jcc`: This package provides driver-specific implementation of JDBC and SQLJ
- `java.sql`: This package provides core JDBC APIs
- `sqlj.runtime`: This package contains SQLJ runtime APIs

Manipulating XML Data in Java applications

XML, as a built-in data type, was introduced in DB2 9.1. XQuery is the language which is used to query XML data, just as SQL is used to query relational data. Apart from using XQuery, DB2 also provides SQLXML and XMLSQL functions that allow us to query the XML data by using SQL queries and vice versa. Like any SQL statement, XQuery can also be embedded in any host language. In this recipe, we will discuss how we can use XML data in Java applications.

Getting ready

We need the IBM Data Server for the JDBC and SQLJ installed. This driver is shipped as part of DB2.

How to do it...

1. **Retrieving XML Data**: XML data can be retrieved in several Java forms such as XML, Object, String, Reader, InputStream, and so on. XML can be retrieved by methods available in the `ResultSet` class.

```
PreparedStatement selectStmt = con.prepareStatement("SELECT info
FROM customer WHERE cid = 1000");
ResultSet rs = selectStmt.executeQuery();
```

   Once we have the result set, we can use the corresponding methods to read XML in different forms.

2. **Retrieving XML as SQLXML objects**: We can use the `ResultSet.getSQLXML` method to retrieve XML data as XML Java objects.

```
while (rs.next()) {
java.sql.SQLXML xml = rs.getSQLXML(1);
}
```

3. **Retrieving XML as String data**: We can use the `ResultSet.getString()` method to read XML data as `String` objects.

```
while (rs.next()) {
String xml = rs.getString(1);
System.out.println (xml);
}
```

4. **Retrieving XML as InputStream**: We can use the `ResultSet.getAsciiStream()` or `ResultSet.getBinaryStream()` methods to read XML as an `InputStream` object.

```
while (rs.next()) {
InputStream xml = rs.getAsciiStream(1);
byte[] buff = new byte[lengthXml];
int bytesRead = xml.read(buff);
String value = new String(buff);
System.out.println (value);
}
```

5. **Retrieving XML as Reader object**: We can use the `ResultSet`.
   `getCharacterStream()` method to read XML data as `Reader Objects`.

```
while (rs.next()) {
  Reader xml = rs.getCharacterStream(1);
char[] buff = new char[100];
int bytesRead = xml.read(buff);
String value = new String(buff);
System.out.println (value);
}
```

6. **Inserting/Updating XML data**: Just like reading XML data, an update or
   insert operation can also be done by using XML as SQLXML, String, Reader,
   InputStream objects, and so on. We can use a set of methods available for the
   `PreparedStatement` class to process XML data. Let's prepare an `INSERT`
   statement that will be used to insert an XML document in a test table.

```
Connection con = DriverManager.getConnection(url);
PreparedStatement insertStmt = null;
String xmldata = "<customerinfo xmlns=""http://posample.org""
Cid=""1000"">…</customerinfo>";
sqls = "INSERT INTO CUSTOMER (CID, INFO) VALUES (?)";
insertStmt = con.prepareStatement(sqls);
```

7. **Inserting XML as a SQLXML object**: We can use the `PreparedStatement.`
   `setSQLXML()` method to insert or update XML as a SQLXML object.

```
SQLXML info = con.createSQLXML();
info.setString(xmldata);
insertStmt.setSQLXML(2, info);
insertStmt.executeUpdate();
```

8. **XML as a string**: XML can be processed as a `String` object by using the
   `setString()` method.

```
String info = new String(xmldata);
insertStmt.setString(2, info);
insertStmt.executeUpdate();
```

9. **XML as BinaryStream**: XML can be processed as a `Binarystream` object by using
   the `setBinaryStream()` method.

```
PreparedStatement insertStmt = null;
try {
  String sqls = "INSERT INTO CUSTOMER (CID, INFO) VALUES (?)";
  insertStmt = conn.prepareStatement(sqls);
  File file = new File("c1.xml");
  insertStmt.setBinaryStream(1, new FileInputStream(file),
    (int)file.length());
  insertStmt.executeUpdate();
```

10. **Inserting XML as clob**: XML can be processed as a `clob` object, bu, using the `setClob()` method.

```
String xsdData = new String();
xsdData=returnFileValues("cust1023.xml");

java.sql.Clob clobData = com.ibm.db2.jcc.t2zos.DB2LobFactory.
createClob(xsdData);

PreparedStatement pstmt = con.prepareStatement(
"INSERT INTO customer(cid,info)" +
"VALUES(1023,XMLPARSE(document cast(? as Clob) strip
whitespace))");

pstmt.setClob(1, clobData);
pstmt.execute();
pstmt.close();
```

How it works...

`pureXML` was introduced in DB2 9. DB2 has a hybrid engine where relational and XML data is stored in separate storage areas. XML is stored in native form, that is, in a hierarchical manner. When an XML document is inserted or updated, DB2 checks the format of the XML document. Any error in the format results in failure of the `INSERT` or `UPDATE` statements. DB2 also allows us to validate the XML documents against a registered XML schema while inserting them. Once an XML document is inserted in the database, it can be queried completely as a whole XML document or partially by selecting only an attribute of it. DB2 provides various interfaces in the JDBC driver that allow us to use XML documents in Java applications.

There's more...

We can call stored procedures that accept XML as `IN` or `OUT` parameters. While calling the procedures, we need to register the parameters as XML types.

▸ We need to use the `java.sql.SQLXML` or `com.ibm.db2.jcc.DB2Xml` type for `IN` parameters.

▸ We need to use the `java.sql.Types.SQLXML` or `com.ibm.db2.jcc.DB2Types.XML` type to register `OUT` parameters.

For example, if we want to call a stored procedure that has one IN, one OUT, and one INOUT parameter, then this can be done as follows:

```
CallableStatement cstmt;
cstmt = con.prepareCall("CALL SP_xml(?,?,?)");
cstmt.setObject (1, in_xml);
cstmt.setObject (3, inout_xml);
cstmt.registerOutParameter (2, java.sql.Types.SQLXML);
cstmt.registerOutParameter (3, java.sql.Types.SQLXML);
cstmt.executeUpdate();
out_xml = cstmt.getSQLXML(2);
inout_xml = cstmt.getSQLXML(3);
```

Batch processing in JDBC applications

Instead of updating one row at a time, we can also update multiple rows simultaneously. We can create a batch from a set of statements and execute them at once. This is mainly done for better performance, as compared to updating a single row at a time. We can only create a batch for similar update statements (also known as batch-compatible statements). All statements must have similar types of input parameters. Either all statements should have input parameters or none of them should have input parameters.

Getting ready

A batch update can be done by using the following methods on the PreparedStatement object.

- ▸ addBatch()
- ▸ executeBatch()
- ▸ clearBatch()

How to do it...

A batch can be created for a Statement object or a PreparedStatement object. If we want to execute multiple SQL statements as part of a batch, then we need to create a batch for a Statement object. If we want to execute a single SQL statement with different values for the parameter markets, then we can create a batch on the PreparedStatement object.

Running SQL multiple times with different values for parameter markers

1. **Creating a prepared statement**: We can prepare a SQL statement that has parameter markers as follows:

    ```
    PreparedStatement preps = conn.prepareStatement("UPDATE DEPT SET
    MGRNO=? WHERE DEPTNO=?");
    ```

2. **Adding a batch**: To add a batch, we need to set the parameter marker values, and then add a batch against the prepared statement.

    ```
    ps.setString(1,mgrnum1);
    ps.setString(2,deptnum1);
    ps.addBatch();

    ps.setString(1,mgrnum2);
    ps.setString(2,deptnum2);
    ps.addBatch();
    ```

3. **Executing the batch**: Now, we have our batch created with two sets of parameter values. We can use the `executeBatch()` method to execute the complete batch:

    ```
    int [] numUpdates=ps.executeBatch();
    ```

    This method returns an integer array of return codes for all the statements that were executed as part of this batch.

4. **Checking the return codes for each statement in the batch**: We can check the returned array values of return codes to check if there were any failures.

    ```
    for (int i=0; i < numUpdates.length; i++) {
      if (numUpdates[i] == SUCCESS_NO_INFO)
        System.out.println("Execution " + i +
          ": unknown number of rows updated");
      else
        System.out.println("Execution " + i +
          "successful: " numUpdates[i] + " rows updated");
    }
    ```

Running multiple SQL statements in a batch

1. **Creating a Statement object**: The batch can also be created in a `Statement` object, where we can add multiple SQL statements to the `Statement` object.

    ```
    Statement stmt = con.createStatement();
    ```

2. **Adding a batch**: We can use the `addBatch()` method for the `Statement` class to add different SQL statements that we wish to execute as part of the batch.

```
stmt.addBatch("INSERT INTO DETAILS VALUES('DTL1', 49, 9.99, 0,
0)");

stmt.addBatch("INSERT INTO DETAILS VALUES('DTL2', 49, 9.99, 0,
0)");

stmt.addBatch("INSERT INTO DETAILS VALUES('DTL3', 49,10.99, 0,
0)");

stmt.addBatch("INSERT INTO DETAILS VALUES('DTL4', 49, 10.99, 0,
0)");
```

4. **Executing the batch**: Now, we have our batch created with a set of SQL statements. We can use the `executeBatch()` method to execute the complete batch.

```
int [] numUpdates=stmt.executeBatch();
```

This method returns an integer array of return codes for all the statements that were executed as part of the batch.

5. **Checking the return codes for each statement in the batch**: We can check the returned array values of return codes to check if there were any failures.

```
for (int i=0; i < numUpdates.length; i++) {
  if (numUpdates[i] == SUCCESS_NO_INFO)
    System.out.println("Execution " + i +
      ": unknown number of rows updated");
  else
    System.out.println("Execution " + i +
      "successful: " numUpdates[i] + " rows updated");
}
```

How it works...

Batch processing is a mechanism where multiple SQL statements are grouped together and submitted to the database at once in a single database call. The database also returns the results for all SQL statements as a batch or as an array. When an SQL statement is added to a batch, it is not sent to the database for execution until the batch execution command is submitted. This mechanism improves the overall performance as the number of to and fro messages is reduced significantly. It reduces the overall communication overhead as well. The methods needed for batch processing in Java are provided by the JDBC and SQLJ drivers shipped with DB2.

There's more...

A `BatchUpdateException` is thrown when the `executeBatch()` method is called with an SQL statement that produces a result set. This exception is also thrown if any SQL contained in the batch fails. The information available in `BatchUpdateException` is similar to that returned by the `executeBatch()` method, which is an integer array of update counts. `BatchUpdateException` is extended from the `SQLException` class, which allows us to use methods available for the `SQLException` class.

```
try {
 // Batch Update
} catch(BatchUpdateException b) {
System.err.println("SQLState:  " + b.getSQLState());
  System.err.println("Message:  " + b.getMessage());
  System.err.println("Error Code:  " + b.getErrorCode());
  System.err.print("Update counts:  ");
  int [] updateCounts = b.getUpdateCounts();
  for (int i = 0; i < updateCounts.length; i++) {
    System.err.print(updateCounts[i] + "   ");
  }
}
```

We cannot retrieve a result set or any output parameter from a `CallableStatement`, which is executed as part of a batch. There is no exception thrown if the `CallableStatement` returns any result set or has any output parameter .

Restrictions on executing statements in a batch

A `CallableStatement` object that you execute in a batch can contain output parameters. However, you cannot retrieve the values of the output parameters. If you try to do so, a `BatchUpdateException` is thrown.

You cannot retrieve the `ResultSet` objects from a `CallableStatement` object that you execute in a batch. A `BatchUpdateException` is not thrown, but the `getResultSet` method invocation returns a null value.

Batch processing in SQLJ applications

We can also use batch processing in SQLJ applications. Similar to JDBC batch processing, SQLJ also involves creating a batch of statements and executing them all at once. SQLJ allows heterogeneous batches as well, where we can include statements with various parameters.

A batch in an SQLJ application can include any of the following statements:

- ▸ INSERT, UPDATE, DELETE, and MERGE
- ▸ CREATE, ALTER, and DROP
- ▸ GRANT and REVOKE
- ▸ CALL (with input parameters)

Getting ready

Batch update can be done by using the following methods in the execution context:

- ▸ setBatching()
- ▸ setBatchLimit()
- ▸ executeBatch()
- ▸ cancel()

How to do it...

The SQL statements in SQLJ applications are executed with an execution context. We can control batch processing by enabling batching in execution contexts.

We use the following steps to execute SQL statements as batches:

1. Create an execution context:

   ```
   ExecutionContext execCtx = new ExecutionContext();
   ```

2. Enable batching on the above-created execution context:

   ```
   execCtx.setBatching(true);
   ```

   Now, all the subsequent statements that are associated with this execution context will be added to the batch.

3. **Setting the batch size**: We can limit the number of SQL statements in a batch by using the setBatchLimit() method:

   ```
   execCtx.setBatchLimit(n);
   ```

   n can be one of the following:

   - ❏ **Positive integer**: This indicates the number of SQL statements that this batch can have
   - ❏ ExecutionContext.UNLIMITED_BATCH: This indicates an unlimited batch.
   - ❏ ExecutionContext.AUTO_BATCH: This indicates the batch size, as set by SQLJ.

4. **Adding SQL statements to the batch**: This includes the above-created execution context against the SQL statements, which should be added to the batch:

```
#sql [ctx, execCtx] {UPDATE EMPLOYEE SET SALARY=10000 WHERE
EMPNO='000100'};
#sql [ctx, execCtx] {UPDATE EMPLOYEE SET SALARY=20000 WHERE
EMPNO='000200'};
```

5. **Verifying the batch**: We can use the `ExecutionContext.getUpdateCount()` method to determine whether the previously-added SQL statement was added to the batch or if it was the first statement in the batch.

```
execCtx.getUpdateCount();
```

This method returns one of the following values:

- ❏ `ExecutionContext.ADD_BATCH_COUNT`: This indicates that the SQL statement was added to the batch.
- ❏ `ExecutionContext.NEW_BATCH_COUNT`: This indicates that the SQL statement was added to the batch and is the first statement in this batch.
- ❏ `ExecutionContext.EXEC_BATCH_COUNT`: This indicates that the SQL statement was part of a batch and the batch has been executed.

Any other value: This indicates if the SQL statement was executed rather than added to the batch. This value is the number of rows updated by this SQL statement.

6. **Executing the batch**: Use the `executeBatch()` method to execute the batch.

```
execCtx.executeBatch();
```

7. **Implicit execution of the batch**: If a SQL statement is not compatible with the other SQL statements in a batch, then the batch gets executed by itself and a new batch created, and this SQL statement is added to the newly-created batch. This is also true if the SQL statement that you attempt to add to the batch is not batchable or if the number of statements in a batch exceeds its limit.

8. **Analyzing the results**: Similar to batches in the JDBC application, this method returns an integer array containing the number of rows updated by each SQL statement in a batch in the order of the SQL statements. Each integer value can have one of the following values:

- ❏ **-2**: Statement executed successfully, but the row count cannot be determined.
- ❏ **-3**: Statement failed.
- ❏ **Any other integer value**: The number of rows updated.

9. **Disabling batching**: Once the batch processing is done, we can disable the batching.

```
execCtx.setBatching(false);
```

10. **Clearing the batch**: If we don't want to execute the batch and just cancel it, we can do so with:

```
execCtx.cancel();
```

How it works...

Batch processing is a mechanism where multiple SQL statements are grouped together and submitted to the database at once in a single database call. The database also returns the results for all the SQL statements as a batch or array. When an SQL statement is added to a batch, it is not sent to the database for execution until the batch execution command is submitted. This mechanism improves overall performance, as the number of "to and fro" messages is reduced significantly. It reduces the overall communication overhead as well. The methods needed for batch processing in SQLJ applications are provided by the JDBC and SQLJ drivers shipped with DB2.

Working with scrollable result sets

One of the new features in the JDBC 2.0 API is the ability to move a result set's cursor backward as well as forward. There are also methods that move the cursor to a particular row and that check the position of the cursor. Scrollable result sets make it easy to create a graphical interface for browsing the result set data, which will probably be one of the main uses for this feature. Another important use of scrollable cursors is to move it to a row that needs to be updated. In this recipe, we will discuss how we can create and use scrollable cursors.

Getting ready

To navigate through scrollable result sets, we should know the following methods, provided by the `ResultSet` class:

The navigation methods are as follows:

- `first()`: Moves the cursor to the first row of the result set
- `last()`: Moves the cursor to the last row of the result set
- `next()`: Moves the cursor to the next row in the result set
- `previous()`: Moves the cursor to the previous row in the result set
- `absolute(int n)`: Moves the cursor to the nth row in the result set. If n is negative, then the position is calculated as (Number of rows + n + 1)

- ▸ `relative(int n)`: Moves the cursor to the nth row from the relative position. n can be negative or positive, depending upon whether we want to move forward or backward respectively.
- ▸ `afterLast()`: Moves the cursor after the last row
- ▸ `beforeFirst()`: Moves the cursor before the first row

The different cursor position methods are as follows (we can use them to know the current cursor position):

- ▸ `getRow()`: Gets the row number
- ▸ `isFirst()`: Tells whether the cursor is positioned at the first row
- ▸ `isLast()`: Tells whether the cursor is positioned at the last row
- ▸ `isBeforeFirst()`: Tells whether the cursor is positioned before the first row
- ▸ `isAfterLast()`: Tells whether the cursor is positioned after the last row

The following are the cursor information methods:

- ▸ The `getType()` method provides information about the scroll property of the `resultSet` object. It returns the following values for different scroll attributes.
  - ❏ `TYPE_FORWARD_ONLY: 1003`
  - ❏ `TYPE_SCROLL_INSENSITIVE: 1004`
  - ❏ `TYPE_SCROLL_SENSITIVE: 1005`

How to do it ...

1. **Creating a scrollable resultSet object**: The scrolling property of a result set is set at the statement level and not at the result set level. To define a statement with scroll properties, we can use any one form of the `createStatement()` or `preparedStatement()` methods:

```
createStatement(int resultSetType, int resultSetConcurrency);

createStatement(int resultSetType, int resultSetConcurrency, int
resultSetHoldability);

prepareStatement(String sql, int resultSetType, int
resultSetConcurrency);

prepareStatement(String sql, int resultSetType, int
resultSetConcurrency, int resultSetHoldability);
```

If the `SELECT` statement does not include any parameter marker, then we can use the `createStatement()` method to create a statement object. Otherwise, if it has any parameter markers, then we need to first prepare it by using the `preparedStatement()` method and use the `setXXX()` methods to set the parameter values. For example, we can create an insensitive-scrollable result set for read-only operations, as shown next:

```
Statement stmt = con.createStatement(ResultSet.TYPE_SCROLL_
INSENSITIVE, ResultSet.CONCUR_READ_ONLY);
```

Scrollable result sets are expensive because of the overhead involved. So they should be declared only when actually needed. By default, all result sets are set to a non-scrollable type.

2. **Executing the statement**: Once we have created or prepared a statement object, we can execute them to get the scrollable result set object, which can be retrieved in a `ResultSet` object.

```
ResultSet rs = stmt.executeQuery("SELECT EMPNO, FIRSTNME,
LASTNAME, WORKDEPT FROM EMPLOYEE");
```

3. **Refreshing the current set**: If the cursor is defined as sensitive, then we need to refresh the current row to see the changes:

```
Rs.refreshRow();
```

4. **Updating current row**: Use the `updateXXX()` methods to update the current row:

```
rs.updateString("WORKDEPT", 'D11');

rs.updateRow();
```

5. **Deleting the current row**: Use `deleteRow()` to delete the current row:

```
rs.deleteRow();
```

6. **Checking the update or delete row**: When we have sensitive cursors and if we have updated or deleted any row and if the new row doesn't fit the current search criteria of the result set definition, then that becomes a hole. Before we attempt to retrieve the row, we need to check if it's a hole or not. To check whether the current row is a hole or not, use the following steps:

   ❑ Create a `DatabaseMetaData` object as follows:

   ```
   DatabaseMetaData dbmd = con.getMetaData();
   ```

   ❑ Check if the result set can have delete holes:

   ```
   boolean dbSeesDeletes = dbmd.deletesAreDetected(ResultSet.
   TYPESCROLL_SENSITIVE);

   int isDeleted = rs.rowDeleted();
   ```

❑   Check the update hole:

```
boolean dbSeesDeletes = dbmd.updatesAreDetected(ResultSet.
TYPESCROLL_SENSITIVE);
int isDeleted = rs.rowUpdated();
```

7.   **Inserting a row in the result set**: If the cursor is updatable, we can insert a row in the result set. We can use the following steps to insert a row:

❑   Create a place holder for the new row:

```
rs.moveToInsertRow();
```

❑   Use the updateXXX() methods to set the values for the new row:

```
rs.updateString("DEPT_NO", "M13");
rs.updateString("DEPTNAME", "TECHNICAL SUPPORT");
rs.updateString("MGRNO", "000010");
rs.updateString("ADMRDEPT", "A00");
```

❑   Insert the new row:

```
rs.insertRow();
```

❑   Move to the previous current row:

```
rs.moveToCurrentRow();
```

❑   Once the cursor is positioned to a new value, the insert buffer is cleared.

❑   Check if the row was inserted or not:

```
DatabaseMetaData dbmd = con.getMetaData();
boolean dbSeesDeletes = dbmd.insertsAreDetected(ResultSet.
TYPESCROLL_SENSITIVE);
int isInserted = rs.rowInserted();
```

How it works...

The scrollable result sets allow the cursor to be moved in both directions. The scrolling mechanism is provided by the JDBC API version 2.0 and higher. A JDBC result set is created with three properties, namely, type, holdability, and concurrency. The scrollable result set is a type of result set. Define a result set of the type TYPE_SCROLL_SENSITIVE or TYPE_SCROLL_INSENSITIVE to make it scrollable.

DB2 maintains the results of an SQL query in a temporary table and uses this to send the result to a client application. If the result set is sensitive, then DB2 has to check the data on every fetch to make sure if the data has changed or not. Therefore, the sensitive result sets are expensive, as compared to the insensitive result sets. When the cursor is opened and the first row is fetched, the client application receives a certain number of rows at once, as defined by the fetch size. If more records are needed, then the client application receives the next set of rows from the database. When a result set is defined as scrollable, the client application keeps all fetched records in memory to allow backward traversal. This can consume a lot of memory if the number of records in a result set is high. Scrollable cursors should be avoided in such cases.

When the result set is defined as scroll-sensitive, it can see the changes made in the database. The changes are only visible if the data is refreshed implicitly. This happens automatically when the next set of rows are passed from the database to the client application. Because the rows are sent to the client application in chunks, DB2 refreshes the data before sending the next chunk with sensitive result sets.

There's more...

DB2 provides support for scrollable, updatable, and holdable cursors. It allows us to traverse a cursor in forward and reverse directions, use them beyond the transaction boundary, and update or delete the rows. This functionality is also available for Java result sets. DB2 supports the following cursor properties:

Property Name	Description
CONCUR_READ_ONLY	This is used for read-only result sets.
CONCUR_UPDATABLE	This allows data-modification operations on result sets.
HOLD_CURSORS_OVER_COMMIT	These result sets can be used across transaction boundaries.
TYPE_FORWARD_ONLY	This is a default. The result set can only be traversed in a forward direction.
TYPE_SCROLL_INSENSITIVE	This result set is scrollable but is insensitive in nature, which means the changes made while traversing the result set are not visible if traversed again, though the changes can be seen if the result set is closed and opened again.
TYPE_SCROLL_SENSITIVE	This result set is also scrollable and is sensitive to the changes made during the result set traversal.

While creating a scrollable result set, we can specify the scrollable attribute only along with the cursor concurrency attribute. DB2 allows the following combinations for these attributes:

Result Set Type	Concurrency
TYPE_FORWARD_ONLY	CONCUR_READ_ONLY
TYPE_FORWARD_ONLY	CONCUR_UPDATABLE
TYPE_SCROLL_INSENSITIVE	CONCUR_READ_ONLY
TYPE_SCROLL_SENSITIVE	CONCUR_READ_ONLY
TYPE_SCROLL_SENSITIVE	CONCUR_UPDATABLE

Using scrollable iterators in SQLJ applications

We can also use a scrollable iterator to traverse a cursor in forward and backward directions. Just like result sets in JDBC applications, we can have sensitive or insensitive iterators. Sensitive iterators can see the changes made by the application, whereas insensitive iterators cannot see any changes made. We can also have asensitive iterators that act as sensitive when they are not read-only and insensitive when they are read-only. We can have a concept of dynamic and static iterators, but DB2 LUW only supports static iterators. The categorization is as follows:

1. **Static iterators**: The size of a static iterator cannot change. It means that new rows cannot be inserted in the result set. Also, it may create holes when any row is updated or deleted in the result set. Any attempt to fetch the data from a hole raises a SQLException.

2. **Dynamic iterators**: The size of a dynamic iterator can change. Rows can be inserted, updated, and deleted within the application and are visible immediately. They can also see committed changes made by other applications.

We can use the following steps to implement scrollable iterators in SQLJ applications:

1. Declare an iterator with sensitivity and dynamic properties:

```
#sql public iterator ScrlItr
    implements sqlj.runtime.Scrollable
    with (sensitivity=SENSITIVE, dynamic=false)  (String, String);
```

   - The values for "sensitivity" can be INSENSITIVE, SENSITIVE, or ASENSITIVE
   - The values for "dynamic" can be true or false

2. Create an iterator object.

```
ScrlItr itr;
```

3. Traverse through the iterator:

```
#sql [ctxt] itr = {SELECT EMPNO, FIRSTNME, LASTNAME FROM
EMPLOYEE};
```

We can use following set of methods to traverse through a named iterator:

- ❑ `rs.first()`: Moves the cursor to the first row of the result set.
- ❑ `rs.last()`: Moves the cursor to the last row of the result set.
- ❑ `rs.next()`: Moves the cursor to the next row in the result set.
- ❑ `rs.previous()`: Moves the cursor to the previous row in the result set.
- ❑ `rs.absolute(int n)`: Moves the cursor to the nth row in the result set. If n is negative, then the position is calculated as (Number of rows + n + 1).
- ❑ `rs.relative(int n)`: Moves the cursor to the nth row from the relative position. n can be negative or positive, depending upon whether we want to move forward or backward.
- ❑ `rs.afterLast()`: Moves the cursor after the last row.
- ❑ `rs.beforeFirst()`: Moves the cursor before the first row.

If we are using positioned iterators, then we can use the following clauses in the `FETCH` statement:

- ❑ `FIRST`: Moves to the first row
- ❑ `LAST`: Moves to the last row
- ❑ `PRIOR`: Moves to the previous row
- ❑ `NEXT`: Moves to the next row
- ❑ `ABSOLUTE(n)`: Moves the cursor to the nth absolute position from the starting of the cursor
- ❑ `RELATIVE(n)`: Moves the cursor to the nth relative position
- ❑ `AFTER`: Moves the cursor after the last row
- ❑ `BEFORE`: Moves the cursor before the first row.

We can use the following methods to know the current cursor position:

- ❑ `getRow()`: Gets the row number
- ❑ `isFirst()`: Tells whether the cursor is positioned at the first row
- ❑ `isLast()`: Tells whether the cursor is positioned on the last row
- ❑ `isBeforeFirst()`: Tells whether the cursor is positioned before the first row
- ❑ `isAfterLast()`: Tells whether the cursor is positioned after the last row

Handling errors and warnings in JDBC applications

A Java application uses its own way of catching exceptions. An error is commonly referred to as an exception in Java applications. An exception can be recognized by an exception class. A try block can have multiple catch blocks. The idea is to handle every possibility of the error condition. JDBC also provides some standard exception classes that can be used to capture the basic information. Apart from them, DB2 also provides its own exception classes that can be used for better diagnosis. In this recipe, we will focus on exception handling in Java applications.

Getting ready

JDBC applications use try and catch blocks to handle different exceptions. There is no exception thrown in the case of warnings. To handle warnings in JDBC applications, we need to explicitly check for warnings. We can use the getWarning() method to retrieve warnings as a SQLWarning object that has the following information:

- Description of the warning
- SQLSTATE
- Error code
- Pointer to the next SQLWarning

 The IBM Data Server Driver for JDBC and SQLJ does not raise a warning condition when no records are found in a result set.

The IBM Data Server Driver for JDBC and SQLJ provides the following classes for handling exceptions in JDBC applications:

- SQLException: This class provides the following information:
    - Error code
    - SQLSTATE
    - Error description
    - Pointer to the next error
- DB2Diagnosable: This class extends the SQLException class. This class provides more information about the error that occurred. When the JDBC driver detects an error, then this class returns the same information as the SQLException class, but if the error was detected by the DB2 server this class returns additional information. We can get the following additional information by using this class.

- ▸ `DB2Sqlca` object: A `DB2Sqlca` object contains following information:
    - ❑ Error code
    - ❑ `SQLERRMC` values
    - ❑ `SQLERRP` values
    - ❑ `SQLERRD` values
    - ❑ `SQLWARN` values
    - ❑ `SQLSTATE`

- ▸ `SQLException Subclasses`: DB2 also provides subclasses that extend the `SQLException` class. These subclasses help in capturing more specific information about the error.

- ▸ `SQLNonTransientException`: This exception is thrown when an SQL operation fails, even after retry. This exception class has the following subclasses that can be used to narrow the error criteria:
    - ❑ `SQLFeatureNotSupportedException`
    - ❑ `SQLNonTransientConnectionException`
    - ❑ `SQLDataException`
    - ❑ `SQLIntegrityConstraintViolationException`
    - ❑ `SQLInvalidAuthorizationSpecException`
    - ❑ `SQLSyntaxException`

- ▸ `SQLTransientException`: This exception is thrown when an SQL statement might succeed if retried without any intervention from the application. This class has the following subclasses:
    - ❑ `SQLTransientConnectionException`
    - ❑ `SQLTransientRollbackException`
    - ❑ `SQLTimeoutException`

- ▸ `SQLRecoverableException`: This exception is thrown when an application needs to perform a recovery action before retrying the SQL statements.

- ▸ `SQLClientInfoException`: This exception is thrown by the `Connection.setClientInfo` method, if any client property can't be set.

How to do it...

JDBC applications use try and catch blocks to handle errors. Only errors can be handled by catch blocks and not warnings.

1. Import the `DB2Diagnosable` and `DB2Sqlca` packages:

```
import com.ibm.db2.jcc.DB2Diagnosable;
import com.ibm.db2.jcc.DB2Sqlca;
```

2. By default, the error message text retrieved from the DB2 server is truncated to a fixed length. Set the following connection property to enable the full message text from the server:

```
String url = "jdbc:db2://localhost:50000/sample:retrieveMessagesFr
omServerOnGetMessage=true;";
```

3. The entire application logic that can generate any kind of error or exception can be coded in a try block.

```
try {
// application Logic
}
```

4. You can catch all exceptions of the `SQLException` class in a catch block.

```
catch (SQLException sqle) {
   // exception handling steps as explained in next step
}
```

5. Get the information about the exception using the methods provided by the `SQLException` class.

```
while(sqle != null) {
        System.out.println(sqle.getErrorCode());
      System.out.println(sqle.getSQLState());
      System.out.println(sqle.getMessage());
    sqle=sqle.getNextException();
}
```

6. Within the catch block, check whether the exception has DB2 driver-specific information by checking if `SQLException` is an instance of the `DB2Diagnosable` class. This can be checked as follows:

```
 if (sqle instanceof DB2Diagnosable) {
   // processing as explained in further steps
}
```

7. Cast the object to the `DB2Diagnosable` object:

```
com.ibm.db2.jcc.DB2Diagnosable diagnosable = (com.ibm.db2.jcc.
DB2Diagnosable)sqle;
```

8. Retrieve the `DB2Sqlca` object:

```
DB2Sqlca sqlca = diagnosable.getSqlca();
```

9. Get `SQLCODE`: This is the SQL error code, defined in DB2.

```
int sqlCode = sqlca.getSqlCode();
```

10. Get the `SQLERRMC` values: We can either get a string of all `SQLERRMC` values or a `String` array of the `SQLERRMC` values.

```
String sqlErrmc = sqlca.getSqlErrmc();
String[] sqlErrmcTokens = sqlca.getSqlErrmcTokens();

if (sqlErrmcTokens != null) {
  for (int i=0; i< sqlErrmcTokens.length; i++) {
    System.err.println (" token " + i + ": " +
sqlErrmcTokens[i]);
  }
}
```

11. Get the `SQLERRP` value: `SQLERRP` is a 3-letter identifier of the DB2 product, which is followed by five alphanumeric characters indicating the version, release, and the level of the product . If `SQLCODE` indicates an error condition, this field identifies the module that returned the error.

```
String sqlErrp = sqlca.getSqlErrp();
```

12. Get the `SQLERRD` value: It consists of six types of `INTEGER` variables that provide diagnostic information.

```
int[] sqlErrd = sqlca.getSqlErrd();
System.out.println (
  "SQLERRD(1): " + sqlErrd[0] + "\n" +
  "SQLERRD(2): " + sqlErrd[1] + "\n" +
  "SQLERRD(3): " + sqlErrd[2] + "\n" +
  "SQLERRD(4): " + sqlErrd[3] + "\n" +
  "SQLERRD(5): " + sqlErrd[4] + "\n" +
  "SQLERRD(6): " + sqlErrd[5] );
```

13. Get the `SQLWARN` values: This is a set of warning indicators, each containing a blank or a W:

```
char[] sqlWarn = sqlca.getSqlWarn();
System.err.println (
                "SQLWARN1: " + sqlWarn[0] + "\n" +
                "SQLWARN2: " + sqlWarn[1] + "\n" +
                "SQLWARN3: " + sqlWarn[2] + "\n" +
                "SQLWARN4: " + sqlWarn[3] + "\n" +
                "SQLWARN5: " + sqlWarn[4] + "\n" +
                "SQLWARN6: " + sqlWarn[5] + "\n" +
                "SQLWARN7: " + sqlWarn[6] + "\n" +
                "SQLWARN8: " + sqlWarn[7] + "\n" +
                "SQLWARN9: " + sqlWarn[8] + "\n" +
                "SQLWARNA: " + sqlWarn[9] );
```

14. Get the `SQLSTATE` values:

```
String sqlState = sqlca.getSqlState();
```

15. Get the error message:

```
String errMessage = sqlca.getMessage();
```

How it works...

Errors and warnings in DB2 are identified by examining the `SQLCODE` and `SQLSTATE` values. DB2 maintains error and warning details in a collection known as **SQLCA (SQL Communication Area)**. It maintains a separate SQLCA for each thread or database connection. DB2 updates SQLCA after the execution of every SQL statement. We can use the `com.ibm.db2.jcc.DB2Sqlca` class in Java applications, which is an encapsulation of SQLCA. The following methods are available in this class, which can be used to access individual members of SQLCA:

- `getMessage()`: Returns the error message text
- `getSqlCode()`: Returns an SQL error code value
- `getSqlErrd()`: Returns an array of the SQLCA SQLERRD element values
- `getSqlErrmc()`: Returns a string that contains the SQLCA SQLERRMC values, delimited with spaces
- `getSqlErrmcTokens()`: Returns an array, each element of which contains an SQLCA SQLERRMC token
- `getSqlErrp()`: Returns the SQLCA SQLERRP value
- `getSqlState()`: Returns the SQLCA SQLSTATE value
- `getSqlWarn()`: Returns an array, each element of which contains an SQLCA SQLWARN value

Error handling in Java applications is implemented by try/catch blocks. Error codes are retrieved by using the `DB2Sqlca` class methods that are then used to raise and handle Java exceptions

Handling SQL warnings

SQL warnings are not thrown as exceptions, so we need to check for warnings after executing SQL statements. We can use the `getWarnings()` methods available for `Connection`, `Statement`, `PreparedStatement`, `CallableStatement`, and `ResultSet` classes.

```
rs = stmt.executeQuery("SELECT * FROM EMPLOYEE");
SQLWarning sqlwarn = stmt.getWarnings();
while (sqlwarn != null) {
   System.out.println ("Warning description: " + sqlwarn.
getMessage());
   System.out.println ("SQLSTATE: " + sqlwarn.getSQLState());
   System.out.println ("Error code: " + sqlwarn.getErrorCode());
   sqlwarn=sqlwarn.getNextWarning();
}
```

Using SQLException subclasses

`SQLException` class is useful for capturing basic information about the exception. DB2 provides the `DB2Diagnosable` class that extends the `SQLException` class. This exception class can be used to capture more specific information about the exception:

1. Check if the exception is an instance of the `DB2Diangnonsable` exception class:

```
catch (SQLException sqle) {
   while(sqle != null) {
   if (sqle instanceof DB2Diagnosable) {
     System.out.println("DB2Diagnosable exception");
   }
}
```

2. Check if the exception is an instance of the `DB2Diagnosable` exception subclasses.

   ❑ The `SQL NonTransientException` exception is thrown when the retry of an operation would fail if corrective action is not taken.

```
if (sqle instanceof SQLNonTransientException) {
   System.out.println("SQLNonTransientException exception");
}
```

- The `SQLTransientException` exception is thrown when the failed statement might succeed if retried without any intervention from the application:

```
if (sqle instanceof SQLTransientException) {
   System.out.println("SQLTransientException exception");
}
```

- The `SQLRecoverableException` exception is thrown when the failed statement might succeed if the application performs some recovery action.

```
if (sqle instanceof SQLRecoverableException) {
   System.out.println("SQLRecoverableException exception");
}
```

- The `SQLClientInfoException` exception is thrown if any client information property cannot be set on a connection.

```
if (sqle instanceof SQLClientInfoException) {
   System.out.println("SQLClientInfoException exception");
}
```

2. Check if the exception can be classified into further subclasses

3. Check if the exception is an instance of the `SQLNonTransientException` exception class. If yes, then we can check if the exception is an instance of its subclasses.

```
if (sqle instanceof SQLNonTransientException) {
   System.out.println("SQLNonTransientException exception");
```

- The `SQLSyntaxErrorException` exception is thrown when there is any syntax error in the SQL statement.

```
if (sqle instanceof SQLSyntaxErrorException ) {
   System.out.println("SQLSyntaxErrorException  exception");
}
```

- The `SQLFeatureNotSupportedException` exception is thrown when the requested function is not supported by the JDBC driver.

```
if (sqle instanceof SQLFeatureNotSupportedException ) {
   System.out.println("SQLFeatureNotSupportedException
exception");
}
```

- The `SQLNonTransientConnectionException` exception is thrown when a connection operation fails.

```
if (sqle instanceof SQLNonTransientConnectionException ) {
   System.out.println("SQLNonTransientConnectionException
exception");
}
```

- ❏ The `SQLDataException` exception is thrown when any data error is encountered. For example, divide by zero error.

```
if (sqle instanceof SQLDataException ) {
   System.out.println("SQLDataException  exception");
}
```

- ❏ The `SQLIntegrityConstraintViolationException` exception is thrown when there is an integrity issue with the data.

```
if (sqle instanceof SQLIntegrityConstraintViolationException
) {
   System.out.println("SQLIntegrityConstraintViolationExcepti
on  exception");
}
```

- ❏ The `SQLInvalidAuthorizationSpecException` exception is thrown when the authorization credentials are invalid.

```
if (sqle instanceof SQLInvalidAuthorizationSpecException ) {
   System.out.println("SQLInvalidAuthorizationSpecException
exception");
}
}
```

4. Check if the exception is an instance of the `SQLTransientException` exception class. If yes, then we can check if the exception is an instance of its subclasses.

```
if (sqle instanceof SQLTransientException) {
   System.out.println("SQLTransientException exception");
```

- ❏ The `SQLTransientConnectionException` exception is thrown when a connection operation fails, but it might succeed if retried.

```
if (sqle instanceof SQLTransientConnectionException ) {
   System.out.println("SQLTransientConnectionException
exception");
}
```

- ❏ The `SQLTransactionRollbackException` exception is thrown when a transaction is rolled back because of a deadlock or some other issue.

```
if (sqle instanceof SQLTransactionRollbackException ) {
   System.out.println("SQLTransactionRollbackException
exception");
}
```

- ❏ The `SQLTimeoutException` exception is thrown when the timeout condition is encountered by a statement.

```
if (sqle instanceof SQLTimeoutException ) {
    System.out.println("SQLTimeoutException  exception");
  }
}
```

Developing Java applications for high availability

DB2 provides high availability solutions (also known as HA) to handle site failures. HA involves two clone servers that act as primary and secondary. When the primary server goes down, DB2 allows the secondary server to take over automatically. Once the secondary server takes over, the entire database traffic is automatically routed to the secondary server. This rerouting is implemented at the server and client side. In this recipe, we will discuss how we can make our Java applications use high-availability features to reroute to the secondary server.

Getting ready

The client applications can use the following features to achieve high availability:

- **Automatic client reroute**: The rerouting information that includes the information about the secondary server is available at the database server. At the client side, the client application uses this information for routing to the secondary server when the primary server goes down. This rerouting is also knows as failover .

- **Client affinity**: This failover solution is controlled by the client. We can configure client affinities for database applications in such a way that if the primary server goes down, the application reroutes the traffic to an alternate or secondary server. The information about the secondary server is configured at the client. The servers are chosen according to a specific order, configured at the client.

- **Workload balancing**: This feature is used to balance the workload among different servers in order to get better throughput. This is only available in DB2 `pureScale`.

The high-availability features are available for JDBC, SQLJ, and pureQuery applications. To implement the high-availability features, we need to use the IBM Data Server Driver for JDBC and SQLJ type-4 connectivity (version 3.58 or 4.8 or later).

To use the automatic client reroute feature, we need a connection from any one of the following interfaces:

- `javax.sql.DataSource`
- `javax.sql.ConnectionPoolDataSource`
- `javax.sql.XADataSource`
- `java.sql.DriverManager`

How to do it...

As discussed previously, we have three features that can be used to design high availability solutions in java applications. Let's discuss how we can implement each of them.

Configuring an automatic client reroute

If we are using the `DriverManager` interface for creating the database connection objects, then we can use the following steps to configure automatic rerouting:

1. Specify the server name and port number of the primary server in the connection URL.

    ```
    String url = "jdbc:db2://prmsrvr:50000/sample:user=dbuser;password
    =dbpassword;";
    ```

2. Specify the server name and the port number of the secondary or alternate server as the client reroute alternate server properties.

    ```
    props.setProperty("clientRerouteAlternateServerName", "secsrvr");
    props.setProperty("clientRerouteAlternatePortNumber", "51000") ;
    ```

3. Setting additional properties: Set the properties to specify the retry count and retry intervals.

    ```
    props.setProperty("maxRetriesForClientReroute", "3");
    props.setProperty("retryIntervalForClientReroute", "2") ;
    ```

If we are using the `DataSource` interface for creating database connection objects, then we can use the following steps to configure automatic reroute:

1. Specify the server name and port number of the primary server as the properties for the primary server.

    ```
    ds.setDriverType(4);
    ds.setServerName("mysrv.in.ibm.com");
    ds.setPortNumber("50000");
    ```

2. Specify the server name and port number of the secondary or alternate server as client reroute alternate server properties. We can set an array of alternate servers for rerouting:

    ```
    ds.setClientRerouteAlternateServerName("mysrv2.in.ibm.com");
    ds.setClientRerouteAlternatePortNumber("50002");
    ```

If we are using JNDI to get the data source, then we can configure JNDI for automatic client rerouting as follows:

1. Create a starting context, required for JNDI naming operations:

```
InitialContext registry = new InitialContext();
```

2. Create a DB2ClientRerouteServerList object

```
DB2ClientRerouteServerList serverAddress = new
DB2ClientRerouteServerList();
```

3. Set the primary and alternate server information

```
serverAddress.setPrimaryPortNumber(50000);
serverAddress.setPrimaryServerName("mysrv.in.ibm.com");

int[] port = {50002};
String[] server = {" mysrv2.in.ibm.com"};
serverAddress.setAlternatePortNumber(port);
serverAddress.setAlternateServerName(server);
```

4. Register and assign JNDI names for the alternate server list

```
registry.rebind("serverList", serverAddress);
datasource.setClientRerouteServerListJNDIName("serverList");
```

Configuring client affinity

1. Create a connection URL for the primary server:

```
String url = "jdbc:db2://prmsrvr:50000/sample:user=dbuser;password
=dbpassword;";
```

2. Enable support for client affinity in Java applications:

```
props.setProperty("enableClientAffinitiesList",
"DB2BaseDataSource.YES (1)");
```

3. Set the properties to specify alternate server details:

```
props.setProperty("clientRerouteAlternateServerName", "secsrvr");
props.setProperty("clientRerouteAlternatePortNumber", "51000") ;
```

 We can also set multiple servers for client affinity so that the application keeps on retrying until it gets a connection.

```
props.setProperty("clientRerouteAlternateServerName",
"host1,host2,host3");
props.setProperty("clientRerouteAlternatePortNumber", "
port1,port2,port3");
```

4. Set the additional properties to control the retry count and retry intervals:

```
props.setProperty("maxRetriesForClientReroute", "3");
props.setProperty("retryIntervalForClientReroute", "2") ;
```

5. Optional: Set the seamless failover mode. If seamless failover is enabled, then no warning is returned when the failover happens.

```
props.setProperty("enableSeamlessFailover", "DB2BaseDataSource.YES
(1)");
```

Workload balancing by using DB2 pureScale

To configure the client application to exploit the workload balancing provided by DB2 `pureScale`, we need to connect to a member of the `pureScale` instance and set additional properties to enable workload balancing and the maximum number of connections. The Java applications support transaction-level workload balancing.

1. Create a URL to connect to a `pureScale` instance:

```
String url = "jdbc:db2://prmsrvr:50000/sample:user=dbuser;password
=dbpassword;";
```

2. Enable the support for workload balancing in Java applications:

```
props.setProperty("enableSysplexWLB", "true");
```

3. Set the maximum number of connections required:

```
props.setProperty("maxTransportObjects", "100");
```

4. Optional: Set the additional global properties to fine-tune the configuration. These properties are specified in the driver configuration property file and hence are globally applied.

   ❑ `db2.jcc.maxRefreshInterval`: The time interval for refreshing the server list at the client. The default is 30.

   ❑ `db2.jcc.maxTransportObjectIdleTime`: The maximum time required to wait before an idle transport is dropped.

   ❑ `db2.jcc.maxTransportObjectWaitTime`: The maximum time required for a client to wait for a transport to become available.

   ❑ `db2.jcc.minTransportObjects`: The lower limit of the number of transport objects in a global transport pool.

How it works...

Automatic client rerouting and *Client affinity* solutions are very much similar. The only difference between the two is the location where the information about secondary server is maintained. These two are intended for maintaining application uptime even when primary server goes down. On the other hand, workload balancing is used to balance the total system load between multiple servers to get better performance. Let's discuss the two concepts in detail.

Automatic client rerouting

The key to automatic client rerouting is in knowing the alternate servers. DB2 gets this information when the first connection is made. If the `clientRerouteAlternateServerName` and `clientRerouteAlternatePortNumber` properties are set, then DB2 loads them into memory along with the primary server details. If alternate server details are not set, and if `clientRerouteServerListJNDIName` is available at the data source, then DB2 gets the primary and alternate server information from the JNDI directory and loads them into memory. If the server information is not available in JNDI as well, then DB2 checks DNS tables for the primary and alternate server details and loads them into memory, if found. If no primary and alternate server information is available in any way, then the connection cannot be established and the DB2 driver throws an exception. For subsequent connections, DB2 gets the information about primary and alternate server details from the driver memory.

Once DB2 has the information about the primary and secondary servers, it attempts to make a connection with the primary server. If this connection attempt fails, it retries the connection to the same primary server, depending on the values of the `maxRetriesForClientReroute` and `retryIntervalForClientReroute` properties. If the connection to the primary still fails, it routes to the alternate server and attempts to get a connection with the alternate server. This attempt is followed by the subsequent attempts, depending on the values of the `maxRetriesForClientReroute` and `retryIntervalForClientReroute` properties. If the failover is successful, DB2 returns an `SQLWarning` to indicate the failover. If the failover is seamless, no warning is returned. We can use the `DB2Connection.alternateWasUsedOnConnect` method to determine whether alternate server information was used to establish the connection. After the successful failover, the driver memory is updated with the new primary and secondary server information.

Workload balancing in a pureScale environment

When the client establishes the first connection to any member of the `pureScale` instance, it gets the list of member servers with the connection details such as the server name, port numbers, and weight. Before starting a new transaction, the client reads a cached server list to identify a server with unused capacity. It then looks for an idle transport object for the above-identified member server. If no idle transport object is found, then the member server tries to allocate a new transport object.

If a new transport object cannot be allocated, depending upon the maximum size of the transport pool, then an error is returned to the application. If an idle transport object is found, then the client uses this transport object to associate the connection. The transaction uses the associated transport object to run. When the transaction ends, the client checks whether the transport object can be reused for other transactions. This reusability of transport objects is configured at the server. If the transport object is reusable, then the server sends a list of instructions that can be applied to the execution environment of the connection.

These instructions initialize special register values. The client replays these instructions to create the execution environment. When not in use, the client disassociates with the transport object. The client copy of the server list is refreshed when a new connection is made to the `pureScale` instance. This can also be controlled by setting the refresh interval. This process is repeated for any incoming transaction.

Using SSL in Java applications

Secure Socket layer (**SSL**) is a security mechanism that creates a secured channel between an application and the database. The data transmitted across this channel is encrypted and hence secure. The IBM Data Server Driver for JDBC and SQLJ provides support for using SSL connections in Java applications. In this recipe, we will discuss how to set up SSL at the database server and how to enable a Java application to make use of it.

Getting ready

The following are the prerequisites for this recipe:

1. The IBM Data Server Driver for JDBC and SQLJ needs to be installed (this is installed by default as part of the DB2 installation).

2. Java Secure Socket Extension needs to be installed (the IBM JSSE provider is also automatically installed as part of the DB2 installation).

3. The IBM Global Security Kit (GSKit) must be installed on the server.

How to do it...

In this recipe, we will see how we can configure server-side and client-side Java environments to support SSL connections. We will also see how to configure DB2 to allow secured connections.

Step 1: Configuring JRE for SSL Support

1. Configure JRE for Java security providers by adding entries in the `java.security` file. The format of an entry is as follows:

   ```
   security.provider.n=provider-package-name
   ```

2. If we need FIPS (Federal Information Processing Standard) compatibility, then add an entry for the `IBMJCEFIPS` provider to the `java.security` file before the entry of the IBMJCE provider.

   ```
   security.provider.1=com.ibm.jsse2.IBMJSSEProvider2
   security.provider.2=com.ibm.crypto.fips.provider.IBMJCEFIPS
   security.provider.3=com.ibm.crypto.provider.IBMJCE
   ```

3. If we don't need FIPS compatibility, then add an entry for the IBMJSSE2Provider provider to the `java.security` file. Make sure that the security file also has an entry for the IBMJCE provider. With IBM SDK for Java 1.4.3 onwards, these provider entries are present by default in the `java.security` file.

```
security.provider.1=com.ibm.jsse2.IBMJSSEProvider2
security.provider.2=com.ibm.crypto.provider.IBMJCE
```

Based on the security providers, we will create a key database. A key database is a file that the server uses to store key pairs and certificates. One database file can hold multiple key pairs and certificates. CMS is the most commonly used key database type. This type is provided by the following provider:

```
security.provider.X=com.ibm.security.cmskeystore.CMSProvider
```

For this recipe, the `java.security` file has the following security providers:

```
security.provider.1=com.ibm.jsse2.IBMJSSEProvider2
security.provider.2=com.ibm.crypto.provider.IBMJCE
security.provider.3=com.ibm.security.cmskeystore.CMSProvider
```

4. If we need FIPS compatibility, then we need to enable FIPS mode. To enable FIPS mode, set the Java system's property com.ibm.jsse2.JSSEFIPS to true.

```
com.ibm.jsse2.JSSEFIPS=true
```

5. Configure JRE for SSL socket factory providers: Add the following entries in the `java.security` file.

```
ssl.SocketFactory.provider=provider-package-name
ssl.ServerSocketFactory.provider=provider-package-name
```

   ❑ If we need FIPS mode in the IBMJSSE2 provider, then we use:

```
ssl.SocketFactory.provider=com.ibm.jsse2.
SSLSocketFactoryImpl
ssl.ServerSocketFactory.provider=com.ibm.jsse2.
SSLServerSocketFactoryImpl
```

   ❑ If we need FIPS mode in the Sun JSSE provider, then we use:

```
ssl.SocketFactory.provider=com.sun.net.ssl.internal.ssl.
SSLSocketFactoryImpl
ssl.ServerSocketFactory.provider=com.sun.net.ssl.internal.
ssl.SSLServerSocketFactoryImpl
```

   ❑ And if we need FIPS mode in the IBMJSSE2 provider, we can go ahead as follows:

```
ssl.SocketFactory.provider=com.ibm.jsse2.
SSLSocketFactoryImpl
ssl.ServerSocketFactory.provider=com.ibm.jsse2.
SSLServerSocketFactoryImpl
```

Step 2: Setting up the server environment

1. **Configuring the system environment variables**: Set the following environment variables to include the GSKit libraries:

    ❑ `JAVA_HOME`: Add the JRE path, which is installed with DB2.

       `JAVA_HOME= $JAVA_HOME; C:\Program Files\IBM\SQLLIB\java\jdk\jre;`

    ❑ `PATH`: Include the GSKit library location.

       `PATH = C:\Program Files\IBM\gsk7\lib;$PATH;`

    ❑ `CLASSPATH`: Include the GSKit classes:

       `CLASSPATH= C:\Program Files\IBM\gsk7\classes\cfwk.zip;C:\Program Files\IBM\gsk7\classes\gsk7cls.jar;$CLASSPATH;`

    ❑ `LIB`: Add the GSKit libraries.

       `LIB = C:\Program Files\IBM\gsk7\lib;$LIB ;`

2. **Creating a server keystore and certificate**: We can proceed as follows:

    ❑ Start the IBM Key Management utility: This executable is available in the `C:\Program Files\IBM\gsk7\bin` directory as `gsk7ikm.exe`.

❑ Create a new key database file, `key.kdb`, of the type CMS.

❑ Choose a password. Make sure you select the **Stash password to a file** option.

❑ Create a new certificate by clicking on the new self-signed button. We can use any name for the certificate. The optional fields can be ignored.

❑ View the certificate by first clicking on the certificate and then clicking on the **View/Edit** button.

❑ Extract the certificate as `cert.arm`.

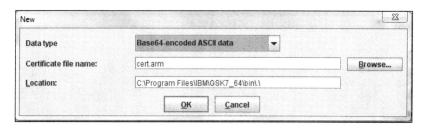

3. **Configuring the DB2 environment** : Proceed as follows:

   ❑ Update the following database manager configuration parameters with these values:

   ```
   UPDATE DBM CFG USING SSL_SVR_KEYDB C:\key.kdb
   UPDATE DBM CFG USING SSL_SVR_STASH C:\key.sth
   UPDATE DBM CFG USING SSL_SVR_LABEL MYSSLLBL
   UPDATE DBM CFG USING SSL_SVCENAME 30112
   ```

   ❑ Set the DB2COMM special register value to SSL.

   ```
   db2set DB2COMM=SSL
   ```

   ❑ Restart the DB2 instance:

   ```
   db2stop force
   db2start
   ```

If the instance starts without any error or warning, it means DB2 is now configured for SSL connections.

```
C:\Windows\system32>db2 "UPDATE DBM CFG USING SSL_SVR_KEYDB C:\key.kdb"
DB20000I  The UPDATE DATABASE MANAGER CONFIGURATION command completed
successfully.

C:\Windows\system32>db2 "UPDATE DBM CFG USING SSL_SVR_STASH C:\key.sth"
DB20000I  The UPDATE DATABASE MANAGER CONFIGURATION command completed
successfully.

C:\Windows\system32>db2 "UPDATE DBM CFG USING SSL_SVR_LABEL MYSSLLBL"
DB20000I  The UPDATE DATABASE MANAGER CONFIGURATION command completed
successfully.

C:\Windows\system32>db2 "UPDATE DBM CFG USING SSL_SVCENAME 30112"
DB20000I  The UPDATE DATABASE MANAGER CONFIGURATION command completed
successfully.

C:\Windows\system32>db2set DB2COMM=SSL

C:\Windows\system32>db2stop force
08/31/2011 02:17:09     0   0   SQL1064N  DB2STOP processing was successful.
SQL1064N  DB2STOP processing was successful.

C:\Windows\system32>db2start
08/31/2011 02:17:15     0   0   SQL1063N  DB2START processing was successful.
SQL1063N  DB2START processing was successful.
```

Step 3: Setting up the client environment

Before we can use SSL connections in Java applications, we need to configure the Java runtime environment (JRE) to use SSL.

1. Import the certificate from the database server to the Java trust store on the client. This can be done by using the keytool utility to import the certificate. For example, if we want to import the certificate stored in `cert.arm`, then we can use the following command, which will store this certificate in the trust store `mycerts`.

    ```
    keytool -import -file cert.arm -keystore mycerts
    ```

    ```
    C:\>keytool -import -file cert.arm -keystore keystore
    Enter keystore password:
    Re-enter new password:
    Owner: CN=Sanju
    Issuer: CN=Sanju
    Serial number: 4e5802ca
    Valid from: 8/27/11 2:02 AM until: 8/26/12 2:02 AM
    Certificate fingerprints:
             MD5:  40:C6:B5:17:F8:AF:58:B1:B9:EB:05:3E:7A:3F:F5:81
             SHA1: 41:E3:0E:38:11:AA:13:8D:67:B9:86:FC:AA:F7:05:49:D6:E1:E3:51
    Trust this certificate? [no]:  yes
    Certificate was added to keystore

    C:\>_
    ```

2. Configure the Java system properties to use the trust store. Set the following properties to configure JRE to use the trust store:

    ❏ `javax.net.ssl.trustStore`: This specifies the name of the trust store.

    ❏ `javax.net.ssl.trustStorePassword`: This specifies the password for the trust store.

Alternatively, we can use the following command to execute the client program with SSL support

```
java -Djavax.net.ssl.trustStore=mycerts -Djavax.net.ssl.
trustStorePassword=mypasword sampleProgram
```

This can also be included in applications directly.

Step 4: Configuring connections to use SSL

To configure database connections to use SSL, we need to set the `sslConnection` property to `true`.

```
java.util.Properties properties = new java.util.Properties();
properties.put("user", "db2user");
properties.put("password", "password");
properties.put("sslConnection", "true");
java.sql.Connection con = java.sql.DriverManager.getConnection(url,
properties);
```

We can also set some optional properties to identify the location of the trust store by setting the `sslTrustStoreLocation` and `sslTrustStorePassword` properties.

How it works...

SSL is a security communication protocol that provides mechanisms for message encryption, integrity, and authentication.

- Authentication is achieved by verifying the certificates which are issued by a trusted certificate authority.
- Message encryption is achieved by using a symmetric key. A symmetric key allows encryption and decryption of a message using the same key.
- Message integrity is achieved by using a message digest or a hash checksum.

SSL uses public key cryptography for a handshake between the client and server. In this technique, each participant has its own public key and private key. A message encrypted by one's public key can only be decrypted by its private key.

The following steps are involved in SSL handshake:

1. The client sends a hello message to the server. This hello message has information about the SSL version, cipher suites, and hashing protocols supported by the client.
2. The server responds with a hello message that includes the chosen SSL version, cipher suite, and hashing algorithm details. The server also sends its certificate, which includes a server's public key.
3. The client verifies the server's certificate and ensures its identity.
4. The client sends a random number to the server. This is encrypted by using the server's public key. This random number will be used by the client and server to generate a symmetric key.
5. The server receives the random number decrypting the message received from the client.
6. The client sends a finish message, indicating to the server that all further messages will be encrypted by the symmetric key.
7. The server sends a finish message, indicating to the client that all further messages will be encrypted by the symmetric key.
8. Now the server and client both have the same symmetric key, which will be used for encryption and decryption of data, thus creating a secured communication channel.
9. With each message, the server and client also sends a message digest generated by the hash function. When this message is received, the client/server generates a new digest and compares it with the message digest received. This ensures the integrity of the message.

6

DB2 9.7 Application Enablement

In this chapter, we will focus on the DB2 9.7 application enablement recipes, which help our other data server developer community to effortlessly code or enable the application on to DB2 data server.

We will cover the following recipes:

- First step towards enabling Oracle application to DB2 9.7
- Using ROWNUM and DUAL in DB2 9.7
- Using CUR_COMMIT concurrency-control isolation level
- Implementing hierarchical queries for recursion support
- Using PL/SQL ANONYMOUS block statements
- Handling RAISE_APPLICATION_ERROR in DB2 PL/SQL
- Migrating Oracle database objects on to DB2 9.7
- Porting multi-action triggers from Oracle to DB2 9.7

Introduction

DB2 9.7 introduces numerous features, which greatly reduce the application developer efforts, while enabling the application from a different data server to DB2. Earlier, DB2 9.5 introduced many features including implicit casting, synonym for DISCTINCT, EXCEPT, and SEQUENCES, global variables in packages, ARRAY collections, and large RID, ROWID support for fast enablement. Now in DB2 9.7, we have many more features, which can be enabled by setting the new DB2 registry variable, DB2_COMPATIBILITY_VECTOR, to a specific value, based on the need.

First step towards enabling Oracle application to DB2 9.7

The new DB2 registry variable, DB2_COMPATIBILITY_VECTOR, can be used to enable one or more compatibility features. These features bottom out the effort of an application developer, while migrating the code written for other relational databases to DB2 9.5 or later.

Getting ready

You need to have the SYSADM privilege on the instance, which needs the compatibility feature to be enabled.

How to do it...

The DB2 registry variable, DB2_COMPATIBILITY_VECTOR, takes hexadecimal value 00 to FFFF. To take advantage of the DB2 compatibility feature for **Oracle** applications, use ORA, and for **Sybase** applications use SYB. The first step towards setting the DB2 9.7 database for the other data server compatibility, includes setting the registry settings at instance level.

1. Setting the instance-level registry for compatibility, we can only set any one of the following, based on the requirement, ORA in case of Oracle to DB2, and SYB in case of Sybase to DB2.

   ```
   db2set DB2_COMPATIBILITY_VECTOR=ORA
   ```

   ```
   db2set DB2_COMPATIBILITY_VECTOR=SYB
   ```

2. An optional complier registry variable, DB2_DEFERRED_PREPARE_SEMANTICS, can be set to enhance the compatibility between Oracle and DB2 applications. When set to YES, the dynamic SQL statements will be evaluated in an OPEN or an EXECUTE call, instead of evaluating at the PREPARE phase. This setting is pretty much required in order to use the DB2 feature called **implicit casting**, which will automatically convert the data of one type to another, based on the conversion rule. If this is not set, the PREPARE phase may fail when un-typed parameter markers are present. The un-typed parameter markers are parameter markers, which are specified without a target data type.

   ```
   db2set DB2_DEFERRED_PREPARE_SEMANTICS=YES
   ```

3. An instance restart is mandatory after enabling the compatibility feature to take effect.

   ```
   Force applications all
   db2stop
   db2start
   ```

4. Now create a `UNICODE` database, which supports PL/SQL statements and new data types.

   ```
   db2sampl -xml -sql
   ```

5. We can enable the `set` decimal floating-point rounding database-configuration parameter to make our setup look similar to Oracle. By default, `DECFLT_ROUNDING` is set to `ROUND_HALF_EVEN`, but Oracle decimal rounding works similar to `ROUND_HALF_UP`.

   ```
   UPDATE DB CFG FOR SAMPLE USING DECFLT_ROUNDING ROUND_HALF_UP
   ```

```
D:\>db2set DB2_COMPATIBILITY_VECTOR=ORA

D:\>db2set DB2_DEFERRED_PREPARE_SEMANTICS=YES

D:\>db2stop
06/18/2011 12:39:00     0   0   SQL1064N  DB2STOP processing was successful.
SQL1064N  DB2STOP processing was successful.

D:\>db2start
06/18/2011 12:50:06     0   0   SQL1063N  DB2START processing was successful.
SQL1063N  DB2START processing was successful.

D:\>db2sampl -sql -xml

  Creating database "SAMPLE"...
  Connecting to database "SAMPLE"...
  Creating tables and data in schema "MOHAN"...
  Creating tables with XML columns and XML data in schema "MOHAN"...

  'db2sampl' processing complete.
```

6. Once we have the database readily configured for Oracle compatibility, we can connect to the database just as Oracle does, and also DB2 in the traditional way. The Oracle way is to invoke `clpplus` from the command window.

   ```
   clpplus
   ```

7. The command `clpplus` launches Oracle like the SQL window to key in the connection string, such as the username, the server host name, and the port number at which the database is listening, and also the database name.

CONNECT <username>@<server hostname>:<port number>/<database name>;

```
CLPPlus: Version 1.4
Copyright (c) 2009, 2011, IBM CORPORATION.  All rights reserved.

SQL> CONNECT mohan@INLAPGS0049:50001/sample;
Enter password: **********


Database Connection Information :
---------------------------------
Hostname = INLAPGS0049
Database server = DB2/NT  SQL09074
SQL authorization ID = mohan
Local database alias = SAMPLE
Port = 50001

SQL> |
```

How it works...

To allow an application running on Oracle or Sybase to run on DB2 9.7 with a different locking mechanism, data types and PL/SQL statements are virtually made simple, as all these steps have been taken care of in the DB2 settings that we performed earlier. So, changes to an application are really exceptional, instead of just a rule.

There's more...

One can set the `DB2_COMPATIBILITY_VECTOR` variable to a required value based on the need, instead of enabling all the compatibility features. If DB2 compatibility features are enabled, some SQL statements may have a change in behavior.

The following table depicts the complete values for the `DB2_COMPATIBILITY_VECTOR`:

Hexadecimal value	Bit position	Compatibility feature
0x01	1	ROWNUM
0x02	2	DUAL
0x04	3	Outer join
0x08	4	Hierarchical queries
0x10	5	NUMBER data type
0x20	6	VARCHAR2 data type
0x40	7	DATE data type
0x80	8	TRUNCATE table
0x100	9	Character literals
0x200	10	Collection methods
0x400	11	Data dictionary compatible views
0x800	12	PL/SQL compilation
0x1000	13	Insensitive cursor
0x2000	14	INOUT parameter

Using ROWNUM and DUAL in DB2 9.7

The ROWNUM and DUAL supports are enabled by setting the DB2_COMPATIBILITY_VECTOR registry variable to ORA.

Oracle programmers use ROWNUM quite often to retrieve a controlled number of rows from a SQL statement. The same can be applied in DB2 9.7.

Getting ready

Enable the compatibility feature by setting the DB2_COMPATIBILITY_VECTOR registry to ORA.

How to do it...

In earlier versions of DB2, when we wanted to return only a specific number of rows of an SQL statement, we used the FETCH FIRST clause. Now that we have the Oracle compatibility feature enabled in DB2 9.7, we can use ROWNUM as in Oracle. In DB2, ROWNUM supports <, >, >=, <=, =, and BETWEEN operators.

We can combine ROWID and ROWNUM together to display the physical address of the row in the database. This value is a unique identifier of the row, and does not change over until a REORG occurs on the table.

Let's start using the ROWNUM on the existing sample database tables. With ROWNUM, we can easily fetch the actual row that we want to read. In the following example, we are retrieving the first row and fifteenth row of the table. In the earlier versions of DB2, we only had the option to use the FETCH FIRST n ROWS ONLY statement to do it, but not to accurately get the row that we wanted.

```
SELECT EMPNO, FIRSTNME, LASTNAME, WORKDEPT, SALARY FROM EMPLOYEE WHERE
ROWNUM <2;
```

```
SELECT EMPNO, FIRSTNME, LASTNAME, WORKDEPT, SALARY FROM EMPLOYEE WHERE
ROWNUM=15;
```

It was difficult to fetch a couple of rows in the middle of a table, unless we had a right to filter the column to choose. Now, it is so simple to fetch data using ROWNUM with the BETWEEN operator.

```
SELECT EMPNO, FIRSTNME, LASTNAME, WORKDEPT, SALARY FROM EMPLOYEE WHERE
ROWNUM BETWEEN 6 AND 8;
```

```
SELECT ROWID, EMPNO, FIRSTNME, LASTNAME, WORKDEPT, SALARY FROM EMPLOYEE
WHERE ROWNUM BETWEEN 6 AND 8;
```

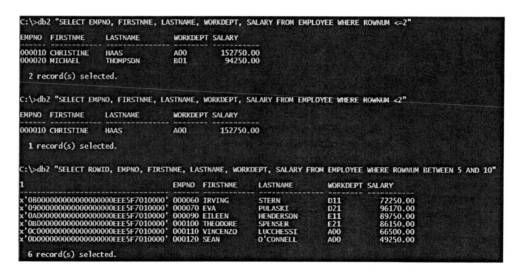

We can also use ROWNUM while performing the UPDATE and the DELETE operations.

```
UPDATE EMPLOYEES SET EDLEVEL=50 WHERE EDLEVEL=12 AND ROWNUM <=1000;
```

```
C:\>db2 "SELECT EDLEVEL, COUNT(*) FROM EMPLOYEES GROUP BY EDLEVEL"

EDLEVEL 2
------- -----------
     12        3072
     14        7168
     15        2048
     16       14336
     17        7168
     18        7168
     19        1024
     20        1024

  8 record(s) selected.

C:\>db2 "UPDATE EMPLOYEES SET EDLEVEL=50 WHERE EDLEVEL=12 AND ROWNUM <=1000"
DB20000I  The SQL command completed successfully.

C:\>db2 "SELECT EDLEVEL, COUNT(*) FROM EMPLOYEES GROUP BY EDLEVEL"

EDLEVEL 2
------- -----------
     12        2072
     14        7168
     15        2048
     16       14336
     17        7168
     18        7168
     19        1024
     20        1024
     50        1000

  9 record(s) selected.
```

In the previous example, we were able to update only the first `1000` records out of the `3072` records. This wasn't possible in the earlier versions of DB2, without using a cursor. Similarly, one can perform the `DELETE` action of only a couple of records in the matching record set.

We are very familiar with using `SYSIBM.SYSDUMMY1` as a dummy table. Now we have an Oracle-like `DUAL` dummy table available to make Oracle customers happy.

```
SELECT 31 * 24 * 60 AS MINUTESINMONTH FROM SYSIBM.SYSDUMMY1;
SELECT 31 * 24 * 60 AS MINUTESINMONTH FROM DUAL;
```

```
C:\>db2 "SELECT 31 * 24 * 60 AS MINUTESINMONTH FROM SYSIBM.SYSDUMMY1"

MINUTESINMONTH
--------------
         44640

  1 record(s) selected.

C:\>db2 "SELECT 31 * 24 * 60 AS MINUTESINMONTH FROM DUAL"

MINUTESINMONTH
--------------
         44640

  1 record(s) selected.
```

How it works...

In Oracle, you can use ROWNUM only with < and <= operators, but DB2 supports all of the major operators for ROWNUM. The DB2 base developers can still use the DB2-specific syntax to get the number of records, using SELECT .... FETCH FIRST <n> ROWS ONLY.

There's more...

Starting from DB2 9.7.2, we can use the LIMIT and the OFFSET syntax to fetch a limited number of rows in an SQL statement.

To enable the LIMIT and the OFFSET syntax of MySQL, DBA has to set the DB2 registry variable DB2_COMPATIBILITY_VECTOR to MYS, and restart the instance.

```
db2set DB2_COMPATIBILITY_VECTOR=MYS

db2stop

db2start
```

The LIMIT clause helps while limiting number of records to be retrieved from a table, and OFFSET helps in skipping a number of rows from the beginning and retrieving records.

```
SELECT EMPNO, FIRSTNME, LASTNAME, WORKDEPT, SALARY FROM EMPLOYEE LIMIT 2

SELECT EMPNO, FIRSTNME, LASTNAME, WORKDEPT, SALARY FROM EMPLOYEE LIMIT 2
OFFSET 5
```

```
C:\>db2 "SELECT EMPNO, FIRSTNME, LASTNAME, WORKDEPT, SALARY FROM EMPLOYEE LIMIT 2"

EMPNO  FIRSTNME     LASTNAME         WORKDEPT SALARY
------ ------------ ---------------- -------- -----------
000010 CHRISTINE    HAAS             A00         152750.00
000020 MICHAEL      THOMPSON         B01          94250.00

  2 record(s) selected.

C:\>db2 "SELECT EMPNO, FIRSTNME, LASTNAME, WORKDEPT, SALARY FROM EMPLOYEE LIMIT 2 OFFSET 5"

EMPNO  FIRSTNME     LASTNAME         WORKDEPT SALARY
------ ------------ ---------------- -------- -----------
000070 EVA          PULASKI          D21          96170.00
000090 EILEEN       HENDERSON        E11          89750.00

  2 record(s) selected.
```

Using CUR_COMMIT concurrency control isolation level

DB2 9.7 introduces a new isolation level called **Currently Committed** (**CC**), wherein readers don't block writers, and writers don't block readers. In earlier versions of DB2, there were chances that a reader would block a writer and a writer would block a reader.

The isolation level currently committed will be set at the database level using the CUR_ COMMIT parameter. When one creates a database on DB2 9.7, by default, CUR_COMMIT will be ON, and in case if one migrates the database from an older version on to DB2 9.7, one has to update the configuration parameter explicitly.

Getting ready

To update the database configuration parameter CUR_COMMIT, one should have the SYSADM or the DBADM privilege.

How to do it...

In this section, we'll look at extracting the current database configuration parameter CUR_COMMIT, and update it, if it's not active. We will also look at the ways of overriding the database-level parameter at the application layer.

1. As the first step towards setting the new isolation level, update the database configuration parameter CUR_COMMIT to ON, in case if you have migrated the database from older versions of DB2. Otherwise, the parameter is ON by default in DB2 9.7.

    UPDATE DB CFG FOR SAMPLE USING CUR_COMMIT ON

    GET DB CFG FOR SAMPLE SHOW DETAIL

    ```
    Auto-Revalidation                      (AUTO_REVAL)     = DEFERRED      DEFERRED
    Currently Committed                    (CUR_COMMIT)     = ON            ON
    CHAR output with DECIMAL input         (DEC_TO_CHAR_FMT) = NEW          NEW
    Enable XML Character operations        (ENABLE_XMLCHAR) = YES           YES
    WLM Collection Interval (minutes)      (WLM_COLLECT_INT) = 0            0
    ```

2. At the application level, one can override the database configuration setting, using the :db2dsdriver.cfg settings.

    ```
    <parameter name="ConcurrentAccessResolution" value=" 0 |
    CurrentlyCommitted |
      WaitForOutcome | SkipLockedData"/>
    ```

    Once you set the ConcurrentAccessResolution to CurrentlyCommitted, the database manager uses the currently committed version of the data. The special registry variables DB2_EVALUNCOMMITTED, DB2_SKIPDELETED, and DB2_ SKIPINSERTED do not provide much value when we have currently committed the version available.

4. Let's try working on two tables in parallel along with turning AUTO COMMIT off. In **Session #1**, execute a DML UPDATE statement on table T1, and in **Session #2**, execute a DML UPDATE statement on table T2. You will see DMLs running successfully in both sessions, but please be aware the we turned off AUTO COMMIT for both the statements. Even though the statements ran successfully, they are not committed yet. Now, let's run SELECT on table T2 from **Session #1**, and T1 from **Session #2**. This is a very good example to create a **deadlock** in a RDBMS. Are you not expecting a deadlock situation in DB2 9.7?

Session #1

```
db2 +c "UPDATE T1 SET ID=10 WHERE ID=5"
db2 +c "SELECT ID, COUNT(*) FROM T2 GROUP BY ID"
```

Session #2

```
db2 +c "UPDATE T2 SET ID=10 WHERE ID=5"
db2 +c "SELECT ID, COUNT(*) FROM T1 GROUP BY ID"
```

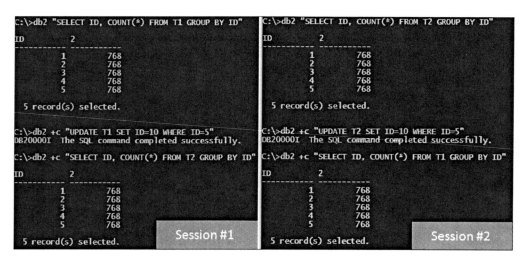

Surprised not to see a deadlock? This is what happens in DB2 9.7. Readers will never block the writer, and writers will never block the reader. The only blockers in DB2 9.7 are the writers blocking another writer. In this case, DB2 managed to retrieve the last committed data from the log buffer or from the active transaction log file.

How it works...

In DB2 9.7, there has been an enhancement in the LOCK attribute to identify the log record, which modified the row. In the case of any lock conflict, the lock manager will provide the log record detail, to fetch the last committed data.

Implementing hierarchical queries for recursion support

The hierarchical query is a new type of SQL statement in DB2 9.7, which enables the retrieval of the hierarchical data. One can enable this feature by setting the DB2_COMPATIBILITY_ VECTOR registry variable to ORA.

We can build the hierarchical queries by using the CONNECT BY clause, pseudo columns such as LEVEL, unary operators such as CONNECT_BY_ROOT and PRIOR, and using a new scalar function, SYS_CONNECT_BY_PATH.

Getting ready

We will run though CONNECT BY, LEVEL, CONNECT_BY_ROOT, and PRIOR to see how easy it is to get the hierarchical data in DB 9.7

How to do it...

If a database table contains hierarchical data, then we can use hierarchical queries to extract the data in a hierarchical order. Let's go through an example, and understand how to use it.

1. In most of the organizations, we will have hierarchical reporting structure. Let's create a table to capture all the employee information, and key in the employee details for analysis:

```
CREATE TABLE HQEMPLOYEE (
   EMPID INTEGER NOT NULL PRIMARY KEY,
   FIRSTNAME VARCHAR (10),
   LASTNAME VARCHAR (10),
   SALARY DECIMAL (8, 2),
   MGRID INTEGER);

INSERT INTO HQEMPLOYEE VALUES (1, 'John', 'Brett', 66000, 6);
INSERT INTO HQEMPLOYEE VALUES (2, 'Peter', 'Robert', 35000, 5);
INSERT INTO HQEMPLOYEE VALUES (3, 'Kim', 'Reynolds', 40000, 5);
```

```
INSERT INTO HQEMPLOYEE VALUES (4, 'Lindsey', 'Bowen', 80000,
NULL);

INSERT INTO HQEMPLOYEE VALUES (5, 'Paul', 'Taylor', 80000, 4);

INSERT INTO HQEMPLOYEE VALUES (6, 'Tim', 'Johnson',  41000, 5);

INSERT INTO HQEMPLOYEE VALUES (7, 'Lauren', 'Brook', 36000, 5);

INSERT INTO HQEMPLOYEE VALUES (8, 'Smith', 'Wright', 34000, 4);

INSERT INTO HQEMPLOYEE VALUES (9, 'Mohan', 'Kumar', 50000, 5);
```

2. If the requirement is to find all the employees working for Lindsey, as well as to display the reporting chain, this can easily be achieved using the following hierarchical queries:

```
SELECT FIRSTNAME,
    LEVEL, SALARY,
    CONNECT_BY_ROOT FIRSTNAME AS ROOT,
    SUBSTR (SYS_CONNECT_BY_PATH (FIRSTNAME, '->'), 1, 25) AS CHAIN
    FROM HQEMPLOYEE
    START WITH FIRSTNAME = 'Lindsey'
    CONNECT BY PRIOR EMPID = MGRID
    ORDER SIBLINGS BY SALARY
```

```
C:\>db2 -tvf HQ2.txt
SELECT FIRSTNAME, LEVEL, SALARY, CONNECT_BY_ROOT FIRSTNAME AS ROOT, SUBSTR(SYS_CONNECT_BY_PATH(FIRSTNAME, '->'), 1, 25)
AS CHAIN FROM HQEMPLOYEE START WITH FIRSTNAME = 'Lindsey' CONNECT BY PRIOR EMPID = MGRID ORDER SIBLINGS BY SALARY

FIRSTNAME  LEVEL      SALARY     ROOT       CHAIN
---------- ---------- ---------- ---------- -------------------------
Lindsey          1    80000.00 Lindsey     ->Lindsey
Smith            2    34000.00 Lindsey     ->Lindsey->Smith
Paul             2    80000.00 Lindsey     ->Lindsey->Paul
Peter            3    35000.00 Lindsey     ->Lindsey->Paul->Peter
Lauren           3    36000.00 Lindsey     ->Lindsey->Paul->Lauren
Kim              3    40000.00 Lindsey     ->Lindsey->Paul->Kim
Tim              3    41000.00 Lindsey     ->Lindsey->Paul->Tim
John             4    66000.00 Lindsey     ->Lindsey->Paul->Tim->Joh
Mohan            3    50000.00 Lindsey     ->Lindsey->Paul->Mohan

  9 record(s) selected.
```

How it works...

DB2 9.7 introduced the CONNECT BY clause to define the relationship between two columns, as follows:

```
SELECT EMPID, FIRSTNAME, LASTNAME, MGRID, LEVEL FROM HQEMPLOYEE CONNECT
BY PRIOR EMPID=MGRID
```

```
c:\>db2 "SELECT EMPID, FIRSTNAME, LASTNAME, MGRID, LEVEL FROM HQEMPLOYEE CONNECT BY PRIOR EMPID=MGRID"

EMPID       FIRSTNAME  LASTNAME   MGRID        LEVEL
---------   ---------- ---------- -----------  -----------
        1   John       Brett              6             1
        2   Peter      Robert             5             1
        3   Kim        Reynolds           5             1
        4   Lindsey    Bowen              -             1
        5   Paul       Taylor             4             2
        2   Peter      Robert             5             3
        3   Kim        Reynolds           5             3
        6   Tim        Johnson            5             3
        1   John       Brett              6             4
        7   Lauren     Brook              5             3
        9   Mohan      Kumar              5             3
        8   Smith      Wright             4             2
        5   Paul       Taylor             4             1
        2   Peter      Robert             5             2
        3   Kim        Reynolds           5             2
        6   Tim        Johnson            5             2
        1   John       Brett              6             3
        7   Lauren     Brook              5             2
        9   Mohan      Kumar              5             2
        6   Tim        Johnson            5             1
        1   John       Brett              6             2
        7   Lauren     Brook              5             1
        8   Smith      Wright             4             1
        9   Mohan      Kumar              5             1

  24 record(s) selected.
```

The CONNECT BY clause describes the relationship between the parent and the child rows of the hierarchy. The LEVEL pseudo column describes the recursion level, and the conditional expression must be qualified by the PRIOR unary operator to refer back to parent. The CONNECT_BY_ROOT is a unary operator, which returns the expression for a root's ancestor, for every row in the hierarchy.

The hierarchical query, START WITH, specifies the root row of the hierarchy, and SYS_CONNECT_BY_PATH combines the second argument with the first, and appends the previous recursive step results with the combined arguments. There is a catch while using this binary function—the arguments must always be of character data type.

We have certain restrictions in DB2 while using recursion, which are as follows:

- A maximum of 64 levels are supported
- Hierarchical queries cannot be used in **Materialized Query Tables** (**MQT**)

Using PL/SQL ANONYMOUS block statements

The ANONYMOUS blocks are standard PL/SQL blocks that provide the ability to build and execute the procedures at runtime, without storing the information in the system catalog. Anonymous blocks do not carry names, and so, can't be referenced by other database objects.

The ANONYMOUS block can contain three sections, which are the **declaration** section, the **execution** section, and the **exceptional handling** section. We can execute these ANONYMOUS blocks from DB2 CLP, DB2 APIs, and various tools, such as **Optim database administrator**, **CLPPlus**, and so on.

Getting ready

Interestingly, we do not require any privilege to invoke an anonymous block, but necessary privileges should be available in the base table to invoke the SQL statements.

How to do it...

1. Let's start writing a simple ANONYMOUS block statement. Remember that ANONYMOUS blocks will have no names associated with it.

    ```
    SET SERVEROUTPUT ON;

    BEGIN

    NULL;--

    END;
    ```

    This ANONYMOUS block will not return anything on to the screen, and you will not be able to see the existence of the code in the system catalog table.

2. We will now create an ANONYMOUS block statement to prepare a report, based on the HQEMPLOYEE table.

    ```
    SET SERVEROUTPUT ON;


    DECLARE
      v_empname VARCHAR2(400);--
      v_totalsalary NUMBER(12,2);--
    BEGIN
      DBMS_OUTPUT.PUT_LINE('            Salary Report        ');--


      DBMS_OUTPUT.PUT_LINE('---------------------------------------
    ');--
      DBMS_OUTPUT.PUT('Employee List: ');--
      FOR row IN
        (SELECT distinct(empid),firstname, lastname FROM hqemployee)
        LOOP
    ```

```
        v_empname := v_empname || '"' || row.firstname || ' ' ||
row.lastname ||
            '", '; --

    END LOOP;--

    DBMS_OUTPUT.PUT_LINE(v_empname); --

    SELECT NVL(SUM(salary),0) INTO v_totalsalary FROM hqemployee
;--

    DBMS_OUTPUT.PUT_LINE('----------------------------------------
');--

    DBMS_OUTPUT.PUT_LINE('Total Salary: ' || TO_CHAR(v_
totalsalary,
        '$99,999,999.99')); --


    END;
```

```
C:\>db2 -tvf A8.db2
SET SERVEROUTPUT ON
DB20000I  The SET SERVEROUTPUT command completed successfully.

DECLARE v_empname VARCHAR2(400);--
v_totalsalary NUMBER(12,2);--
BEGIN DBMS_OUTPUT.PUT_LINE('              Salary Report      ');--
DBMS_OUTPUT.PUT_LINE('--------------------------------------');--
DBMS_OUTPUT.PUT('Employee List: ');--
FOR row IN (SELECT distinct(empid),firstname, lastname FROM hqemployee) LOOP v_empname := v_empname || '"' || row.first
name || ' ' || row.lastname || '", '; --
END LOOP;--
DBMS_OUTPUT.PUT_LINE(v_empname); --
SELECT NVL(SUM(salary),0) INTO v_totalsalary FROM hqemployee ;--
DBMS_OUTPUT.PUT_LINE('--------------------------------------');--
DBMS_OUTPUT.PUT_LINE('Total Salary: ' || TO_CHAR(v_totalsalary, '$99,999,999.99')); --
END
DB20000I  The SQL command completed successfully.

             Salary Report
--------------------------------------
Employee List: "John Brett", "Peter Robert", "Kim Reynolds", "Lindsey Bowen", "Paul Taylor", "Tim Johnson", "Lauren Broo
k", "Smith Wright", "Mohan Kumar",
--------------------------------------
Total Salary: $     462,000.00
```

How it works...

Any reporting requirement is to aggregate the data from more than one column into a single value. It is possible to implement the reporting SQL statements with complex recursions. However, one can use ANONYMOUS blocks to perform this quickly, with dynamic formatting options and simple logic flow.

The ANONYMOUS code block retrieves the list of all employees and the total salary. The names are displayed in one line, and are separated by commas, and the summarized value is available at the end with a specific reporting format.

There's more...

ANONYMOUS blocks can also be used with statement attributes, such as SQL%FOUND, SQL%NOTFOUND, and SQL%ROWCOUNT to determine the result of the previous SQL statement execution.

The SQL%FOUND attribute returns a Boolean value TRUE, if one or more rows are affected by an INSERT, UPDATE, or DELETE statement. The following example demonstrates how an ANONYMOUS block can be used to insert a row, and display a status message:

```
SET SERVEROUTPUT ON;


BEGIN
INSERT INTO HQEMPLOYEE (EMPID, FIRSTNAME, LASTNAME, SALARY, MGRID)
VALUES (10, 'JONES', 'ALEX', 8250.00, 6);--
IF SQL%FOUND THEN
DBMS_OUTPUT.PUT_LINE ('The new row has been inserted');--
END IF;--
END;
```

In a similar way, the SQL%NOTFOUND attribute returns a Boolean value TRUE, if no records were affected by the INSERT, UPDATE, or DELETE statements.

```
SET SERVEROUTPUT ON;


BEGIN
DELETE FROM HQEMPLOYEE WHERE EMPID=12; --
IF SQL%NOTFOUND THEN
DBMS_OUTPUT.PUT_LINE ('No rows were deleted');--
END IF;--
END;
```

The SQL%ROWCOUNT attribute returns an integer value equal to the number of rows that were affected by an INSERT, UPDATE, or DELETE statement.

```
SET SERVEROUTPUT ON;


BEGIN
UPDATE HQEMPLOYEE SET SALARY = 60000 WHERE EMPID = 9;--
DBMS_OUTPUT.PUT_LINE ('# Number of Records Updated: ' || SQL%ROWCOUNT);--
END;
```

Handling RAISE_APPLICATION_ERROR in DB2 PL/SQL

Exception handling is a mechanism to capture the application error, and process it conditionally. While writing SQL-stored procedures, one can write without any error-handling mechanism in place. In this case, if there is any runtime error, the execution stops and the procedure will terminate. In earlier versions of DB2, the basic error checking was mainly using `SQLCODE` and `SQLSTATE` values of the DB2 communication area.

Along with earlier exception handlers, DB2 9.7 supports most of Oracle PL/SQL exception handlers, such as defining exception blocks, customized exception-handler declaration, and raising custom-defined errors.

Getting ready

DB2 9.7 supports almost all the Oracle pre-defined exceptions, such as `NO_DATA_FOUND`, `TOO_MANY_ROWS`, `INVALID_CURSOR`, `ZERO_DIVIDE`, `DUP_VAL_ON_INDEX`, `VALUE_ERROR`, and many more in the list. Now we will look at the way in which one can raise a customized application error.

How to do it...

The built-in procedure, `RAISE_APPLICATION_ERROR`, provides a way to intentionally abort a process, based on a condition. In addition, this also makes a user-defined code and error message available to the program for analysis.

We will look at the `RAISE_APPLICATION_ERROR` API, and the ways of implementing it.

```
RAISE_APPLICATION_ERROR (ERRORNUMBER, MESSAGE);
```

Let's build a SQL procedure to verify if the employee is present in the organization, based on the employee number:

```
CREATE OR REPLACE PROCEDURE verify_HQEmployee
( p_empid INT
) IS
v_ename hqemployee.firstname%TYPE;--
v_mgr employees.mgrid%TYPE;--


BEGIN
SELECT firstname,  mgrid
INTO v_ename, v_mgr FROM hqemployee WHERE empid = p_empid;--
```

```
IF v_ename IS NULL THEN
RAISE_APPLICATION_ERROR (-20010, 'No name entered for ' || p_empid);--
END IF;--


IF v_mgr IS NULL THEN
RAISE_APPLICATION_ERROR (-20020, 'No manager entered for ' || p_empid);--
END IF;--


DBMS_OUTPUT.PUT_LINE ('Employee ' || p_empid || ' Validation
Successful');--
EXCEPTION
WHEN OTHERS THEN
DBMS_OUTPUT.PUT_LINE ('SQLCODE: ' || SQLCODE);--
DBMS_OUTPUT.PUT_LINE ('SQLERRM: ' || SQLERRM);--
END;
```

```
C:\>db2 -tvf AppException.db2
CREATE OR REPLACE PROCEDURE verify_HQEmployee
( p_empid INT
) IS
v_ename hqemployee.firstname%TYPE;--
v_mgr hqemployee.mgrid%TYPE;--

BEGIN
SELECT firstname, mgrid
INTO v_ename, v_mgr FROM hqemployee WHERE empid = p_empid;--

IF v_ename IS NULL THEN
RAISE_APPLICATION_ERROR (-20010, 'No name entered for ' || p_empid);--
END IF;--

IF v_mgr IS NULL THEN
RAISE_APPLICATION_ERROR (-20020, 'No manager entered for ' || p_empid);--
END IF;--

DBMS_OUTPUT.PUT_LINE ('Employee ' || p_empid || ' Validation Successful');--
EXCEPTION
WHEN OTHERS THEN
DBMS_OUTPUT.PUT_LINE ('SQLCODE: ' || SQLCODE);--
DBMS_OUTPUT.PUT_LINE ('SQLERRM: ' || SQLERRM);--
END
DB20000I  The SQL command completed successfully.
```

How it works...

This procedure expects an employee ID as an input, and if the employee is not present, it raises an application error with error number -20020. These error numbers are built specific to the application for troubleshooting purposes. And, if there is no manager for an employee, it raises error -20020. There are flexibilities available to display SQLCODE and SQLERRM from the DB2 communication area to get a database-specific error.

```
C:\>db2 "CALL verify_HQEmployee(4)"

  Return Status = 0

SQLCODE: -438
SQLERRM: SQL0438N Application raised error or warning with diagnostic text: "No manager entered for 4".  SQLSTATE=UD020

C:\>db2 "CALL verify_HQEmployee(15)"

  Return Status = 0

SQLCODE: -438
SQLERRM: SQL0438N Application raised error or warning with diagnostic text: "NO_DATA_FOUND".  SQLSTATE=ORANF

C:\>db2 "CALL verify_HQEmployee(1)"

  Return Status = 0

Employee 1 Validation Successful
```

Migrating Oracle database objects on to DB2 9.7

In earlier days, it was a little difficult to migrate the database from one server to another. The reasons were many, for example data type portability was not efficient, database objects, such as procedures, functions, sequences, and triggers needed application development team efforts to modify to another database server code base, and so on. After having the **Oracle Compatibility Feature** enabled in DB2 9.7, the database migration including all the database objects and data is made so simple, that a 4~5 TB of data can be migrated in less than two days. The reason behind this efficient database server-enablement is code compatibility between Oracle and DB2 9.7.

Getting ready

The migration activity can be carried out using many migration tools, such as IBM Migration Tool Kit (MTK), Data Movement Tool (DMT) and other external vendor products. We have installed IBM Data Movement Tool for the demonstration of object migration such as tables, procedures, triggers, and views. In this recipe, we have migrated the Oracle 11g database to DB2 9.7.

How to do it...

The prerequisite is to have the Oracle and DB2 client installed on the machine, where the migration activity is going to take place.

1. Let's get the source Oracle data server version:

    ```
    SELECT * FROM v$version;
    ```

    ```
    SQL> SELECT * FROM v$version;

    BANNER
    ---------------------------------------------------------------------------
    Oracle Database 11g Enterprise Edition Release 11.2.0.1.0 - Production
    PL/SQL Release 11.2.0.1.0 - Production
    CORE    11.2.0.1.0      Production
    TNS for 32-bit Windows: Version 11.2.0.1.0 - Production
    NLSRTL Version 11.2.0.1.0 - Production
    ```

2. Let's take a look at the DB2 version on the target data server:

    ```
    db2level
    ```

    ```
    D:\Data\mohan>db2level
    DB21085I  Instance "DB2" uses "32" bits and DB2 code release "SQL09075" with
    level identifier "08060107".
    Informational tokens are "DB2 v9.7.500.702", "s111017", "IP23286", and Fix Pack
    "5".
    Product is installed at "C:\PROGRA~1\IBM\SQLLIB" with DB2 Copy Name "DB2COPY1".
    ```

3. Configure the Oracle connectivity at the migration server.

    We need to edit the `tnsnames.ora` file at the Oracle installation path `C:\app\Mohan\product\11.2.0\dbhome_1\NETWORK\ADMIN`, to add the server name and port in which it is listening to the client. By default, Oracle listens at `1521`.

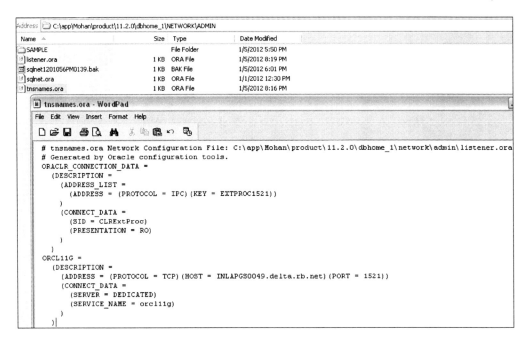

3. Now, we will enable the target DB2 9.7 database for easy database object migration.

    Starting from version 9.1, DB2 recommends using automatic storage along with a 32K page size. While enabling Oracle on to DB2, make sure we turn on the compatibility feature using the following steps:

    db2set DB2_COMPATIBILITY_VECTOR=ORA

    db2set DB2_DEFERRED_PREPARE_SEMANTICS=YES

    UPDATE DB CFG FOR SAMPLE USING AUTO_REVAL DEFERRED_FORCE

    UPDATE DB CFG FOR SAMPLE USING DECFLT_ROUNDING ROUND_HALF_UP

    FORCE APPLICATIONS ALL

    db2stop

    db2start

4. Catalog the DB2 node and the database at the migration server, using the following command syntax and the actual command:

```
CATALOG [ADMIN] {TCPIP | TCPIP4 | TCPIP6} NODE node-name REMOTE
hostname

[SERVER service-name] [SECURITY {SOCKS | SSL}] [REMOTE_INSTANCE
instance-
   name][SYSTEM system-name] [OSTYPE os-type] [WITH "comment
string"]
```

```
CATALOG DATABASE database-name [AS alias] [ON drive | AT NODE
node-name]
[AUTHENTICATION {SERVER | CLIENT | DCS | DCE SERVER PRINCIPAL
principalname
   | KERBEROS TARGET PRINCIPAL principalname | SERVER_ENCRYPT |
   SERVER_ENCRYPT_AES | DCS_ENCRYPT | DATA_ENCRYPT | GSSPLUGIN}]
[WITH "comment-
   string"]
```

For example:

```
C:\>db2 "CATALOG TCPIP NODE DB2NODE REMOTE 10.160.26.119 SERVER db2c_DB2"
DB20000I  The CATALOG TCPIP NODE command completed successfully.
DB21056W  Directory changes may not be effective until the directory cache is
refreshed.
C:\>db2 "CATALOG DATABASE SAMPLE AS SAMPLE2 AT NODE DB2NODE"
DB20000I  The CATALOG DATABASE command completed successfully.
DB21056W  Directory changes may not be effective until the directory cache is
refreshed.
```

Download the no-charge migration tool called the **IBM Data Movement Tool** (**DMT**) from the following link, and install it on the target server: `https://www14.software.ibm.com/webapp/iwm/web/reg/pick.do?source=idmt&lang=en_US`

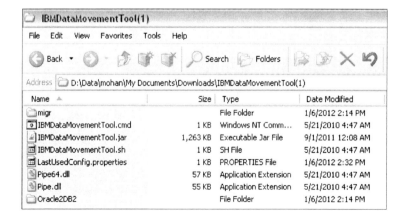

5. Select the project name and the path in which you would like to create the project, based on the space requirement. If the project is in terms of TBs, with lots of database objects, it's better to choose the right filesystem for the project path. Launch `IBMDataMovementTool.cmd` in the Microsoft Windows platform, and `IBMDataMovementTool.sh` in the UNIX platform. Key in all the information required, such as source and target **Database Name**, **Server Name**, **Port Number**, **UserID**, and **Password**, as shown in the following screenshot:

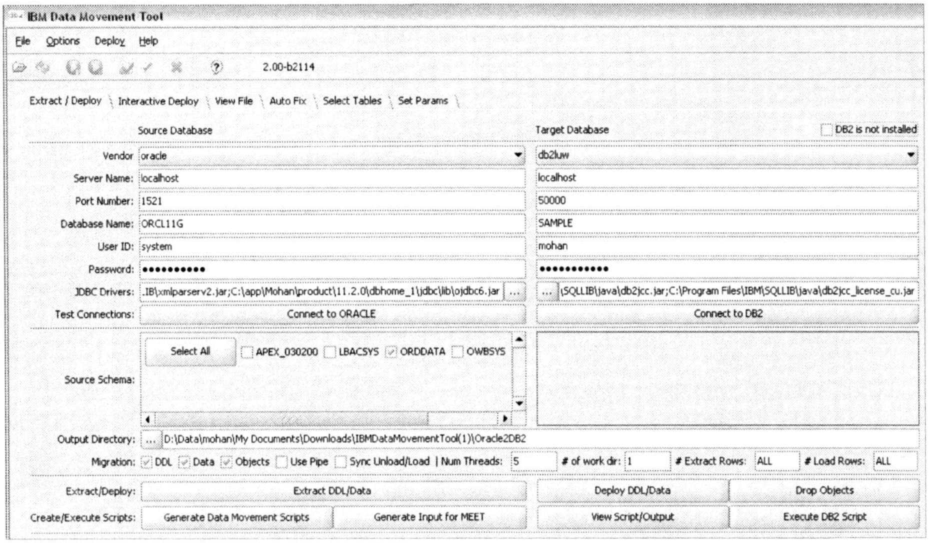

6. Test the connection with the source Oracle 11g database `ORCL11G`, and select the schema which you want to migrate from the source Oracle database to the target DB2 database, as shown in the following screenshot:

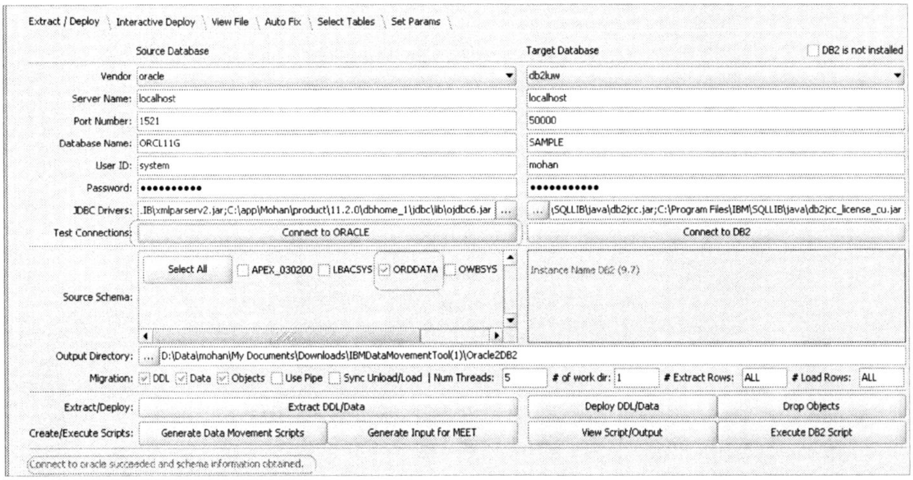

7. Now test the connection for target DB2 9.7 database: `SAMPLE`:

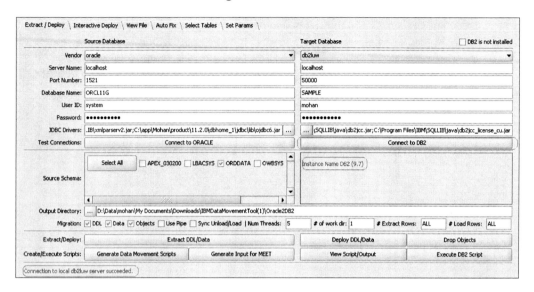

8. The IBM DMT tool has many features, and it is beneficial to know the important ones before starting with the migration activity. Let's start with the options that are available in DMT.

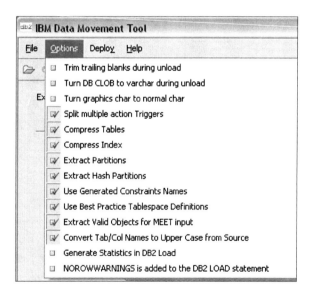

Enabling **Extract Hash Partitions** will be beneficial when migrating data from an Oracle RAC environment to the DB2 DPF environment. We may have to change the code to accommodate the change in syntax.

Oracle syntax for Hash partitioning—PARTITION BY HASH

DB2 syntax for Hash partitioning—DISTRIBUTE BY HASH

One can also select the TABLE and the INDEX compression, so that we can save the disk space on the target server. Oracle supports multi-action triggers, and DB2 started supporting them from DB2 9.7.4, which was released in April 2011. We can ask IBM DMT to split the multi-action triggers into multiple triggers.

9. The next step is to choose the deployment options before starting to deploy the database objects from source to target, and is very much self-explanatory.

10. Let's look at the output directory and the migration options.

We can choose the output directory based on the disk space requirement. In case the source database is very huge in size, then we may need a good amount of storage space to keep the extracted data before loading it into the target.

There are multiple migration options available in DMT, and are listed as follows:

- ❑ **DDL**: Only extracts **Data Definition Language** to create a similar object in the target database.

- ❑ **Data**: Along with DDL, data will also be ported to the target database server.

- ❑ **Use Pipes**: This is a very interesting option in DMT, and is very useful when we have less space available on the source or target to store the extracted data. In this method, DMT creates an operating system pipe, and performs data export and import without storing the intermediate data files.

- ❑ **Sync Unload/Load**: This will be used when we have IBM Optim data unload to help in unloading and loading the data.

Now let's look at the deployment options available in IBM DMT.

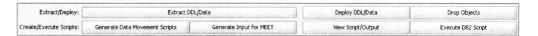

Once all the setup processes are complete, we can migrate the whole Oracle database to DB2, or we can migrate only the schemas which are required. One can also select only the tables required to migrate from the source to the target database, by selecting tables in the **Select Tables** tab in the IBM DMT.

We can complete the migration process in one go by selecting **Extract DDL/Data** and **Deploy DDL/Data**, or go in steps such as **Generate Data Movement Scripts** and **Execute DB2 Script**.

In order to evaluate the migration process by analyzing the objects in the source Oracle database and score them based on the percentage of attention required for the object modification.

12. Let's start with actual database migration from Oracle to DB2. In this example, we will migrate the ORDDATA schema to DB2 9.7. We have about 282 objects present in the ORDDATA schema, which needs to be ported to DB2, and the important objects are shown in the following screenshot:

OBJECT_NAME	OBJECT_TYPE
REGIONS	TABLE
REG_ID_PK	INDEX
COUNTRIES	TABLE
COUNTRY_C_ID_PK	INDEX
LOCATIONS	TABLE
LOC_ID_PK	INDEX
LOC_CITY_IX	INDEX
LOC_STATE_PROVINCE_IX	INDEX
LOC_COUNTRY_IX	INDEX
DEPARTMENTS	TABLE
DEPT_ID_PK	INDEX
DEPT_LOCATION_IX	INDEX
JOBS	TABLE
JOB_ID_PK	INDEX
EMPLOYEES	TABLE
EMP_EMAIL_UK	INDEX
EMP_EMP_ID_PK	INDEX
EMP_DEPARTMENT_IX	INDEX
EMP_JOB_IX	INDEX
EMP_MANAGER_IX	INDEX
EMP_NAME_IX	INDEX
JOB_HISTORY	TABLE
JHIST_EMP_ID_ST_DATE_PK	INDEX
JHIST_JOB_IX	INDEX
JHIST_EMPLOYEE_IX	INDEX
JHIST_DEPARTMENT_IX	INDEX
LOCATIONS_SEQ	SEQUENCE
DEPARTMENTS_SEQ	SEQUENCE
EMPLOYEES_SEQ	SEQUENCE
EMP_DETAILS_VIEW	VIEW
SECURE_DML	PROCEDURE
SECURE_EMPLOYEES	TRIGGER
ADD_JOB_HISTORY	PROCEDURE
UPDATE_JOB_HISTORY	TRIGGER

13. When we click on the **Extract DDL/Data** button in DMT, it asks for a confirmation to run the tool. Upon successful completion of the extraction, we can see all the extracted data files in the **Output Directory**, and also in the **View File** log in DMT, as shown in the following screenshot:

Extract / Deploy   Interactive Deploy   View File   Auto Fix   Select Tables   Set Params

```
[2012-01-08 12.18.28.994] Blade_2 unloaded 0 rows in 0.63 sec ORDDATA.ORDDCM_MAPPED_PATHS_TMP [64/80]
[2012-01-08 12.18.29.009] Blade_3 unloaded 2415 rows in 0.312 sec ORDDATA.ORDDCM_STD_ATTRS [65/80]
[2012-01-08 12.18.29.025] Blade_1 unloaded 9 rows in 0.203 sec ORDDATA.ORDDCM_DOCS [66/80]
[2012-01-08 12.18.29.040] Blade_4 unloaded 0 rows in 0.46 sec ORDDATA.ORDDCM_RT_PREF_PARAMS_TMP [67/80]
[2012-01-08 12.18.29.087] Blade_1 unloaded 0 rows in 0.62 sec ORDDATA.ORDDCM_CT_ACTION_TMP [68/80]
[2012-01-08 12.18.29.087] Blade_4 unloaded 0 rows in 0.47 sec ORDDATA.ORDDCM_CT_DAREFS_TMP [69/80]
[2012-01-08 12.18.29.103] Blade_2 unloaded 0 rows in 0.109 sec ORDDATA.ORDDCM_PRV_ATTRS_TMP [70/80]
[2012-01-08 12.18.29.103] Blade_0 unloaded 0 rows in 0.109 sec ORDDATA.ORDDCM_DOC_REFS_TMP [71/80]
[2012-01-08 12.18.29.119] Blade_1 unloaded 0 rows in 0.32 sec ORDDATA.ORDDCM_CT_PRED_TMP [72/80]
[2012-01-08 12.18.29.134] Blade_3 unloaded 8 rows in 0.125 sec ORDDATA.ORDDCM_DOC_TYPES [73/80]
[2012-01-08 12.18.29.150] Blade_1 unloaded 0 rows in 0.31 sec ORDDATA.ORDDCM_ANON_RULES_TMP [74/80]
[2012-01-08 12.18.29.165] Blade_3 unloaded 0 rows in 0.31 sec ORDDATA.ORDDCM_CT_PRED_PAR_TMP [75/80]
[2012-01-08 12.18.29.181] Blade_4 unloaded 0 rows in 0.94 sec ORDDATA.ORDDCM_DOCS_TMP [76/80]
[2012-01-08 12.18.29.259] Blade_1 unloaded 0 rows in 0.109 sec ORDDATA.ORDDCM_DICT_ATTRS_TMP [77/80]
[2012-01-08 12.18.29.259] Blade_3 unloaded 0 rows in 0.94 sec ORDDATA.ORDDCM_UID_DEFS_TMP [78/80]
[2012-01-08 12.18.29.290] Blade_3 unloaded 0 rows in 0.31 sec ORDDATA.ORDDCM_MAPPING_DOCS_TMP [79/80]
[2012-01-08 12.18.29.322] Blade_3 unloaded 0 rows in 0.32 sec ORDDATA.ORDDCM_STD_ATTRS_TMP [80/80]
[2012-01-08 12.18.29.572] done Blade_0
[2012-01-08 12.18.29.822] done Blade_1
[2012-01-08 12.18.30.072] done Blade_2
[2012-01-08 12.18.30.322] done Blade_3
[2012-01-08 12.18.30.572] done Blade_4
[2012-01-08 12.18.30.603] Starting extract of other metadata. Please wait ....
[2012-01-08 12.18.30.744] Work completed
[2012-01-08 12.18.30.744] ====  Total time: 963.3 KB unloaded in 23.282 sec
[2012-01-08 12.18.30.744] ==== Unload rate: 145.46 MB / hour
```

14. Now that we have the data extracted from Oracle, let's start importing it to DB2 by clicking on the **Deploy DDL/Data** in the **Target Database** section of the tool. Once it starts deploying the objects to the DB2 database, we will start seeing the log in **View File**, as shown in the following screenshot. The DMT tool deploys all the objects to the target database with the same schema as in the source.

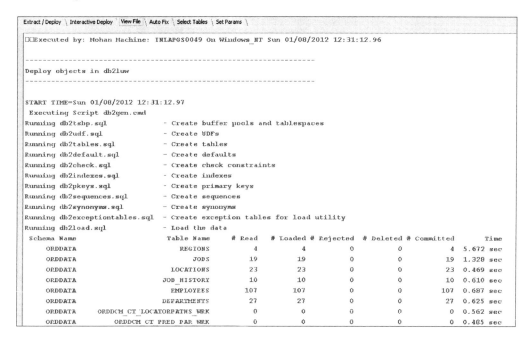

Make sure to check all the objects, as the table would go for a **Check Pending** state because of the use of the LOAD command, and because of having constraints on the table.

```
Running db2tabcount.sql        - Count rows from all tables
Running db2excepttabcount.sql  - Exception table row count
Running db2tabstatus.sql       - Show status of tables after load
```

TABLE_NAME	FK_CHECKED	CC_CHECKED	STATUS
ORDDATA.JOBS	Y	Y	NORMAL
ORDDATA.JOB_HISTORY	Y	N	CHECK PENDING
ORDDATA.LOCATIONS	Y	Y	NORMAL
ORDDATA.EMPLOYEES	Y	N	CHECK PENDING
ORDDATA.DEPARTMENTS	Y	Y	NORMAL
ORDDATA.ORDDCM_CT_LOCATORPATHS_WRK	Y	Y	NORMAL
ORDDATA.ORDDCM_CT_PRED_PAR_WRK	Y	Y	NORMAL
ORDDATA.ORDDCM_CT_ACTION_WRK	Y	Y	NORMAL
ORDDATA.ORDDCM_CT_MACRO_PAR_WRK	Y	Y	NORMAL
ORDDATA.ORDDCM_CT_MACRO_DEP_WRK	Y	Y	NORMAL
ORDDATA.ORDDCM_STORED_TAGS_WRK	Y	Y	NORMAL
ORDDATA.ORDDCM_DATA_MODEL_WRK	Y	Y	NORMAL
ORDDATA.ORDDCM_CT_PRED_WRK	Y	Y	NORMAL
ORDDATA.ORDDCM_MAPPED_PATHS_WRK	Y	Y	NORMAL
ORDDATA.ORDDCM_CT_PRED_SET_WRK	Y	Y	NORMAL
ORDDATA.ORDDCM_ANON_RULES_WRK	Y	N	CHECK PENDING
ORDDATA.ORDDCM_ANON_ATTRS_WRK	Y	N	CHECK PENDING
ORDDATA.ORDDCM_UID_DEFS_WRK	Y	Y	NORMAL
ORDDATA.ORDDCM_DICT_ATTRS_WRK	Y	Y	NORMAL
ORDDATA.ORDDCM_STD_ATTRS_WRK	Y	Y	NORMAL
ORDDATA.ORDDCM_CT_PRED_OPRD_WRK	Y	Y	NORMAL
ORDDATA.ORDDCM_MAPPING_DOCS_WRK	Y	Y	NORMAL
ORDDATA.ORDDCM_CT_VLD_MSG	Y	Y	NORMAL
ORDDATA.ORDDCM_CT_MACRO_PAR	Y	Y	NORMAL

IBM DMT creates temporary tables in the target DB2 database while deploying the objects for every single table, and drops it when the copy is done completely.

```
D:\Data\mohan>db2 list tables for schema ORDDATA

Table/View                   Schema     Type   Creation time
------------------------------------------------------------------------
ORDDCM_CT_LOCATORPATHS       ORDDATA      T     2012-01-08-12.31.26.853002
ORDDCM_CT_LOCATORPATHS_TMP   ORDDATA      G     2012-01-08-12.31.30.540002
ORDDCM_CT_LOCATORPATHS_WRK   ORDDATA      T     2012-01-08-12.31.23.587002
```

We can see the logs for all the IBM DMT object movements at the installation location, and review them before handing over the system for application usage. In some cases, DMT leaves the _TMP and the _WRK in the database after the migration, so application DBA needs to proactively drop those tables.

Address	D:\Data\mohan\My Documents\Downloads\IBMDataMovementTool(1)\Oracle2DB2\logs			
Name ▲		Size	Type	Date Modified
db2check.log		2 KB	Text Document	1/8/2012 12:31 PM
db2default.log		9 KB	Text Document	1/8/2012 12:31 PM
db2exceptiontables.log		24 KB	Text Document	1/8/2012 12:32 PM
db2excepttabcount.log		2 KB	Text Document	1/8/2012 12:33 PM
db2fkeys.log		9 KB	Text Document	1/8/2012 12:33 PM
db2indexes.log		10 KB	Text Document	1/8/2012 12:31 PM
db2load.log		8 KB	Text Document	1/8/2012 12:33 PM
db2loadmessages.log		82 KB	Text Document	1/8/2012 12:33 PM
db2pkeys.log		7 KB	Text Document	1/8/2012 12:31 PM
db2sequences.log		4 KB	Text Document	1/8/2012 12:31 PM
db2synonyms.log		1 KB	Text Document	1/8/2012 12:31 PM
db2tabcount.log		2 KB	Text Document	1/8/2012 12:33 PM
db2tables.log		9 KB	Text Document	1/8/2012 12:31 PM
db2tabstatus.log		8 KB	Text Document	1/8/2012 12:33 PM
db2tsbp.log		2 KB	Text Document	1/8/2012 12:31 PM
db2udf.log		1 KB	Text Document	1/8/2012 12:31 PM
fixcheck.log		2 KB	Text Document	1/8/2012 12:33 PM

How it works...

As we discussed in *Chapter 1, DB2 9.7 Application Enhancements*, the DB2 9.7 compatibility feature has made the application-enablement team's life easier. There's is no need to change the base application code, as almost all of Oracle procedures, triggers, functions, built-in packages, and commands are available in DB2 with the same Oracle behavior.

Porting multi-action triggers from Oracle to DB2 9.7

A **trigger** is a database object, which does a set of actions in response to a DML operation, such as insert, update, and delete, against a specific table. DB2 9.7 supports two types of triggers in PL/SQL; they are **row-level** triggers and **statement-level** triggers. A row-level trigger fires for every single row-level change, and a statement-level trigger fires for every single statement, even though one statement affects multiple rows in the table.

Triggers are being supported even by Oracle with an exception, that is, Oracle allows a single trigger to handle multiple actions. These are known as multi-action triggers, which were not being supported by earlier versions of DB2, but DB2 9.7 supports it.

Getting ready

Let's start looking at the multi-action trigger, and create some base tables to work on.

How to do it...

We will create a sample trigger on the employee table. Whenever there are any changes made to the employee table, it will log the action in the logging table for audit purposes.

1. As a first step towards logging the activity, create a logging table, as follows:

   ```
   CREATE TABLE LOG_EMP_OPERATION (OPDATE TIMESTAMP, ACTION VARCHAR2
   (40));
   ```

   ```
   C:\>db2 "CREATE TABLE LOG_EMP_OPERATION (OPDATE TIMESTAMP, ACTION VARCHAR2(40))"
   DB20000I  The SQL command completed successfully.
   ```

   Take an example Oracle multi-trigger, which does insert the activity in the log table that we created in *step 1*:

   ```
   CREATE OR REPLACE TRIGGER UpdateEmployee

   AFTER INSERT OR DELETE OR UPDATE ON employees FOR EACH ROW

   BEGIN

   IF DELETING THEN

   INSERT INTO log_emp_operation VALUES (SYSDATE, 'Deleted Rows -
   Employee
     Table');

   ELSIF INSERTING THEN

   INSERT INTO log_emp_operation VALUES (SYSDATE, 'Inserted Rows -
   Employee
     Table');

   ELSIF UPDATING THEN

   INSERT INTO log_emp_operation VALUES (SYSDATE, 'Updated Rows -
   Employee
     Table');

   END IF;

   END UpdateEmployee;
   ```

2. We will now work on converting the Oracle multi-trigger into the DB2 PL/SQL trigger. The same Oracle code works without any change, including the `sysdate`. But, we have used CURRENT TIMESTAMP instead of SYSDATE:

```
C:\>db2 -td@ -vf UpdateEmployee.db2
CREATE OR REPLACE TRIGGER UpdateEmployee
        AFTER INSERT OR DELETE OR UPDATE ON employees FOR EACH ROW
BEGIN
IF DELETING THEN
INSERT INTO log_emp_operation VALUES(CURRENT TIMESTAMP, 'Deleted Rows - Employee Table');
        ELSIF INSERTING THEN
        INSERT INTO log_emp_operation VALUES(CURRENT TIMESTAMP, 'Inserted Rows - Employee Table');
                ELSIF UPDATING THEN
                INSERT INTO log_emp_operation VALUES(CURRENT TIMESTAMP, 'Updated Rows - Employee Table');
END IF;
END UpdateEmployee
DB20000I  The SQL command completed successfully.
```

3. We will validate the functioning of the trigger by performing the DML operation on the table `Employees`. When we queried the `log_emp_operation` table, before the DML operation found no rows in it and after the insert, the update, and the delete on the base table, we found three log records for each action.

```
C:\>db2 -x "SELECT * FROM log_emp_operation"

C:\>db2 "INSERT INTO EMPLOYEES VALUES ('100200','MOHANKUMAR','P','SARASWATIPURA','CS','8102','2010-01-01-00.00.00','LEAD
  DB2',5,'M','1980-01-01-00.00.00',80000.00, 10000.00,10000.00)"
DB20000I  The SQL command completed successfully.

C:\>db2 "UPDATE EMPLOYEES SET SALARY=85000.00 WHERE EMPNO='100200'"
DB20000I  The SQL command completed successfully.

C:\>db2 "DELETE FROM EMPLOYEES WHERE EMPNO='100200'"
DB20000I  The SQL command completed successfully.

C:\>db2 -x "SELECT * FROM log_emp_operation"
2011-07-03-22.58.23.616000 Inserted Rows - Employee Table
2011-07-03-22.59.20.028000 Updated Rows - Employee Table
2011-07-03-23.00.32.532000 Deleted Rows - Employee Table
```

How it works...

The Oracle multi-actions trigger, with INSERT, UPDATE, and DELETE actions on EMPLOYEES table, can easily be ported on to DB2 with the help of new trigger event predicates, namely DELETING, INSERTING, and UPDATING. These new set of event predicates help in identifying the event that fired the trigger.

7

Advanced DB2 Application Features and Practices

In this chapter, we will focus on following recipes related to advanced database features that include:

- ▶ Working with OLAP functions
- ▶ Using optimizer profiles
- ▶ Using explain utilities
- ▶ Using section explain information
- ▶ Interpreting db2exfmt output
- ▶ Application development in partitioned databases

Introduction

In this chapter, we will focus on some advanced DB2 features that are useful for analyzing and troubleshooting application performance. We will discuss some OLAP functions, which are very powerful in computing complex use cases in a very simple manner. Then we will discuss how we can influence DB2 optimizer to choose our guidelines. We will also look at different tools available for capturing and analyzing SQL explain information. Then, we will also touch upon different partitioning techniques available in DB2, and what a developer needs to know, to make sure that the application is well suited for such an environment.

Working with OLAP functions

Consider a scenario where we have a **sales** table that holds sales data for different regions, and we want to rank all regions based on their total sales. We might also want to rank them based on their contribution to the total profit. This can certainly be achieved by writing complex SQL statements. Let's see what DB2 offers in such situations. DB2 provides a rich set of **Online Analytical Processing** (**OLAP**) functions that provide us with the ability to perform complex ordering and aggregation of result sets, in a very simple manner. OLAP functions do not perform any kind of filtering, and act on every row in the result set. They are always applied on a window. We can also use scalar functions and aggregate functions over OLAP windows. In this recipe, we will discuss how we can use the different OLAP functions provided by DB2.

Getting ready

This recipe uses the T_SALES table as an example. The sample table and data can be created by the following set of SQL statements:

```
-- Create sample table
CREATE TABLE T_SALES
(COUNTRY VARCHAR(20),
 CITY VARCHAR(20),
 AMOUNT DECIMAL(10,2),
 DATE DATE);

-- Create a view that lists total sales for each city.
CREATE VIEW V_TOTAL_SALES AS
  SELECT COUNTRY,
  CITY,
  SUM(AMOUNT) AS SALES_AMT
  FROM T_SALES GROUP BY COUNTRY, CITY;

-- Insert sample T_SALES data
INSERT INTO T_SALES VALUES ('USA', 'New York', 200, '2011-10-01');
INSERT INTO T_SALES VALUES ('USA', 'New York', 800, '2011-09-01');
INSERT INTO T_SALES VALUES ('USA', 'New York', 190, '2011-08-01');
INSERT INTO T_SALES VALUES ('USA', 'New York', 230, '2011-10-03');

INSERT INTO T_SALES VALUES ('USA', 'California', 200, '2011-10-05');
```

```
INSERT INTO T_SALES VALUES ('USA', 'California', 390, '2011-09-05');
INSERT INTO T_SALES VALUES ('USA', 'California', 720, '2011-08-05');
INSERT INTO T_SALES VALUES ('USA', 'California', 110, '2011-10-05');

INSERT INTO T_SALES VALUES ('USA', 'Los Angeles', 160, '2011-08-03');
INSERT INTO T_SALES VALUES ('USA', 'Los Angeles', 500, '2011-10-05');
INSERT INTO T_SALES VALUES ('USA', 'Los Angeles', 330, '2011-09-05');
INSERT INTO T_SALES VALUES ('USA', 'Los Angeles', 120, '2011-08-05');

INSERT INTO T_SALES VALUES ('USA', 'Alaska', 360, '2011-08-03');
INSERT INTO T_SALES VALUES ('USA', 'Alaska', 600, '2011-10-05');
INSERT INTO T_SALES VALUES ('USA', 'Alaska', 450, '2011-09-05');
INSERT INTO T_SALES VALUES ('USA', 'Alaska', 720, '2011-08-05');

INSERT INTO T_SALES VALUES ('UK', 'London', 450, '2011-10-05');
INSERT INTO T_SALES VALUES ('UK', 'London', 530, '2011-09-05');
INSERT INTO T_SALES VALUES ('UK', 'London', 790, '2011-08-05');
INSERT INTO T_SALES VALUES ('UK', 'London', 330, '2011-07-05');

INSERT INTO T_SALES VALUES ('UK', 'Manchester', 200, '2011-08-01');
INSERT INTO T_SALES VALUES ('UK', 'Manchester', 330, '2011-07-01');
INSERT INTO T_SALES VALUES ('UK', 'Manchester', 120, '2011-10-03');
INSERT INTO T_SALES VALUES ('UK', 'Manchester', 640, '2011-09-03');
```

How to do it...

All OLAP functions are computed on a **window**. If the window is not defined, then OLAP functions use the entire result set as a window. Let's see how we can create a result set window, and use different OLAP functions on it.

Using RANK function: Considering the previous `total_sales` table. If we want to rank different cities based on their total sales, then we can use the RANK function, which allows us to rank the rows within a result set window. This function can only be applied on a window, which can be defined by using the PARTITION BY clause. Since ranking needs an ordered sequence, we need to specify the order on which ranking should be computed.

In our example, we first need to calculate the total sales amount for each city, and then rank them on total sales. This can be achieved as follows:

```
SELECT CITY, SALES_AMT,
  RANK() OVER (ORDER BY SALES_AMT DESC) AS RANK
  FROM V_TOTAL_SALES;
```

```
db2 => SELECT CITY, SALES_AMT,
db2 (cont.) =>        RANK() OVER (ORDER BY SALES_AMT DESC) AS RANK
db2 (cont.) =>    FROM V_TOTAL_SALES;

CITY                     SALES_AMT                     RANK
------------------------ --------------------------    --------------------
Alaska                                   2130.00                          1
London                                   2100.00                          2
California                               1420.00                          3
New York                                 1420.00                          3
Manchester                               1290.00                          5
Los Angeles                              1110.00                          6

   6 record(s) selected.
```

If we observe, the rows with the same value are assigned the same rank. The RANK() function may result in gaps in the ranks, in case of duplicate values. An alternative to the RANK() function can be DENSE_RANK(), where there are no gaps in the rank sequence.

```
SELECT COUNTRY, CITY, SALES_AMT,
  RANK() OVER (PARTITION BY COUNTRY
  ORDER BY SALES_AMT DESC) AS RANK,
  DENSE_RANK() OVER (PARTITION BY COUNTRY
  ORDER BY SALES_AMT DESC) AS DENSE_RANK
  FROM V_TOTAL_SALES;
```

```
db2 => SELECT COUNTRY, CITY, SALES_AMT,
db2 (cont.) =>        RANK() OVER (PARTITION BY COUNTRY
db2 (cont.) =>                     ORDER BY SALES_AMT DESC) AS RANK,
db2 (cont.) =>        DENSE_RANK() OVER (PARTITION BY COUNTRY
db2 (cont.) =>                     ORDER BY SALES_AMT DESC) AS DENSE_RANK
db2 (cont.) =>    FROM V_TOTAL_SALES;

COUNTRY              CITY                   SALES_AMT       RANK    DENSE_RANK
-------------------- ---------------------- --------------- ------- ----------
UK                   London                      2100.00       1         1
UK                   Manchester                  1290.00       2         2
USA                  Alaska                      2130.00       1         1
USA                  California                  1420.00       2         2
USA                  New York                    1420.00       2         2
USA                  Los Angeles                 1110.00       4         3

   6 record(s) selected.
```

A slight modification of this scenario could be to rank the cities within each country. In that case, we would need to define a window for each country.

```
SELECT COUNTRY, CITY, SALES_AMT,
  RANK() OVER (PARTITION BY COUNTRY ORDER BY SALES_AMT DESC) AS RANK
  FROM V_TOTAL_SALES;
```

```
db2 => SELECT COUNTRY, CITY, SALES_AMT,
db2 (cont.) =>       RANK() OVER (PARTITION BY COUNTRY ORDER BY SALES_AMT DESC) AS RANK
db2 (cont.) =>   FROM V_TOTAL_SALES;

COUNTRY              CITY               SALES_AMT                    RANK
-------------------- ------------------ ---------------------------- --------------------
UK                   London             2100.00                         1
UK                   Manchester         1290.00                         2
USA                  Alaska             2130.00                         1
USA                  California         1420.00                         2
USA                  New York           1420.00                         2
USA                  Los Angeles        1110.00                         4

  6 record(s) selected.
```

If the FETCH FIRST n ROWS (where n is the number of rows) clause is specified, then we may not get the expected results. In such cases, the ranking might not be in order, or we may see some missing ranks. This is because the FETCH FIRST clause is computed even after the OLAP functions are calculated. To understand it better, let's sort the result set by the country's name, and observe the results.

```
SELECT CITY, SALES_AMT,
  RANK() OVER (ORDER BY SALES_AMT DESC) AS RANK
  FROM V_TOTAL_SALES
ORDER BY CITY FETCH FIRST 3 ROWS ONLY;
```

```
db2 => SELECT CITY, SALES_AMT,
db2 (cont.) =>       RANK() OVER (ORDER BY SALES_AMT DESC) AS RANK
db2 (cont.) =>   FROM V_TOTAL_SALES
db2 (cont.) => ORDER BY COUNTRY FETCH FIRST 3 ROWS ONLY;

CITY                 SALES_AMT                    RANK
-------------------- ---------------------------- --------------------
London               2100.00                         2
Manchester           1290.00                         5
Alaska               2130.00                         1

  3 record(s) selected.
```

Using aggregate functions: An aggregate function can be applied on a set of rows. The result of an aggregate function is a scalar value. We can use aggregate functions as part of OLAP specifications as well, but there is one difference: the result of an aggregate function is a scalar value and is available to all the rows, as OLAP functions do not filter the result set rows. For example, if we use the SUM() function for a result set, then we will see the same result of SUM() for all the rows in a data window. The total number of rows will still be same whether or not we use OLAP functions. The window for aggregate functions can be defined by using the PARTITON BY clause. Consider following example, where we calculate the total sales for each country:

```
SELECT COUNTRY, SUM(SALES_AMT) OVER (PARTITION BY COUNTRY)
  FROM V_TOTAL_SALES;
```

```
db2 => SELECT COUNTRY, SUM(SALES_AMT) OVER (PARTITION BY COUNTRY)
db2 (cont.) =>   FROM V_TOTAL_SALES;

COUNTRY                  2
-------------------- --------------------------------
UK                                            3390.00
UK                                            3390.00
USA                                           6080.00
USA                                           6080.00
USA                                           6080.00
USA                                           6080.00
```

In this example, the SUM() function will be applied on all rows that belong to one window, that is; one COUNTRY, and is reported once per each row. We can use other aggregate functions, such as AVG, COUNT, and so on, in the same fashion.

Deriving cumulative functionality: If we introduce ordering in an aggregate function partition window, then we can achieve cumulative functions. With the following query, we are only calculating the SUM of all AMOUNT values for each CITY window:

```
SELECT CITY,
  SUM(AMOUNT) OVER (PARTITION BY CITY)
  FROM T_SALES;
```

If we introduce the ORDER BY clause within the partition window, then we can achieve a cumulative sum. In the following example, SUM() will be computed on the current row and all rows preceding the current row, within the window boundary. In our example, it would mean the total cumulative sales for each city over daily sales.

```
SELECT CITY, DATE, AMOUNT,
  SUM(AMOUNT) OVER (PARTITION BY CITY ORDER BY DATE ASC) AS CUMM_SUM
  FROM T_SALES;
```

```
db2 => SELECT CITY, DATE, AMOUNT,
db2 (cont.) =>          SUM(AMOUNT) OVER (PARTITION BY CITY ORDER BY DATE ASC) AS CUMM_SUM
db2 (cont.) =>     FROM T_SALES;

CITY                DATE          AMOUNT        CUMM_SUM
------------------  ----------    ----------    -------------------
Alaska              08/03/2011     360.00                    360.00
Alaska              08/05/2011     720.00                   1080.00
Alaska              09/05/2011     450.00                   1530.00
Alaska              10/05/2011     600.00                   2130.00
California          08/05/2011     720.00                    720.00
California          09/05/2011     390.00                   1110.00
California          10/05/2011     200.00                   1420.00
California          10/05/2011     110.00                   1420.00
London              07/05/2011     330.00                    330.00
London              08/05/2011     790.00                   1120.00
London              09/05/2011     530.00                   1650.00
London              10/05/2011     450.00                   2100.00
:
:
```

Referencing relative rows: With LEAD and LAG functions, we can refer to the previous and preceding rows in aggregate functions. LEAD and LAG functions take an offset as a parameter to refer to relative rows. Consider the following example where we are selecting the total sales for a city along with the next highest sales.

```
SELECT CITY, SALES_AMT,

  LAG(SALES_AMT, 1) OVER (ORDER BY SALES_AMT DESC) AS NEXT_HIGH_SALES_AMT

  FROM V_TOTAL_SALES;
```

```
db2 => SELECT CITY, SALES_AMT,
db2 (cont.) =>          LAG(SALES_AMT, 1) OVER (ORDER BY SALES_AMT DESC) AS NEXT_HIGH_SALES_AMT
db2 (cont.) =>     FROM V_TOTAL_SALES;

CITY                SALES_AMT                    NEXT_HIGH_SALES_AMT
------------------  ---------------------------  -------------------------------
Alaska              2130.00                                              -
London              2100.00                                        2130.00
California          1420.00                                        2100.00
New York            1420.00                                        1420.00
Manchester          1290.00                                        1420.00
Los Angeles         1110.00                                        1290.00

  6 record(s) selected.
```

LEAD and LAG functions also allow us to calculate measures, based on current and relative row values. For example, in the previous query, if we also wanted to compute the difference in sales, then it could be done as follows:

```
SELECT CITY, RANK() OVER (ORDER BY SALES_AMT DESC),

   SALES_AMT, LAG(SALES_AMT, 1) OVER (ORDER BY SALES_AMT DESC) AS
      NEXT_HIGH_SALES_AMT,

   LAG(SALES_AMT, 1) OVER (ORDER BY SALES_AMT DESC)  - SALES_AMT AS SALES_
DIFF

      FROM V_TOTAL_SALES;
```

```
db2 => SELECT CITY, RANK() OVER (ORDER BY SALES_AMT DESC)AS RANK,
db2 (cont.) =>        SALES_AMT, LAG(SALES_AMT, 1) OVER (ORDER BY SALES_AMT DESC) AS NEXT_HIGH_SALES_AMT,
db2 (cont.) =>        LAG(SALES_AMT, 1) OVER (ORDER BY SALES_AMT DESC)  - SALES_AMT AS SALES_DIFF
db2 (cont.) =>    FROM V_TOTAL_SALES;

CITY                 RANK         SALES_AMT   NEXT_HIGH_SALES_AMT  SALES_DIFF
-------------------- ------------ ----------- -------------------- ------------
Alaska                          1    2130.00                    -            -
London                          2    2100.00              2130.00        30.00
California                      3    1420.00              2100.00       680.00
New York                        3    1420.00              1420.00         0.00
Manchester                      5    1290.00              1420.00       130.00
Los Angeles                     6    1110.00              1290.00       180.00

  6 record(s) selected.
```

Another typical use case for using the LAG function is to compare the total sales with the previous month. In such a case, the query will look something like this:

```
WITH TEMP AS
(SELECT DISTINCT CITY,
   MONTH(DATE) AS REPORTING_MONTH,
   SUM(AMOUNT) OVER (PARTITION BY CITY, MONTH(DATE)) AS CURRENT_SALES
   FROM T_SALES)
SELECT CITY, REPORTING_MONTH, CURRENT_SALES,
   LAG(CURRENT_SALES, 1) OVER (PARTITION BY CITY ORDER BY REPORTING_MONTH)
AS
      PRE_SALES
   FROM TEMP;
```

Referencing boundary rows: The FIRST_VALUE function can be used to refer the first row in an OLAP window boundary. Similarly, the LAST_VALUE function refers to the last row in an OLAP window boundary. These functions can be useful when we have a requirement that compares the current value with the first value. For example, we might want to compare the sales for a city with the one having the highest sales. In such a case the query will look like the following:

```
SELECT CITY,
   RANK() OVER ( PARTITION BY COUNTRY
```

```
ORDER BY SALES_AMT DESC) AS RANK, SALES_AMT,
FIRST_VALUE(SALES_AMT) OVER (PARTITION BY COUNTRY
ORDER BY SALES_AMT DESC) AS FIRST_SALES_AMT
FROM V_TOTAL_SALES;
```

```
db2 => SELECT CITY,
db2 (cont.) =>        RANK() OVER ( PARTITION BY COUNTRY
db2 (cont.) =>                        ORDER BY SALES_AMT DESC) AS RANK, SALES_AMT,
db2 (cont.) =>        FIRST_VALUE(SALES_AMT) OVER (PARTITION BY COUNTRY
db2 (cont.) =>                        ORDER BY SALES_AMT DESC) AS FIRST_SALES_AMT
db2 (cont.) => FROM V_TOTAL_SALES;

CITY                 RANK    SALES_AMT          FIRST_SALES_AMT
-------------------- ------- ------------ ------------------------
London               1       2100.00            2100.00
Manchester           2       1290.00            2100.00
Alaska               1       2130.00            2130.00
California           2       1420.00            2130.00
New York             2       1420.00            2130.00
Los Angeles          4       1110.00            2130.00

  6 record(s) selected.
```

How it works...

OLAP functions can be referenced in expressions in the SELECT list and in the ORDER BY clause. These functions are calculated after all other operators are calculated. In general, DB2 evaluates different parts of a query in the following order:

- FROM clause
- WHERE clause
- GROUP BY clause
- HAVING clause
- OLAP functions
- FETCH FIRST n ROWS

Once all the clauses other than OLAP functions are computed, we get a result set. When OLAP functions are applied to this result set, the total number of rows does not change. This is true even if we use aggregate functions, such as SUM(), MIN(), MAX(), and so on, over OLAP windows.

There's more...

Since OLAP functions are computed after all other parts of the query, it introduces a restriction of not being able to use OLAP functions in a predicate. If we still want to use OLAP functions in a predicate, then we can use nested queries or common table expressions. For example, if we need to select the top three regions that have the highest sales, then we can use the following query where we are using OLAP functions in a common table expression.

```
WITH TOP_CITIES AS

  (SELECT CITY, SALES_AMT, RANK() OVER (ORDER BY SALES_AMT) AS RANK

  FROM V_TOTAL_SALES)

SELECT * FROM TOP_CITIES

WHERE RANK <= 3;
```

Other ways of defining an OLAP window

We can further define the granularity of an OLAP window by using the ROWS BETWEEN clause. It allows us to apply aggregate functions on a set of rows instead of the entire window. Consider the following example:

```
SELECT CCY, DATE,

  AVG(USD_EQ) OVER (PARTITION BY CCY

  ORDER BY DATE

  ROWS BETWEEN 9 PRECEDING AND CURRENT ROW)

  FROM CCY_EXCHANGE_RATES;
```

 CCY stands for CURRENCY in this example.

In this example, we are calculating the average USD equivalent of a currency over the past ten days (including the current day). In this case, we defined our window as a PARTITION BY CCY that creates one window for each currency symbol. Within this window, we wanted to apply the AVG function only on ten values instead of entire window. We limited this by using the ROWS BETWEEN clause. Now, the AVG will be computed only on ten values of CCY, sorted by DATE.

We can also define our window as UNBOUND PRECEDING or UNBOUND FOLLOWING that includes all the rows before or after the current row. For example:

```
SELECT CCY, DATE,

  AVG(USD_EQ) OVER (PARTITION BY CCY

  ORDER BY DATE
```

```
ROWS BETWEEN UNBOUND PRECEDING AND CURRENT ROW)
FROM CCY_EXCHANGE_RATES;
```

Using optimizer profiles

DB2 uses cost-based optimization for choosing the access plan for a query. The total cost depends on various factors, such as system configuration, database and database manager configuration, memory available (buffer pool, sort heap, and so on), current optimization level, CPU parallelism, IO characteristics, and so on, and most importantly information regarding the actual data. In the DB2 terminology, this is also known as **catalog statistics**. Therefore, it is always recommended to keep the statistics updated. These statistics include information about the following:

- Number of rows, data pages, active blocks, data range information, data length, and so on
- Most frequent values
- Number of distinct values for a column, and clustering details
- Column group statistics

These details are stored in the system catalog tables, and are used by the optimizer to calculate the cost of each possible query execution plan. The DB2 optimizer is intelligent enough to come up with the best access plan. In some cases, if we come across some SQL queries, which are not performing well even after all possibilities of tuning, then we might want to provide some information to the optimizer that can override some actions in the chosen access plan, so that we can get better performance. This becomes more important if we don't want to make application-level changes, and instead give this information directly to DB2 in terms of a configuration file for that SQL query. In the DB2 terminology, these are known as **Optimizer profiles**. In this recipe, we will see how to create and use optimizer profiles.

Getting ready

An optimization profile is an XML document that has optimization instructions for one or more SQL statements. If an optimization profile is available for a particular SQL statement, then it forces the optimizer to use the guidelines contained in the profile. Hence, it is extremely important to understand why an optimizer chose a particular plan. Also, we should have a proper understanding of the guidelines that we place in the optimizer profiles. The structure of an optimization profile is as follows:

```
<?xml version="1.0" encoding="UTF-8"?>
<OPTPROFILE VERSION="9.1.0.0">
  <!-- Global optimization guidelines section. -->
  <OPTGUIDELINES>............</OPTGUIDELINES>

  <!-- Statement profile section. -->
```

```
<STMTPROFILE ID="Guidelines for Q1">
  <STMTKEY SCHEMA="TEST">
    <![CDATA[SQL Query]]>
  </STMTKEY>
  <OPTGUIDELINES>..........</OPTGUIDELINES>
</STMTPROFILE>
</OPTPROFILE>
```

How to do it...

We can create more than one optimization profile and register them in the database, but having one master optimization profile is a better option as it eases the maintenance. Let's see how to create and enable optimization profiles.

1. **Create an optimization profile**: Create the optimization profile as an XML document following the schema mentioned above. To create an optimization profile, we would need SQL query and optimization instructions. Save this as an xml document (e.g. test_profile.xml).

    For example, if we want to force an index scan, the optimizer profile will look like:

    ```
    <STMTPROFILE ID="Guideline for query 1">
        <STMTKEY SCHEMA="DBUSER">
            <![CDATA[SELECT COL1 FROM TBL1 WHERE COL2=?]]>
        </STMTKEY>
        <OPTGUIDELINES>
            <IXSCAN TABID="TBL1" INDEX="IDX1"/>
        </OPTGUIDELINES>
    </STMTPROFILE>
    ```

    In this example, we want the optimizer to always use the index idx1, which is defined on col1 and col2. See the *There's more* section, for some examples of optimization profiles.

2. **Create** the SYSTOOLS.OPT_PROFILE **table**: This table is a place holder for all optimization profiles. Once an optimization profile XML document is created, it must be inserted in this table. This table can be created with any of the following commands:

    ```
    CALL SYSINSTALLOBJECTS('OPT_PROFILES', 'C', '', '')
    ```

    Or

    ```
    CREATE TABLE SYSTOOLS.OPT_PROFILE (
        SCHEMA   VARCHAR(128) NOT NULL,
    ```

```
NAME      VARCHAR(128) NOT NULL,

PROFILE BLOB (2M)      NOT NULL,

PRIMARY KEY (SCHEMA, NAME)
)
```

3. **Load the optimization profile**: The optimization profile XML document can either be imported (by using the `IMPORT` or `LOAD` utilities), or inserted directly into the `OPT_PROFILE` table.

   ❑ **Inserting an optimization profile**: The optimizer profile XML can be directly inserted into the `OPT_PROFILE` table as follows:

```
INSERT INTO SYSTOOLS.OPT_PROFILE VALUES

  ('DBUSER',' TESTPROF',

    CAST('<?xml version="1.0" encoding="UTF-8"?>

      <OPTPROFILE VERSION="9.7.00">

        <STMTPROFILE ID="Guideline for query 1">

          <STMTKEY SCHEMA="DBUSER">

            <![CDATA[SELECT COL1 FROM TBL1 WHERE COL2=?]]>

          </STMTKEY>

          <OPTGUIDELINES>

            <IXSCAN TABID="TBL1" INDEX="IDX1"/>

          </OPTGUIDELINES>

        </STMTPROFILE>

      </OPTPROFILE>' AS BLOB));
```

   ❑ **Importing an optimization profile**: Consider the following data file (`test_file.dat`) that we can use for importing an optimization profile.

```
"DBUSER","TESTPROF","test_profile.xml"
```

   We can also import multiple optimization at once, by adding them to the data file (`test_file.dat`). Each profile must appear on a separate line. Once we have the data file ready, we can use the following command to import it.

```
IMPORT FROM test_file.dat OF DEL MODIFIED BY LOBSINFILE INSERT INTO
   SYSTOOLS.OPT_PROFILE;
```

4. **Set an optimization profile for a session**: We can associate an optimization profile at a CLP session-level, by using the following command:

```
SET CURRENT OPTIMIZATION PROFILE=DBUSER.TESTPROF
```

Once set, this profile will be in use until the connection terminates. This statement can also be embedded in an application program, allowing us to associate optimization profiles at the session level.

5. **Set an optimization profile for SQL stored procedures**: Call SET_ROUTINE_OPTS procedure before creating the SQL procedures.

```
CALL SYSPROC.SET_ROUTINE_OPTS('OPTPROFILE  DBUSER.TESTPROF ')
```

We can also associate optimization profiles at application bind time by using the OPTPROFILE bind option.

```
BIND prog1.bnd OPTPROFILE KCHEN.PROF1
```

For SQLJ applications, we can use the BINDOPTIONS parameter to associate an optimization profile during the customization phase.

```
sqlj test.sqlj db2sqljcustomize -url jdbc:db2://localhost:50000/
SAMPLE -user dbuser -password password -bindoptions "OPTPROFILE
DBUSER.TESTPROF " -storebindoptions test_SJProfile0
```

How it works...

Once an optimization profile is associated with an application, every SQL query is compared against the guidelines present in the optimization profile. If any match is found, then the corresponding guidelines will be picked up to choose the access plan, otherwise a warning (SQL0473W) will be returned. If the guidelines are selected for any SQL query, then it also reflects in the explain information, if captured.

Once an optimization profile is associated with a session, it remains effective until the session terminates or the profile is explicitly disassociated. This can be done by setting the current optimization profile to a NULL or an EMPTY string. If set to an EMPTY string, then it disables the use of optimization profiles. If set to NULL, then the optimization profile specified by OPTPROFILE option will be used for optimization.

```
SET CURRENT OPTIMIZATION PROFILE NULL

SET CURRENT OPTIMIZATION PROFILE = ''
```

There's more...

It is important to note that, since SQLJ generates an implicit DECLARE CURSOR clause for a SELECT SQL statement, it is necessary to also include the DECLARE CURSOR clause along with the SELECT statement in the optimization profile, in order for the guideline to be picked up.

If we choose to delete an existing optimization profile, we can delete it from the system catalogs as follows:

```
DELETE FROM SYSTOOLS.OPT_PROFILE WHERE SCHEMA = 'DBUSER' AND NAME =
'MYPROFILE'
```

Once a profile is deleted, it is still available in cache, so we should flush the cache. When we flush the optimization profile cache, any dynamic SQL statements which were prepared with that profile become invalid in the dynamic plan cache.

Examples of optimization profiles

- ▶ **Changing the current optimization**: We can choose to use a different optimization level for a particular query, by overriding the current optimization level as follows:

```
<OPTGUIDELINES>
   <QRYOPT VALUE="0"></QRYOPT>
</OPTGUIDELINES>
```

- ▶ **Changing** the REOPT **option to** ALWAYS: We can override the REOPT value for a particular query, by overriding it as follows:

```
<OPTGUIDELINES>
   <REOPT VALUE='ALWAYS'/>
</OPTGUIDELINES>
```

- ▶ **Changing the table join order**: In this example, we are guiding the table order in a merge join as follows:

```
<OPTGUIDELINES>
   <MSJOIN FIRST="TRUE" outermost="true">
     <ACCESS TABLEID="tbl2"/>
     <MSJOIN>
       <ACCESS TABLEID="tbl3"/>
       <ACCESS TABLEID="tbl1"/>
     </MSJOIN>
   </MSJOIN>
</OPTGUIDELINES>
```

- ▶ **Query rewrite request**: We can tell the optimizer to join the tables instead of using a sub query as follows:

```
<OPTGUIDELINES>
   <SUBQ2JOIN OPTION="ENABLE" />
</OPTGUIDELINES>
```

▶ **Request for an index scan instead of a table scan**: We can force a particular index scan instead of a table scan, by using the following guideline:

```
<OPTGUIDELINES>
  <IXSCAN TABLE='TAB1' INDEX='IDX1' />
</OPTGUIDELINES>
```

▶ **Request a different join method**: We can ask the optimizer to choose MERGE join for the given query. This can be requested for any two tables, including the result of another type of join.

```
<OPTGUIDELINES>
  <MSJOIN>
    <ACCESS TABLEID="tbl1"/>
    <ACCESS TABLEID="tbl2"/>
  </MSJOIN>
</OPTGUIDELINES>
```

```
<OPTGUIDELINES>
  <MSJOIN>
    <NLJOIN>
      <IXSCAN TABLE='tbl1'/>
      <IXSCAN TABLE="tbl2"/>
    </NLJOIN>
    <IXSCAN TABLE='S'/>
  </MSJOIN>
</OPTGUIDELINES>
```

▶ **Requesting MQT usage**: We can ask optimizer to use MQTs to satisfy the given query as follows:

```
<OPTGUIDELINES>
  <MQTENFORCE>
    <NAME='MQT1'/>
    <TYPE='REPLICATED' />
  </ MQTENFORCE >
<OPTGUIDELINES>
```

List of guidelines available

The optimizer is a part of the SQL engine that creates and chooses the best access plan for an SQL statement. It uses cost-based optimization where it chooses the access plan based on the lowest cost. Every access plan, in itself, is a way to execute an SQL statement. We use optimization profiles to influence the optimizer decision. For example, we can force the optimizer to choose a specific type of join for a given SQL statement. The following table describes the most common optimization guidelines that can be included in an optimization profile:

Category	Guideline	Description
General	REOPT	Overrides the REOPT bind option
	DEGREE	Overrides the current degree
	QRYOPT	Overrides the current optimization level
	RTS	Real-time statistics collection
	DPFXMLMOVEMENT	This affects the optimizer plan when moving XML data between database partitions
Query rewrite request	INLIST2JOIN	Requests the IN list to join
	SUBQ2JOIN	Requests the sub query to join
	NOTEX2AJ	Requests not exists to anti-join
	NOTIN2AJ	Requests not in to anti-join
Access request	TBSCAN	Requests table scan access
	IXSCAN	Requests index scan
	LPREFETCH	Requests list prefetch
	IXAND	Requests index ANDing
	IXOR	Requests index ORing
	XISCAN	Requests XML index access
	XANDOR	Requests XANDOR access
	ACCESS	Requests the optimizer to choose the ACCESS method
Join request	NLJOIN	Requests Nested loop join
	HSJOIN	Requests Hash join
	MSJOIN	Requests Merge join
	JOIN	Requests optimizer to choose the JOIN method

Using explain utilities

An SQL query can have more than one possible way or path of execution (also known as access plan). **Access plan** is also known as **explain plan**, and these two terms are used interchangeably. The DB2 optimizer uses a cost-based optimization to choose the path with the most efficient cost. The cost of each plan is determined from the latest database statistics available. That's why it is very important to make sure that the system statistics are up-to-date. Access plans provide the following information:

▸ Decision criteria that were used to choose the access plan

- ▸ Sequence of operations that were performed to process the query
- ▸ Cost of each step performed
- ▸ Selectivity estimate for each predicate
- ▸ Values of special registers and other variables (host variables, parameter markers, and so on)
- ▸ Optimization level in effect
- ▸ All objects that were used to process the query

DB2 provides different utilities that can be used to get the access plan chosen for a query execution. The access plan can be very useful to evaluate performance tuning actions. We can compare access plans before and after any performance tuning step is performed. This way we can make sure that the desired action is in effect. Analyzing access plans is also very helpful in identifying problems with slow running queries. In this recipe, we will discuss different methods to capture access plans.

Getting ready

We can capture explain information as plain text, or record it in EXPLAIN tables. Capturing the information in EXPLAIN tables allows us to capture every fine detail of the explain information, and hence allows for detailed analysis of access plans.

- ▸ **Capturing explain information as plain text**: This can be done by using the db2expln utility. This tool is commonly used for quick examination of the chosen access plan. This can be used for both static and dynamic SQL and XQuery statements. It also allows us to capture access plans for multiple SQL statements at once.

- ▸ **Capturing explain information in EXPLAIN tables**: Before we can capture explain information in EXPLAIN tables, we need to create them. This can be done as follows:

  - Executing SQLLIB/MISC/EXPLAIN.DDL script or
  - CALL SYSPROC.SYSINSTALLOBJECTS('EXPLAIN', 'C', CAST(NULL AS VARCHAR(128)),
    CAST (NULL AS VARCHAR(128)))

There are different methods to capture explain information in EXPLAIN tables, which are described in the next section. We can capture the explain information for both static and dynamic SQL statements in EXPLAIN tables. In addition, we can capture explain information for CLI applications. As mentioned earlier, EXPLAIN tables can capture detailed information about the optimizer and statements being explained. EXPLAIN tables can be queried just like a regular table, allowing us to use explain information from within the application. Another option is to use the db2exfmt tool to format the contents of EXPLAIN tables.

How to do it...

1. **Get the access plan of an SQL statement**: We can use the `db2expln` utility to get the basic access plan for a given SQL statement. We can pass the SQL statement as an argument to the `db2expln` command.

   ```
   db2expln -database SAMPLE -statement "SELECT EMP.EMPNO, EMP.JOB,
   DEPT.DEPTNAME
      FROM EMPLOYEE EMP, DEPARTMENT DEPT WHERE EMP.WORKDEPT = DEPT.
   DEPTNO " -
      terminal -graph -opids
   ```

   The first section in the output includes the database version information along with the environment information, such as the isolation level in effect while the SQL is being explained, and so on.

```
C:\Windows\system32>db2expln -database SAMPLE -statement "SELECT EMP.EMPNO, EMP.JOB, DEPT.
DEPTNAME FROM EMPLOYEE EMP, DEPARTMENT DEPT WHERE EMP.WORKDEPT = DEPT.DEPTNO " -terminal -
graph -opids

DB2 Universal Database Version 9.7, 5622-044 (c) Copyright IBM Corp. 1991, 2008
Licensed Material - Program Property of IBM
IBM DB2 Universal Database SQL and XQUERY Explain Tool

DB2 Universal Database Version 9.7, 5622-044 (c) Copyright IBM Corp. 1991, 2008
Licensed Material - Program Property of IBM
IBM DB2 Universal Database SQL and XQUERY Explain Tool

******************* DYNAMIC *****************************************

==================== STATEMENT ==========================================================

     Isolation Level      = Cursor Stability
     Blocking             = Block Unambiguous Cursors
     Query Optimization Class = 5

     Partition Parallel    = No
     Intra-Partition Parallel = No

     SQL Path             = "SYSIBM", "SYSFUN", "SYSPROC", "SYSIBMADM",
                            "DBUSER"
```

The next section displays the SQL statement which is being explained, and the total cost estimate:

```
Statement:

 SELECT EMP.EMPNO, EMP.JOB, DEPT.DEPTNAME
 FROM EMPLOYEE EMP, DEPARTMENT DEPT
 WHERE EMP.WORKDEPT = DEPT.DEPTNO


Section Code Page = 1208

Estimated Cost = 15.240876
Estimated Cardinality = 42.000000
```

This section shows the detailed explain plan in a sequential manner. The order of steps appearing in the following section is the actual order of execution chosen by the optimizer:

```
(   4) Access Table Name = DBUSER.DEPARTMENT  ID = 2,5
      |  #Columns = 2
      |  Skip Inserted Rows
      |  Avoid Locking Committed Data
      |  Currently Committed for Cursor Stability
      |  May participate in Scan Sharing structures
      |  Scan may start anywhere and wrap, for completion
      |  Fast scan, for purposes of scan sharing management
      |  Scan can be throttled in scan sharing management
      |  Relation Scan
      |  |  Prefetch: Eligible
      |  Lock Intents
      |  |  Table: Intent Share
      |  |  Row  : Next Key Share
      |  Sargable Predicate(s)
(   2) |  |  Process Build Table for Hash Join
(   2) Hash Join
      |  Early Out: Single Match Per Outer Row
      |  Estimated Build Size: 4000
      |  Estimated Probe Size: 4000
(   3) |  Access Table Name = DBUSER.EMPLOYEE  ID = 2,6
      |  |  #Columns = 3
      |  |  Skip Inserted Rows
      |  |  Avoid Locking Committed Data
      |  |  Currently Committed for Cursor Stability
      |  |  May participate in Scan Sharing structures
      |  |  Scan may start anywhere and wrap, for completion
      |  |  Fast scan, for purposes of scan sharing management
      |  |  Scan can be throttled in scan sharing management
      |  |  Relation Scan
      |  |  |  Prefetch: Eligible
      |  |  Lock Intents
      |  |  |  Table: Intent Share
      |  |  |  Row  : Next Key Share
      |  |  Sargable Predicate(s)
(   2) |  |  |  Process Probe Table for Hash Join
(   1) Return Data to Application
      |  #Columns = 3

End of section
```

The following section displays the access plan in a graphical representation. This access plan is read from bottom to top:

```
Optimizer Plan:

              Rows
            Operator
              (ID)
              Cost

               42
              n/a
             RETURN
             ( 1)
            15.2409
               |
               42
              n/a
             HSJOIN
             ( 2)
            15.2409
            /        \
        42              14
       n/a             n/a
      TBSCAN          TBSCAN
      ( 3)            ( 4)
     7.63065         7.60332
        |               |
        42              14
       n/a             n/a
     Table:          Table:
     DBUSER          DBUSER
     EMPLOYEE        DEPARTMENT
```

2. **Get access plans for a set of SQL statements**: We can use the db2expln method to get the access plans for multiple SQL statements at once, by defining them in a statement file. This also allows us to define different environment options, such as CURRENT OPTIMIZATION LEVEL, CURRENT DEGREE, CURRENT REFRESH AGE, and so on. This helps in comparing the access plan results with modified environment options, without actually changing them.

Sample statement file:

```
SET CURRENT QUERY OPTIMIZATION 1;

SELECT EMP.EMPNO, EMP.JOB, DEPT.

DEPTNAME FROM EMPLOYEE EMP, DEPARTMENT DEPT WHERE EMP.WORKDEPT =
DEPT.DEPTNO;


SET CURRENT QUERY OPTIMIZATION 5;

SELECT EMP.EMPNO, EMP.JOB, DEPT.

DEPTNAME FROM EMPLOYEE EMP, DEPARTMENT DEPT WHERE EMP.WORKDEPT =
DEPT.DEPTNO;
```

```
SET CURRENT QUERY OPTIMIZATION 9;

SELECT EMP.EMPNO, EMP.JOB, DEPT.

DEPTNAME FROM EMPLOYEE EMP, DEPARTMENT DEPT WHERE EMP.WORKDEPT =
DEPT.DEPTNO;
```

We can use the following command to get the access plan for this statement file.

```
db2expln -database SAMPLE -stmtfile stmtinputfile.db2 -terminator
; -output
   MyAccessPlans.out -graph -opids
```

The resultant output will have access plans for all these statements one after another.

3. **Get the access plan for a package**: We can use the db2expln method to get the basic access plan for all SQL statements contained in a package. Please note that only static SQL statements will be explained.

   Example: db2expln -d SAMPLE -c DBUSER -p P1154476 -s 0 -g -o P1154476.out

4. **Capturing the access plan for a statement in** EXPLAIN **tables**: One way to capture the explain information in EXPLAIN tables is by using the EXPLAIN statement. EXPLAIN tables must be created before using the EXPLAIN statement. EXPLAIN statements can be executed against SQL and XQuery as well.

   Example: EXPLAIN ALL WITH SNAPSHOT FOR SELECT EMP.EMPNO, EMP.JOB, DEPT.

   DEPTNAME FROM EMPLOYEE EMP, DEPARTMENT DEPT WHERE EMP.WORKDEPT = DEPT.DEPTNO

   The SQL statement is not executed, and only the access plan is captured in EXPLAIN tables.

5. **Capturing access plan for static SQL during bind time**: We can also capture the access plan information in EXPLAIN tables during package binding time. This can be done by using the EXPLAIN YES clause in the BIND statement. If we also want to capture an explain snapshot, then use the EXPLSNAP clause.

   Example:

```
BIND MyProgram.bnd EXPLAIN YES

BIND MyProgram.bnd EXPLAIN YES EXPLSNAP YES

BIND MyProgram.bnd EXPLSNAP YES
```

   When the EXPLAIN YES clause is specified, the access plan information will be captured for static SQL at bind time, and incremental bind statements at run time. Other options available for the EXPLAIN clause are:

- ❑ NO: No explain formation will be collected
- ❑ ALL: In addition to information captured by the EXPLAIN YES clause, this clause also captures access plan information for dynamic SQL statement at runtime
- ❑ REOPT: Explain information for each re-optimizable incremental bind statement and re-optimizable dynamic SQL statement is captured in EXPLAIN tables
- ❑ ONLY: If this clause is specified, then only the explain information is captured, and no package is created in the database

If the package is for a routine, if it contains incremental bind statements, and if EXPLAIN clauses are specified to capture the explain information, then the routine must be specified with MODIFIES SQL DATA.

Just like EXPLAIN clause options, we have similar clauses for EXPLSNAP as well that behave in the same manner as EXPLAIN options do.

6. **Capturing explain snapshot at execution time**: This can be controlled by the CURRENT EXPLAIN SNAPSHOT special register.

- ❑ When set to YES, the compiler captures explain snapshot data, and then executes the query
- ❑ When set to EXPLAIN, the compiler only captures the explain snapshot data, and does not execute the query

```
db2 SET CURRENT EXPLAIN SNAPSHOT YES

db2 -tf testsql.db2

db2 SET CURRENT EXPLAIN SNAPSHOT NO

db2exfmt -d SAMPLE -g TIC -w -1 -n % -s % -# 0 -o explain.out
```

7. **Capturing explain information at execution** time: This can be controlled by the CURRENT EXPLAIN MODE special register.

- ❑ When set to YES, the compiler captures the explain information in EXPLAIN tables, and executes the query.
- ❑ When set to EXPLAIN, the compiler only captures the explain information, and does not execute the query.
- ❑ When set to RECOMMEND INDEXES, the compiler captures the explain information and also recommends indexes in the ADVISE_INDEX table. The query is not executed.

❑ When set to `EVALUATE INDEXES`, the compiler uses the indexes suggested by the `ADVISE_INDEX` table, and evaluates their performance benefits.

❑ When set to `REOPT`, the compiler captures the explain information for static and dynamic SQL statements during statement re-optimization at runtime. At runtime, the values for host variables and parameter markers are available to the compiler.

```
db2 SET CURRENT EXPLAIN MODE EXPLAIN

db2 -tf testsql.db2

db2 SET CURRENT EXPLAIN MODE NO

db2exfmt -d SAMPLE -g TIC -w -1 -n % -s % -# 0 -o explain.
out
```

8. **Reading information stored** in `EXPLAIN` **tables**: The `db2exfmt` utility is used to interpret information stored in `EXPLAIN` tables. This is an interactive tool that prompts for input arguments.

For example, if no input arguments are provided, then it uses default options as follows, and enters into an **interactive** mode:

```
db2exfmt [-e % -n % -s % -v % -w -1 -# 0]
```

```
C:\Windows\system32>db2exfmt
DB2 Universal Database Version 9.7, 5622-044 (c) Copyright IBM Corp. 1991, 2008
Licensed Material - Program Property of IBM
IBM DATABASE 2 Explain Table Format Tool

Enter Database Name ==> sample
Connecting to the Database.
Connect to Database Successful.
Binding package - Bind was Successful
Enter Explain table schema (Default is connection id) ==>
Enter up to 26 character Explain timestamp (Default -1) ==>
Enter up to 128 character source name (SOURCE_NAME, Default %%) ==>
Enter source schema (SOURCE_SCHEMA, Default %%) ==>
Enter section number (0 for all, Default 0) ==>
Enter outfile name. Default is to terminal ==>
```

This utility is used once we have captured the explain information in the `EXPLAIN` tables by any means.

For example:

```
db2 explain plan with snapshot for SELECT EMP.EMPNO, EMP.JOB,
DEPT.

DEPTNAME FROM EMPLOYEE EMP, DEPARTMENT DEPT WHERE EMP.WORKDEPT =
DEPT.DEPTNO
```

```
db2exfmt
```

Or

```
db2 set current explain mode yes

db2 set current explain snapshot yes

db2 "SELECT EMP.EMPNO, EMP.JOB, DEPT.
DEPTNAME FROM EMPLOYEE EMP, DEPARTMENT DEPT WHERE EMP.WORKDEPT =
DEPT.DEPTNO"

db2exfmt
```

How it works...

An access plan is very important because it tells us how the query is behaving. This plan consists of a series of operations that will be performed on base tables in order to get the desired results. The access plan is chosen by the DB2 optimizer, based on all information available to it, which is nothing but the statistics.

Some of the most important information available in the explain plan includes:

- Scan type: Table scan or index scan
- Join type: Hash join, nested-loop join, and merge join
- Total cost (in timerons)
- Number of page I/Os
- Communication cost
- Cost of fetching first row
- Set of database objects that will be accessed
- Set of columns that will be accessed
- Set of predicates that will be applied
- Estimated number of rows to be returned

How does the EXPLAIN statement work?

EXPLAIN statements can be embedded in host languages as static or dynamic SQL. The statement to be explained is not executed. For a static EXPLAIN statement, explain information is captured at BIND time. During pre-compilation, the EXPLAIN statement itself is commented out, and is no longer a part of the application, and hence, when the package is run, EXPLAIN statements are not executed. However, the section number will still include EXPLAIN statements.

For dynamic EXPLAIN statements, the explain information is captured when the EXPLAIN statement is submitted for compilation. During execution time, the EXPLAIN statement returns successfully without doing any processing.

There's more...

When we capture explain information, DB2 also captures system statistics that were in effect when the statement was explained. These statistics can be different from the current statistics. This can happen if statistics were collected again after the explain information was captured. This can also happen if real-time statistics gathering is enabled in the database. If only EXPLAIN tables are populated, and no explain snapshot is taken, then DB2 collects only a few statistics, whereas if an explain snapshot is taken, it captures all the statistics relevant to the statement being explained. Once we have the statistics recorded in EXPLAIN tables, we can use the SYSPROC.EXPLAIN_FORMAT_STATS scalar function to format the statistics in the snapshot in a readable format. If we are using db2exfmt to format the content of EXPLAIN tables then db2exfmt internally uses this table function to display the recorded statistics.

For example, we can use the following information to get the snapshot information:

```
SELECT EXPLAIN_FORMAT_STATS(SNAPSHOT)
  FROM EXPLAIN_STATEMENT
  WHERE EXPLAIN_REQUESTER = 'DBUSER' AND
    SOURCE_NAME = 'SQLC2H20' AND
    STMTNO = 1;
```

The results of this SQL query contain detailed information about the statistics captured in the explain_statement table. The first section in the output shows the Tablespace statistics, as shown in the following screenshot:

```
Tablespace Context:
-------------------
              Name:                     USERSPACE1
              Overhead:                 7.500000
              Transfer Rate:            0.060000
              Prefetch Size:            32
              Extent Size:              32
              Type:                     Database managed
              Partition Group Name:     NULLP
              Buffer Pool Identifier:   0
```

The next section displays table statistics including information such as the total number of data pages, average width of row, and so on:

```
Base Table Statistics:
----------------------
Name    :        EMPLOYEE
Schema:          DBUSER
                 Number of Columns:                        14
                 Number of Pages with Rows:                1
                 Number of Pages:                          1
                 Number of Rows:                           42
                 Table Overflow Record Count:              0
                 Width of Rows:                            49
                 Time of Creation:                         2011-06-08-00.06.57.313001
                 Last Statistics Update:                   2011-08-29-00.00.00.000000
                 Primary Tablespace:                       USERSPACE1
                 Tablespace for Indexes:                   USERSPACE1
                 Tablespace for Long Data:                 NULLP
                 Number of Referenced Columns:             3
                 Number of Indexes:                        2
                 Volatile Table:                           No
                 Number of Active Blocks:                  -1
                 Number of Column Groups:                  0
                 Number of Data Partitions:                1
                 Average Row Compression Ratio:            -1.000000
                 Percent Rows Compressed:                  -1.000000
                 Average Compressed Row Size:              -1
                 Statistics Type:                          S
```

The next section displays the column level details. It includes information about all columns selected or referred to in the SQL query.

```
Column Information:
-------------------
        Number:                                       8
        Name:                                         JOB
        Statistics Available:                         Yes

        Column Statistics:
        ------------------
                Schema name of the column type:        SYSIBM
                Name of column type:                   CHARACTER
                Maximum column length:                 8
                Scale for decimal or timestamp column: 0
                Number of distinct column values:      8
                Average column length:                 9
                Number of most frequent values:        7
                Number of quantiles:                   15
                Second highest data value:             PRES
                Second lowest data value:              CLERK
                Column sequence in partition key:      0
                Average number of sub-elements:        -1
                Average length of delimiters:          -1

        Column Distribution Statistics:
        -------------------------------
                Frequency Statistics:
                Valcount        Value
                ------------------------------------
                10              DESIGNER
                8               CLERK
                7               MANAGER
                6               OPERATOR
                .......

                Quantile Statistics:
                Valcount        Value       Distcount
                --------------------------------------------------
                0               ANALYST     0
                3               ANALYST     0
                3               CLERK       0
                11              CLERK       0
                11              DESIGNER              0
                21              DESIGNER              0

                .......
```

The last section displays information about indexes available for the referenced table.

```
Indexes defined on the table:
-----------------------------
Name  : XEMP2
Schema: DBUSER
        Unique Rule:                          Duplicate index
        Used in Operator:                     No
        Page Fetch Pairs:                     Not Available
        Number of Columns:                    1
        Index Leaf Pages:                     1
        Index Tree Levels:                    1
        Index First Key Cardinality:          8
        Index Full Key Cardinality:           8
        Index Cluster Ratio:                  100
        Index Cluster Factor:                 -1.000000
        Time of Creation:                     2011-06-08-00.06.57.572000
        Last Statistics Update:               2011-08-29-00.00.00.000000
        Index Sequential Pages:               0
        Index First 2 Keys Cardinality:       -1
        Index First 3 Keys Cardinality:       -1
        Index First 4 Keys Cardinality:       -1
        Index Avg Gap between Sequences:      0.000000
        Fetch Avg Gap between Sequences:      -1.000000
        Index Avg Sequential Pages:           0.000000
        Fetch Avg Sequential Pages:           -1.000000
        Index Avg Random Pages:               1.000000
        Fetch Avg Random Pages:               -1.000000
        Index RID Count:                      42
        Index Deleted RID Count:              0
        Index Empty Leaf Pages:               0
        Avg Partition Cluster Ratio:          -1
        Avg Partition Cluster Factor:         -1.000000
        Data Partition Cluster Factor:        1.000000
        Data Partition Page Fetch Pairs:      Not Available
```

Capturing explain information for a routine

When we create a stored procedure or any other routine, it is stored as a package in the database. If we want to capture the access plan for all SQL statements contained in a routine, then we first need to find the routine package registered in the database. To get the procedure to package name mapping, we can use the following SQL query:

```
SELECT PROCSCHEMA, PROCNAME, BNAME AS PACKAGENAME

   FROM SYSCAT.PROCEDURES, SYSCAT.ROUTINEDEP

   WHERE SYSCAT.PROCEDURES.SPECIFICNAME = SYSCAT.ROUTINEDEP.ROUTINENAME
```

Once we have the package name, we can use any of the following methods to capture the explain information for the routine.

```
db2expln -d SAMPLE -c DBUSER -p P1154476 -s 0 -g -o P1154476.out
```

Explain tables

The following table summarizes the EXPLAIN tables, which are used for capturing explain information:

Table name	Description
EXPLAIN_ACTUALS	Stores the explain section's actuals information.
EXPLAIN_ARGUMENT	Stores information about the unique characteristics of each individual operator.
EXPLAIN_DIAGNOSTIC	Contains diagnostic messages produced for the explained statement.
EXPLAIN_DIAGNOSTIC_DATA	Contains message tokens for diagnostic messages recorded in EXPLAIN_DIAGNOSTIC table.
EXPLAIN_INSTANCE	Contains environment information about the explained statement. This is the main table among all EXPLAIN tables – each EXPLAIN table links to this one.
EXPLAIN_OBJECT	Identifies the data objects used in the access plan generated.
EXPLAIN_OPERATOR	Contains all operators present in the access plan.
EXPLAIN_PREDICATE	Identifies all predicates applied by each operator in the access plan.
EXPLAIN_STATEMENT	Contains the SQL statement information which is explained. If an explain snapshot is also requested, then this table also holds the explain snapshot in the SNAPSHOT column.
EXPLAIN_STREAM	Contains input and output data streams between individual operators and data objects.

Using section explain information

Starting from DB2 9.7 Fix Pack 1, DB2 introduced the **section explain functionality** that allows us to capture explain information using the contents of a run-time section. Using section explains, we can get information about the actual execution values along with the estimated values provided by the EXPLAIN command. In this recipe, we will discuss how we can extract explain information from a section, and compare the estimated and actual values in the access plan.

Getting ready

We should have EXPLAIN tables created before we can capture any explain information.

How to do it...

To obtain the estimated and actual explain information, perform the following steps:

1. **Enable section actuals**: Update the SECTION_ACTUALS database manager configuration parameter value to BASE.

   ```
   UPDATE DATABASE CONFIGURATION USING SECTION_ACTUALS BASE
   ```

2. Create a workload to collect the activities submitted by the target application, and enable section data collection for these activities.

```
CREATE WORKLOAD MYWL

  APPLNAME( 'TESTAPP.EXE')

  COLLECT ACTIVITY DATA WITH DETAILS,SECTION;


GRANT USAGE ON WORKLOAD MYWL TO PUBLIC;
```

 We could use the system default workload instead of creating a new one, but in that case, we couldn't limit the amount of information captured by the activity event monitor.

3. Create an activity monitor, and activate it to start collecting the activity information.

```
CREATE EVENT MONITOR ACTEVMON FOR ACTIVITIES WRITE TO TABLE;
SET EVENT MONITOR ACTEVMON STATE 1;
```

4. Run the application that we want to analyze. In this example, our application's name is testApp.exe.

5. Find the statement ID information from the activity event monitor tables, by using the following SQL command:

```
SELECT APPL_ID, UOW_ID, ACTIVITY_ID,

  STMT_TEXT

FROM ACTIVITYSTMT_ACTEVMON
```

6. Use this activity ID information as input to the EXPLAIN_FROM_ACTIVITY stored procedure, and obtain the section explain with actuals.

```
CALL EXPLAIN_FROM_ACTIVITY( ' *LOCAL.DB2.110918175715 ', 1, 1,
'ACTEVMON',

  'DBUSER', ?, ?, ?, ?, ? )
```

7. Format the explain information by using the db2exfmt utility.

```
db2exfmt -d sample -w 2011-09-18-11.54.23.345321 -n SQLC2H10 -s
NULLID -# 0 -t
```

The following image displays the sample output for this SQL query. We can observe that the access plan highlights the estimated versus the actual values for each operator:

```
Access Plan:
-----------
        Total Cost:             15.2409
        Query Degree:           1

              Rows
           Rows Actual
            RETURN
            (   1)
             Cost
             I/O
              |
              42                        <-- Estimated number of rows
              42                        <-- Actual number of rows
            ^HSJOIN
            (   2)
            15.2409
              NA
         /-----+------\
        42            14               <-- Estimated number of rows
        42            14               <-- Actual number of rows
      TBSCAN         TBSCAN
      (   3)         (   4)
     7.63065        7.60332
        NA            NA
        |             |
        42            14               <-- Estimated number of rows
        NA            NA               <-- Actual number of rows
   TABLE: DBUSER  TABLE: DBUSER
     EMPLOYEE       DEPARTMENT
```

It also indicates the estimated versus the actual statistics in a detailed section for each operator as shown in the following screenshot. This helps us in identifying cardinality issues.

```
1) RETURN: (Return Result)
        Cumulative Total Cost:          15.2409
        Cumulative First Row Cost:      15.2409
        Estimated Bufferpool Buffers:   1

        Arguments:
        ---------
        BLDLEVEL: (Build level)
                DB2 v9.7.100.166 : s091103
        EXECUTID: (Executable ID)
                0100000000000000320000000000000000000000002002011091823294 3402000
        HEAPUSE : (Maximum Statement Heap Usage)
                80 Pages
        STMTHEAP: (Statement heap size)
                2048

        Input Streams:
        -------------
                5) From Operator #2

                        Estimated number of rows:       42
                        Actual number of rows:          42
```

Examine the actual versus the estimated values for different operators in the access plan. In this way, the section actually provides us the exact information that will be available at run-time, giving us the ability to identify the problem areas, if any.

How it works

With regular explain modes, we must re-run the SQL statement in the `explain` mode. With section explain, we do not need to re-run the SQL statement, the explain information can be obtained directly from the section, as long as the section is still available in memory or system catalogs.

When the explain information is obtained from the section or catalogs, it doesn't retrieve all the information that is available to a regular explain. This is because everything is stored in the section or catalogs. Some non-critical information is excluded to limit the section size.

There's more...

DB2 provides four procedures to perform section explain. These four stored procedures differ only in their way of getting inputs.

- ▶ EXPLAIN_FROM_ACTIVITY: This is useful when we have the SQL statement captured by an activity event monitor. This is particularly used to capture section actuals information in explain plans.

- ▶ EXPLAIN_FROM_CATALOG: This is useful when the section of a static SQL statement is stored in a database package or a catalog. In other words, the statement must be available in the `syscat.statements` table.

- ▶ EXPLAIN_FROM_DATA: This is useful if we already have section data stored in a monitor table.

- ▶ EXPLAIN_FROM_SECTION: This is useful for obtaining explain information, if we know the execution ID of the SQL statement. This statement must be available in the package cache.

Interpreting db2exfmt output

In the previous recipe, we discussed how to use different explain utilities. `db2exfmt` is the most commonly-used utility for troubleshooting a performance problem. This utility gives very detailed information captured in EXPLAIN tables in the form of an ASCII text report. This report contains textual information, as well as the access plan in a graphical format, which is extremely useful for query analysis. In this recipe, we will discuss how to interpret the results from the `db2exfmt` utility.

How to do it...

As mentioned in the previous recipe, the output of the db2exfmt tool contains very detailed information about the query execution plan. In this section, we will discuss how to interpret each section.

1. **Verifying the database information**: The top section of the db2exfmt output contains DB2 version information, and the time when the db2exfmt tool was run.

```
DB2 Universal Database Version 9.7, 5622-044 (c) Copyright IBM Corp. 1991, 2008
Licensed Material - Program Property of IBM
IBM DATABASE 2 Explain Table Format Tool


******************** EXPLAIN INSTANCE ********************

DB2_VERSION:         09.07.1
SOURCE_NAME:         SQLC2H20
SOURCE_SCHEMA:       NULLID
SOURCE_VERSION:
EXPLAIN_TIME:        2011-09-04-00.24.34.513001
EXPLAIN_REQUESTER:   DBUSER
```

2. **Check the database context area**: This section contains the configuration parameter values that have the most significant impact on query performance. We can also get this information by querying the database configuration parameter values.

```
Database Context:
----------------
        Parallelism:          None
        CPU Speed:            5.668131e-007
        Comm Speed:           100
        Buffer Pool size:     250
        Sort Heap size:       256
        Database Heap size:   600
        Lock List size:       4096
        Maximum Lock List:    22
        Average Applications: 1
        Locks Available:      28835
```

3. **View package context area**: This section indicates whether the SQL query explained was static or dynamic, along with other details, such as optimization level in effect and isolation levels. This gives the environment in which a given SQL statement is explained.

```
Package Context:
----------------
        SQL Type:            Dynamic
        Optimization Level: 5
        Blocking:            Block All Cursors
        Isolation Level:    Cursor Stability

---------------- STATEMENT 1   SECTION 203 ----------------
        QUERYNO:            1
        QUERYTAG:
        Statement Type:    Select
        Updatable:          No
        Deletable:          No
        Query Degree:       1
```

4. **Original statement**: This is the SQL statement submitted by the application.

```
Original Statement:
-------------------
SELECT e.lastname, e.job, d.deptname, d.location, p.projname
FROM employee AS e, department AS d, project AS p
WHERE e.workdept = d.deptno AND e.workdept = p.deptno
```

5. **Optimized statement**: Once an SQL query is submitted for execution, the first step performed is query rewrite. DB2 optimizer rewrites the query in a more optimized form. If any **Materialized Query Table** (**MQT**) is being used in a query execution, then we can see the MQT name in re-written SQL. Also, if we have any view in our SQL query, then the view reference is also replaced with its definition. Any kind of push-down logic is reflected in this rewritten SQL statement. Constant expressions are also computed and substituted in re-written SQL statement. The optimizer may choose to embed or remove nested sub-selects.

```
Optimized Statement:
--------------------
SELECT Q3.LASTNAME AS "LASTNAME", Q3.JOB AS "JOB", Q2.DEPTNAME AS "DEPTNAME",
       Q2.LOCATION AS "LOCATION", Q1.PROJNAME AS "PROJNAME"
FROM DBUSER.PROJECT AS Q1, DBUSER.DEPARTMENT AS Q2, DBUSER.EMPLOYEE AS Q3
WHERE (Q3.WORKDEPT = Q1.DEPTNO) AND (Q1.DEPTNO = Q2.DEPTNO)
```

Table names are replaced with Q(n) in the order of their position in the SQL query.

6. **Access plan**: This is the graphical representation of an access plan. The access plan is read from bottom-to-top and left-to-right. The total cost mentioned on top of an access plan is the estimated cost of the query in timerons. A **timeron** is a relative unit of measurement introduced in DB2. It signifies the cost of an SQL query, based on factors such as CPU usage, I/O characteristics, and so on. This unit is primarily used by the optimizer to calculate and compare the execution cost for an SQL query.

```
Access Plan:
-----------
          Total Cost:          22.8578
          Query Degree:        1

                   Rows
                  RETURN
                  (   1)
                   Cost
                   I/O
                    |
                   105
                  HSJOIN
                  (   2)
                  22.8578
                    3
            /-------+-------\
          42                 20
        TBSCAN             HSJOIN
        (   3)             (   4)
        7.63065           15.2172
          1                  2
          |            /-----+------\
          42          14             20
    TABLE: DBUSER    TBSCAN         TBSCAN
       EMPLOYEE      (   5)         (   6)
         Q3          7.60332        7.60917
                       1              1
                       |              |
                      14             20
                 TABLE: DBUSER   TABLE: DBUSER
                  DEPARTMENT       PROJECT
                     Q2             Q1
```

Each operator has information about the rows received and rows returned, along with the cost estimates. We can recognize these values as follows:

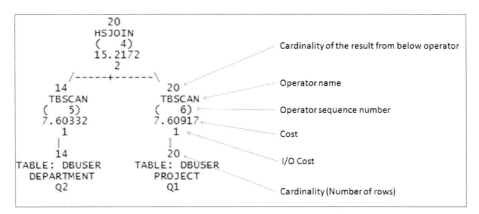

7. **Extended diagnostic information**: This section is just informational, and lists all database objects being used or considered in choosing the access plan for a query. It also gives diagnostic information about table statistics. This section also warns us if the statistics are not up-to-date. If we are expecting an MQT or statistical view to be used for an SQL statement, and if it is not used, then this section tells us why it wasn't used. The optimizer might have found some better alternative, or maybe the MQT or statistical view cannot be used because of the predicates applied in the SQL statement. In such cases, we might want to tune the MQT or statistical view definition to make it more usable.

```
Extended Diagnostic Information:
--------------------------------

Diagnostic Identifier:    1
Diagnostic Details:       EXP0062W  The following MQT or statistical view was
                          not eligible because one or more columns or
                          expressions referenced in the query were not found
                          in the MQT: "DBUSER    "."ADEFUSR".
Diagnostic Identifier:    2
Diagnostic Details:       EXP0148W  The following MQT or statistical view was
                          considered in query matching: "DBUSER    "."ADEFUSR".
```

8. **Getting detailed information about each operation**: The access plan graph does not give complete information. To know more details about any operator, we need to see the detailed information contained in the `db2exfmt` output. It contains detailed information for each and every node in the access plan, in an ordered fashion.

   For example, as per the `db2exfmt` output, the detailed information for **Operator #1** is as follows:

```
1) RETURN: (Return Result)
        Cumulative Total Cost:        22.8578
        Cumulative CPU Cost:          313719
        Cumulative I/O Cost:          3
        Cumulative Re-Total Cost:     22.8578
        Cumulative Re-CPU Cost:       313719
        Cumulative Re-I/O Cost:       3
        Cumulative First Row Cost:    22.8578
        Estimated Bufferpool Buffers: 1

        Arguments:
        ---------
        BLDLEVEL: (Build level)
                DB2 v9.7.100.166 : s091103
        HEAPUSE  : (Maximum Statement Heap Usage)
                80 Pages
        PREPTIME: (Statement prepare time)
                439 milliseconds
        STMTHEAP: (Statement heap size)
                2048

        Input Streams:
        -------------
                8) From Operator #2

                        Estimated number of rows:     105
                        Number of columns:            5
                        Subquery predicate ID:        Not Applicable

                        Column Names:
                        ------------
                        +Q4.PROJNAME+Q4.LOCATION+Q4.DEPTNAME+Q4.JOB
                        +Q4.LASTNAME
```

From this section, we can observe the following information:

- Detailed cost information
- Relevant database arguments
- Input stream details:
- Number of input rows
- Number of input columns
- Column names

Similarly, the detailed information for **Operator #2** is as follows:

```
2) HSJOIN: (Hash Join)
             Cumulative Total Cost:          22.8578
             Cumulative CPU Cost:            313719
             Cumulative I/O Cost:            3
             Cumulative Re-Total Cost:       22.8578
             Cumulative Re-CPU Cost:         313719
             Cumulative Re-I/O Cost:         3
             Cumulative First Row Cost:      22.8578
             Estimated Bufferpool Buffers:   1

             Arguments:
             ----------
             BITFLTR : (Hash Join Bit Filter used)
                    FALSE
             EARLYOUT: (Early Out flag)
                    NONE
             HASHCODE: (Hash Code Size)
                    24 BIT
             HASHTBSZ: (Number of hash table entries)
                    8
             TEMPSIZE: (Temporary Table Page Size)
                    8192
             TUPBLKSZ: (Unrecognized Argument)
                    4000

             Predicates:
             ----------
             2) Predicate used in Join,
                    Comparison Operator:       Equal (=)
                    Subquery Input Required:   NO
                    Filter Factor:             0.0714286

                    Predicate Text:
                    ---------------
                    (Q2.DEPTNO = Q3.WORKDEPT)
```

In the previous section, we can observe the following information for **Operator #2**:

- **Detailed cost information**: This cost is the cumulative cost for this node that includes the cost of all nodes below the current node).
- Bufferpool buffers: These represent the number of bufferpool pages required by given operator.

❏ **Relevant database arguments**: These arguments indicate different options that are in effect while the given SQL statement is prepared. Only options/ arguments that are relevant to the given operator are listed here.

❏ **Predicates used**: This gives the information about join predicates. It helps us identify the part of the SQL statement being executed here. It also shows the estimated selectivity of the predicate, based on table and column statistics, and the predicate being applied.

```
Input Streams:
--------------
        2) From Operator #3

                Estimated number of rows:       42
                Number of columns:              3
                Subquery predicate ID:          Not Applicable

                Column Names:
                ------------
                +Q3.JOB+Q3.LASTNAME+Q3.WORKDEPT

        7) From Operator #4

                Estimated number of rows:       20
                Number of columns:              5
                Subquery predicate ID:          Not Applicable

                Column Names:
                ------------
                +Q1.PROJNAME+Q1.DEPTNO+Q2.LOCATION+Q2.DEPTNAME
                +Q2.DEPTNO


Output Streams:
---------------
        8) To Operator #1

                Estimated number of rows:       105
                Number of columns:              5
                Subquery predicate ID:          Not Applicable

                Column Names:
                ------------
                +Q4.PROJNAME+Q4.LOCATION+Q4.DEPTNAME+Q4.JOB
                +Q4.LASTNAME
```

The previous section from the db2exfmt output shows information about the input and the output streams for **Operator #2**. The two input streams represent outer and inner tables along with input and output stream cardinalities.

9. **Objects used in access plan**: The next section shows all objects being used in the access plan.

```
Objects Used in Access Plan:
----------------------------

        Schema: DBUSER
        Name:   ADEFUSR
        Type:   Materialized View (reference only)

        Schema: DBUSER
        Name:   PROJACT
        Type:   Table (reference only)

        Schema: DBUSER
        Name:   DEPARTMENT
        Type:   Table

        Schema: DBUSER
        Name:   EMPLOYEE
        Type:   Table

        Schema: DBUSER
        Name:   PROJECT
        Type:   Table
```

Tablespace context: This section has information about the tablespaces that will be accessed.

```
Tablespace Context:
-------------------
        Name:                        USERSPACE1
        Overhead:                    7.500000
        Transfer Rate:               0.060000
        Prefetch Size:               32
        Extent Size:                 32
        Type:                        Database managed
        Partition Group Name:        NULLP
        Buffer Pool Identifier:      0
```

10. **Table information**: This section contains information about all tables referenced in an access plan, along with column details. This can be very useful to check whether the statistics are up-to-date. It can also suggest if we should collect column level statistics as well.

```
Base Table Statistics:
----------------------
Name   :       EMPLOYEE
Schema:        DBUSER
               Number of Columns:            14
               Number of Pages with Rows:    1
               Number of Pages:              1
               Number of Rows:               42
               Table Overflow Record Count:  0
               Width of Rows:                60
               Time of Creation:             2011-06-08-00.06.57.313001
               Last Statistics Update:       2011-08-29-00.00.00.000000
               .....
               Number of Referenced Columns: 3
               .....
               Number of Data Partitions:    1
               .....
```

The subsequent section includes information about all columns used or referenced in the SQL query being explained. If the distribution statistics are available at column level, then `db2exfmt` shows them as well, as shown in the following screenshot:

```
Column Information:
--------------------
        Number:                                  8
        Name:                                    JOB
        Statistics Available:                    Yes

        Column Statistics:
        ------------------
                Schema name of the column type:          SYSIBM
                Name of column type:                     CHARACTER
                Maximum column length:                   8
                ...
                Number of distinct column values:        8
                Average column length:                   9
                Number of most frequent values:          7
                Number of quantiles:                     15
                Second highest data value:               PRES
                Second lowest data value:                CLERK
                Column sequence in partition key:        0
                ...

        Column Distribution Statistics:
        -------------------------------
                Frequency Statistics:
                Valcount        Value
                --------------------------------
                10              DESIGNER
                8               CLERK
                ...

                Quantile Statistics:
                Valcount        Value           Distcount
                --------------------------------------------
                0               ANALYST         0
                3               ANALYST         0
                3               CLERK           0
                ...
```

The last section shows information about indexes available for the referenced table:

```
Indexes defined on the table:
--------------------------------
Name   : XEMP2
Schema: DBUSER
        Unique Rule:                            Duplicate index
        Used in Operator:                       No
        Page Fetch Pairs:                       Not Available
        Number of Columns:                      1
        Index Leaf Pages:                       1
        Index Tree Levels:                      1
        Index First Key Cardinality:            8
        Index Full Key Cardinality:             8
        Index Cluster Ratio:                    100
        Index Cluster Factor:                   -1.000000
        Time of Creation:                       2011-06-08-00.06.57.572000
        Last Statistics Update:                 2011-08-29-00.00.00.000000
        ...

Name   : PK_EMPLOYEE
Schema: DBUSER
        Unique Rule:                            Primary key index
        Used in Operator:                       No
        Page Fetch Pairs:                       Not Available
        Number of Columns:                      1
        Index Leaf Pages:                       1
        Index Tree Levels:                      1
        Index First Key Cardinality:            42
        Index Full Key Cardinality:             42
        Index Cluster Ratio:                    100
        Index Cluster Factor:                   -1.000000
        Time of Creation:                       2011-06-08-00.06.57.313001
        Last Statistics Update:                 2011-08-29-00.00.00.000000
        ...
```

How it works

The db2exfmt utility uses information available in the EXPLAIN tables, and formats them in a readable format. If the SQL statement was explained with the snapshot option, then it also captures catalog statistics in EXPLAIN tables. The db2exfmt utility uses the SYSPROC. EXPLAIN_FORMAT_STATS function to format the catalog statistics captured in the snapshot.

There's more...

When analyzing the access plan, we should keep following things in mind:

- **Cardinality of all tables referenced in SQL query**: This is useful to recognize wrong cardinality estimates by the optimizer. The primary reason for such issues is old statistics.

- **Algorithm of optimizer joins**: This helps us to understand if the join method used is proper, and if the inner and outer tables are also chosen properly. For example, if we observe a bigger table being chosen as the inner table, then there is some problem with the current statistics. Ideally, we will want the smaller table to be chosen as the inner table.

- **Underlying database partition information (if any)**: This will help us to ensure that a large portion of data is not transferred in the form of table queues. Also, we should know what type of table queues we can expect.

- ▶ **Table range partition information (if any)**: This will help us to ensure that proper partition elimination is taking place.

- ▶ **Information about indexes used in the access plan**: This helps us understand why a particular index is being used or chosen. It also helps us identify new indexes that might benefit the given SQL statement.

Understanding optimizer joins

A join is a process of combining data from two tables, based on some join criteria. Only two tables are joined at a time. One of the tables is selected as the outer table, and is traversed only once. Another table is the inner table that can be traversed multiple times, depending upon the join technique. The DB2 optimizer uses three types of join techniques to combine data from two tables.

- ▶ Nested loop join
- ▶ Merge join
- ▶ Hash join

Nested loop join: The operation of a nested loop join can be summarized as follows:

1. Read the first row in the outer table.

2. Scan the inner table until a match is found. When matched, join the two rows. This step is repeated until the end of the inner table row matches.

3. Read the next row in the outer table and perform *step 2*.

In this way, all rows in the outer table are matched with the inner table.

This join can be used if the predicate is of the following form:

Expr(outer table columns) OPERATOR (inner table column).

The OPERATOR can be =, <, >, <=, or >=.

For example, C1 + C2 = C3, where C1 and C2 are from the outer table, and C3 is from the inner table.

When the optimizer selects this join method, it also decides whether to sort the outer table. If the outer table is sorted before the join, then an overhead is incurred because of sorting. The cost estimated for the sort operation takes the **sortheap** into consideration, as spilling this memory area can significantly increase sorting cost. When the inner table is sorted, it is more likely to fit in the bufferpool, thus giving better performance in terms of I/O cost. So, whichever is most cost-efficient is chosen for the join. If we have ORDER BY, GROUP BY, or DISTINCT in the query, which would mean sorting is necessary, then the optimizer may choose to sort the table before joining, if it can reduce the cost of the future sort operation.

Merge join: The operation of a merge join can be summarized as follows:

1. The data should be ordered in both the outer and the inner table. This ordering can be achieved by either sorting or by using an index.

2. Read the first row in the outer table, and scan the inner table until a match is found.

3. Scanning of inner table continues until it finds a mismatch.

4. When a mismatch is found in the inner table, go back to the outer table and read the next row.

5. Scan the outer table until it finds a mismatch.

6. Read the next row in the outer table, then again go back to the inner table and read the first row from where it came back to the outer table. The optimizer keeps a track of current positions.

7. In this way, the outer table is scanned only once, and the inner table may be scanned multiple times, in case of duplicate values. But only duplicate rows will be scanned multiple times.

This type of join requires an equality predicate, such as `C1 = C2`. The column cannot be of LOB type or a LONG field.

Hash join: The hash join operation can be summarized as follows:

1. The inner table is scanned and copied to a memory area drawn from the sortheap. This memory area is divided into sections, based on the hash value computed on columns of the join predicate. If the size of this memory area exceeds the sortheap size, then the extra sections are written to temporary tables.

2. Once the inner table is processed, it starts reading the outer table row by row. First, the hash value is computed for this row, and the resultant hash value is compared with the hash value of the inner table. If these values match, it proceeds with comparing the actual values. If they match, the row is selected.

3. If the corresponding sections from the inner table are available in memory buffers, then this comparison happens immediately. If the sections from the inner table are written to temporary tables, then the row from the outer table is first written to a temporary table. Then, the matching pairs from the temporary table are read, and hash values of their rows are matched. If the hash values match, then the actual join predicates are compared.

4. Hash join performance is best if we can avoid section overflow to temporary tables.

This type of join can only be used for equality predicates where the column types are the same, and their lengths and precisions are also the same. The column cannot be of LOB type or a LONG field.

Operators in an access plan

To understand the `db2exfmt` output, we should understand the basic elements of optimizer operators. An **access plan** is a sequence of operations signified by operators. We can observe the following operators in an access plan:

Operator	Description
DELETE	Represents the deletion of rows from a table
EISCAN	**(Extended Index Scan)** scans a user defined index to produce a reduced stream of rows
FETCH	Represents fetching of columns from a table
FILTER	Represents how data is filtered
GENROW	This operator is used by the optimizer to generate rows of data.
GRPBY	Represents the grouping of rows
SUM	Represents addition of numeric data values usually for the GROUP BY clause
HSJOIN	Represents hash joins
INSERT	Represents the insertion of rows into a table
IXAND	**(Dynamic Bitmap Index ANDing)** this operator represents ANDing of the results of multiple index scans
IXSCAN	Represents the scanning of an index
MSJOIN	**(Merge Scan Join)** this operator represents a merge join
NLJOIN	Represents a nested loop join
RETURN	Represents the return of data from a query
RIDSCN	Represents the scan of a list of **Row Identifiers** (**RIDs**)
RPD	**(Remote PushDown)** This operator retrieves data from a remote data source
SHIP	**(Ship query to remote system)** This operator sends data from a remote data source
SORT	Represents the sorting of rows in a table
TBSCAN	Represents table scans
TEMP	Represents the storage of data in a temporary table
TQ	Represents a table queue
LTQ	**(Local table queue)** Represents table queues, which are used to pass data between database agents within a database partition
DTQ	**(Directed table queue)** Represents the transmission of hashed data to one or more database partitions
BTQ	**(Broadcast table queue)** Represents the transmission of non-hashed data to all database partitions
MDTQ	**(Merge directed table queue)** Represents a table queue in which rows are hashed to one of the receiving database partitions, and the order is preserved

Operator	Description
MBTQ	(**Merge broadcast table queue**) Represents a table queue in which rows are not hashed and transferred to all database partitions with the order preserved
UNION	Represents the concatenation of steams of rows from multiple tables
UNIQUE	Represents rows with duplicate values
UPDATE	Represents the updating of data in the rows of a table
XISCAN	(**Index scan over XML data**) This operation is performed for a single query predicate
XSCAN	This operator is used to navigate XML fragments to evaluate XPath expressions, and to extract document fragments if needed
XANDOR	(**Index ANDing and ORing over XML data**) This operator allows ANDed predicates to be applied to multiple indexes, to reduce the underlying table accesses to a minimum
AVG	Represents the average of numeric values for a GROUP BY clause
MIN	Represents the minimum of numeric values for a GROUP BY clause
MAX	Represents the maximum of numeric values for a GROUP BY clause
GENROW	Represents the generation of rows of data

Application development in partitioned databases

Database partitioning works on the _divide and conquer_ rule. When the data grows, we can use different partitioning techniques to divide the data into smaller chunks, and then process it, resulting in very good performance. Typically, we come across large data volumes in business intelligence environments where we perform deep analysis on historical data. A typical installation of a data warehouse involves more than one partitioning technique. When we are designing applications for large databases that are partitioned, we need to make sure that our applications are also designed in a way that they can get benefit from the underlying partitioned database. In this recipe, we will discuss the different partitioning techniques that DB2 provides, and what should be considered for designing applications in such an environment.

How to do it

DB2 provides three main techniques for partitioning:

- Database partitioning
- Range partitioning
- Multidimensional clustering

In this recipe, we will see how we can implement these three techniques, and what best practices should be considered while writing SQL statements in such an environment.

Considering partitioned architecture: Here we are referring to the **Database Partitioning Feature** (**DPF**) architecture where the database is partitioned across multiple partitions. In such cases, the data in each table is split across different partitions, chosen by hash values on partitioning keys. When we are querying a table which is partitioned across multiple partitions, then the SQL query will be divided into sub-queries, and each sub-query is passed on to a database partition. This results in inter-partition parallelism. As a developer, we don't need to think much about the DPF nature of tables, as the SQL query will always be executed in parallel across different partitions.

The following table is distributed by a FACT_KEY on different partitions:

```
CREATE TABLE FACT_TABLE
   (FACT_KEY BIGINT NOT NULL PRIMARY KEY,
     DIM1_KEY INTEGER,
     DIM2_KEY INTEGER,
     MEASURE1 DECIMAL(30,2),
     MEASURE2 DECIMAL(30,2))
   DISTRIBUTE BY HASH(FACT_KEY);
```

Considering range-partitioned table layout: When we have a table, partitioned by range of data values, then we can design SQL queries that can benefit from the table layout. When the table is partitioned by range, we should try to include the partition column in our SQL query, and apply filters on it. This directly leads to less table data to be scanned, resulting in better performance. This performance is then complemented by partitioned indexes, where DB2 maintains a separate index for each table partition. Partitioned indexes mean fewer levels in the index tree, which in turn results in better performance.

For example, consider the following table definition:

```
CREATE TABLE FACT_TABLE
   (FACT_KEY BIGINT NOT NULL PRIMARY KEY,
     SALES_DATE DATE,
     DIM1_KEY INTEGER,
     DIM2_KEY INTEGER,
     MEASURE1 DECIMAL(30,2),
     MEASURE2 DECIMAL(30,2))
   DISTRIBUTE BY HASH(FACT_KEY)
   PARTITION BY RANGE (SALES_DATE)
     (STARTING FROM '2011-01-01'
     ENDING AT '2011-12-01'
     EVERY 1 MONTH);
```

This table is partitioned on SALES_DATE for each month. This means that every partition will store the data for the respective month. We should try to include SALES_DATE in our query, so that partition elimination can happen. In this example, it's very obvious that we will definitely need SALES_DATE to calculate monthly reports. Let's consider a different scenario:

Fact Table		
Column Name	Data Type	Generated By
FACT_KEY	BIGINT	
DIM1_KEY	INTEGER	
DIM2_KEY	INTEGER	
DIM3_KEY	INTEGER	
DATE_KEY	INTEGER	
RP_DATE	DATE	GENERATED ALWAYS AS(DATE(TO_DATE(CHAR(DATE_KEY), 'YYYYMMDD')))
MEASURE1	DECIMAL	
MEASURE2	DECIMAL	

Dimension Table	
Column Name	Data Type
DATE_KEY	INTEGER
DATE	DATE
DAY	INTEGER
MONTH	INTEGER
YEAR	INTEGER
QUARTER	INTEGER

Definition of the fact table:

```
CREATE TABLE FACT_TABLE
  (FACT_KEY BIGINT NOT NULL PRIMARY KEY,
    DIM1_KEY INTEGER,
    DIM2_KEY INTEGER,
    DIM3_KEY INTEGER,
    DATE_KEY INTEGER,
    RP_DATE DATE GENERATED ALWAYS AS (DATE(TO_DATE(CHAR(DATE_KEY),
      'YYYYMMDD')))
    MEASURE1 DECIMAL(30,2),
    MEASURE2 DECIMAL(30,2))
DISTRIBUTE BY HASH(FACT_KEY)
PARTITION BY RANGE (RP_DATE)
  (STARTING FROM '2011-01-01'
    ENDING AT '2011-12-01'
    EVERY 1 MONTH);
```

In this scenario, if we apply a filter on the DATE_KEY column, then partition elimination will not happen, because the optimizer will not be able to make out if it can use RP_DATE as an alternative. In such cases, we should apply a predicate on the range partition column.

Considering MDC tables: When a table is clustered on multiple dimensions, it is referred to as a multi-dimensional clustered table. The power of **Multidimensional Clustering** (**MDC**) lies in using its dimensions wisely. MDC tables maintain block indexes on its dimensions. Block indexes are very small in size compared to relational indexes. It also means that traversal is very fast in block indexes. To make sure that our queries use block indexes, we should try to include the dimensions of an MDC in our SQL queries.

Consider the following table definition:

```
CREATE TABLE REGION_SALES
   (REGION VARCHAR(20),
     AMOUNT DECIMAL(20,2),
     DATE DATE)
ORGANIZE BY DIMENSIONS(REGION);
```

For this table, the following SQL query will have good performance, as this will use block indexes:

```
SELECT DATE, SUM(AMOUNT)
   FROM REGION_SALES
   WHERE REGION ='NY'
   GROUP BY DATE
```

Verify partition elimination: If we expect partition elimination to happen, then we can verify it by using the explain utility. Consider the following SQL statement:

```
SELECT ORDERDATE, PARTKEY, RETURNSTATUS
   FROM SALES_DTL
   WHERE ORDERDATE BETWEEN '01/01/2011' AND '03/31/2011'
      AND PARTKEY=43283
```

The following screenshot shows the plan information for this SQL statement given by the db2expln utility. The output clearly shows that partition elimination will happen only on the ninth, tenth, and eleventh data partitions.

```
Estimated Cost = 67.235824
Estimated Cardinality = 3.938294
( 2) Access Table Name = DBUSER.SALES_DTL ID = -2,-32768
|  Index Scan: Name = DBUSER.IDXPK ID = 2
|  | Regular Index (Not Clustered)
|  | Index Columns:
|  | | 1: PARTKEY (Ascending)
| #Columns = 2
| Data-Partitioned Table
| Scan Direction = Reverse
| Data Partition Elimination Info:
|  | Range 1:
|  | | #Key Columns = 1
|  | | | Start Key: Inclusive value
|  | | | | 1: 2011-01-01
|  | | | Stop Key: Inclusive value
|  | | | | 1: 2011-03-31
| Active Data Partitions: 09-11
| #Key Columns = 1
|  | Start Key: Inclusive value
|  | | | 1: 49981
||
............ . .
||
||
| Data Partition Elimination Info:
|  | Range 1:
|  | | #Key Columns = 1
|  | | | Start Key: Inclusive value
|  | | | | 1: 2011-01-01
|  | | | Stop Key: Inclusive value
|  | | | | 1: 2011-03-31
```

Verifying block index usage: Just like partition elimination, we can also observe block indexes in the explain plan for MDC tables. Consider the following SQL statement:

```
SELECT DATE, SUM(AMOUNT)
FROM REGION_SALES
    WHERE REGION ='NY'
GROUP BY DATE
```

The REGION_SALES table is an MDC table with REGION as its dimension. Looking at the explain information for this SQL, it shows that optimizer has chosen the SYSIBM. SQL110918025821420 index, which is a block index for scanning the data.

```
(    5) Access Table Name = DBUSER.REGION_SALES  ID = 3,26
       |  Index Scan:  Name = SYSIBM.SQL110918025821420  ID = 1
       |  | Composite Dimension Block Index
       |  | Index Columns:
       |  | | 1: REGION (Ascending)
       |  #Columns = 2
```

| Clustered by Dimension for Block Index Access

| Skip Inserted Rows

| Avoid Locking Committed Data

| Currently Committed for Cursor Stability

There's more

DB2 provides different techniques that allow us to spread data across multiple database partitions. DB2 implements the **shared-nothing** architecture, where each database partition consists of its own data, indexes, configuration environment, and transaction logs. A partition is also referred to as a **node**. DB2 provides the following partitioning features:

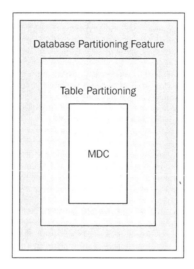

Database partitioning feature

The main goal behind implementing DPF is to divide the data across multiple partitions, where each partition of data is serviced by its own processor and memory. The database manager uses a hashing algorithm to decide the partition in which the target row will be stored. The same logic is used with data retrieval as well. This hashing is done on the partitioning key. Hence, it becomes very important to choose a proper partitioning key. A good partitioning key will ensure that all partitions have an equal amount of data. If the data is skewed among different partitions, then the partition with more data can become a bottleneck, and we will not get optimum performance.

The following screenshot shows the architecture of a partitioned database:

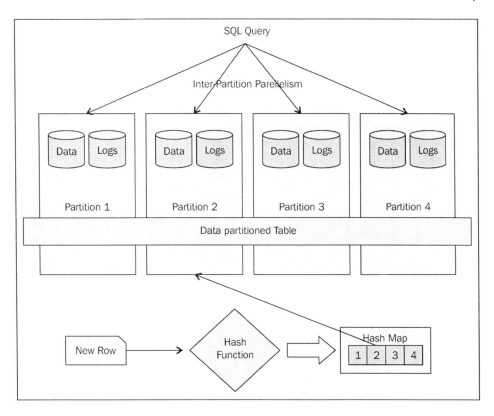

Range partitioning

Range partitioned tables are another way of dividing the data in the form of ranges. These ranges cannot overlap. For example, we can create a range partitioned table with ranges defined on month. In that case, our table layout will appear as follows:

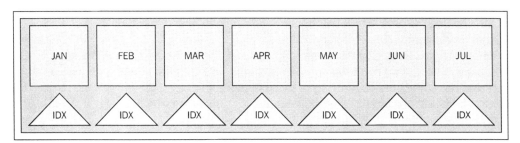

We can see that the table is divided into different ranges, and each range has its own index. These indexes are also known as **local indexes**. Local indexes were introduced in DB2 9.7. In this example, whenever we have an SQL query that has filters on a range partition column, then DB2 knows which partitions it should scan. This is known as **partition elimination**.

Multidimensional clustering

Multidimensional Clustering allows us to define our table as clustered in multiple dimensions. A table clustered in three dimensions appears as follows:

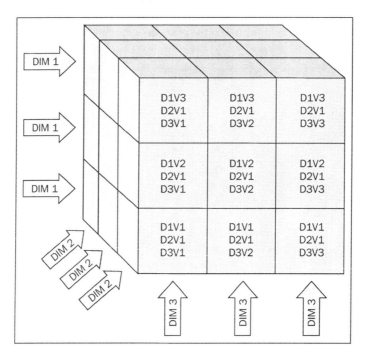

We can see that the data, which belongs to one combination of dimension values, sits together (or clustered). Each combination of dimension values form one block. MDC tables are different from clustered indexes, as MDC allows data to cluster a table on multiple dimensions, whereas we can have only one clustered index per table. When we have an SQL query that has some predicate on any of these dimensions, then DB2 knows which blocks to access. This is achieved by using block indexes. MDC tables are very powerful in terms of performance.

In the previous example, let's consider that each dimension has ten different values. Then the table will have at least `10x10x10` which is equal to `1000` blocks. Now, if we have an SQL query that has filters on all three dimensions, then we get a filter factor of `1/1000`, which means only one-thousandth part of the table will be scanned. In this way, MDCs are extremely useful in handling large volumes of data.

Putting everything together

All of the previous examples that explained partitioning techniques are mostly used together. In such cases, we get the performance benefit from all three techniques combined.

1. First of all, we get inter-partition parallelism, where the query is divided into sub-queries, and each query is passed on to one database partition, where they are executed in parallel. This gives us a first-level of performance.

2. Secondly, we get a performance benefit from table partition. Depending on the query predicates, DB2 finds out which range partition to access. This reduces the total amount of data to be scanned.

3. Within a range, the data is clustered depending on the dimension values. This gives us a third-level of performance benefit. This also reduces the amount of data to be scanned.

The following diagram demonstrates how these three techniques appear at the data storage level:

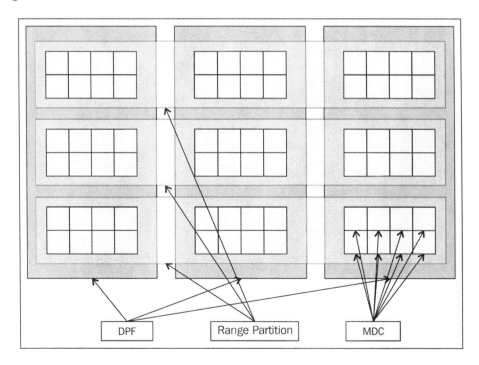

From this illustration, we can observe the following:

- ▶ We can see that the table is split across multiple database partitions.

- ▶ A table on each database partition, in turn, is divided into separate ranges. Each database partition will have all the ranges defined for the table.

- ▶ Each table partition, in turn, is clustered on multiple dimensions.

8
Preparing and Monitoring Database Applications

In this chapter, we will focus on recipes related to application preparation and performance monitoring:

- ▸ Preparing applications for execution
- ▸ Rebinding existing packages
- ▸ Customizing application behavior using registry variables
- ▸ Monitoring application performance

Introduction

In this chapter, we will focus on various tips and techniques that can be used to prepare an application. We will discuss some registry variables that can impact the overall application behavior. We will then discuss the latest monitoring techniques introduced in DB2 9.7. These monitoring techniques can be used by application developers to proactively monitor application performance and also troubleshoot performance problems.

Preparing applications for execution

A database application coded in a high-level language has SQL statements embedded in it. Before we can execute the application, it is precompiled, bound to the database, and then compiled to generate an assembly code. During the precompilation and binding processes, we have many options that can control the environment for application execution.

Precompilation is the process of separating SQL statements from application logic. Applications that do not have any embedded SQL statements don't need to be precompiled. When an application is precompiled, a bind file is generated. This bind file has information on all SQL statements contained in the application. All SQL statements in the application source file are commented as a result of precompilation and are replaced with DB2 runtime API calls for these statements.

Binding is the process of compiling all SQL statements contained in the bind file. The result of binding is a **package**. This package contains access plans for all static SQL statements. Access plans for dynamic SQL statements are generated during application execution time.

In this recipe, we will focus on the different precompilation and bind options.

Getting ready

We need the following privileges to use the PRECOMPILE and BIND commands:

- ▸ BINDADD authority to bind a package
- ▸ IMPLICIT_SCHEMA or CREATEIN privilege on the package schema
- ▸ ALTERIN and BIND privileges, if the package already exists
- ▸ If explain information is also captured during the BIND operation, then we need INSERT privileges on the explain tables
- ▸ Privileges needed to compile static SQL statements

Group privileges are not considered during the PRECOMPILE or BIND operations. We should either have direct user privileges or by roles.

How to do it...

When an application is precompiled, it generates a host language file containing only host language calls and a package. We have an option to create a bind file that can be used to bind the package against any database in the future. In this recipe, we will discuss the different options available for the PRECOMPILE and BIND operations.

1. **Precompiling an application**: We can use the PRECOMPILE statement to precompile an application. It accepts the application source file and produces a modified source file that only contains host language specific calls. All SQL statements contained in the application are separated and stored in a package.

   In the following example, we are precompiling a sample application tbread.sqc. By default, the PRECOMPILE or PREP command also compiles the SQL statements contained in the application and creates a package.

   ```
   C:\test>db2 prep tbread.sqc

       LINE     MESSAGE FOR tbread.sqc

       ------   -------------------------------------------------------
   ------

   SQL0060W  The "C" precompiler is in progress.

   SQL0091W  Precompilation or binding was ended with "0"

   errors and "0" warnings.
   ```

   We also have an option to create a bind file containing all SQL statements. This can be done by using the BINDFILE clause in the PRECOMPILE statement. Once we have the bind file, we can create a package at any later point in time. This is particularly useful when we want to create the package after collecting the latest statistics.

   ```
   C:\test>db2 prep tbreadtbread.sqc BINDFILE USING tbreadtbread.bnd

       LINE     MESSAGE FOR tbreadtbread.sqc

       ------   -------------------------------------------------------
   ------

   SQL0060W  The "C" precompiler is in progress.

   SQL0091W  Precompilation or binding was ended with "0"

   errors and "0" warnings.
   ```

    The sample program tbread.sqc can be located at the <DB2-install-path>/SQLLIB/samples/c directory.

2. **Binding a package**: **Binding** is the process of creating a package from an application bind file. This bind file can be generated from precompilation of an application. Binding is implicitly done when an application is precompiled but a separate bind file allows us to bind an application at a later point in time.

   The following statement binds a `.bnd` file and creates a package in the database.

```
C:\test>db2 bind tbread.bnd

    LINE     MESSAGE FOR tbread.bnd

    ------   -----------------------------------------------------------
    ------
SQL0061W  The binder is in progress.
SQL0091W  Binding was ended with "0" errors and "0" warnings.
```

3. **Viewing the bound packages**: All packages bound to a database can be found in the `SYSCAT.PACKAGES` table. It also has information on all the options used during package binding.

```
SELECT PKGSCHEMA, PKGNAME, BOUNDBY, VALID, TOTAL_SECT, ISOLATION,
 BLOCKING, QUERYOPT, DEGREE, INTRA_PARALLEL, VALIDATE, REOPTVAR,
PKGVERSION, EXPLICIT_BIND_TIME, LAST_BIND_TIME, PKG_CREATE_TIME
 FROM SYSCAT.PACKAGES
WHERE PKGSCHEMA='SANJU'
```

PKGSCHEMA	PKGNAME	BOUNDBY	VALID	TOTAL_SECT	ISOLATION	BLOCKING	QUERYOPT
SANJU	P3114849	SANJU	Y	4	CS	U	5
SANJU	P3114858	SANJU	Y	4	CS	U	5
SANJU	P4444361	SANJU	Y	3	CS	U	5
SANJU	P4444412	SANJU	Y	5	CS	U	5
SANJU	P7262233	SANJU	Y	1	CS	U	5
....							
....							

DEGREE	INTRA_PARALLEL	VALIDATE	REOPTVAR	EXPLICIT_BIND_TIME
ANY	N	B	N	2011-11-16-23.11.48.495008
ANY	N	B	N	2011-11-16-23.11.48.605003
ANY	Y	B	N	2011-11-16-14.44.43.651001
ANY	Y	B	N	2011-11-16-14.44.44.155002
ANY	N	B	N	2011-11-16-17.26.22.429001
....				
....				

LAST_BIND_TIME	PKG_CREATE_TIME
2011-11-16-23.11.48.495008	2011-11-16-23.11.48.495008
2011-11-16-23.11.48.605003	2011-11-16-23.11.48.605003
2011-11-16-14.44.43.651001	2011-11-16-14.44.43.651001
2011-11-16-14.44.44.155002	2011-11-16-14.44.44.155002
2011-11-16-17.26.22.429001	2011-11-16-17.26.22.429001
....	
....	

4. **Enabling cursor blocking**: If we have cursors defined in our application, then we can control the block size of cursors by using the BLOCKING clause in the BIND or PRECOMPILE statement. When enabled, DB2 fetches blocks of rows instead of individual rows from database and passes them to the client application. This results in better performance.

   The following statements can be used to enable cursor blocking either at precompile time or at bind time for the given application tbread.sqc.

   ```
   PRECOMPILE tbread.sqc BLOCKING ALL;

   BIND tbread.bnd BLOCKING ALL;
   ```

5. **Using different schema names for packages**: We can use the COLLECTION clause of the BIND or PRECOMPILE statement to specify a schema name for a given package. It allows us to group related packages together.

   In the following examples, a package will be created in the DBUSER schema:

   ```
   PRECOMPILE tbread.sqc COLLECTION DBUSER;

   BIND tbread.bnd COLLECTION DBUSER;
   ```

6. **Changing default date/time format**: We can change the default format of dates or times returned to the caller by using the DATETIME clause in the BIND or PRECOMPILE statement.

   In the following examples, we are changing the default date/time format to European:

   ```
   PRECOMPILE tbread.sqc DATETIME EUR;

   BIND tbread.bnd DATETIME EUR;
   ```

7. **Specifying default isolation level**: The default isolation level for all SQL statements in a package can be changed by using the ISOLATION clause.

   In the following examples, we are setting the default isolation level to UR (Uncommitted Read):

   ```
   PRECOMPILE tbread.sqc ISOLATION UR;

   BIND tbread.bnd ISOLATION UR;
   ```

8. **Specifying schema names for unqualified objects**: We may have SQL statements referring to database objects without using their fully qualified names. In such cases, we can provide the schema name for all unqualified objects by using the QUALIFIER clause in the BIND or PRECOMPILE statement. This becomes handy if we have different schema names in different environments, such as dev, qa, or prod.

   In the following examples, we are setting the DBUSER schema for the unqualified database objects:

   ```
   PRECOMPILE tbread.sqc QUALIFIER DBUSER;

   BIND tbread.bnd QUALIFIER DBUSER;
   ```

9. **Changing query optimization for embedded SQL statements**: We can override the default optimization level for a given package by using the QUERYOPT clause in the BIND or PRECOMPILE statement. This optimization level overrides the system default optimization level for this package.

In the following examples, we are setting the current optimization level to 4:

```
PRECOMPILE tbread.sqc QUERYOPT 4;
```

```
BIND tbread.bnd QUERYOPT 4;
```

10. **Specifying the authorization ID for dynamic SQL statements**: When we have dynamic SQL statements in our applications, then we can specify which authorization ID to choose for checking authorization on various database objects.

```
PRECOMPILE tbread.sqc DYNAMICRULES RUN;
```

```
BIND tbread.bnd DYNAMICRULES RUN;
```

The possible options for the DYNAMICRULES clause are:

- RUN: Authorization ID of user executing the package is chosen for authorization checking and implicit schema qualifier for unqualified objects.
- BIND: Authorization ID of user binding the package is chosen for authorization checking and implicit schema qualifier for unqualified objects.
- DEFINERUN: This behaves similarly to the RUN option unless the package is used within a routine. In that case, the authorization ID of the user who defined the routine will be used for authorization checking and implicit schema qualifier for unqualified objects.
- INVOKERUN: This behaves similarly to the RUN option unless the package is used within a routine. In that case, the authorization ID of the user who invokes the routine will be used for authorization checking and implicit schema qualifier for unqualified objects.

11. **Granting EXECUTE to users and groups**: While binding a package, we also have an option to grant the EXECUTE privilege on this package to any user, role, or group. This can be granted either to a user, role, or group.

In the following examples, we are granting the EXECUTE privilege on the newly created package to PUBLIC:

```
PRECOMPILE tbread.sqc GRANT PUBLIC;
```

```
BIND tbread.bnd GRANT PUBLIC;
```

12. **Changing package owner**: We can use the OWNER clause in the BIND or PRECOMPILE statement to change the package owner to a user other than the binder.

In the following examples, the owner of the newly created package will be DBUSER1.

```
PRECOMPILE tbread.sqc OWNER DBUSER1;
```

```
BIND tbread.bnd OWNER DBUSER1;
```

13. **Checking for authorization errors**: We can choose to check for authorization errors and database object errors at runtime versus bind time. This can be specified by using the VALIDATE clause. When set to BIND, DB2 will check for all objects and authorizations at bind time. When set to RUN, DB2 will still check for objects and authorizations but it will still bind the package and a warning will be returned. If no errors are observed at bind time, then it will not check anything during runtime. However, if any error is observed, DB2 will check for error again during execution time. This is handy, if we have any database objects which are not yet created in the database and will be created before the application is run.

   In the following examples, we are setting the validation to RUN:

   ```
   PRECOMPILE tbread.sqc VALIDATE RUN;

   BIND tbread.bnd VALIDATE RUN;
   ```

How it works...

When a package is created, all SQL statements are compiled and their access plans are generated. This results in better application performance as it saves SQL compilation time. This advantage is only applicable for static SQL statements; dynamic SQL statements are still compiled at runtime. If the application is designed to access more than one database, then we need to create separate packages for each database.

When an application is bound to the database, a package is created. By default, the name of this package contains the first eight characters of the application name. That means, if we have two applications with their initial eight characters matching, then the package of one application will replace the other one and the application will get the *package not found* error. Hence it's a good idea to explicitly set package names and override the default names.

Understanding the consistency token

When an application is precompiled, a package is created along with the modified application source code. The package and application source files are generated with a matching timestamp also referred to as a **consistency token**. When the application is executed, the corresponding package name and timestamp is sent to the database where it checks for the package with given name and timestamp. If multiple versions of a package are available then each version will have a different associated timestamp. The consistency token is an eight-character string representation of the timestamp for the package.

There's more...

`BIND` also provides us the capability to store all SQL statements in catalogs and enable incremental binding for them. When incremental binding is enabled, DB2 processes all SQL statements in a package as dynamic SQL statements, with one difference as the SQL statements are known to DB2 beforehand just as a regular static SQL statement. This option is very helpful if we don't have the complete environment set up at package binding time.

```
BIND tbread.bnd GENERIC 'STATICASDYNAMIC yes'
```

Advantages of deferred binding

We have an option to generate a bind file during application precompilation. Once we have the bind file, we can bind it at a later point in time. This is also known as **deferred binding**. Deferred binding has the following advantages:

- ▶ If we have the bind file, then it can be bound against any database allowing the application to access multiple databases
- ▶ We don't need to provide application source files to end users. Instead, we can just provide them with bind files which can be bound using the `BIND` statement

Packages and SQL routines

When a stored procedure is created, a corresponding package is also registered in the database. This package has information on all SQL statements in the procedure including their access plans.

Consider the following stored procedure definition:

```
CREATE PROCEDURE sample_sp()
RESULT SETS 1
LANGUAGE SQL
BEGIN
    DECLARE c1 CURSOR WITH RETURN FOR SELECT EMPNO, FIRSTNME, LASTNAME,
SALARY
                            FROM EMPLOYEE WHERE WORKDEPT = 'D11';
    OPEN c1;
END@
```

Once created, this procedure can be located in the `SYSCAT.PROCEDURES` table.

```
SELECT CHAR(PROCNAME, 20) AS PROCNAME,
CHAR(PROCSCHEMA, 20) AS PROCSCHEMA,
CHAR(SPECIFICNAME, 20) AS SPECIFICNAME
  FROM SYSCAT.PROCEDURES WHERE PROCNAME='SAMPLE_SP';
```

```
db2 => SELECT CHAR(PROCNAME, 20) AS PROCNAME,
db2 (cont.) =>          CHAR(PROCSCHEMA, 20) AS PROCSCHEMA,
db2 (cont.) =>          CHAR(SPECIFICNAME, 20) AS SPECIFICNAME
db2 (cont.) =>     FROM SYSCAT.PROCEDURES WHERE PROCNAME='SAMPLE_SP';

PROCNAME                PROCSCHEMA              SPECIFICNAME
----------------------- ----------------------- -----------------------
SAMPLE_SP               SANJU                   SQL111118234159600

  1 record(s) selected.
```

The package for this procedure can be found in the SYSCAT.PACKAGES table. When the package is created for a procedure, we can find it as a dependency on the procedure.

SELECT CHAR(ROUTINESCHEMA, 10) AS ROUTINESCHEMA,

CHAR(ROUTINENAME, 20) AS ROUTINENAME,

    BTYPE,

CHAR(BSCHEMA, 20) AS BSCHEMA,

CHAR(BNAME, 20) AS BNAME

  FROM SYSCAT.ROUTINEDEP

  WHERE ROUTINENAME = 'SQL111118234159600';

```
db2 => SELECT CHAR(ROUTINESCHEMA, 10) AS ROUTINESCHEMA,
db2 (cont.) =>          CHAR(ROUTINENAME, 20) AS ROUTINENAME,
db2 (cont.) =>          BTYPE,
db2 (cont.) =>          CHAR(BSCHEMA, 20) AS BSCHEMA,
db2 (cont.) =>          CHAR(BNAME, 20) AS BNAME
db2 (cont.) =>     FROM SYSCAT.ROUTINEDEP
db2 (cont.) =>     WHERE ROUTINENAME = 'SQL111118234159600';

ROUTINESCHEMA ROUTINENAME           BTYPE BSCHEMA               BNAME
------------- --------------------- ----- --------------------- --------------------
SANJU         SQL111118234159600    K     SANJU                 P3415918
SANJU         SQL111118234159600    T     SANJU                 EMPLOYEE

  2 record(s) selected.
```

Once we have the dependency name, we can query the SYSCAT.PACKAGE table to get the package details for the following procedure:

```
SELECT CHAR(PKGSCHEMA, 10) AS PKGNAME,
CHAR(PKGNAME, 20) AS PKGNAME
  FROM SYSCAT.PACKAGES
  WHERE PKGNAME = 'P3415918';
```

```
db2 => SELECT CHAR(PKGSCHEMA, 10) AS PKGNAME,
db2 (cont.) =>        CHAR(PKGNAME, 20) AS PKGNAME
db2 (cont.) =>    FROM SYSCAT.PACKAGES
db2 (cont.) =>    WHERE PKGNAME = 'P3415918';

PKGNAME    PKGNAME
---------- --------------------
SANJU      P3415918

  1 record(s) selected.
```

The preceding SQL statements can be combined into one statement as follows:

```
SELECT CHAR(PROCNAME, 20), CHAR(PROCSCHEMA, 10),
CHAR(PROC.SPECIFICNAME, 20), CHAR(PKGNAME, 20)
  FROM SYSCAT.PROCEDURES PROC,
        SYSCAT.ROUTINEDEP DEP,
        SYSCAT.PACKAGES PKG
  WHERE PROC.PROCNAME = 'SAMPLE_SP' AND
        DEP.ROUTINENAME = PROC.SPECIFICNAME AND
        PKG.PKGNAME = DEP.BNAME;
```

```
db2 => SELECT CHAR(PROCNAME, 20), CHAR(PROCSCHEMA, 10),
db2 (cont.) =>        CHAR(PROC.SPECIFICNAME, 20), CHAR(PKGNAME, 20)
db2 (cont.) =>    FROM SYSCAT.PROCEDURES PROC,
db2 (cont.) =>        SYSCAT.ROUTINEDEP DEP,
db2 (cont.) =>        SYSCAT.PACKAGES PKG
db2 (cont.) =>    WHERE PROC.PROCNAME = 'SAMPLE_SP' AND
db2 (cont.) =>        DEP.ROUTINENAME = PROC.SPECIFICNAME AND
db2 (cont.) =>        PKG.PKGNAME = DEP.BNAME;

1                    2          3                      4
-------------------- ---------- ---------------------- --------------------
SAMPLE_SP            SANJU      SQL111118234159600     P3415918

  1 record(s) selected.
```

Rebinding existing packages

Rebind is the process of recreating a previously bound package. Rebinding becomes necessary in the following scenarios:

- When the database statistics are updated, we should rebind the existing packages so that fresh access plans are generated. These new access plans will be based on the latest statistics. It becomes significant if any new indexes are added to a table. In such cases, rebinding will result in access plans that can use this index. This is necessary for consistent performance.

- If any database object that has a dependency on a package is dropped, then the package becomes invalid. In such cases, we need to rebind the package. This rebinding is optional as all invalid packages are automatically validated and rebound when they are executed. As a best practice, we should rebind even invalid packages once all dependencies are back in place.

- A package that depends on user-defined functions becomes inoperative when the underlying UDF is dropped. In such cases, we need to rebind the package explicitly.

- If the application source has been altered, the existing package is no longer valid. We should rebind the package to pick up the latest changes in the application.

An alternate to REBIND is creating the package again by using the BIND statement. However, REBIND performs better than BIND, so we should try for REBIND if BIND is not necessary.

Getting ready

We need the following privileges to use the REBIND and BIND commands:

- The BINDADD authority to bind a package

- The IMPLICIT_SCHEMA or CREATEIN privilege on package schema

- The ALTERIN and BIND privileges if the package already exists

- If the explain information is also captured during the BIND operation, then we need the INSERT privileges on explain tables

- Privileges needed to compile static SQL statements

The group privileges are not considered during the PRECOMPILE or BIND operation. We should either have direct user privileges or by roles.

How to do it...

Let's discuss how a package can be rebound to a database and the different options that can be used for rebinding.

1. **Finding invalid and inoperative packages**: If we have altered or dropped any database object, it's a good idea to check for invalid and inoperative packages that need a rebind. This can be achieved by querying the `SYSCAT.PACKAGES` tables and checking the `VALID` column values. If this column has anything other than `Y` then it needs a rebind. It can have the following values:

   - `N`: This means the package needs rebinding
   - `V`: This means the package will be automatically validated when invoked
   - `X`: This means the package is in an inoperative state
   - `Y`: This means the package is in a valid state and does not need a rebind

   ```
   SELECT PKGSCHEMA, PKGNAME FROM SYSCAT.PACKAGES WHERE VALID <> 'Y';
   ```

   ```
   db2 => SELECT CHAR(PKGSCHEMA, 10) AS PKGSCHEMA, CHAR(PKGNAME, 20) AS PKGNAME FROM SYSCAT.P
   ACKAGES WHERE VALID <> 'Y'

   PKGSCHEMA  PKGNAME
   ---------- --------------------
   SANJU      P3135945

     1 record(s) selected.
   ```

2. **Rebinding a package**: This is the simplest form of rebind where we need only the package name to be rebound.

   ```
   REBIND PACKAGE <package-name>;
   ```

   This replaces the existing package with a new package with the same name and version.

3. **Customizing the package by using REBIND options**: We cannot change any option that was chosen at package bind time except the `REOPT` and `APREUSE` options. `REOPT` specifies whether host variable values should be considered while compiling an SQL statement or not, whereas `APREUSE` specifies whether access plans for static SQL statements can be reused or not. If these options are not specified during `REBIND`, then the original `BIND` options will be preserved.

   ```
   REBIND PACKAGE packagename REOPT ONCE;
   REBIND PACKAGE packagename APREUSE YES;
   ```

How it works...

When REBIND is used, it replaces the existing package with a new one that has newly generated access plans for SQL statements. To do so, it uses the SYSCAT.STATEMENTS table to find the information on all SQL statements in the package and then creates a fresh package from them. If the package was created with explain enabled then REBIND will re-explain the statements and store the explain information in EXPLAIN tables.

REBIND does not automatically commit a transaction; hence we need to explicitly commit the transaction if autocommit is disabled. We can rebind multiple packages within a single transaction. Once the transaction is committed, the new package becomes available to the application. Since the package information needs an exclusive lock on its corresponding row in the SYSCAT.PACKAGES table, we cannot rebind a package if any user is accessing it.

If we have multiple versions of a package, then we can rebind only one version at a time.

There's more...

When a stored procedure is created, there is no bind file generated. In such cases, we no longer have an option to use BIND to recreate the package for stored procedures or any routine. We can use REBIND in such cases. REBIND for stored procedures is needed when system statistics are updated. We can get the package name for a given stored procedure and use the REBIND command, otherwise we can use the REBIND_ROUTINE_PACKAGE stored procedure. This procedure can be used to rebind packages for stored procedures, user-defined functions, or triggers.

```
CALL SYSPROC.REBIND_ROUTINE_PACKAGE ('P','SAMPLE_SP','');
```

There are two ways to invoke the REBIND_ROUTINE_PACKAGE stored procedure:

```
CALL REBIND_ROUTINE_PACKAGE (type, routine-name, options);
CALL REBIND_ROUTINE_PACKAGE (type, schema, module, routine-name,
options);
```

Here type represents the type of the routine. It can have the following values:

- P: Indicates a procedure
- SP: Indicates the specific name of a procedure
- F: Indicates a function
- SF: Indicates the specific name of a function
- T: Indicates a trigger

The `options` parameter can be a string of all rebind options.

```
CALL SYSPROC.REBIND_ROUTINE_PACKAGE ('P','SAMPLE_SP','REOPT ONCE APREUSE
YES');
```

Customizing application behavior using registry variables

DB2 provides many registry variables that can affect the database environment. If configured properly, they can have a significant impact on application performance. All registry variables are effective at instance level, which means they will affect all databases in a given instance. In this recipe, we will discuss some registry variables which are relevant from an application-behavior perspective. Most of the time, application developers do not have permissions to change any registry variable, but we should know what impact they can have on the way an application behaves.

Getting ready

Registry variables operate at instance level, so we need the SYSADM authority to view or modify their values.

How to do it...

The following steps discuss the most important registry variables that can have a significant impact on application performance and behavior:

Disclaimer: Registry variables are very sensitive and can behave differently in different scenarios. Proper testing should be done before deploying them to production.

► DB2_CONNRETRIES_INTERVAL: This registry variable indicates the time interval between two successive connection retries. This is applicable only when automatic client reroute is enabled.

db2set DB2_CONNRETRIES_INTERVAL=10

The unit for this variable value is in seconds.

See the *Developing Java applications for high availability* recipe discussed in *Chapter 5, Designing Java Applications* for more details on the automatic client reroute feature.

▸ `DB2_MAX_CLIENT_CONNRETRIES`: This variable indicates the maximum number of times a client retries to get a database connection. This is also applicable only when automatic client reroute is enabled.

db2set DB2_MAX_CLIENT_CONNRETRIES =5

The value for this registry variable can be any integer.

`DB2_MAX_CLIENT_CONNRETRIES` and `DB2_CONNRETRIES_INTERVAL` registry variables are used in conjunction with each other. The following table summarizes the application behavior based on values for these two registry variables:

DB2_MAX_CLIENT_CONNRETRIES	DB2_CONNRETRIES_INTERVAL	Behavior
SET	NOT SET	`DB2_CONNRETRIES_INTERVAL` defaults to 30
NOT SET	SET	`DB2_MAX_CLIENT_CONNRETRIES` defaults to 10
NOT SET	NOT SET	Connection retry happens repeatedly for up to 10 minutes

▸ `DB2_VIEW_REOPT_VALUES`: This registry variable enables storing of cached values for all re-optimized SQL statements in the `EXPLAIN_PREDICATE` table when the statement is explained. If disabled, then only users with `DBADM` can store these statements in the `EXPLAIN_PREDICATE` table.

db2set DB2_VIEW_REOPT_VALUES=YES

▸ `DB2_ANTIJOIN`: This registry variable affects the way DB2 optimizer handles `NOT EXISTS` and `NOT IN` subqueries in SQL statements. This variable can have the following impact on the optimizer decisions:

 ❑ In DB2 Enterprise Server Edition, when set to `YES`, the optimizer searches for opportunities to convert the `NOT EXISTS` subqueries into anti joins that can be processed more efficiently. The default value for DB2 Enterprise Server Edition is `NO`.

 ❑ In all DB2 versions, when set to `EXTENT`, the optimizer searches for opportunities to convert `NOT IN` and `NOT EXISTS` sub queries into anti joins.

 ❑ In non-ESE versions, when set to `NO`, then optimizer limits the opportunities to convert `NOT EXISTS` sub queries into anti joins. The default value for non-DB2 Enterprise Server Edition is `YES`.

 db2set DB2_ANTIJOIN=YES

▶ DB2_INLIST_TO_JOIN: The DB2 optimizer can rewrite an IN list predicate to a join. The optimizer will choose to do so only if it can evaluate the performance of both join methods. Sometimes the optimizer is not able to estimate their performances. This may happen if the IN list contains parameter markers that prevent the optimizer from finding the actual selectivity. In such cases, we can use this registry variable to favor the nested loop join over join the list of values. In this case, it treats the IN list as an inner table for the join.

Consider the following SQL statements:

```
SELECT *
  FROM EMPLOYEE
  WHERE DEPTNO IN ('D11', 'D21', 'E21')
```

The preceding SQL statement can be rewritten as follows:

```
SELECT *
  FROM EMPLOYEE, (VALUES 'D11', 'D21', 'E21) AS V(DNO)
  WHERE DEPTNO = V.DNO
```

We can use the following command to change the value for the DB2_INLIST_TO_JOIN registry variable.

db2set DB2_INLIST_TO_JOIN=YES

▶ DB2_REDUCED_OPTIMIZATION: This registry variable can be used to reduce the level of optimization for SQL statements. This is helpful if we have simple SQL statements that do not have too many joins. For example, locating an employee by its employee ID is a simple SQL statement where DB2 can directly pick a primary key index to locate the desired record. In this case, we don't want to spend a lot of time in finding and evaluating many possible access plans. By reducing optimization, we can save total compilation time. This variable can also be used to control the optimization for SQL statements.

db2set DB2_REDUCED_OPTIMIZATION=YES

This variable can have following values:

- ❏ NO: No changes in optimization techniques.
- ❏ YES: Reduces some optimization techniques that can consume significant compilation time.
- ❏ Integer value: This setting is similar to the YES value but has an additional behavior for dynamic SQL statements. If the total number of joins for a query exceeds this integer value, then the optimizer switches to a greedy algorithm instead of disabling some optimization techniques. This is only applicable if the current optimization level is set to 5.

❑ DISABLE: When this registry variable is not in effect, the optimizer sometimes reduces optimization for dynamic SQL statements when operating at optimization level 5. When this variable is set to DISABLE, then the optimizer performs full optimization at level 5.

❑ NO_SORT_NLJOIN: When this setting is in effect, the optimizer does not generate any access plans that require sorts for nested loop joins. Extra care should be taken before using this setting as it may severely impact performance.

❑ NO_SORT_MGJOIN: When this setting is in effect, the optimizer does not generate any access plans that require sorts for merge scan joins. Extra care should be taken before using this setting as it may severely impact performance.

▸ DB2_EXTENDED_OPTIMIZATION: This registry variable indicates whether or not to use additional optimization to improve query performance. We can use multiple optimization extensions as a comma-separated list.

db2set DB2_EXTENDED_OPTIMIZATION=ON,ENHANCED_MULTIPLE_DISTINCT

This variable can have the following values:

❑ OFF: Disables extended optimization.

❑ ON: Enables extended optimization.

❑ ENHANCED_MULTIPLE_DISTINCT: This can improve the performance of SQL statements that involve multiple DISTINCT clauses. This is applicable only in a partitioned environment where the number of processors is less than or equal to the number of partitions.

❑ SNHD: This indicates the optimizer to choose more efficient single partition hash-directed partitioning strategy based on cost. In this case, operations that cannot be executed parallel are more optimized to execute on single partition instead of coordinator partition.

❑ IXOR: This indicates the optimizer to use the index ORing data access method.

▸ DB2ASSUMEUPDATE: This variable indicates the optimizer to assume that all fixed length columns in the SET clause in an UPDATE statement are being changed. This eliminates the need for comparing the existing and new values for every column to check whether a column is actually being changed or not. This option can cause additional logging and index maintenance.

db2set DB2ASSUMEUPDATE=ON

- ▶ DB2_KEEPTABLELOCK: This variable allows an application to retain read-mode table lock even when the read operation is done. Thus when the application re-requests the table lock, the lock is already available. The lock is released at the transaction or connection boundary. However, this might impact the concurrency of other applications.

  db2set DB2_KEEPTABLELOCK=TRANSACTION

  We can use the following values for this variable:

  - ❑ OFF: This registry variable is disabled

  - ❑ ON or TRANSACTION: The lock is retained until the transaction ends

  - ❑ CONNECTION: The lock is retained until the transaction is rolled back or the connection terminates

- ▶ DB2_EVALUNCOMMITTED: This variable allows the optimizer to defer row locking until the data is known to satisfy the predicate wherever possible. In other words, it tries to evaluate the WHERE clause before locking the rows. In such cases, predicate evaluation may occur on uncommitted data. The decision of deferred locking is made at application bind time. This setting is applicable only for cursor stability or read stability isolation levels.

  db2set DB2_EVALUNCOMMITTED=YES

  Consider the following example:

  CREATE TABLE TEST (a INT);

  Application 1 inserts a record and doesn't commit.

  INSERT INTO TEST VALUES (1);

  Application 2 runs the following query:

  SELECT * FROM TEST;

  In this case, application 2 will have to wait until application 1 commits or rolls back. Now consider the following SELECT query:

  SELECT * FROM TEST WHERE a=2;

  In this case also, application 2 will have to wait until application 1 releases the locks. However, if we see the new row inserted by application 1, we can say that application 2 is not interested in this row as it is only looking for a=2. In such cases, if we enable DB2_EVALUNCOMMITTED, then DB2 will not attempt to acquire a lock before checking the data. It will see if the new row can be a part of the result set (that is, it satisfies the predicates). If yes, only then will it wait for application 1 to release the locks, otherwise it will not wait. This results in improved concurrency.

▶ `DB2_SKIPDELETED`: When enabled, this allows the optimizer to skip deleted keys during index scan and deleted rows during table scan for cursor stability and read stability isolation levels. It means that if one application deletes some rows without committing, then the second application assumes that these rows will be deleted. Hence it will not wait for locks on these rows. This results in improved concurrency as it does not wait for locks to get released.

db2set DB2_SKIPDELETED=YES

▶ `DB2_SKIPINSERTED`: This is similar to `DB2_SKIPDELETED` but this ignores the uncommitted new rows. If an application inserts some rows in a table without committing them then second application assumes that no new rows have been inserted. This is applicable only for cursor stability and read stability isolation levels.

db2set DB2_SKIPINSERTED=YES

▶ `DB2LOCK_TO_RB`: This variable indicates whether or not the entire transaction should be rolled back instead of the current statement when a lock timeout occurs. When set to `STATEMENT`, it causes only the current statement to roll back. For all other values, it causes the entire transaction to roll back.

db2set DB2LOCK_TO_RB=NULL

▶ `DB2NOEXITLIST`: This variable indicates whether DB2 should not automatically commit in-flight transactions when the application exits.

db2set DB2NOEXITLIST=ON

How it works...

All DB2 registry variables are applicable at instance level. Whenever we change any registry variable value, we need to restart the instance for the changes to take effect. We can use the `db2start` command to start the instance.

In a partitioned environment, we need to change the registry variable value for each partition.

There are different options available for the `db2set` command that can be used to change the registry variable values.

▶ To change a registry variable for the current instance as follows:

db2set registry_variable_name=new_value

▶ To change a registry variable for a given instance as follows:

db2set registry_variable_name=new_value -iinstance_name

▶ To change a registry variable for a particular given instance as follows:

db2set registry_variable_name=new_value -iinstance_namepartition_number

▶ To change a registry variable for all instances of DB2 as follows:

```
db2set registry_variable_name=new_value -g
```

There's more...

We can use the following command to show all registry variables and their values for a given instance.

```
db2set
```

```
db2set -all
```

```
C:\>db2set
DB2_REDUCED_OPTIMIZATION=YES
DB2_EXTENDED_OPTIMIZATION=ENHANCED_MULTIPLE_DISTINCT
DB2MAXFSCRSEARCH=2
DB2INSTOWNER=SANJU
DB2PORTRANGE=60000:60003
DB2INSTPROF=C:\PROGRAMDATA\IBM\DB2\DB2COPY1
DB2COMM=SSL

C:\>db2set -all
[e]  DB2PATH=C:\Program Files (x86)\IBM\SQLLIB
[i]  DB2_REDUCED_OPTIMIZATION=YES
[i]  DB2_EXTENDED_OPTIMIZATION=ENHANCED_MULTIPLE_DISTINCT
[i]  DB2MAXFSCRSEARCH=2
[i]  DB2INSTOWNER=SANJU
[i]  DB2PORTRANGE=60000:60003
[i]  DB2INSTPROF=C:\PROGRAMDATA\IBM\DB2\DB2COPY1
[i]  DB2COMM=SSL
[g]  DB2_EXTSECURITY=NO
[g]  DB2_DOCPORT=51000
[g]  DB2_DOCHOST=localhost
[g]  DB2SYSTEM=SANJU
[g]  DB2PATH=C:\Program Files (x86)\IBM\SQLLIB
[g]  DB2INSTDEF=DB2
[g]  DB2ADMINSERVER=DB2DAS00
```

Alternatively, we can use the following SQL statement to get the preceding information in a tabular format:

```
SELECT DBPARTITIONNUM, REG_VAR_NAME, REG_VAR_VALUE, LEVEL FROM SYSIBMADM.
REG_VARIABLES
```

```
db2 => SELECT DBPARTITIONNUM, CHAR(REG_VAR_NAME, 30) REG_VAR_NAME, CHAR(REG_VAR_VALUE, 40) REG_VAR_V
ALUE, LEVEL  from SYSIBMADM.REG_VARIABLES

DBPARTITIONNUM REG_VAR_NAME                    REG_VAR_VALUE                            LEVEL
-------------- ------------------------------  ---------------------------------------- -----
             0 DB2ADMINSERVER                  DB2DAS00                                 G
             0 DB2COMM                         SSL                                      I
             0 DB2INSTDEF                      DB2                                      G
             0 DB2INSTPROF                     C:\PROGRAMDATA\IBM\DB2\DB2COPY1          I
             0 DB2PATH                         C:\Program Files (x86)\IBM\SQLLIB        E
             0 DB2SYSTEM                       SANJU                                    G
             0 DB2PORTRANGE                    60000:60003                              I
             0 DB2INSTOWNER                    SANJU                                    I
             0 DB2MAXFSCRSEARCH                2                                        I
             0 DB2_EXTENDED_OPTIMIZATION       ENHANCED_MULTIPLE_DISTINCT               I
             0 DB2_REDUCED_OPTIMIZATION        YES                                      I
             0 DB2_DOCHOST                     localhost                                G
             0 DB2_DOCPORT                     51000                                    G
             0 DB2_EXTSECURITY                 NO                                       G

  14 record(s) selected.
```

Monitoring application performance

Once an application has been deployed and run in production, we should actively monitor it for potential bottlenecks. DB2 provides various tools that can be used to monitor application activities. These include event monitors, snapshots, SQL-based snapshots, and monitoring functions, administrative views, and stored procedures. In this recipe, we will discuss different areas of application monitoring and the preferred tools that an application developer can use.

In this recipe, we will discuss various administrative views, routines, and functions which are very useful for monitoring applications.

How to do it...

There are different aspects of monitoring. Whenever we observe any slowdown in application performance, we need handy scripts that can be used to monitor and identify problems. This recipe provides various monitoring tips and commands that can be used for such monitoring requirements.

- **Monitoring current SQL statements**: The `MON_CURRENT_SQL` administrative view can be used to get information on all SQL statements that are currently running in the database. This includes both static and dynamic SQL statements. This is very useful to identify long running queries and isolate problematic queries.

```
SELECT APPLICATION_HANDLE,
APPLICATION_NAME,
      ELAPSED_TIME_SEC,
  ACTIVITY_STATE,
  ACTIVITY_TYPE,
  TOTAL_CPU_TIME,
  ROWS_READ,
  ROWS_RETURNED,
  QUERY_COST_ESTIMATE,
  DIRECT_READS,
  DIRECT_WRITES,
SUBSTR(STMT_TEXT, 1, 100)
FROM SYSIBMADM.MON_CURRENT_SQL;
```

```
APPLICATION_HANDLE APPLICATION_NAME  ELAPSED_TIME_SEC ACTIVITY_STATE
------------------ ----------------  ---------------- --------------
20                      db2bp.exe                   5       EXECUTING
7                       db2bp.exe                   7       EXECUTING
17                      db2bp.exe                   6       EXECUTING
19                      db2bp.exe                   0       EXECUTING
17                      db2bp.exe                   6       EXECUTING
7                       db2bp.exe                   7       EXECUTING
20                      db2bp.exe                   1       EXECUTING


ACTIVITY_TYPE TOTAL_CPU_TIME ROWS_READ ROWS_RETURNED ROWS_RETURNED
------------- -------------- --------- ------------- ---------------
CALL                       0         4             0               0
CALL                       0         4             0               0
CALL                       0         4             0               0
READ_DML                   0         0             0               0
WRITE_DML                  0         4             0               0
WRITE_DML                  0         4             0               0
WRITE_DML                  0         4             0               0


DIRECT_READS DIRECT_WRITES STMT_TEXT
------------ ------------- ------------------------------------------------
14                       0 CALL iterator2()
12                       0 CALL iterator()
12                       0 CALL iterator1()
0                        0 SELECT APPLICATION_HANDLE,
                              SUBSTR (APPLICATION_NAME, 1, 20),
                              ELAPSED_TIME_SEC,ACTIVITY_STATE,ACTIVITY_T
12                       0 INSERT INTO TEST1 VALUES (3,3,3)
12                       0 INSERT INTO TEST VALUES (1,1,1)
14                       0 UPDATE TEST2 SET (A,B,C) = (2,2,2)
```

► **Monitoring package cache**: The `MON_PKG_CACHE_SUMMARY` administrative view can be used to get key information on static and dynamic SQL statements present in a package cache. The information available in this administrative view is aggregated. This means that if one SQL statement has been executed a number of times then the information returned will be the total of all monitor elements.

```
SELECT SECTION_TYPE,
       EXECUTABLE_ID,
       NUM_COORD_EXEC,
       NUM_COORD_EXEC_WITH_METRICS,
       TOTAL_STMT_EXEC_TIME,
       AVG_STMT_EXEC_TIME,
       TOTAL_CPU_TIME,
       AVG_CPU_TIME,
       TOTAL_LOCK_WAIT_TIME,
       AVG_LOCK_WAIT_TIME,
       TOTAL_IO_WAIT_TIME,
       AVG_IO_WAIT_TIME,
       PREP_TIME,
```

```
        ROWS_READ_PER_ROWS_RETURNED,
    SUBSTR(STMT_TEXT, 1, 100)
        FROM SYSIBMADM.MON_PKG_CACHE_SUMMARY
        ORDER BY TOTAL_CPU_TIME DESC;
```

```
SECTION_TYPE EXECUTABLE_ID NUM_COORD_EXEC NUM_COORD_EXEC_WITH_METRICS
------------ ------------- -------------- ---------------------------
D            x'010....'                 0                           0
D            x'010....'                 0                           0
D            x'010....'                 3                           3
S            x'010....'              1450                        1450
S            x'010....'                 0                           0
S            x'010....'                 3                           3


TOTAL_STMT_EXEC_TIME AVG_STMT_EXEC_TIME TOTAL_CPU_TIME AVG_CPU_TIME
-------------------- ------------------ -------------- ------------
                   0                  -              0            -
                   0                  -              0            -
                 106                 35              0            0
                9071                  6          62400           43
                   0                  -              0            -
               10193               3397        1996812       665604


TOTAL_LOCK_WAIT_TIME AVG_LOCK_WAIT_TIME   TOTAL_IO_WAIT_TIME  PREP_TIME
-------------------- --------------------  ------------------  ---------
                   0                    -                   0        186
                   0                    -                   0          0
                   0                    0                  31        114
                   0                    0                9049          0
                   0                    -                   0          0
                   0                    0                 131          0

AVG_IO_WAIT_TIME  ROWS_READ_PER_ROWS_RETURNED STMT_TEXT
----------------  --------------------------- ---------------------------
               -                            - call iterator()
               -                            - CALL iterator()
              10                            0 SELECT DISTINCT CURRENT
                                                  SQLID FROM SYSIBM.SYSTABLES
               6                            - INSERT INTO TEST1 VALUES (3,3,3)
               -                            - INSERT INTO TEST VALUES (1,1,1)
              43                            - UPDATE TEST2 SET (A,B,C) = (2,2,2)
```

> ▶ **Monitoring lock waits**: The MON_LOCKWAITS administrative view can be used to retrieve information on all applications that are waiting for locks. This can be very useful in identifying problems related to locks.

```
SELECT LOCK_NAME,
       LOCK_WAIT_ELAPSED_TIME,
       TABSCHEMA,
       TABNAME,
       DATA_PARTITION_ID,
```

```
          LOCK_MODE,

          LOCK_CURRENT_MODE,

          LOCK_MODE_REQUESTED,

          REQ_APPLICATION_HANDLE,

          REQ_AGENT_TID,

          REQ_MEMBER,

          REQ_USERID,

    SUBSTR(REQ_STMT_TEXT, 1, 100),

          HLD_APPLICATION_HANDLE,

          HLD_MEMBER,

          HLD_UERSID,

    SUBSTR(HLD_CURRENT_STMT_TEXT, 1, 100)

       FROM SYSIBMADM.MON_LOCKWAITS;
```

```
LOCK_NAME                          LOCK_WAIT_ELAPSED_TIME TABSCHEMA TABNAME
--------------------------         ---------------------- --------- -------
03001A0004000000000000000052                            4 SANJU     TEST1
03001A0004000000000000000052                            5 SANJU     TEST1

DATA_PARTITION_ID LOCK_MODE LOCK_CURRENT_MODE LOCK_MODE_REQUESTED
----------------- --------- ----------------- -------------------
                -         X                 -                   X
                -         X                 -                   X

REQ_APPLICATION_HANDLE REQ_AGENT_TID REQ_MEMBER REQ_USERID
---------------------- ------------- ---------- ----------
                    19          1104          0 SANJU
                    43          1444          0 SANJU

REQ_STMT_TEXT                           HLD_APPLICATION_HANDLE HLD_MEMBER
--------------------------------------- ---------------------- ----------
UPDATE TEST1 SET (A,B,C) = (7,6,5)                          44          0
UPDATE TEST1 SET (A,B,C) = (4,4,4)                          44          0


HLD_UERSID HLD_CURRENT_STMT_TEXT
---------- -----------------------------------
SANJU      UPDATE TEST1 SET (A,B,C) = (7,6,5)
SANJU      UPDATE TEST1 SET (A,B,C) = (7,6,5)
```

► **Monitoring current locks in the database**: MON_GET_LOCKS is a table function that can be used to retrieve information on all the locks currently acquired in the database.

```
SELECT APPLICATION_HANDLE,
       LOCK_OBJECT_TYPE_ID,
       LOCK_OBJECT_TYPE,
       LOCK_MODE,
       LOCK_STATUS,
       LOCK_ATTRIBUTES
  FROM TABLE (MON_GET_LOCKS(NULL, -2));
```

```
APPLICATION_HANDLE LOCK_OBJECT_TYPE_ID LOCK_OBJECT_TYPE
------------------ ------------------- ----------------
                 7               x'56'        VARIATION
                43               x'52'              ROW
                 7               x'41'             PLAN
                43               x'56'        VARIATION
                43               x'43'          CATALOG
                44               x'56'        VARIATION
                44               x'43'          CATALOG
                43               x'53'         SEQUENCE


LOCK_MODE LOCK_STATUS LOCK_ATTRIBUTES
--------- ----------- ----------------
        S           G 0000000000000000
       NS           G 0000000000000000
        S           G 0000000000000000
        X           G 0000000000000000
        S           G 0000000000000000
        S           G 0000000000000000
        S           G 0000000000000000
        S           G 0000000000000000
```

▶ **Monitoring activity on a table**: MON_GET_TABLE is a table function that can be used to retrieve information on all activities happening on a table. These activities include the total number of reads, writes, and so on. The gain of the result set is a table in the database. If the table is range partitioned, then it will have one row for each partition. The function has information only about tables that have been accessed since the database was activated.

```
SELECT TABSCHEMA,
       TABNAME,
       TAB_TYPE,
       TABLE_SCANS,
       ROWS_READ,
       ROWS_INSERTED,
       ROWS_UPDATED,
       ROWS_DELETED,
       OVERFLOW_ACCESSES,
       OVERFLOW_CREATES,
       PAGE_REORGS
FROM TABLE(MON_GET_TABLE('','',-2)) AS t
WHERE TABSCHEMA='SANJU';
```

TABSCHEMA	TABNAME	TAB_TYPE	TABLE_SCANS	ROWS_READ	ROWS_INSERTED
SANJU	TEST1	USER_TABLE	67559	405803002	0
SANJU	TEST	USER_TABLE	40	5281601	2094795
SANJU	TEST2	USER_TABLE	61111	0	0
SANJU	DEPARTMENT	USER_TABLE	2	27	0
SANJU	EMPLOYEE	USER_TABLE	2	42	0

ROWS_UPDATED	ROWS_DELETED	OVERFLOW_ACCESSES	OVERFLOW_CREATES	PAGE_REORGS
288336	0	0	0	0
0	0	0	0	0
0	0	0	0	0
0	0	0	0	0
0	0	0	0	0

▶ **Monitoring connection activities**: The MON_GET_CONNECTION table function can be used to get the activity information on individual database connections. The information returned by this table function is an aggregated result. Metrics collected by this table function are periodically aggregated during the execution of SQL statements. Hence the metrics are always increasing. If we want to get the connection activity during a time interval then we need to analyze the difference between consecutive results. The function returns one row per database connection.

The table function returns different detailed metrics for all activities. The following SQL statements return different wait times that different connections have spent:

```
SELECT APPLICATION_HANDLE, AGENT_WAIT_TIME, POOL_READ_TIME,
    POOL_WRITE_TIME, DIRECT_READ_TIME, DIRECT_WRITE_TIME,
    CLIENT_IDLE_WAIT_TIME, LOCK_WAIT_TIME, TOTAL_CPU_TIME,
    TOTAL_WAIT_TIME, TOTAL_SECTION_SORT_TIME,
    TOTAL_SECTION_SORT_PROC_TIME, TOTAL_COMPILE_TIME,
    TOTAL_COMPILE_PROC_TIME, TOTAL_IMPLICIT_COMPILE_TIME,
    TOTAL_IMPLICIT_COMPILE_PROC_TIME, TOTAL_SECTION_TIME,
    TOTAL_SECTION_PROC_TIME, TOTAL_ROUTINE_TIME, TOTAL_COMMIT_TIME,
    TOTAL_COMMIT_PROC_TIME, TOTAL_ROLLBACK_TIME,
    TOTAL_ROLLBACK_PROC_TIME, TOTAL_LOAD_TIME, TOTAL_LOAD_PROC_TIME
    FROM TABLE(MON_GET_CONNECTION(cast(NULL as bigint), -2)) AS t;
```

```
APPL_HANDLE  AGENT_WAIT_TM POOL_READ_TM POOL_WRITE_TM DIR_READ_TM
-----------  ------------- ------------ ------------- -----------
         19              0          374           304     1969438
         18              0         4453           278         578
         44              0           18             0       28448
         43              0          469             0       10094
          7              0         8728             0        1234

DIR_WRITE_TM CLIENT_IDLE_WAIT_TM LOCK_WAIT_TM TOT_CPU_TM TOT_WAIT_TM
------------ ------------------- ------------ ---------- -----------
           0            20552230      2490501 1396957754     4475621
         199            26445458         6789     265201       12831
           0            19850444      4038746 1367847968     4067465
           0            23211948      1809462  675312730     1824165
           1            26455273            0    1123205       24239

TOT_SECTION_SORT_TM TOT_SECTION_SORT_PROC_TM TOT_COMPILE_TM
------------------- ------------------------ --------------
                  0                        0            130
                  0                        0           1404
                  0                        0            129
                  0                        0            134
                  9                        9           1680

TOT_COMPILE_PROC_TM TOT_IMPLICIT_COMPILE_TM TOT_IMPLICIT_COMPILE_PROC_TM
------------------- ----------------------- ----------------------------
                  8                       0                            0
                178                       0                            0
                  7                       0                            0
                  7                       0                            0
                383                       0                            0

TOT_SECTION_TM TOT_SECTION_PROC_TM TOT_ROUTINE_TM TOT_COMMIT_TM
-------------- ------------------- -------------- -------------
       3866409             1382272        2022714         15848
         11139                 434              0           124
       5823706             1784916          43514           257
       2488743              679029          21168          3810
         43440               23024              0             8

TOT_COMMIT_PROC_TM TOT_RBK_TM TOT_RBK_PROC_TM TOT_LOAD_TM TOT_LOAD_PROC_TM
------------------ ---------- --------------- ----------- ----------------
              1053          8               5           0                0
                56         21               0        4371             3517
                31         56              54           0                0
                24        266              39           0                0
                 8          0               0           0                0
```

The following SQL statement returns read and write metrics for each connection:

```
SELECT APPLICATION_HANDLE,  POOL_DATA_L_READS, POOL_INDEX_L_READS,
       POOL_DATA_P_READS, POOL_INDEX_P_READS, POOL_DATA_WRITES,
       POOL_INDEX_WRITES, DIRECT_READS, DIRECT_WRITES, DIRECT_
READ_REQS,
       DIRECT_WRITE_REQS, ROWS_MODIFIED, ROWS_READ, ROWS_RETURNED
   FROM TABLE(MON_GET_CONNECTION(cast(NULL as bigint), -2)) AS t;
```

APPLICATION_HANDLE	POOL_DATA_L_READS	POOL_INDEX_L_READS	POOL_DATA_P_READS
19	6455318	36915	13
18	1764	3097	275
44	4409268	37055	2
43	1701263	13412	37
7	18724	833	1786

POOL_INDEX_P_READS	POOL_DATA_WRITES	POOL_INDEX_WRITES	DIRECT_READS
8	304	0	72286
349	279	1	776
0	0	0	73728
15	0	0	26576
278	0	0	2384

DIRECT_WRITES	DIRECT_READ_REQS	DIRECT_WRITE_REQS	ROWS_MODIFIED
0	9200	0	2569348
676	80	124	360
0	9234	0	24028
0	3327	0	514265
34	153	17	52

ROWS_READ	ROWS_RETURNED
1293162736	6
395	15
1314218132	6
501460406	5
5286114	30427

The following SQL statement returns various activity details for each connection:

```
SELECT APPLICATION_HANDLE, DEADLOCKS, LOCK_ESCALS, LOCK_TIMEOUTS,
       LOCK_WAITS, TOTAL_SECTION_SORTS, TOTAL_SORTS, POST_
THRESHOLD_SORTS,
       POST_SHRTHRESHOLD_SORTS, SORT_OVERFLOWS, TOTAL_
COMPILATIONS,
       TOTAL_IMPLICIT_COMPILATIONS, TOTAL_APP_SECTION_EXECUTIONS,
       TOTAL_ROUTINE_INVOCATIONS, TOTAL_APP_COMMITS, INT_COMMITS,
       TOTAL_APP_ROLLBACKS, INT_ROLLBACKS
  FROM TABLE(MON_GET_CONNECTION(cast(NULL as bigint), -2)) AS t;
```

APPL_HANDLE	DEADLCKS	LCK_ESCALS	LCK_TMOUTS	LCK_WAITS	TOT_SECTION_SORTS
19	1	0	0	224	0
18	0	0	0	2	6
44	0	0	0	227	0
43	0	0	0	85	0
7	0	0	0	0	4

TOT_SORTS	POST_THRESHOLD_SORTS	POST_SHRTHRESHOLD_SORTS	SORT_OVERFLOWS
0	0	0	0
6	0	0	0
0	0	0	0
0	0	0	0
4	0	0	0

TOT_COMPILATIONS	TOT_IMPLICIT_COMPILATIONS	TOT_APP_SECTION_EXECUTIONS
12	0	2965798
71	0	50
11	0	880014
12	0	315126
32	0	59

TOT_ROUTINE_INVOC	TOT_APP_COMMITS	INT_COMMITS	TOT_APP_RBKS	INT_ROLLBACKS
5	2318	1	5	2
0	44	1	3	0
4	228	1	5	0
5	87	1	5	0
0	59	1	6	0

▸ **Monitoring database activities**: The MON_DB_SUMMARY administrative view provides summary information on all activities happening in the database. The information available in this administrative view is aggregated over a period of time. This is very useful to get high-level information on database activities.

```
SELECT TOTAL_APP_COMMITS, TOTAL_APP_ROLLBACKS, APP_RQSTS_
COMPLETED_TOTAL,
        AVG_RQST_CPU_TIME, ROUTINE_TIME_RQST_PERCENT,
        RQST_WAIT_TIME_PERCENT, ACT_WAIT_TIME_PERCENT,
        LOCK_WAIT_TIME_PERCENT, AGENT_WAIT_TIME_PERCENT,
        NETWORK_WAIT_TIME_PERCENT, SECTION_PROC_TIME_PERCENT,
        SECTION_SORT_PROC_TIME_PERCENT, COMPILE_PROC_TIME_PERCENT,
        TRANSACT_END_PROC_TIME_PERCENT, UTILS_PROC_TIME_PERCENT,
        AVG_LOCK_WAITS_PER_ACT, AVG_LOCK_TIMEOUTS_PER_ACT,
        AVG_DEADLOCKS_PER_ACT, AVG_LOCK_ESCALS_PER_ACT,
        ROWS_READ_PER_ROWS_RETURNED, TOTAL_BP_HIT_RATIO_PERCENT
   FROM SYSIBMADM.MON_DB_SUMMARY;
```

```
TOT_APP_COMMITS TOT_APP_RBKS APP_RQSTS_COMPLETED_TOT AVG_RQST_CPU_TM
--------------- ------------ ----------------------- ---------------
           3835          766                    9251          466323

ROUTINE_TM_RQST_PCT RQST_WAIT_TM_PCT ACT_WAIT_TM_PCT LOCK_WAIT_TM_PCT
------------------- ---------------- --------------- ----------------
              12.68            71.13           70.17            82.14

AGENT_WAIT_TM_PCT NW_WAIT_TM_PCT SEC_PROC_TM_PCT SEC_SORT_PROC_TM_PCT
----------------- -------------- --------------- --------------------
             0.00           0.00           98.39                 0.00

COMPILE_PROC_TM_PCT TRANSACT_END_PROC_TM_PCT UTILS_PROC_TM_PCT
------------------- ------------------------ -----------------
               0.04                     0.03              0.08

AVG_LOCK_WAITS_PER_ACT AVG_LOCK_TMOUTS_PER_ACT AVG_DEADLOCKS_PER_ACT
---------------------- ----------------------- ---------------------
                     0                       0                     0

AVG_LOCK_ESCALS_PER_ACT ROWS_READ_PER_ROWS_RETURNED TOT_BP_HIT_RATIO_PCT
----------------------- --------------------------- --------------------
                      0                       96946                99.97
```

▶ **Monitoring connection summary:** The MON_CONNECTION_SUMMARY administrative view provides summary information on all connections. This provides a high-level overview of connection metrics that are aggregated over a period of time.

```
SELECT APPLICATION_HANDLE, TOTAL_APP_COMMITS, TOTAL_APP_ROLLBACKS,
ACT_COMPLETED_TOTAL, APP_RQSTS_COMPLETED_TOTAL, AVG_RQST_CPU_
TIME, ROUTINE_TIME_RQST_PERCENT, RQST_WAIT_TIME_PERCENT, ACT_
WAIT_TIME_PERCENT, IO_WAIT_TIME_PERCENT, LOCK_WAIT_TIME_PERCENT,
AGENT_WAIT_TIME_PERCENT, NETWORK_WAIT_TIME_PERCENT, SECTION_PROC_
TIME_PERCENT, SECTION_SORT_PROC_TIME_PERCENT, COMPILE_PROC_TIME_
PERCENT, TRANSACT_END_PROC_TIME_PERCENT, UTILS_PROC_TIME_PERCENT,
AVG_LOCK_WAITS_PER_ACT, AVG_LOCK_TIMEOUTS_PER_ACT, AVG_DEADLOCKS_
PER_ACT, AVG_LOCK_ESCALS_PER_ACT, ROWS_READ_PER_ROWS_RETURNED,
TOTAL_BP_HIT_RATIO_PERCENT FROM SYSIBMADM.MON_CONNECTION_SUMMARY
```

APPL_HANDLE	TOT_APP_COMMITS	TOT_APP_RLBCKS	ACT_CMPLTD_TOT	APP_RQSTS_CMPLTD_TOT
7	66	6	66	388
18	44	3	50	125
19	2419	6	3370445	52
43	88	6	315372	49

AVG_RQST_CPU_TM	ROUT_TM_RQST_PCT	RQST_WAIT_TM_PCT	ACT_WAIT_TM_PCT	IO_WAITTM_PCT
3176	0.00	50.33	46.94	42.25
2121	0.00	75.87	74.34	42.92
48080408	27.48	66.07	66.07	40.26
13803859	0.84	72.74	72.74	0.57

LOCK_WAIT_TM_PCT	AGENT_WAIT_TM_PCT	NETWORK_WAIT_TM_PCT	SECTION_PROC_TM_PCT
0.00	0.00	0.00	94.57
52.91	0.00	0.00	10.63
59.43	0.00	0.00	98.22
99.19	0.00	0.00	98.93

SEC_SRT_PROC_TM_PCT	CMPLE_PROC_TM_PCT	TXN_END_PROC_TM_PCT	UTILS_PROC_TM_PCT
0.03	2.01	0.03	0.00
0.00	4.36	1.37	86.93
0.00	0.00	0.05	0.00
0.00	0.00	0.01	0.00

AVG_LOCK_WAITS_PER_ACT	AVG_LOCK_TMOUTS_PER_ACT	AVG_DEADLOCKS_PER_ACT
0	0	0
0	0	0
0	0	0
0	0	0

AVG_LOCK_ESCALS_PER_ACT	ROWS_READ_PER_ROWS_RETURNED	TOT_BP_HIT_RATIO_PCT
0	173	89.61
0	26	87.16
0	322824265	99.99
0	83640341	99.99

▶ **Capturing monitor data for each connection for a given time period**: The
`MONREPORT.CONNECTION()` stored procedure can be used to get the database
activity information for each connection over a given period of time. This procedure
accepts the time interval for which the metrics should be calculated. The default time
interval is 10 seconds.

`CALL MONREPORT.CONNECTION(10);`

The report generated by this procedure is divided into two main parts. The first part
contains a summary of all active connections.

```
===========================================================================
 Part 1 - Summary of connections

  ---------------------------------------------------------------------------
    APPLICATION TOTAL_       TOTAL_     ACT_COMPLETED  TOTAL_WAIT  CLIENT_IDLE
 #   _HANDLE     CPU_TIME     ACT_TIME   _TOTAL          _TIME       _WAIT_TIME
 ---  ----------  ----------  --------  -------------  ----------  -----------
 1    7           0           0         0              0           0
 2    18          0           0         0              0           40060
 3    19          7020045     32949     4004           25887       0
 4    43          2371215     24615     660            22065       0
 5    44          14196091    32526     4004           18222       0
```

The second part contains one section for each connection. It has detailed information
on all activities related to each connection. Apart from basic connection details, it has
the following sections that give a very good overview of the connection:

❑ It gives an overview of the activity information for a given connection, which
includes number of requests completed, total CPU time taken, total wait
times, and so on.

```
Work volume and throughput
  -------------------------------------------------------------------------
                                   Per second            Total
                                   -------------------   ------------------
TOTAL_APP_COMMITS                  0                     1
ACT_COMPLETED_TOTAL                133                   4004
APP_RQSTS_COMPLETED_TOTAL          0                     0

TOTAL_CPU_TIME                     = 7020045
TOTAL_CPU_TIME per request         = 0

Row processing
  ROWS_READ/ROWS_RETURNED          = 0 (6013109/0)
  ROWS_MODIFIED                    = 0

Wait times
  -------------------------------------------------------------------------

-- Wait time as a percentage of elapsed time --

                                        %    Wait time/Total time
                                        ---  ------------------------------
For requests                            78   25887/32948
For activities                          78   25887/32949

-- Time waiting for next client request --

CLIENT_IDLE_WAIT_TIME              = 0
CLIENT_IDLE_WAIT_TIME per second   = 0
```

❑   The next section shows a breakdown of the total wait time and total
     processing time:

```
-- Detailed breakdown of TOTAL_WAIT_TIME --

                                  %    Total
                                  ---  ---------------------------------------
TOTAL_WAIT_TIME                   100  25887

I/O wait time
  POOL_READ_TIME                  0    0
  POOL_WRITE_TIME                 0    0
  DIRECT_READ_TIME                0    19
  DIRECT_WRITE_TIME               0    0
  LOG_DISK_WAIT_TIME              0    0
LOCK_WAIT_TIME                    99   25869
AGENT_WAIT_TIME                   0    0
Network and FCM
  TCPIP_SEND_WAIT_TIME            0    0
  TCPIP_RECV_WAIT_TIME            0    0
  IPC_SEND_WAIT_TIME              0    0
  IPC_RECV_WAIT_TIME              0    0
  FCM_SEND_WAIT_TIME              0    0
  FCM_RECV_WAIT_TIME              0    0
WLM_QUEUE_TIME_TOTAL              0    0

Component times
-------------------------------------------------------------------------------
-- Detailed breakdown of processing time --

                                       %                 Total
                                       ---------------   ---------------------
Total processing                       100               7061

Section execution
  TOTAL_SECTION_PROC_TIME              99                6996
    TOTAL_SECTION_SORT_PROC_TIME       0                 0
Compile
  TOTAL_COMPILE_PROC_TIME              0                 0
  TOTAL_IMPLICIT_COMPILE_PROC_TIME     0                 0
Transaction end processing
  TOTAL_COMMIT_PROC_TIME               0                 2
  TOTAL_ROLLBACK_PROC_TIME             0                 0
Utilities
  TOTAL_RUNSTATS_PROC_TIME             0                 0
  TOTAL_REORGS_PROC_TIME               0                 0
  TOTAL_LOAD_PROC_TIME                 0                 0
```

❑ The next section gives us information on the `Buffer pool` hit ratios that the connection maintained and other I/O details. It also includes the overall locking details for a given connection.

```
Buffer pool
----------------------------------------------------------------------------
Buffer pool hit ratios

Type                  Ratio              Reads (Logical/Physical)
----------------      ----------------   ------------------------------------
Data                  100                20173/0
Index                 100                204/0
XDA                   0                  0/0
Temp data             0                  0/0
Temp index            0                  0/0
Temp XDA              0                  0/0


I/O
----------------------------------------------------------------------------
Buffer pool writes
   POOL_DATA_WRITES        = 0
   POOL_XDA_WRITES         = 0
   POOL_INDEX_WRITES       = 0
Direct I/O
   DIRECT_READS            = 402
   DIRECT_READ_REQS        = 51
   DIRECT_WRITES           = 0
   DIRECT_WRITE_REQS       = 0
Log I/O
   LOG_DISK_WAITS_TOTAL    = 0


Locking
----------------------------------------------------------------------------
                      Per activity                    Total
                      ---------------------------     --------------------
LOCK_WAIT_TIME        6                               25869
LOCK_WAITS            0                               1
LOCK_TIMEOUTS         0                               0
DEADLOCKS             0                               0
LOCK_ESCALS           0                               0
```

❑ The last section gives us detailed information about every connection metric, such as the number of routine calls, sort details, number of compilations, and so on.

```
Routines
--------------------------------------------------------------------------------
                               Per activity              Total
                               ----------------------    ----------------------
TOTAL_ROUTINE_INVOCATIONS      0                         0
TOTAL_ROUTINE_TIME             0                         83

TOTAL_ROUTINE_TIME per invocation   = 0

Sort
--------------------------------------------------------------------------------
TOTAL_SORTS                         = 0
SORT_OVERFLOWS                      = 0
POST_THRESHOLD_SORTS                = 0
POST_SHRTHRESHOLD_SORTS             = 0

Network
--------------------------------------------------------------------------------
Communications with remote clients
TCPIP_SEND_VOLUME per send          = 0              (0/0)
TCPIP_RECV_VOLUME per receive       = 0              (0/0)
...
...

Other
--------------------------------------------------------------------------------
Compilation
   TOTAL_COMPILATIONS               = 0
   PKG_CACHE_INSERTS                = 2053
   PKG_CACHE_LOOKUPS                = 6006
Catalog cache
   CAT_CACHE_INSERTS                = 0
   CAT_CACHE_LOOKUPS                = 2002
Transaction processing
   TOTAL_APP_COMMITS                = 1
   ....
   ....

DB2 utility operations
--------------------------------------------------------------------------------
   TOTAL_RUNSTATS                   = 0
   TOTAL_REORGS                     = 0
   TOTAL_LOADS                      = 0
```

▶ **Capturing current applications details**: The MONREPORT.CURRENTAPPS stored procedure can be used to get information on all applications that are currently connected to the database. The information returned includes summary as well as detailed information for each application. It gives an overview of application activity type and activity state. This is useful for finding the type of workload running on the database.

```
CALL MONREPORT.CURRENTAPPS;
```

The report generated by this procedure is divided into two main parts.

❑ The first part shows a summary of all activities and states for all connected applications.

```
===============================================================================
  Part 1 - Summary of application processing

  Number of connections          = 5
  Number of coordinator activities = 8

  --Units of work by WORKLOAD_OCCURRENCE_STATE--

  WORKLOAD_OCCURRENCE_STATE             Number of units of work
  ------------------------------------  ------------------------------------
  UOWEXEC                               4
  UOWWAIT                               1

  --Active coordinator agents by REQUEST_TYPE--

  REQUEST_TYPE                          Number of agents
  ------------------------------------  ------------------------------------
  EXECUTE                               4

  --All agents by EVENT_OBJECT:EVENT_TYPE--

  EVENT_OBJECT:EVENT_TYPE               Number of agents
  ------------------------------------  ------------------------------------
  LOCK:ACQUIRE                          2
  REQUEST:PROCESS                       1
  ROUTINE:PROCESS                       1

  --Coordinator activities by ACTIVITY_STATE--

  ACTIVITY_STATE                        Number of activities
  ------------------------------------  ------------------------------------
  EXECUTING                             8

  --Coordinator activities by ACTIVITY_TYPE--

  ACTIVITY_TYPE                         Number of activities
  ------------------------------------  ------------------------------------
  CALL                                  4
  OTHER                                 1
  READ_DML                              1
  WRITE_DML                             2
```

❑ The second part has more details on individual applications or connections.

```
=================================================================================
 Part 2 - Details by connection


 --------------------------------------------------------------------------------
 APPLICATION_HANDLE        = 7
 APPLICATION_ID            = *LOCAL.DB2.111116115451
 APPLICATION_NAME          = db2bp.exe

 Unit of work WORKLOAD_OCCURRENCE_STATE = UOWEXEC

 --Agents for this connection--

 MEMBER   AGENT_TYPE:AGENT_SUBTYPE     REQUEST_TYPE        EVENT_OBJECT:EVENT_TYPE
 ------   -------------------------    ----------------    ------------------------
 0        COORDINATOR:                 EXECUTE             ROUTINE:PROCESS

 --Activities for this connection--

 MEMBER                 UOW_ID      ACTIVITY_ID      ACTIVITY_TYPE    ACTIVITY_STATE
 -------------------    ----------  ---------------  ---------------  --------------
 0                      84          1                CALL             EXECUTING
 0                      84          62               READ_DML         EXECUTING

 --------------------------------------------------------------------------------
```

▶ **Capturing current SQL statements information**: The `MONREPORT.CURRENTSQL` stored procedure gives us information on all SQL statements that are currently running on the database. It also lists the top SQL statements measured against various metrics.

```
CALL MONREPORT.CURRENTSQL;
```

❑ We can also get details for a specific application by passing the application handle as an input parameter to this procedure.

```
CALL MONREPORT.CURRENTSQL(44);
```

The report generated by this procedure is divided into three parts.

❏ The first part shows a list of the top activities or SQL statements based on various metrics.

```
================================================================================
 Part 1 - Summaries by 'top' metrics

 Top 10 current activities by TOTAL_CPU_TIME
--------------------------------------------------------------------------------
 ACTIVITY  UOW_ID  APPLICATION  TOTAL_CPU  STMT_TEXT
 _ID               _HANDLE      _TIME
 --------  ------  -----------  ---------  --------------------------------
 1         2350    19           0          CALL lock3()
 2551      265     44           0          UPDATE TEST1 SET (A,B,C) = (7,6,5)
 62        90      7            0          SELECT ARRAY_AGG(A.ACTIVITY_ID
 1         105     43           0          LOCK TABLE TEST1 IN EXCLUSIVE MODE
 1         2488    19           0          UPDATE TEST1 SET (A,B,C) = (7,6,5)
 1         90      7            0          CALL monreport.currentsql()
 1         262     44           0          CALL lock2()
 1         101     43           0          CALL lock1()

 Top 10 current activities by ROWS_READ
--------------------------------------------------------------------------------
 ACTIVITY  UOW_ID  APPLICATION  ROWS_READ    STMT_TEXT
 _ID               _HANDLE
 --------  ------  -----------  -----------  --------------------------------
 1         2350    19           11154        CALL lock3()
 1         101     43           375          CALL lock1()
 1         262     44           339          CALL lock2()
 1         90      7            35           CALL monreport.currentsql()
 1         2488    19           0            UPDATE TEST1 SET (A,B,C) =
 2551      265     44           0            UPDATE TEST1 SET (A,B,C) =
 62        90      7            0            SELECT ARRAY_AGG(A.ACTIVITY_ID
 1         105     43           0            LOCK TABLE TEST1 IN EXCLUSIVE

 Top 10 current activities by DIRECT READS + DIRECT WRITES
--------------------------------------------------------------------------------
 ACTIVITY  UOW_ID  APPLICATION  DIRECT_READS +  STMT_TEXT
 _ID               _HANDLE      DIRECT_WRITES
 --------  ------  -----------  --------------  --------------------------------
 1         2350    19           44430           CALL lock3()
 1         101     43           1480            CALL lock1()
 1         262     44           1348            CALL lock2()
 1         90      7            226             CALL monreport.currentsql()
 1         2488    19           0               UPDATE TEST1 SET (A,B,C) =
 2551      265     44           0               UPDATE TEST1 SET (A,B,C) =
 62        90      7            0               SELECT ARRAY_AGG(A.ACTIVITY_ID
 1         105     43           0               LOCK TABLE TEST1 IN EXCLUSIVE
```

❏ The next part shows the overall ranking of SQL statements or activities which are computed by comparing all metrics.

```
================================================================================
  Part 2 - Overall ranking of activities

  ACTIVITY   UOW_ID  APPLICATION   TOTAL_CPU   ROWS_READ       DIRECT_READS +
  _ID                _HANDLE       _TIME                       DIRECT_WRITES
  --------   ------  -----------   ---------   -------------   --------------------
  1          2350    19            1           1               1
  1          101     43            1           2               2
  1          262     44            1           3               3
  1          90      7             1           4               4
  1          2488    19            1           5               5
  1          105     43            1           5               5
  62         90      7             1           5               5
  2551       265     44            1           5               5
```

☐   The last part shows a complete statement of all activities that have been
    executed during the given time period.

```
================================================================================
Part 3 - Complete statement text for activities

--------------------------------------------------------------------------------
ACTIVITY_ID/UOW_ID/APPLICATION_HANDLE = 1/2350/19

CALL lock3()
--------------------------------------------------------------------------------
ACTIVITY_ID/UOW_ID/APPLICATION_HANDLE = 1/101/43

CALL lock1()
--------------------------------------------------------------------------------
ACTIVITY_ID/UOW_ID/APPLICATION_HANDLE = 1/262/44

CALL lock2()
--------------------------------------------------------------------------------
ACTIVITY_ID/UOW_ID/APPLICATION_HANDLE = 1/90/7

CALL monreport.currentsql()
--------------------------------------------------------------------------------
ACTIVITY_ID/UOW_ID/APPLICATION_HANDLE = 1/2488/19

UPDATE TEST1 SET (A,B,C) = (7,6,5)
```

▶ **Capturing database summary metrics during a given time period**: The
  MONREPORT.DBSUMMARY stored procedure gives information on all activities
  happening on the database during a given time interval. The metrics returned
  are computed at database level and include all applications running against the
  database. This procedure accepts the time interval for which the metrics should be
  calculated. The default time interval is 10 seconds.

  CALLMONREPORT.DBSUMMARY(30);

The report generated is divided into the following sections:.

❑ The first part shows the high-level activity metrics summarized at database level, which includes number of requests completed, total CPU time taken, total wait time, and so on.

```
================================================================================
   Part 1 - System performance

   Work volume and throughput
   --------------------------------------------------------------------------
                                    Per second            Total
                                    --------------------  --------------------
   TOTAL_APP_COMMITS                0                     1
   ACT_COMPLETED_TOTAL              536                   5368
   APP_RQSTS_COMPLETED_TOTAL        0                     0

   TOTAL_CPU_TIME                   = 8954458
   TOTAL_CPU_TIME per request       = 0

   Row processing
     ROWS_READ/ROWS_RETURNED        = 1342587 (8055525/6)
     ROWS_MODIFIED                  = 0

   Wait times
   --------------------------------------------------------------------------

   -- Wait time as a percentage of elapsed time --

                                        %     Wait time/Total time
                                        ---   ------------------------------
   For requests                         59    27893/46867
   For activities                       59    27892/46867

   -- Time waiting for next client request --

   CLIENT_IDLE_WAIT_TIME               = 20030
   CLIENT_IDLE_WAIT_TIME per second    = 2003
```

❑ This section shows a breakdown of total wait time and total processing time
for all activities happening on the database.

```
-- Detailed breakdown of TOTAL_WAIT_TIME --

                             %    Total
                             ---  -------------------------------------------
TOTAL_WAIT_TIME              100  27893

I/O wait time
  POOL_READ_TIME             0    0
  POOL_WRITE_TIME            0    0
  DIRECT_READ_TIME           4    1164
  DIRECT_WRITE_TIME          0    0
  LOG_DISK_WAIT_TIME         0    2
LOCK_WAIT_TIME               95   26726
AGENT_WAIT_TIME              0    0
Network and FCM
  TCPIP_SEND_WAIT_TIME       0    0
........
........

Component times
--------------------------------------------------------------------------
-- Detailed breakdown of processing time --

                                   %                Total
                                   ----------------  ----------------------
Total processing                   100              18974

Section execution
  TOTAL_SECTION_PROC_TIME          46               8882
    TOTAL_SECTION_SORT_PROC_TIME   0                2
Compile
  TOTAL_COMPILE_PROC_TIME          0                0
  TOTAL_IMPLICIT_COMPILE_PROC_TIME 0                0
Transaction end processing
  TOTAL_COMMIT_PROC_TIME           0                0
  TOTAL_ROLLBACK_PROC_TIME         0                0
Utilities
  TOTAL_RUNSTATS_PROC_TIME         0                0
  TOTAL_REORGS_PROC_TIME           0                0
  TOTAL_LOAD_PROC_TIME             0                0
```

❑ The next section gives information on the `Buffer pool` hit ratios that the database maintained and other I/O details. It also includes the overall locking details summarized at database level.

```
 Buffer pool
------------------------------------------------------------------------
Buffer pool hit ratios

Type               Ratio              Reads (Logical/Physical)
-----------------  -----------------  ------------------------------------
Data               100                27032/0
Index              100                276/0
XDA                0                  0/0
Temp data          0                  0/0
Temp index         0                  0/0
Temp XDA           0                  0/0


I/O
------------------------------------------------------------------------
Buffer pool writes
   POOL_DATA_WRITES        = 0
   POOL_XDA_WRITES         = 0
   POOL_INDEX_WRITES       = 0
Direct I/O
   DIRECT_READS            = 752
   DIRECT_READ_REQS        = 74
   DIRECT_WRITES           = 0
   DIRECT_WRITE_REQS       = 0
Log I/O
   LOG_DISK_WAITS_TOTAL    = 1

Locking
------------------------------------------------------------------------
                        Per activity                   Total
                        -----------------------------  -------------------
LOCK_WAIT_TIME          4                              26726
LOCK_WAITS              0                              1
LOCK_TIMEOUTS           0                              0
DEADLOCKS               0                              0
LOCK_ESCALS             0                              0
```

❑ The next section gives detailed information on metrics, such as the number of routine calls, sort details, number of compilations, and so on. The following report gives an overview of detailed activities happening on the database.

```
Routines
----------------------------------------------------------------------
                            Per activity            Total
                            -------------------     -----------------
TOTAL_ROUTINE_INVOCATIONS   0                       1
TOTAL_ROUTINE_TIME          2                       11258

TOTAL_ROUTINE_TIME per invocation    = 11258

Sort
----------------------------------------------------------------------
TOTAL_SORTS                           = 4
SORT_OVERFLOWS                        = 0
POST_THRESHOLD_SORTS                  = 0
POST_SHRTHRESHOLD_SORTS               = 0

Network
----------------------------------------------------------------------
Communications with remote clients
TCPIP_SEND_VOLUME per send            = 0         (0/0)
TCPIP_RECV_VOLUME per receive         = 0         (0/0)
........
........

Other
----------------------------------------------------------------------
Compilation
  TOTAL_COMPILATIONS                  = 0
  PKG_CACHE_INSERTS                   = 2749
  PKG_CACHE_LOOKUPS                   = 8049
Catalog cache
  CAT_CACHE_INSERTS                   = 0
  CAT_CACHE_LOOKUPS                   = 2681
Transaction processing
  TOTAL_APP_COMMITS                   = 1
.........
.........

DB2 utility operations
----------------------------------------------------------------------
  TOTAL_RUNSTATS                      = 0
  TOTAL_REORGS                        = 0
  TOTAL_LOADS                         = 0
```

❑ The next section shows performance metrics for all applications which are currently connected to the database. Each application or connection is assigned to one service class and one workload. The following report shows performance metrics based on different classifications of applications based on their assigned service classes, workloads, and so on.

```
================================================================================
Part 2 - Application performance drill down

Application performance database-wide
--------------------------------------------------------------------------------
TOTAL_CPU_TIME          TOTAL_        TOTAL_APP_      ROWS_READ +
per request             WAIT_TIME %   COMMITS         ROWS_MODIFIED
----------------------  -----------   --------------  -------------------------
0                       59            1               8055525

Application performance by connection
--------------------------------------------------------------------------------
APPLICATION_  TOTAL_CPU_TIME      TOTAL_        TOTAL_APP_   ROWS_READ +
HANDLE        per request         WAIT_TIME %   COMMITS      ROWS_MODIFIED
------------- ------------------- -----------   -----------  ----------
7             0                   0             0            0
18            0                   0             0            0
....
....

Application performance by service class
--------------------------------------------------------------------------------
SERVICE_      TOTAL_CPU_TIME      TOTAL_        TOTAL_APP_   ROWS_READ +
CLASS_ID      per request         WAIT_TIME %   COMMITS      ROWS_MODIFIED
--------      ------------------- -----------   -----------  ----------
11            0                   0             0            0
12            0                   0             0            0
13            0                   59            1            8043511

Application performance by workload
--------------------------------------------------------------------------------
WORKLOAD_     TOTAL_CPU_TIME      TOTAL_        TOTAL_APP_   ROWS_READ +
NAME          per request         WAIT_TIME %   COMMITS      ROWS_MODIFIED
------------- ------------------- -----------   -----------  ----------
SYSDEFAULTADM 0                   0             0            0
SYSDEFAULTUSE 0                   79            2            6019110
```

❑ The last section shows metrics for each database partition.

```
================================================================================
Part 3 - Member level information

- I/O wait time is
  (POOL_READ_TIME + POOL_WRITE_TIME + DIRECT_READ_TIME + DIRECT_WRITE_TIME).

        TOTAL_CPU_TIME      TOTAL_        RQSTS_COMPLETED_  I/O
MEMBER  per request         WAIT_TIME %   TOTAL             wait time
------  ------------------- -----------   ----------------  --------------
0       0                   59            0                 1149
```

▶ **Capturing lock wait information**: The `MONREPORT.LOCKWAIT` stored procedure can be used to capture information about all lock waits happening on the database during a given time interval. The report produced contains information on all the locks, lock holders, lock modes, lock requested, and so on. This procedure accepts the time interval for which the metrics should be calculated. The default time interval is 10 seconds.

```
CALL MONREPORT.LOCKWAIT;
```

The report generated is divided into the following sections:.

❑ The first section shows the information on all lock waits present on the database.

```
===============================================================================
 Part 1 - Summary of current lock waits


 -------------------------------------------------------------------------------

      REQ_APPLICATION  LOCK_MODE   HLD_APPLICATION  LOCK_  LOCK_OBJECT_TYPE
 #    HANDLE           REQUESTED   _HANDLE          MODE
 ---- ---------------  ---------   ---------------  -----  ----------------
 1    19               IX          44               X      TABLE
 2    43               X           44               X      TABLE
```

❑ The next section shows details of each lock wait. It gives information on lock holder and lock requestor applications.

```
===============================================================================
 Part 2 - Details for each current lock wait

 lock wait #:1
 -------------------------------------------------------------------------------

 -- Lock details --

 LOCK_NAME            = 03001A00000000000000000054
 LOCK_WAIT_START_TIME = 2011-11-17-01.24.41.223800
 LOCK_OBJECT_TYPE     = TABLE
 TABSCHEMA            = SANJU
 TABNAME              = TEST1
 ROWID                =
 LOCK_STATUS          = W
 LOCK_ATTRIBUTES      = 0000000000000000
 ESCALATION           = N

 -- Requestor and holder application details --

 Attributes           Requestor                       Holder
 ------------------   -------------------------        -------------------------
 APPLICATION_HANDLE   19                              44
 APPLICATION_ID       *LOCAL.DB2.111116115529         *LOCAL.DB2.111116120728
 APPLICATION_NAME     db2bp.exe                       db2bp.exe
 SESSION_AUTHID       SANJU                           SANJU
 MEMBER               0                               0
 LOCK_MODE            -                               X
 LOCK_MODE_REQUESTED  IX                              -
```

❑ The next section displays the details of both requestor and holder application activity information.

```
-- Lock holder current agents --

AGENT_TID               = 4772
REQUEST_TYPE            = EXECUTE
EVENT_STATE             = EXECUTING
EVENT_OBJECT            = REQUEST
EVENT_TYPE              = PROCESS
ACTIVITY_ID             = 3891
UOW_ID                  = 271

AGENT_TID               = 4264
REQUEST_TYPE            = INTERNAL-2147483648
.....
.....

-- Lock holder current activities --

ACTIVITY_ID             = 3894
UOW_ID                  = 271
LOCAL_START_TIME        = 2011-11-17-01.25.04.898280
ACTIVITY_TYPE           = OTHER
ACTIVITY_STATE          = EXECUTING

STMT_TEXT               =
CALL lock2()

ACTIVITY_ID             = 1
.....
.....

-- Lock requestor waiting agent and activity --

AGENT_TID               = 1104
REQUEST_TYPE            = EXECUTE
ACTIVITY_ID             = 1
UOW_ID                  = 2494
LOCAL_START_TIME        = 2011-11-17-01.24.41.218447
ACTIVITY_TYPE           = WRITE_DML
ACTIVITY_STATE          = EXECUTING

STMT_TEXT               =
UPDATE TEST1 SET (A,B,C) = (7,6,5)
```

▶ **Capturing package cache information during a given time interval**: The
MONREPORT.PKGCACHE stored procedure returns information on all SQL statements
contained in the package cache. The report also lists the top SQL statements based
on various metrics. This procedure accepts the time interval for which the metrics
should be calculated. The default time interval is 10 seconds.

```
CALL MONREPORT.PKGCACHE(10);
```

We can limit the results to just static or dynamic SQL statements by passing s or d
as follows:

```
CALL MONREPORT.PKGCACHE(10, 'd');
```

The following report generated by this procedure contains summaries by top metrics:

```
================================================================================
 Part 1 - Summaries by 'top' metrics

 Top 10 statements by TOTAL_CPU_TIME
 --------------------------------------------------------------------------------
 #    TOTAL_       STMT_TEXT
      CPU_TIME
 --   -----------  ------------------------------------------------------------
 1    156001       UPDATE TEST1 SET (A,B,C) = (7,6,5)
 2    15600        CALL SYSIBM.SQLCAMESSAGECCSID (:HV00010  :HI00010 , 80, NULL, N
 3    15600        LOCK TABLE TEST1 IN EXCLUSIVE MODE
 4    0            CALL lock2()
 5    0            CALL lock1()
 .....
 .....


 Top 10 statements by TOTAL_CPU TIME per exec
 --------------------------------------------------------------------------------
 #    TOTAL_       STMT_TEXT
      CPU_TIME
 --   -----------  ------------------------------------------------------------
 1    6541         UPDATE TEST1 SET (A,B,C) = (7,6,5)
 2    205          CALL SYSIBM.SQLCAMESSAGECCSID (:HV00010  :HI00010 , 80, NULL, N
 3    154          LOCK TABLE TEST1 IN EXCLUSIVE MODE
 7    0            LOCK TABLE TEST2 IN EXCLUSIVE MODE
 ......
 ......


 Top 10 statements by TOTAL_ACT_WAIT_TIME
 --------------------------------------------------------------------------------
 #    TOTAL_ACT    LOCK_WAIT    STMT_TEXT
      _WAIT_TIME   _TIME
 --   -----------  -----------  ------------------------------------------------
 15   1            0            CALL SAVE_EXEC_INFO (CAST(:HV00040  :HI00040  AS "
 16   0            0            CALL monreport.PKGCACHE(?)
 4    0            0            CALL lock2()
 5    0            0            CALL lock1()
 1    0            0            UPDATE TEST1 SET (A,B,C) = (7,6,5)
 ......
 ......
```

The other top reports generated are based on the following metrics:

```
Top 10 statements by TOTAL_ACT_WAIT_TIME per exec
-----------------------------------------------------------------------------
......
......

Top 10 statements by ROWS_READ + ROWS_MODIFIED
-----------------------------------------------------------------------------
.......
.......

Top 10 statements by ROWS_READ + ROWS_MODIFIED per exec
-----------------------------------------------------------------------------
......
......

Top 10 statements by number of executions
-----------------------------------------------------------------------------
.....
.....

Top 10 statements by I/O wait time
-----------------------------------------------------------------------------
......
......

Top 10 statements by I/O wait time per exec
-----------------------------------------------------------------------------
......
......
```

Each top report identifies the executable SQL statements by a serial number. The last part in the generated report contains the mapping of these serial numbers to SQL statements. All SQL statements contained in the package cache are assigned a unique ID which is a binary token.

```
================================================================================
  Part 2 - EXECUTABLE_IDs for statements in Part 1

  #    EXECUTABLE_ID
  --   -------------------------------------------------------------------------
  1    x'01000000000000007B01000000000000010000000100201111116231149681003'
  2    x'01000000000000000E500000000000000010000000100201110092313338863001'
  3    x'01000000000000007B01000000000000020000000100201111116231149681003'
  4    x'0100000000000000019F61400000000000000000200201111170120537037003005'
  5    x'010000000000000090F514000000000000000000200201111170120532219003'
  6    x'01000000000000000BA2516000000000000000000200201111170126222127005'
  ......
  ......
  ......
```

How it works...

DB2 provides different ways of monitoring applications. It includes event monitors, SQL-based snapshots, administrative views, monitoring functions, monitoring routines, and so on. DB2 9.7 introduced a number of monitoring functions. These functions have names prefixed with MON_. These functions are very light-weight when compared to snapshot monitor table functions and hence are recommended for monitoring. These new monitoring functions also report many new monitoring elements that give time-spent breakdown information that allows us to clearly identify where an SQL statement is spending most of the time.

The information returned from these monitoring functions represents the total metrics from database start. In other words, these metrics are always increasing. To actively monitor the application behavior, we should examine the difference between two successive outputs.

9
Advanced Performance Tuning Tips

In this chapter, we will focus on following recipes related to application performance tuning:

- ▶ Understanding predicates in SQL statements
- ▶ Improving `INSERT` performance
- ▶ Writing effective SQL statements

Introduction

In this chapter, we will focus on various tips and techniques that can be used to enhance application performance. We will discuss different types of predicates that DB2 considers while compiling an SQL statement. We will also discuss how we can exploit the optimizer using better predicates. Then, we will discuss different ways to improve the `INSERT` performance. Towards the end, we will talk about many techniques that we can consider while writing better quality SQL statements.

Understanding predicates in SQL statements

A **predicate** is an element of SQL that is used for **search** operations. These are specified in the WHERE and the HAVING clause. Every database has its own set of predicates, which are used to filter the table data. There are different types of predicates in DB2, and DB2 has its own way of evaluating them. Based on the cost and the efficiency of a predicate, we can classify them as follows:

- ▶ Range delimiting predicates
- ▶ Index SARGable predicates
- ▶ Data SARGable predicates
- ▶ Residual predicates

 SARGable is a term used for Search Argument

In this recipe, we will discuss these predicates, and analyze their impact on query performance.

Getting ready

All the examples used in this recipe use the tables in the SAMPLE database. A SAMPLE database can be created by using the db2sampl command.

How to do it...

While applying predicates in an SQL statement, we should aim for the highest selectivity possible, so that the fewest rows are returned. Depending upon feasibility, the DB2 optimizer tries to rewrite the given SQL statement to promote better predicates, but as a developer, we should try to use the best predicates wherever possible.

Understanding range delimiting predicates: We all know that an **index scan** is much better when compared to a **table scan**, but that is not the end of optimization. We can further reduce the amount of index scan. In a regular index scan, all the leaf nodes in an index tree are scanned. If we can provide **start** and **stop** keys in the index tree, then the optimizer doesn't need to scan the entire index. Predicates that allow this kind of range delimiting are considered to be the best amongst all. We should try and use them as much as possible. To enforce range delimiting predicates, we need an index on the search column, and we can have search operators, such as =, <, >, BETWEEN, and so on, where we can define a range on an index scan.

For example, the predicate in the following SQL statement is a range delimiting predicate.

```
SELECT EMPNO, FIRSTNME, SALARY
FROM EMPLOYEE
WHERE EMPNO='000200';
```

Identifying range delimiting predicates in an access plan: We can identify range delimiting predicates in an access plan as well. If this type of predicate is used, then DB2 marks the start key and the stop key in the `IXSCAN` operator details, implying a range delimiting predicate.

Consider following SQL statement:

```
SELECT EMPNO, SALARY
FROM EMPLOYEE
WHERE EMPNO = '000200';
```

The access plan for this SQL statement looks as follows:

```
Optimized Statement:
-------------------
SELECT '000200' AS "EMPNO", Q1.SALARY AS "SALARY"
FROM SANJU.EMPLOYEE AS Q1
WHERE (Q1.EMPNO = '000200')

Access Plan:
-----------
        Total Cost:          0.0274065
        Query Degree:        1

        Rows
       RETURN
       (   1)
        Cost
        I/O
         |
         1
       IXSCAN
       (   2)
     0.0274065
         0
         |
         42
  INDEX: SANJU
     TEST_IDX
         Q1
```

As we can see, looking at the access plan graph alone, may not give a clear picture of the start and stop keys. To get more details, we need to see the operator details for IXSCAN. We can see that DB2 has marked the start and the stop keys, which means that the range delimiting predicate is in effect.

```
Predicates:
----------
2) Start Key Predicate,
        Comparison Operator:            Equal (=)
        Subquery Input Required:        No
        Filter Factor:                  0.0238095

        Predicate Text:
        ---------------
        (Q1.EMPNO = '000200')

2) Stop Key Predicate,
        Comparison Operator:            Equal (=)
        Subquery Input Required:        No
        Filter Factor:                  0.0238095

        Predicate Text:
        ---------------
        (Q1.EMPNO = '000200')
```

Understanding index SARGable predicates: This type of predicate does not limit the index scan, so the entire index needs to be scanned. But the benefit is that we can get the result rows directly from the index scan, without traversing the table data. This type of predicate should be our second choice. The requirement for this type of predicate is an index with referenced columns as a part of the index. We can use operators, such as <>, IS NOT NULL, LIKE, and so on, which are index SARGable, where the optimizer will have to scan the entire index to get the result row IDs.

For example, the predicate in the following SQL statement is an index SARGable predicate.

```
SELECT EMPNO, FIRSTNME, SALARY
FROM EMPLOYEE
WHERE EMPNO <> '000200';
```

 <> (not equal to) is not range delimiting, because it only tells which value is not valid. The optimizer will still have to scan all the values.

Identifying index SARGable predicates in an access plan: DB2 explicitly marks SARGable predicates as **Sargable Predicate** in the *operator details* section. If this clause is against the `IXSCAN` operator, then it means that it's an index SARGable predicate. Looking at the graph as well, we can tell that some filtering is happening, as the rows selected reduce from the total cardinality of the index.

For example, observe following access plan where we can see an index scan:

```
Original Statement:
-------------------
SELECT EMPNO, SALARY
FROM EMPLOYEE
WHERE SALARY > 10000


Optimized Statement:
--------------------
SELECT Q1.EMPNO AS "EMPNO", Q1.SALARY AS "SALARY"
FROM SANJU.EMPLOYEE AS Q1
WHERE (10000 < Q1.SALARY)

Access Plan:
-----------
        Total Cost:           1227.74
        Query Degree:         1

      Rows
     RETURN
     (   1)
      Cost
      I/O
       |
     999999
     IXSCAN
     (   2)
     1227.74
        0
       |
     1e+006
  INDEX: SANJU
    TEST_IDX
        Q1
```

If we look at the operator details, we can see that the optimizer has marked this predicate as SARGable, which, in this case, is index SARGable.

```
Predicates:
----------
2) Sargable Predicate,
        Comparison Operator:          Less Than (<)
        Subquery Input Required:      NO
        Filter Factor:                0.999999

        Predicate Text:
        --------------
        (10000 < Q1.SALARY)
```

Understanding data SARGable predicates: This type of predicate cannot be satisfied by an index scan, it needs a table scan. The filtering will be done by reading the columns from a table, and then searching this list.

For example, if we don't have any index on the EMPNO column of the EMPLOYEE table, then the following predicate becomes data SARGable:

```
SELECT EMPNO, FIRSTNME, SALARY

FROM EMPLOYEE

WHERE EMPNO='000200';
```

Identifying data SARGable predicates in an access plan: Just as index SARGable predicates, data SARGable predicates are also identified by the SARGable predicate in the TBSCAN operator details section in the access plan. The only way to distinguish the index SARGable and the data SARGable predicates is by looking at the operator. For index SARGable, it will be IXSCAN and for data SARGable, it will be TBSCAN. Looking at the access plan graph, we can observe that the rows selected from TBSCAN are less than the table cardinality. This also implies that some filtering is happening.

For example, observe the following access plan where we can see a table scan:

```
Original Statement:
------------------
SELECT EMPNO, SALARY
FROM EMPLOYEE
WHERE EDLEVEL = 14


Optimized Statement:
-------------------
SELECT Q1.EMPNO AS "EMPNO", Q1.SALARY AS "SALARY"
FROM SANJU.EMPLOYEE AS Q1
WHERE (Q1.EDLEVEL = 14)

Access Plan:
-----------
        Total Cost:            7.64124
        Query Degree:          1

      Rows
     RETURN
     (   1)
      Cost
      I/O
       |
      1.68
     TBSCAN
     (   2)
     7.64124
        1
        |
       42
  TABLE: SANJU
    EMPLOYEE
       Q1
```

If we look at the operator details, we can observe that the optimizer has marked this predicate as SARGable, which, in this case, is a data SARGable predicate.

```
Predicates:
----------
2) Sargable Predicate,
        Comparison Operator:              Equal (=)
        Subquery Input Required:          No
        Filter Factor:                    0.04

        Predicate Text:
        ---------------
        (Q1.EDLEVEL = 14)
```

Understanding residual predicates: This type of predicate is the most expensive one, compared to the other three, and should be avoided as much as possible. These predicates may be a result of using correlated queries, using LONG VARCHAR, or LOB columns, and so on in SQL statements that cannot use indexes, and need I/O beyond normal table access.

Consider the following table definition:

```
db2 => describe table emp_photo

                              Data type                    Column
Column name                   schema     Data type name    Length     Scale Nulls
----------------------------- ---------- ----------------- ---------- ----- ------
EMPNO                         SYSIBM     CHARACTER                  6     0 No
PHOTO_FORMAT                  SYSIBM     VARCHAR                   10     0 No
PICTURE                       SYSIBM     BLOB                  102400     0 Yes

  3 record(s) selected.
```

We can see that the PICTURE column in this table is a BLOB column. If we have any SQL statement that filters on this column, then it would need additional I/O to fetch the BLOB columns. This is an example of a **residual predicate**.

```
SELECT EMPNO, PICTURE

FROM EMP_PHOTO

WHERE LENGTH(PICTURE) = 29540
```

Identifying residual predicates in access plan: Residual predicates can be identified by observing **Residual Predicate** under the TBSCAN operator details section in an access plan.

For example, observe the following access plan, where we can see a table scan:

```
Original Statement:
-------------------
SELECT EMPNO, PICTURE
FROM EMP_PHOTO
WHERE LENGTH(PICTURE) = 29540


Optimized Statement:
--------------------
SELECT Q1.EMPNO AS "EMPNO", Q1.PICTURE AS "PICTURE"
FROM SANJU.EMP_PHOTO AS Q1
WHERE (LENGTH(Q1.PICTURE) = 29540)

Access Plan:
-----------
        Total Cost:            7.6015
        Query Degree:          1

      Rows
     RETURN
     (   1)
      Cost
      I/O
       |
      0.32
     TBSCAN
     (   2)
     7.6015
       1
       |
       8
  TABLE: SANJU
    EMP_PHOTO
       Q1
```

If we look at the operator details, we can observe that the optimizer has marked this predicate as residual.

```
Predicates:
----------
2) Residual Predicate,
        Comparison Operator:         Equal (=)
        Subquery Input Required:     NO
        Filter Factor:               0.04

        Predicate Text:
        ---------------
        (LENGTH(Q1.PICTURE) = 29540)
```

How it works...

The following diagram shows the order in which different predicates are applied during SQL execution:

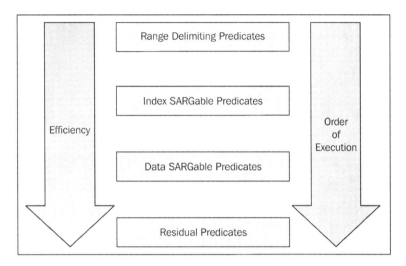

As we can see, since the range delimiting predicates are best in terms of efficiency, they are computed first. As a developer, we should encourage range delimiting and index SARGable predicates, as they are best in terms of performance. Data SARGable and residual predicates can impact performance drastically, as they involve a lot of I/O, so we should avoid them as much as possible.

There's more...

The following table summarizes the characteristics of each type of predicate:

Predicate type	Reduces index I/O	Reduces data pages	Filters intermediate result set	Filters final result set
Range delimiting	yes	yes	yes	yes
Index SARGable	no	yes	yes	yes
Data SARGable	no	no	yes	yes
Residual	no	no	no	yes

From this table, it's clear that the residual predicates are worst in terms of performance. We should try to make data SARGable and residual predicates into range delimiting or index SARGable predicates.

For example, consider the following SQL statement where we are filtering on the `PICTURE` column `length` in the `EMP_PHOTO` table:

```
SELECT EMPNO, PICTURE
FROM EMP_PHOTO
WHERE LENGTH(PICTURE) = 29540;
```

If we can add a generated column in `EMP_PHOTO`, defined as `LENGTH (PICTURE)`, then we can avoid this residual predicate. If we can index this generated column, it will make it a range delimiting predicate, which is preferred for performance.

Improving INSERT performance

Many-a-times, we have requirements for a bulk load of data. DB2 provides different utilities for loading data, such as import, load, and so on. Each of these utilities have their own advantages and disadvantages. Import is preferred for a low volume of data, whereas load is commonly used for a high volume of data. But, load makes the database non-recoverable, as it does not log anything. Because of this, many application designs do not prefer load, and hence the only option available is to use import or regular inserts. In such cases, we can use some techniques to improve INSERT performance. This recipe will focus on these techniques.

Getting Ready

Before we discuss the INSERT performance, we should know the basics of DB2 storage. The lowest storage unit in DB2 is a page. A **page** is a block of physical memory located in a `tablespace` container. A table can have data in multiple pages, but one page can have rows from only one table. As and when the data comes in, DB2 keeps on assigning pages to a table, and stores the rows in them. We can perform `INSERT`, `UPDATE`, and `DELETE` operations on a table that can change the table data. If we `DELETE` any row in a table, then it creates a gap in the data page. This is also known as **fragmentation**. It can also happen as a result of an `UPDATE` statement. One obvious result of fragmentation is space wastage. It reduces the data density on pages. So, to get a set of rows in bufferpool, DB2 now has to read more pages causing more I/O, which directly affects the system performance. Hence, it is recommended to use `REORG` on tables, depending on the table activity. DB2, in itself, tries to fill the gaps created by `DELETE`, by inserting new records in these gaps. The downside of this approach is that it has to search the data pages to find a suitable gap. If a gap is found, it will insert a row in it, else it will insert the new row at the end. To make this searching efficient, DB2 maintains a **Free Space Control Record** (**FSCR**) in every page header. So, instead of checking the whole page, DB2 can get the free space information from the page header itself.

With this background, let's discuss how we can improve `INSERT` performance.

How to do it...

Use buffered INSERTs: Buffered INSERTs allow us to send more than one row to the database server for insertion. It saves overhead in processing individual `INSERT` statements, plus it also saves the number of messages transmitted over the network. Every language provides some interface for buffered inserts or batch inserts. It can also be done by using simple SQL statements, as follows:

```
INSERT INTO TEST_TABLE VALUES (), (), (),();
```

We can also use compound statements to send multiple `INSERT` statements at once, as follows:

```
BEGIN ATOMIC
INSERT INTO TEST_TABLE VALUES ();
INSERT INTO TEST_TABLE VALUES ();
INSERT INTO TEST_TABLE VALUES ();
INSERT INTO TEST_TABLE VALUES ();
END ATOMIC @
```

Using prepared statements: When DB2 gets an `INSERT` request, it compiles the statement and then executes it. Just as any other statement, if an `INSERT` statement needs to be executed multiple times, we should first prepare a statement with parameter markers and then execute the prepared statement with different values for `INSERT`.

```
BEGIN
    -- declare variables
DECLARE stmtVARCHAR(1000);
  DECLARE val1 INTEGER;
  DECLARE val2 INTEGER;

    -- prepare an insert statement without actual values
  SET stmt = 'INSERT INTO TEST_TABLE VALUES (?, ?)';
  PREPARE s1 FROM stmt;

    -- execute the above prepared insert statement with actual values
  SET val1 = 10;
  SET val2 = 110;
  EXECUTE s1 USING :val1 :val2;

-- execute the above prepared insert statement with next set of values
  SET val1 = 20;
```

```
   SET val2 = 220;
   EXECUTE s1 USING :val1 :val2;
END @
```

Aggressive page cleaning: When a row is inserted or updated in a bufferpool page, it becomes dirty, and it will eventually be written to a disk. This transferring of dirty pages to the disk is done by **page cleaners**. For a better INSERT performance, we can use aggressive page cleaning, by using the following recommendations:

> ▶ **Reduce the** CHNGPGS_THRESH parameter: This database configuration parameter indicates the threshold percentage of dirty pages in the bufferpool. Once this threshold is crossed, DB2 invokes page cleaners to move dirty pages to the disk. The default value of this parameter is 60. For better INSERT performance, we can reduce it to a low value.
>
> UPDATE DB CFG FOR SAMPLE USING CHNGPGS_THRESH 10;

 Once the bulk insert is complete, we should set it back to the normal value, depending on the type of workload

> ▶ **Tune the** NUM_IOCLEANERS **parameter**: This configuration parameter indicates the number of asynchronous page cleaners for the database. This parameter should be set to at least the number of physical storage devices in the database. For example, if we have 10 storage devices, then we should set it as follows:
>
> UPDATE DB CFG FOR SAMPLE USING NUM_IOCLEANERS 10;

 As best practice, we should set this parameter to AUTOMATIC

Enable alternate page cleaning: This is an alternative to the previous step, and is the most aggressive page cleaning algorithm. Once enabled, page cleaners no longer respond to the CHNGPS_THRESH parameter and the LSN gap triggers. When the number of dirty pages exceeds an acceptable value, the page cleaners search the entire bufferpool, and clean all victim pages, by writing them on the disk. In this mode, pages are written to the disk more frequently, but fewer pages at a time. It allows page cleaners to work more effectively, as they have less number of pages to write for each invocation. Alternate page cleaning can be enabled by setting DB2_USE_ALTERNATE_PAGE_CLEANING to ON.

```
db2set DB2_USE_ALTERNATE_PAGE_CLEANING=ON
```

Lock the table: When a row is inserted, it is locked until the INSERT is committed. When we are doing bulk inserts, DB2 has to acquire a lot of locks. This is an overhead. Another problem with so many locks is that it consumes a lot of locklist space, which affects the overall system concurrency. If we are doing huge INSERTs on a table, it's a good idea to lock the table explicitly in an exclusive mode, and then run the INSERT commands. Once all rows are inserted, we can release the table lock.

```
ALTER TABLE tablename LOCKSIZE TABLE;
```

When the lock size is set to `TABLE`, DB2 will use a table lock for all subsequent SQL statements until this `LOCKSIZE` is set back to `ROW`, which is the default.

Or

```
LOCK TABLE tablename IN EXCLUSIVE MODE
```

This will lock the table in `EXCLUSIVE` mode. This exclusive lock will be released as soon as the transaction completes (`COMMIT` or `ROLLBACK`).

Once the `INSERT` is done, we can release the lock as follows:

```
ALTER TABLE tablename LOCKSIZE ROW;
```

Or

```
COMMIT/ROLLBACK;
```

Control transaction logs: Transaction log is another area that consumes time in `INSERT`. Each row inserted is recorded in the transaction logs. We can disable logging for a table that can improve the `INSERT` performance. This might not be a suitable choice in many cases, as it makes the table non-recoverable. Once the transaction is committed or rolled back, logging is re-enabled for the table automatically.

```
ALTER TABLE tablename ACTIVATE NOT LOGGED INITIALLY
```

Reduce FSCR searching: When an `INSERT` command is submitted, DB2 searches a certain number of FSCRs to find a suitable gap in data pages. The number of FSCR searches can be controlled by the `DB2MAXFSCRSEARCH` registry variable. The unit for this value is **percentage**. The default value for this registry variable is **five** percent. We can set it to a lower value to reduce the searching. This will improve the `INSERT` performance, but it may leave gaps in data pages, making the table more fragmented. This solution works very well when we are storing historical information in a table, where `UPDATES` and `DELETES` are not frequent.

```
C:\>db2set DB2MAXFSCRSEARCH=2

C:\>db2 terminate
DB20000I  The TERMINATE command completed successfully.

C:\>db2stop force
11/03/2011 16:15:06      0   0   SQL1064N  DB2STOP processing was successful.
SQL1064N  DB2STOP processing was successful.

C:\>db2start
11/03/2011 16:15:14      0   0   SQL1063N  DB2START processing was successful.
SQL1063N  DB2START processing was successful.

C:\>db2set
DB2_REDUCED_OPTIMIZATION=YES
DB2_EXTENDED_OPTIMIZATION=ENHANCED_MULTIPLE_DISTINCT
DB2MAXFSCRSEARCH=2
DB2INSTOWNER=SANJU
DB2PORTRANGE=60000:60003
DB2INSTPROF=C:\PROGRAMDATA\IBM\DB2\DB2COPY1
```

Disable FSCR searching: We can also disable the FSCR search by enabling the `APPEND` mode for the table. This is the fastest approach to improve the `INSERT` performance. When the `APPEND` mode is set to `ON` for a table, all new rows are stored at the end. When the `APPEND` mode is enabled, DB2 does not maintain free space information. This mode cannot be used when the table has clustered indexes. At any time, we can disable the `APPEND` mode, if no longer needed.

We can use following statement to enable the `APPEND` mode for a table:

`ALTER TABLE tablename APPEND ON`

Use the following statement to disable APPEND mode for given table.

`ALTER TABLE tablename APPEND OFF`

Reserve PCTFREE space: If we have clustered indexes defined for a table, then DB2 stores every record close to other records with similar index values. This adds an overhead of searching for the proper space. If no space is found at the desired location, DB2 searches FSCRs to find a gap. To avoid this overhead, we can set a certain amount of free space identified by the `PCTFREE` clause. If done before `REORG`, DB2 will reserve some free space for new rows during `REORG`, thus avoiding the need of search, which results in improved `INSERT` performance. This increases the probability of finding a suitable place at the appropriate place.

`ALTER TABLE tablename PCTFREE <integer-value>`

How it works...

As mentioned in the previous section, a row in a table is eventually stored in a data page. DB2 uses write-ahead logging, which means that the row will first be written to transaction logs, and then to a cached data page in the bufferpool. The row is not written to the disk even at `COMMIT`. This is done asynchronously by page cleaners. Page cleaners monitor the pages in the bufferpool, and look for a dirty page. A **dirty page** is a page in which any insert or update has been performed. Page cleaners move these dirty pages to a physical disk. Once a page is moved from the bufferpool to the disk, it can safely be overwritten by other data pages, as we have preserved a copy. When we are doing bulk inserts, we are changing a lot of data pages. We need to make sure that the bufferpool has enough space for dirty pages. If all the pages in the bufferpool are dirty pages, then an `INSERT` will pause until the page cleaners clean some dirty pages and make space for fresh pages.

Writing effective SQL statements

A majority of the application performance can be addressed or avoided by writing good quality SQL queries. Many-a-times, we underestimate the power of SQL writing techniques. We can write an SQL statement in many different ways to get the desired result set. The key lies in identifying the best SQL query amongst them. When an SQL query is submitted for execution, the DB2 optimizer rewrites the SQL in the most efficient way it can, but that does not mean we can get away with bad SQL queries. Inefficient SQL queries may confuse the optimizer, resulting in a suboptimal access plan. As a developer, we should always consider best practices in writing SQL queries. In this recipe, we will discuss some best practices that can help us write good quality SQL queries. We will also analyze the different ways of writing SQL statements, by comparing their access plans.

Getting Ready

We should be familiar with different tools to capture information. In this recipe, we will use the `db2exfmt` utility to get the access plans for SQL statements.

How to do it...

While writing SQL queries, we should focus on each and every attribute that we are referencing in the statement, whether it's in the `SELECT` list or in the `WHERE` clause. We will address both these sections in this recipe, in different steps. Each step here is one independent tip that can be used in any SQL statement. Some of the following tips are also recommended by IBM as part of their best practices for **performance tuning**.

Avoid column expressions in join predicates: Instead of applying expressions on column predicates, use **inverse expressions**. If we have any expression on columns, it prevents DB2 from using index scans. It also leads to inaccurate selectivity estimates and query rewrite efficiency. When we have expressions over columns, it makes it difficult for an optimizer to recognize similar columns, which is useful when columns can be replaced with constants. It also prevents the optimizer from estimating the number of rows returned.

```
EXPRESSION(COL) = 'constant'
```

You can rewrite this predicate as follows:

```
COL = INVERSEXPRESSION('constant')
```

Consider the following example, where we don't have any expression in the `join` predicate. We can observe that the optimizer is using an index to get the results:

```
Original Statement:
-------------------
select empno, firstnme
from employee
where WORKDEPT = 'E21'


Optimized Statement:
--------------------
SELECT Q1.EMPNO AS "EMPNO", Q1.FIRSTNME AS "FIRSTNME"
FROM DBUSER.EMPLOYEE AS Q1
WHERE (Q1.WORKDEPT = 'E21')

Access Plan:
-----------
        Total Cost:              7.60312
        Query Degree:            1

            Rows
           RETURN
           (   1)
            Cost
            I/O
             |
            5.25
           FETCH
           (   2)
           7.60312
             1
        /----+----\
     5.25           42
    IXSCAN      TABLE: DBUSER
    (   3)         EMPLOYEE
  0.0325278          Q1
      0
      |
      42
  INDEX: DBUSER
      XEMP2
       Q1
```

If we modify this SQL statement (see the previous image), and add an expression in the predicate column, we can see that the index is no longer useful. In this case the optimizer chose to do a table scan, which is way more costlier than an index scan.

```
Original Statement:
-------------------
select empno, firstnme
from employee
where LCASE(WORKDEPT) = 'e21'


Optimized Statement:
--------------------
SELECT Q1.EMPNO AS "EMPNO", Q1.FIRSTNME AS "FIRSTNME"
FROM SANJU.EMPLOYEE AS Q1
WHERE (LCASE(Q1.WORKDEPT) = 'e21')

Access Plan:
-----------
        Total Cost:              7.65183
        Query Degree:           1

      Rows
     RETURN
     (   1)
      Cost
      I/O
        |
      1.68
     TBSCAN
     (   2)
     7.65183
        1
        |
       42
  TABLE: SANJU
    EMPLOYEE
       Q1
```

If we can convert the previous expression (`LCASE(WORKDEPT) = 'e21'`) as an inverse expression, we should see an index scan again.

```
Original Statement:
------------------
SELECT empno, firstnme
from employee
where workdept = UCASE('e21')


Optimized Statement:
-------------------
SELECT Q1.EMPNO AS "EMPNO", Q1.FIRSTNME AS "FIRSTNME"
FROM DBUSER.EMPLOYEE AS Q1
WHERE (Q1.WORKDEPT = 'E21')

Access Plan:
-----------
        Total Cost:             7.60424
        Query Degree:           0

            Rows
           RETURN
           (   1)
            Cost
            I/O
             |
             6
           FETCH
           (   2)
           7.60424
             1
        /----+----\
       6            42
    IXSCAN     TABLE: DBUSER
    (   3)        EMPLOYEE
   0.0332595         Q1
       0
       |
       42
  INDEX: DBUSER
      XEMP2
       Q1
```

Many-a-times, we don't have any other option, but to use the expressions. In such cases, we can use generated columns with the matching definition, and define an index on this generated column. Now, we can either rewrite our SQL statement to directly refer to this generated column, else the optimizer will try to rewrite the SQL statement to use this generated column. With the previous example, we can define a generated column, as follows:

```
-- put the table in check pending state
SET INTEGRITY FOR EMPLOYEE OFF;
-- add a generated column with required definition
ALTER TABLE EMPLOYEE
ADD COLUMN L_WORKDEPT CHAR(3) GENERATED ALWAYS AS (LCASE(WORKDEPT));
```

```
-- run set integrity with FORCE GENERATED option to generate values for
all generated columns

SET INTEGRITY FOR DEPAARTMENT, EMPLOYEE IMMEDIATE CHECKED FORCE
GENERATED;

-- create an index on generated column

CREATE INDEX EMP_IDX_GEN ON EMPLOYEE(L_WORKDEPT);

-- collect table statistics

RUNSTATS ON TABLE DBUSER.EMPLOYEE;
```

Now, if we observe the access plan, we can see that the optimizer has rewritten the SQL statement to use the generated column. Since we have an index on this generated column, it's an added advantage in terms of performance. This means that we don't have to change the application to make use of this generated column; it is handled by the optimizer automatically.

```
Original Statement:
------------------
select empno, firstnme
from employee
where LCASE(WORKDEPT) = 'e21'


Optimized Statement:
-------------------
SELECT Q1.EMPNO AS "EMPNO", Q1.FIRSTNME AS "FIRSTNME"
FROM SANJU.EMPLOYEE AS Q1
WHERE (Q1.L_WORKDEPT = 'e21')

Access Plan:
-----------
        Total Cost:            7.60312
        Query Degree:          1

            Rows
            RETURN
            (   1)
            Cost
             I/O
              |
            5.25
            FETCH
            (   2)
            7.60312
              1
         /----+----\
      5.25           42
     IXSCAN      TABLE: SANJU
     (   3)        EMPLOYEE
   0.0325278         Q1
       0
       |
       42
  INDEX: SANJU
   EMP_IDX_GEN
       Q1
```

Avoid complex expressions in the WHERE clause: If we have complex expressions in the search criteria, it can impact the cardinality estimation for the optimizer, resulting in a suboptimal access plan.

Consider following the SQL statement, where we don't have any expression in the WHERE clause predicate. If we observe the cardinality of the rows selected, it is 41, which is approximately equal to the number of rows in the EMPLOYEE table. The optimizer uses the information stored in the catalog statistics to estimate this cardinality, and the following access plan seems to be estimating it correctly.

```
Original Statement:
-------------------
SELECT EMPNO, SALARY, WORKDEPT
FROM EMPLOYEE
WHERE SALARY > 4000


Optimized Statement:
-------------------
SELECT Q1.EMPNO AS "EMPNO", Q1.SALARY AS "SALARY", Q1.WORKDEPT AS "WORKDEPT"
FROM SANJU.EMPLOYEE AS Q1
WHERE (4000 < Q1.SALARY)

Access Plan:
-----------
          Total Cost:           7.59552
          Query Degree:         1

       Rows
      RETURN
      (   1)
       Cost
       I/O
        |
       41  <>----------------- Cardinality
      TBSCAN
      (   2)
      7.59552
        1
        |
       42
  TABLE: SANJU
    EMPLOYEE
        Q1
```

The following screenshot shows the values for the expression SALARY * EDLEVEL/3. We can see that all values are greater than 4000:

```
C:\Windows>db2 "select salary, SALARY * EDLEVEL/3 from employee order by 1 asc, 2 asc"

SALARY        2
----------    -------------------------------
   35024.00          186794.6666666666666666
   38874.00          155496.0000000000000000
   38907.00          181566.0000000000000000
   39490.00          157960.0000000000000000
   39490.00          157960.0000000000000000
   39875.00          225958.3333333333333333
   41118.00          205590.0000000000000000
   41525.00          193783.3333333333333333
   41536.00          235370.6666666666666666
   43175.00          201483.3333333333333333
   43945.00          234373.3333333333333333
   46398.00          216524.0000000000000000
   48224.00          257194.6666666666666666
   49148.00          262122.6666666666666666
   49907.00          232899.3333333333333333
   50875.00          288291.6666666666666666
```

Now, let's observe the access plan when we include an expression in the WHERE clause. We can see that the cardinality estimate is now 14, which doesn't seem right. If we look at the actual values, we should get all rows satisfying this criteria. The point is that the optimizer is not able to estimate the cardinality properly, if we have any sort of complex expressions in predicates.

```
Original Statement:
-------------------
SELECT EMPNO, SALARY, WORKDEPT
FROM EMPLOYEE
WHERE SALARY * EDLEVEL/3 > 4000


Optimized Statement:
--------------------
SELECT Q1.EMPNO AS "EMPNO", Q1.SALARY AS "SALARY", Q1.WORKDEPT AS "WORKDEPT"
FROM SANJU.EMPLOYEE AS Q1
WHERE (4000 < ((Q1.SALARY * Q1.EDLEVEL) / 3))

Access Plan:
-----------
        Total Cost:           7.61082
        Query Degree:         1

      Rows
     RETURN
     (   1)
      Cost
      I/O
       |
     ( 14 )  <-------------------------- Cardinality
     TBSCAN
     (   2)
     7.61082
        1
       |
       42
 TABLE: SANJU
   EMPLOYEE
      Q1
```

In such cases, we can either define a generated column as SALARY * EDLEVEL / 3, or we can use statistical views. **Statistical views** are similar to normal views but they also allow a collection of statistics on them. DB2 uses the statistics on these views for better cardinality estimation. For example, we can define a statistical view, as follows, that can help our query:

```
CREATE VIEW SV_EMP_SAL AS (SELECT EMPNO
                              FROM EMPLOYEE
                              WHERE SALARY * EDLEVEL / 3 > 4000);


-- Enable view for use in query optimization.
ALTER VIEW SV_EMP_SAL ENABLE QUERY OPTIMIZATION;


-- Collect statistics on this view.
RUNSTATS ON TABLE SANJU.SV_EMP_SAL WITH DISTRIBUTION;
```

Now, since we are providing the correct statistics for our expression (SALARY * EDLEVEL / 3), it should now reflect in the access plan as well.

```
Original Statement:
-------------------
SELECT EMPNO, SALARY, WORKDEPT
FROM EMPLOYEE
WHERE SALARY * EDLEVEL / 3 > 4000


Optimized Statement:
--------------------
SELECT Q1.EMPNO AS "EMPNO", Q1.SALARY AS "SALARY", Q1.WORKDEPT AS "WORKDEPT"
FROM DBUSER.EMPLOYEE AS Q1
WHERE (4000 < ((Q1.SALARY * Q1.EDLEVEL) / 3))

Access Plan:
-----------
        Total Cost:           7.66243
        Query Degree:         0

     Rows
    RETURN
    (   1)
     Cost
      I/O
       |
     ( 42 ) <----------------- Cardinality
    TBSCAN
    (   2)
    7.66243
       1
       |
      42
  TABLE: DBUSER
     EMPLOYEE
        Q1
```

Avoid joins on expressions: Joining expression predicates can limit the `join` method to the nested loop, as it causes inaccurate cardinality estimates.

Let's consider the following example, where we don't have any expression in joining columns. We can observe that the optimizer has chosen `HSJOIN` (hash join) to join the two tables, which is considered to be a better join.

 The preference of joins depends on the use case; it can't be generalized to say which join is better.

```
Original Statement:
-------------------
SELECT EMP.EMPNO, EMP.JOB, DEPT.DEPTNAME
FROM EMPLOYEE EMP, DEPARTMENT DEPT
WHERE EMP.WORKDEPT = DEPT.DEPTNO


Optimized Statement:
-------------------
SELECT Q2.EMPNO AS "EMPNO", Q2.JOB AS "JOB", Q1.DEPTNAME AS "DEPTNAME"
FROM SANJU.DEPARTMENT AS Q1, SANJU.EMPLOYEE AS Q2
WHERE (Q2.WORKDEPT = Q1.DEPTNO)

Access Plan:
-----------
        Total Cost:             15.2409
        Query Degree:           1

             Rows
            RETURN
            (   1)
             Cost
             I/O
              |
              42
           ^HSJOIN
            (   2)
           15.2409
              2
         /-----+------\
        42             14
      TBSCAN         TBSCAN
      (   3)         (   4)
      7.63065        7.60332
        1              1
        |              |
        42             14
    TABLE: SANJU   TABLE: SANJU
     EMPLOYEE       DEPARTMENT
        Q2             Q1
```

If we modify the previous example, and add an expression to the `join` condition, we can now observe that the `join` method is changed to `NLJOIN` (**nested loop join**). For small tables, it doesn't make much difference, but this is very dangerous, if any of the table is bigger in size.

```
Original Statement:
-------------------
SELECT EMP.EMPNO, EMP.JOB, DEPT.DEPTNAME
FROM EMPLOYEE EMP, DEPARTMENT DEPT
WHERE UPPER(EMP.WORKDEPT) = DEPT.DEPTNO


Optimized Statement:
-------------------
SELECT Q2.EMPNO AS "EMPNO", Q2.JOB AS "JOB", Q1.DEPTNAME AS "DEPTNAME"
FROM SANJU.DEPARTMENT AS Q1, SANJU.EMPLOYEE AS Q2
WHERE (UPPER(Q2.WORKDEPT) = Q1.DEPTNO)

Access Plan:
-----------
        Total Cost:              16.0762
        Query Degree:            1

                 Rows
                RETURN
                (   1)
                 Cost
                 I/O
                  |
                  42
                NLJOIN
                (   2)
               16.0762
                  2
            /-----+-----\
         14                 3
      TBSCAN            TBSCAN
      (   3)            (   4)
      7.60332           7.65183
         1                 1
         |                 |
         14                42
   TABLE: SANJU       TABLE: SANJU
    DEPARTMENT          EMPLOYEE
        Q1
```

The previous problem can be solved by using generated columns defined as `UPPER(WORKDEPT)`.

Avoid joining different data types: When two columns of different data types are joined, it prevents DB2 from using the `Hash` join. If we encounter such a case, we should consider the option of using generated columns. Let's compare the two use cases by analyzing their access plans.

For this example, we will join the `EMPLOYEE` and `DEPARTMENT` tables on the work department. The table definitions show that `DEPTNO` and `WORKDEPT` are both `CHAR(3)`.

```
db2 => DESCRIBE TABLE DEPARTMENT

                             Data type            Column
Column name                  schema   Data type name    Length    Scale Nulls
---------------------------  -------  --------------  ----------  ----- ------
DEPTNO                       SYSIBM   CHARACTER             3      0 No
DEPTNAME                     SYSIBM   VARCHAR              36      0 No
MGRNO                        SYSIBM   CHARACTER             6      0 Yes
ADMRDEPT                     SYSIBM   CHARACTER             3      0 No
LOCATION                     SYSIBM   CHARACTER            16      0 Yes

  5 record(s) selected.

db2 => DESCRIBE TABLE EMPLOYEE

                             Data type            Column
Column name                  schema   Data type name    Length    Scale Nulls
---------------------------  -------  --------------  ----------  ----- ------
EMPNO                        SYSIBM   CHARACTER             6      0 No
FIRSTNME                     SYSIBM   VARCHAR              12      0 No
MIDINIT                      SYSIBM   CHARACTER             1      0 Yes
LASTNAME                     SYSIBM   VARCHAR              15      0 No
WORKDEPT                     SYSIBM   CHARACTER             3      0 Yes
PHONENO                      SYSIBM   CHARACTER             4      0 Yes
HIREDATE                     SYSIBM   DATE                  4      0 Yes
JOB                          SYSIBM   CHARACTER             8      0 Yes
EDLEVEL                      SYSIBM   SMALLINT              2      0 No
SEX                          SYSIBM   CHARACTER             1      0 Yes
BIRTHDATE                    SYSIBM   DATE                  4      0 Yes
SALARY                       SYSIBM   DECIMAL               9      2 Yes
BONUS                        SYSIBM   DECIMAL               9      2 Yes
COMM                         SYSIBM   DECIMAL               9      2 Yes

  14 record(s) selected.
```

Consider the following SQL statement and its access plan. We can see that the optimizer has chosen HSJOIN to join both the tables, as both the columns involved in the join are of the same data type:

```
Original Statement:
-------------------
SELECT EMP.EMPNO, EMP.JOB, DEPT.DEPTNAME
FROM TEST_EMP EMP, TEST_DEPT DEPT
WHERE EMP.WORKDEPT = DEPT.DEPTNO

Optimized Statement:
--------------------
SELECT Q2.EMPNO AS "EMPNO", Q2.JOB AS "JOB", Q1.DEPTNAME AS "DEPTNAME"
FROM SANJU.TEST_DEPT AS Q1, SANJU.TEST_EMP AS Q2
WHERE (Q2.WORKDEPT = Q1.DEPTNO)

Access Plan:
-----------
        Total Cost:            15.2409
        Query Degree:          1

              Rows
             RETURN
             (   1)
              Cost
              I/O
               |
               42
             HSJOIN
             (   2)
            15.2409
               2
         /-----+------\
       42               14
     TBSCAN          TBSCAN
     (   3)          (   4)
     7.63065         7.60332
        1               1
        |               |
       42               14
  TABLE: SANJU     TABLE: SANJU
    TEST_EMP         TEST_DEPT
      Q2               Q1
```

Let's test the same join operation on two dummy tables that are similar to EMPLOYEE and DEPARTMENT, but with varied lengths of joined columns.

```
-- create test tables similar to EMPLOYEE and DEPARTMENT and copy sample
data in them.
CREATE TABLE TEST_EMP LIKE EMPLOYEE;
INSERT INTO TEST_EMP SELECT * FROM EMPLOYEE;

CREATE TABLE TEST_DEPT LIKE DEPARTMENT;
INSERT INTO TEST_DEPT SELECT * FROM DEPARTMENT;

-- add a dummy column with different data type.
ALTER TABLE TEST_DEPT ADD COLUMN D_DEPTNO VARCHAR(10);

-- populate this dummy column from existing DEPTNO column from DEPARTMENT
table.
UPDATE TEST_DEPT SET D_DEPTNO = DEPTNO;

-- collect statistics on both sample tables
RUNSTATS ON TABLE DBUSER.TEST_EMP;
RUNSTATS ON TABLE DBUSER.TEST_DEPT;
```

If we observe the access plan now, we can see that HSJOIN is no longer useful. Hence, the optimizer now chose MSJOIN to join the two tables.

```
Access Plan:
-----------
        Total Cost:              15.2702
        Query Degree:           1

            Rows
            RETURN
            (   1)
            Cost
             I/O
              |
             42
            MSJOIN
            (   2)
           15.2702
              2
         /---+---\
        14           3
      TBSCAN      FILTER
      (   3)      (   6)
      7.60768     7.64552
         1           1
         |           |
        14          42
       SORT       TBSCAN
      (   4)      (   7)
      7.60695     7.64552
         1           1
         |           |
        14          42
      TBSCAN       SORT
      (   5)      (   8)
      7.60332     7.64479
         1           1
         |           |
        14          42
  TABLE: SANJU    TBSCAN
   TEST_DEPT      (   9)
      Q1          7.63065
                     1
                     |
                    42
              TABLE: SANJU
                TEST_EMP
                   Q2
```

Avoid joining non-equality predicates: When two columns are joined with non-equality operators, it limits the join method to the nested loop, as hash join and merge join cannot be used with inequality predicates. As far as possible, we should try to avoid such joins. It might not always be possible to get rid of such predicates, but in such a case, we should make sure that we have proper indexes created with the latest statistics. DB2 chooses the inner table on the basis of table cardinality. Hence, it is extremely important to make sure that the statistics are up-to-date.

```
Original Statement:
-------------------
SELECT E1.EMPNO, COUNT(*)
FROM EMPLOYEE E1, EMPLOYEE E2
WHERE E1.SALARY > E2.SALARY
GROUP BY E1.EMPNO


Optimized Statement:
--------------------
SELECT Q4.EMPNO AS "EMPNO", Q4.$C1
FROM
    (SELECT Q3.EMPNO, COUNT(*)
    FROM
        (SELECT Q2.EMPNO
        FROM SANJU.EMPLOYEE AS Q1, SANJU.EMPLOYEE AS Q2
        WHERE (Q1.SALARY < Q2.SALARY)) AS Q3
    GROUP BY Q3.EMPNO) AS Q4

Access Plan:
------------
        Total Cost:            0.749479
        Query Degree:          1

            Rows
            RETURN
            (   1)
            Cost
            I/O
             |
            42
            GRPBY
            (   2)
            0.738634
             0
             |
            859.95
            NLJOIN
            (   3)
            0.616634
             0
        /-----+------\
      42                 20.475
    IXSCAN             IXSCAN
    (   4)             (   5)
    0.0510835          0.0554024
      0                  0
      |                  |
      42                 42
INDEX: SANJU        INDEX: SANJU
   TEST_IDX            TEST_IDX
      Q2                 Q1
```

When two tables are joined with NLJOIN (**nested loop join**), one table is chosen as the inner table and the other one as the outer table. The smaller table is chosen as the inner table, as it can be easily accommodated in memory. If the bigger table is chosen as the inner table, then it will be traversed completely against every row of the outer table. It may add overflows, as data might get spilled on disk, reducing overall performance.

Avoid unnecessary outer joins: If we have the LEFT OUTER JOIN, or the RIGHT OUTER JOIN, or the FULL OUTER JOIN in the SQL query, it prevents a lot of optimization. For example, if we have OUTER JOINS in an SQL query, then it prevents the usage of **Materialized Query Tables (MQTs)**. In many cases, we can handle it at data loading time, by making sure that no orphan entries exist in the fact table (for example), which do not have any match in the parent dimension table. In such cases, we can use INNER JOINS instead of OUTER JOINS. If we have a scenario where an OUTER JOIN is needed, and we want to use MQTs, then it can be used as follows:

Consider the following SQL statement where we have an MQT, but it will not be picked up by the optimizer:

```
Original Statement:
-------------------
SELECT LOCATION, EMPNO
FROM DEPARTMENT D LEFT OUTER JOIN EMPLOYEE E ON E.WORKDEPT = D.DEPTNO

Optimized Statement:
--------------------
SELECT Q2.LOCATION AS "LOCATION", Q1.EMPNO AS "EMPNO"
FROM SANJU.EMPLOYEE AS Q1 RIGHT OUTER JOIN SANJU.DEPARTMENT AS Q2 ON
        (Q1.WORKDEPT = Q2.DEPTNO)

Access Plan:
-----------
        Total Cost:            15.1667
        Query Degree:          1

            Rows
            RETURN
            (   1)
            Cost
             I/O
              |
              42
            HSJOIN<
            (   2)
            15.1667
              2
        /-----+------\
      42                14
    TBSCAN            TBSCAN
    (   3)            (   4)
    7.58306           7.57406
      1                 1
      |                 |
      42                14
  TABLE: SANJU     TABLE: SANJU
    EMPLOYEE         DEPARTMENT
      Q1                Q2
```

In such cases, we can create a view with an MQT definition, and create an MQT on this view instead of base tables. Now, this MQT will be picked up by the optimizer. This is a new enhancement in DB2 9.7.

```
-- create a view with desired SQL statement that we want an MQT for.
CREATE VIEW TEST_VIEW AS
```

```
SELECT LOCATION, EMPNO
FROM DEPARTMENT D LEFT OUTER JOIN EMPLOYEE E
ON E.WORKDEPT = D.DEPTNO;

-- create an MQT on this view
CREATE TABLE TEST_MQT AS (SELECT * FROM TEST_VIEW) DATA INITIALLY
DEFERRED REFRESH DEFERRED;

-- refresh MQT to populate the data in it
REFRESH TABLE TEST_MQT;

-- collect statistics on the table created
RUNSTATS ON TABLE DBUSER.TEST_MQT;

-- set the current refresh age to any to allow the above MQT be picked up
by the optimizer
SET CURRENT REFRESH AGE ANY;
```

Once we have this MQT created, and if we observe the access plan, we can see that the MQT is being picked up as expected.

```
Original Statement:
-------------------
SELECT *
FROM TEST_VIEW

Optimized Statement:
--------------------
SELECT Q1.LOCATION AS "LOCATION", Q1.EMPNO AS "EMPNO"
FROM SANJU.TEST_MQT AS Q1

Access Plan:
-----------
        Total Cost:          7.58579
        Query Degree:        1

     Rows
    RETURN
    (   1)
     Cost
     I/O
      |
     48
    TBSCAN
    (   2)
    7.58579
      1
      |
     48
  TABLE: SANJU
    TEST_MQT
       Q1
```

Avoid redundant predicates: The DB2 optimizer is good in rewriting SQL queries, and eliminating redundant predicates, but this may not happen every time. Consider a scenario where we have predicates from two different tables, and they are similar from a business rules point of view. In that case, the optimizer cannot interpret it as duplicate. In such cases, the optimizer may not estimate the cardinality accurately. As best practice, such redundancy should be handled at SQL development time. Consider the following example, where the optimizer removes redundant predicates on its own.

```
SELECT EMPNO, SALARY, MGRNO

FROM EMPLOYEE E, DEPARTMENT D

WHERE D.DEPTNO = E.WORKDEPT AND

E.WORKDEPT='E21' AND

D.DEPTNO='E21'
```

```
Original Statement:
-------------------
SELECT EMPNO, SALARY, MGRNO
FROM EMPLOYEE E, DEPARTMENT D
WHERE D.DEPTNO = E.WORKDEPT AND E.WORKDEPT='E21' AND D.DEPTNO='E21'


Optimized Statement:
-------------------
SELECT Q2.EMPNO AS "EMPNO", Q2.SALARY AS "SALARY", Q1.MGRNO AS "MGRNO"
FROM SANJU.DEPARTMENT AS Q1, SANJU.EMPLOYEE AS Q2
WHERE (Q1.DEPTNO = 'E21') AND (Q2.WORKDEPT = 'E21')
```

Avoid using SELECT *: Do not select everything from a table. Select only the required columns. It keeps the application running in an expected manner, even if the base table is recreated with a different column order. It also saves the extra processing needed to fetch other columns from the base tables, and it also consumes less memory. It may affect the access plan as well. Needless to say, it also makes the application code easier to understand.

Consider the following example where we are only interested in the EMPNO and the SALARY information from the EMPLOYEE table. Let's say that this table has one index created on the EMPNO column with SALARY in it's include list.

```
CREATE UNIQUE INDEX test_idx ON EMPLOYEE(EMPNO) INCLUDE (SALARY).
```

If we use `SELECT *`, then DB2 has to fetch all the columns, and hence, it can't use this index.

`SELECT * FROM EMPLOYEE;`

```
Original Statement:
-------------------
SELECT *
FROM EMPLOYEE
WHERE SALARY > 5000


Optimized Statement:
--------------------
SELECT Q1.EMPNO AS "EMPNO", Q1.FIRSTNME AS "FIRSTNME", Q1.MIDINIT AS
       "MIDINIT", Q1.LASTNAME AS "LASTNAME", Q1.WORKDEPT AS "WORKDEPT",
       Q1.PHONENO AS "PHONENO", Q1.HIREDATE AS "HIREDATE", Q1.JOB AS "JOB",
       Q1.EDLEVEL AS "EDLEVEL", Q1.SEX AS "SEX", Q1.BIRTHDATE AS "BIRTHDATE",
       Q1.SALARY AS "SALARY", Q1.BONUS AS "BONUS", Q1.COMM AS "COMM"
FROM SANJU.EMPLOYEE AS Q1
WHERE (5000 < Q1.SALARY)

Access Plan:
-----------
        Total Cost:            7.61902
        Query Degree:          1

      Rows
     RETURN
     (   1)
      Cost
      I/O
       |
       42
     TBSCAN
     (   2)
     7.61902
       1
       |
       42
  TABLE: SANJU
     EMPLOYEE
        Q1
```

On the other hand, if we only select the columns, which are required, then the chances of using the index are higher. In this example, since we have an index that can satisfy the query, it will be used:

```
Original Statement:
-------------------
SELECT EMPNO, SALARY
FROM EMPLOYEE
WHERE SALARY > 5000


Optimized Statement:
--------------------
SELECT Q1.EMPNO AS "EMPNO", Q1.SALARY AS "SALARY"
FROM SANJU.EMPLOYEE AS Q1
WHERE (5000 < Q1.SALARY)

Access Plan:
-----------
        Total Cost:           0.0616772
        Query Degree:         1

      Rows
     RETURN
     (   1)
      Cost
      I/O
       |
       42
     IXSCAN
     (   2)
    0.0616772
        0
        |
       42
  INDEX: SANJU
    TEST_IDX
       Q1
```

Filter maximum rows: Avoid applying any kind of filter logic in the application. Instead, apply it in the SQL query itself. It will reduce the number of rows in the result set, saving a lot of network traffic, thus improving the overall performance.

Avoid counting to check the existence of rows: If we only want to find whether a table has data or not, avoid using SELECT COUNT(*), and just select one row from the table. Counting all rows is expensive.

Observe the following access plan. We can see that DB2 has to do a GROUP BY after the table scan just to count the total number of rows, which is expensive.

```
Original Statement:
-------------------
SELECT COUNT(*)
FROM EMP_TEST1


Optimized Statement:
--------------------
SELECT Q3.$C0
FROM
    (SELECT COUNT(*)
     FROM
         (SELECT $RID$
         FROM SANJU.EMP_TEST1 AS Q1) AS Q2) AS Q3

Access Plan:
-----------
        Total Cost:              7.5855
        Query Degree:           1

     Rows
     RETURN
     (    1)
      Cost
       I/O
        |
        1
     GRPBY
     (    2)
     7.58499
        1
        |
        42
     TBSCAN
     (    3)
     7.5789
        1
        |
        42
  TABLE: SANJU
     EMP_TEST1
        Q1
```

If we use the following query, then DB2 does not have to do any GROUP BY. Also, observe the difference in the cardinality of the rows selected from the table scan. Since we are selecting only one row, the total cost gets further reduced.

```
SELECT 1 FROM TABLE_NAME FETCH FIRST ROW ONLY OPTIMIZE FOR 1 ROW;
```

```
Original Statement:
-------------------
SELECT 1
FROM EMP_TEST1
FETCH FIRST ROW ONLY
OPTIMIZE
FOR 1 ROW


Optimized Statement:
--------------------
SELECT 1
FROM SANJU.EMP_TEST1 AS Q1

Access Plan:
-----------
        Total Cost:            7.56835
        Query Degree:          1

      Rows
     RETURN
     (   1)
      Cost
       I/O
        |
        1
     TBSCAN
     (   2)
     7.59748
        1
        |
        42
  TABLE: SANJU
    EMP_TEST1
        Q1
```

Consider using UNION ALL **as well:** It's a common tendency to join the two result sets by a UNION operator. When we do a UNION of two result sets, DB2 automatically sorts the result sets, and then removes the duplicate rows. There could be many scenarios where we are sure that there will not be any duplicates. For example, if we are calculating some measures on two different product lines, then we can be sure that there will not be any duplicates. In such cases, use UNION ALL instead of UNION. It will avoid the extra SORT operation.

Observe following access plan for a UNION SQL statement. We can see that DB2 sorts the result set to remove duplicate rows:

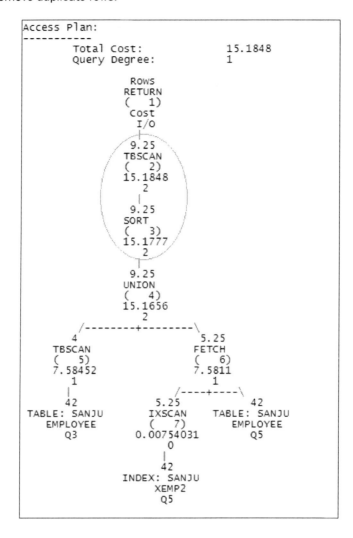

On the other hand, the following access plan for UNION ALL prevents the SORT operation, resulting in better performance:

```
Access Plan:
-----------
         Total Cost:              15.1682
         Query Degree:            1
                    ROWS
                  RETURN
                  (    1)
                   Cost
                   I/O
                    |
                  9.25
                  UNION
                  (    2)
                 15.1656
                    2
          /--------+--------\
         4                   5.25
      TBSCAN               FETCH
      (    3)              (    4)
      7.58452             7.5811
         1                   1
         |              /----+----\
        42           5.25          42
   TABLE: SANJU    IXSCAN     TABLE: SANJU
    EMPLOYEE       (    5)     EMPLOYEE
       Q3        0.00754031       Q5
                     0
                     |
                    42
               INDEX: SANJU
                 XEMP2
                   Q5
```

Use uncommitted read if possible: If we are querying a read-only table, or if the business logic permits to read uncommitted data, always use the `WITH UR` clause or the `FOR FETCH ONLY` clause in the `SELECT` statement. This prevents the rows or the tables from being locked, thus giving us better performance and better concurrency.

```
SELECT EMPNO, SALARY FROM EMPLOTEE WITH UR;
```

```
SELECT EMPNO, SALARY FROM EMPLOTEE FOR FETCH ONLY;
```

Reduce the number of database calls: Try to retrieve as much as possible in a single database call, instead of multiple calls. This saves network traffic and the overhead of processing individual statements, such as compilation, and so on. If we need to process some set of data, and based on this, if we want to retrieve some more data, then we should consider using a compound SQL or a stored procedure.

```
BEGIN
    -- declare variables
    DECLARE SQLSTATE CHAR(5);
    DECLARE v_empnoVARCHAR(6);
```

```
DECLARE v_workdeptVARCHAR(2);

DECLARE at_end INT DEFAULT 0;

-- declare condition for row not found state

DECLARE not_found CONDITION FOR SQLSTATE '02000';

-- declare the cursor and a condition handler to handle row not found
condition.
DECLARE C1 CURSOR FOR

   SELECT EMPNO, WORKDEPT FROM EMPLOYEE;

DECLARE CONTINUE HANDLER FOR not_found

   SET at_end = 1;

-- process the cursor

OPEN C1;

FETCH C1 INTO v_empno, v_workdept;

WHILE at_end = 0 DO

  IF (v_workdept = 'E21')

      THEN

         UPDATE EMPLOYEE

             SET salary = salary * 1.20

             WHERE EMPNO = v_empno;

         ELSE UPDATE EMPLOYEE

             SET salary = salary * 1.10

             WHERE EMPNO = v_empno;

   END IF;

   FETCH C1 INTO v_empno, v_workdept;

  END WHILE;

  CLOSE C1;

END @
```

Use `SELECT INTO`: If we are expecting a single row from an SQL statement, then use `SELECT INTO` instead of opening a cursor, and iterating through it. This gives better performance.

```
SELECT MAX(SALARY)

  INTO V_MAXSALARY

  FROM EMPLOYEE;
```

In such cases, an error is returned if multiple rows are retrieved from an SQL statement.

Apply predicates in sub select queries: DB2 processes the inner `SELECT` query, before the other parts of the SQL query. We should try to limit the rows returned from the inner query. The optimizer will rewrite the query anyway, but we should keep it easy for the optimizer. Let's take both examples.

In the following example, the predicate is applied after joining two tables. If we observe the rewritten SQL statement, we can see that the optimizer is applying a predicate filter before joining the two tables:

```
Original Statement:
------------------
SELECT emp.empno, emp.lastname, dept.deptname
FROM emp LEFT OUTER JOIN dept ON emp.workdept = dept.deptno
WHERE emp.salary > 50000.00


Optimized Statement:
------------------
SELECT Q4.EMPNO AS "EMPNO", Q4.LASTNAME AS "LASTNAME", Q4.DEPTNAME AS
        "DEPTNAME"
FROM
    (SELECT Q3.DEPTNAME, Q2.LASTNAME, Q2.EMPNO
    FROM
        (SELECT Q1.EMPNO, Q1.LASTNAME, Q1.WORKDEPT
        FROM SANJU.EMPLOYEE AS Q1
        WHERE (+50000.00 < Q1.SALARY)) AS Q2 LEFT OUTER JOIN SANJU.DEPARTMENT
            AS Q3 ON (Q2.WORKDEPT = Q3.DEPTNO)) AS Q4
```

But as best practice, we should filter the result sets before joining them. We can write the previous SQL statement as follows:

```
Original Statement:
------------------
SELECT e.empno, e.lastname, dept.deptname
FROM
    (SELECT empno, lastname, workdept
    FROM emp
    WHERE salary > 50000.00) as e LEFT OUTER JOIN dept ON e.workdept =
        dept.deptno


Optimized Statement:
------------------
SELECT Q3.EMPNO AS "EMPNO", Q3.LASTNAME AS "LASTNAME", Q1.DEPTNAME AS
        "DEPTNAME"
FROM SANJU.DEPARTMENT AS Q1 RIGHT OUTER JOIN
    (SELECT Q2.EMPNO, Q2.LASTNAME, Q2.WORKDEPT
    FROM SANJU.EMPLOYEE AS Q2
    WHERE (+50000.00 < Q2.SALARY)) AS Q3 ON (Q3.WORKDEPT = Q1.DEPTNO)
```

Use the `LIKE` **clause wisely:** Always avoid using the `LIKE` clause with % or _ at the beginning, as it prevents the optimizer from using any matching index, and might result in a table scan. If needed, use the `LIKE` clause with % or _, at the end of expression value.

Consider the following example, where we have `LIKE '%string%'`. We can observe that the index is not being used:

```
Original Statement:
-------------------
select empno, firstnme, lastname, workdept
from employee
where workdept like '%E2%'

Optimized Statement:
-------------------
SELECT Q1.EMPNO AS "EMPNO", Q1.FIRSTNME AS "FIRSTNME", Q1.LASTNAME AS
       "LASTNAME", Q1.WORKDEPT AS "WORKDEPT"
FROM SANJU.EMPLOYEE AS Q1
WHERE (Q1.WORKDEPT LIKE '%E2%')

Access Plan:
-----------
        Total Cost:          7.59611
        Query Degree:        1

    Rows
    RETURN
    (   1)
     Cost
      I/O
       |
      4.2
    TBSCAN
    (   2)
    7.59611
       1
       |
       42
  TABLE: SANJU
    EMPLOYEE
        Q1
```

If we rewrite the above SQL statement as `LIKE 'string%'` then the index can be used.

```
Original Statement:
------------------
select empno, firstnme, lastname, workdept
from employee
where workdept like 'E2%'


Optimized Statement:
-------------------
SELECT Q1.EMPNO AS "EMPNO", Q1.FIRSTNME AS "FIRSTNME", Q1.LASTNAME AS
       "LASTNAME", Q1.WORKDEPT AS "WORKDEPT"
FROM SANJU.EMPLOYEE AS Q1
WHERE (Q1.WORKDEPT LIKE 'E2%')

Access Plan:
-----------
        Total Cost:            7.58339
        Query Degree:          1

             Rows
            RETURN
            (   1)
             Cost
             I/O
              |
              6
            FETCH
            (   2)
            7.58339
              1
        /----+----\
       6           42
    IXSCAN    TABLE: SANJU
    (   3)       EMPLOYEE
   0.00918804       Q1
       0
       |
       42
   INDEX: SANJU
       XEMP2
        Q1
```

Prefer `IN` over the `LIKE` clause: If we are certain about different values that may exist, we can rewrite the SQL to use the `IN` clause instead of the `LIKE` clause. This results in better performance. If the `IN` clause is not feasible, then we should consider using the `BETWEEN` clause. Consider the following example:

```
SELECT EMPNO, FIRSTNME, LASTNAME, SALARY
  FROM EMPLOYEE
  WHERE WORKDEPT LIKE 'E2_';
```

We can rewrite this SQL statement, as follows:

```
SELECT EMPNO, FIRSTNME, LASTNAME, SALARY
  FROM EMPLOYEE
  WHERE WORKDEPT IN ('E21', 'E22', 'E23');
```

Index

C

CACHE 80
CallableStatement object 198
CallableStatement.setArray method 143
CALL MONREPORT.CURRENTSQL; 353
CALL MONREPORT.CURRENTSQL(44); 353
CALLMONREPORT.DBSUMMARY(30); 355
CALL MONREPORT.LOCKWAIT; 361
CALL statement 129, 138
CASE_NOT_FOUND exception 155
CC 238, 239
CGTT
  creating 66, 67
  dropping 68
  referencing 68
character literals 235
CHNGPGS_THRESH parameter
  about 378
  reducing 378
Class.forName() method 75, 77, 183
client affinity
  configuring 218
client environment
  setting up 228
clientRerouteAlternatePortNumber property
  220
clientRerouteAlternateServerName property
  220
clientRerouteServerListJNDIName 220
clob
  XML, inserting as 194
CLOSE CALL 174
close() method 53
clpplus command 234
COLLECTION clause 321
collection methods 235
column data type 18
column expressions
  in join predicates, avoiding 382-385
column names
  creating online, ALTER TABLE operation used
    8, 9
com.ibm.db2.jcc.DB2ConnectionPoolData-
    Source interface 186
com.ibm.db2.jcc.DB2SimpleDataSource
    interface 186
com.ibm.db2.jcc.DB2XADataSource
    interface 186

com.ibm.db2.jcc package 191
COM.ibm.db2.jdbc.DB2DataSource interface
    186
COM.ibm.db2.jdbc.DB2XADataSource
    interface 186
COMMIT ON RETURN 128
complex expressions
  in WHERE clause, avoiding 386-388
compound statement 127
CONCUR_READ_ONLY property 205
concurrency
  improving, connection concentrator used
    86-89
  improving, enhanced optimistic locking used
    106
CONCUR_UPDATABLE property 205
conditional triggers 160
CONNECT authority 46
CONNECT BY clause 241, 242
CONNECT BY, LEVEL operator 241
CONNECT_BY_ROOT operator 241
connection activities, monitoring 342, 343,
    345
connection concentrator
  and connection pooling, differences 90
  enabling 87
  used, for improving concurrency 86-89
  values, tuning 88
connection objects, JDBC applications
  creating 182
  DataSource interface, used for connection
    185, 186
  DB2 JDBC Type-2 driver 182
  IBM Data Server Driver for JDBC and SQLJ
    182
  Type-2 connectivity 182
  Type-2 connectivity, DB2 JDBC driver used
    182
  Type-2 connectivity, IBM DB2 Data Server
    used 183
  Type-4 connectivity 182-184
connection objects, SQLJ applications
  about 188, 189
  DataSource interface used 189, 190
  DriverManager interface used 189
  Java packages 191
  JDBC DriverManager interface used 188, 189
connection pooling
  about 86

R

RAISE_APPLICATION_ERROR
about 247
in DB2 PL/SQL 247, 248
range delimiting predicate
about 368
characteristics 375
identifying, in access plan 369, 370
range-partitioned table layout 308
range partitioning 307, 313, 314
range partitioning key
generated columns as 70
RANK function
using 265
RANK() function 266
READS SQL DATA 128
REAL to DOUBLE conversions 18
rebind
about 327
invalid and inoperative packages, finding 328
options 328
package 328
package rebinding, REBIND options used 328
privileges 327
REBIND command 54, 329
**REBIND_ROUTINE_PACKAGE stored proce-
dure 329**
recursion support
hierarchical query, implementing for 241-243
redundant predicates
avoiding 397
REGION_SALES table 311
registry variables
DB2_ANTIJOIN 331
DB2_CONNRETRIES_INTERVAL 330
DB2_EXTENDED_OPTIMIZATION 333
DB2_INLIST_TO_JOIN 332
DB2_MAX_CLIENT_CONNRETRIES 331
DB2_REDUCED_OPTIMIZATION 332
db2set DB2ASSUMEUPDATE=ON 333
db2set DB2_CONNRETRIES_INTERVAL=10
330
db2set DB2_EVALUNCOMMITTED=YES 334
db2set DB2_INLIST_TO_JOIN=YES 332
db2set DB2_KEEPTABLELOCK=TRANSACTION
334
Db2set DB2LOCK_TO_RB=NULL 335

db2set DB2_MAX_CLIENT_CONNRETRIES =5
331
Db2set DB2NOEXITLIST=ON 335
db2set DB2_REDUCED_OPTIMIZATION=YES
332
db2set DB2_SKIPDELETED=YES 335
db2set DB2_SKIPINSERTED=YES 335
db2set DB2_VIEW_REOPT_VALUES=YES 331
DB2_SKIPDELETED 335
DB2_VIEW_REOPT_VALUES 331
used, for customizing application behavior
330-336
RELATIVE(n) clause 207
RELEASE SAVEPOINT statement 72
REOPT ALWAYS statement 58
REOPT option 328
REOPT value 277
REORG command 376
REPLACE clause
about 9
used, for creating objects 9-11
REOPT bind option 54
residual predicate
about 368, 373
characteristics 375
identifying, in access plan 373, 374
RESIGNAL statement 146
ResultSet class 192, 213
ResultSet.getAsciiStream() method 192
ResultSet.getBinaryStream() method 192
ResultSet.getCharacterStream() method 193
ResultSet.getSQLXML method 192
ResultSet.getString() method 192
result sets
in stored procedure 135
multiple result sets, returning 140
returning 135
returning, to caller 136
returning, to client 137
using, from nested stored procedure 138,
139
retryIntervalForClientReroute property 220
RETURN operator 306
return_to_client_sp 138
reuseDB2Connection() method 99
REUSE STORAGE clause 22, 23
REVALIDATION options 14
RFETCH FIRST clause 267

Thank you for buying
IBM DB2 9.7 Advanced Application Developer Cookbook

About Packt Publishing

Packt, pronounced 'packed', published its first book "*Mastering phpMyAdmin for Effective MySQL Management*" in April 2004 and subsequently continued to specialize in publishing highly focused books on specific technologies and solutions.

Our books and publications share the experiences of your fellow IT professionals in adapting and customizing today's systems, applications, and frameworks. Our solution-based books give you the knowledge and power to customize the software and technologies you're using to get the job done. Packt books are more specific and less general than the IT books you have seen in the past. Our unique business model allows us to bring you more focused information, giving you more of what you need to know, and less of what you don't.

Packt is a modern, yet unique publishing company, which focuses on producing quality, cutting-edge books for communities of developers, administrators, and newbies alike. For more information, please visit our website: www.PacktPub.com.

About Packt Enterprise

In 2010, Packt launched two new brands, Packt Enterprise and Packt Open Source, in order to continue its focus on specialization. This book is part of the Packt Enterprise brand, home to books published on enterprise software – software created by major vendors, including (but not limited to) IBM, Microsoft and Oracle, often for use in other corporations. Its titles will offer information relevant to a range of users of this software, including administrators, developers, architects, and end users.

Writing for Packt

We welcome all inquiries from people who are interested in authoring. Book proposals should be sent to author@packtpub.com. If your book idea is still at an early stage and you would like to discuss it first before writing a formal book proposal, contact us; one of our commissioning editors will get in touch with you.

We're not just looking for published authors; if you have strong technical skills but no writing experience, our experienced editors can help you develop a writing career, or simply get some additional reward for your expertise.

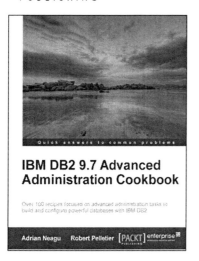

IBM DB2 9.7 Advanced Administration Cookbook

ISBN: 978-1-84968-332-6   Paperback: 480 pages

Over 100 recipes focused on advanced administration tasks to build and configure powerful databases with IBM DB2

1. Master all the important aspects of administration from instances to IBM's newest High Availability technology pureScale

2. Learn to implement key security features to harden your database's security against hackers and intruders

3. Empower your databases by building efficient data configuration using MDC and clustered tables

IBM Sametime 8.5.2 Administration Guide

ISBN: 978-1-84968-304-3   Paperback: 484 pages

A comprehensive, practical book for the planning, installation, and maintenance of your Sametime 8.5.2 environment

1. Discover all the servers and components included in the new Sametime 8.5.2 architecture

2. Quickly zero in on which server components provide the features you need for your Sametime environment

3. Understand the dependencies between different servers and how to design both a pilot and production environment

Please check **www.PacktPub.com** for information on our titles

IBM Cognos TM1 Cookbook

ISBN: 978-1-84968-210-7   Paperback: 490 pages

Build real world planning, budgeting, and forecastingsolutions with a collection of over 60 simple but incredibly effective recipes

1. A comprehensive developer's guide for planning, building, and managing practical applications with IBM TM1

2. No prior knowledge of TM1 expected

3. Complete coverage of all the important aspects of IBM TM1 in carefully planned step-by-step practical demos

4. Part of Packt's Cookbook series: Practical recipes that illustrate the use of various TM1 features

IBM Rational Team Concert 2 Essentials

ISBN: 978-1-84968-160-5   Paperback: 308 pages

Improve team productivity with Integrated Precesses, Planning, and Collaboration using Team Concert Enterprise Edition

1. Understand the core features and techniques of Rational Team Concert and Jazz platform through a real-world Book Manager Application

2. Expand your knowledge of software development challenges and find out how Rational Team Concert solves your tech, team, and collaboration worries

3. Complete overview and understanding of the Jazz Platform, Rational Team Concert, and other products built on the Jazz Platform

Please check **www.PacktPub.com** for information on our titles

CPSIA information can be obtained at www.ICGtesting.com
Printed in the USA
LVOW071526200612

286970LV00007B/149/P